The Life of The
BLESSED VIRGIN MARY

The Life of The
BLESSED VIRGIN MARY

FROM THE VISIONS OF

Anne Catherine Emmerich

Translated by

SIR MICHAEL PALAIRET

With supplementary notes by

REV. SEBASTIAN BULLOUGH, O.P.

TAN Books
An Imprint of Saint Benedict Press, LLC
Charlotte, North Carolina

Nihil Obstat: Ricardvs Roche, S.T.D.
                  Censor Depvtatvs

Imprimatur: ✠ Humphrey Bright
                  Episcopvs Tit. Solensis
                  Vicarivs Capitvlaris Birmingamiensis

Birmingamiae: Die II JVNII MCMLIV

First published by Burns and Oates, Limited; London, England
1954.

ISBN: 978-0-89555-048-4

Printed and bound in the United States of America.

TAN Books
An Imprint of Saint Benedict Press, LLC
Charlotte, North Carolina

2013

PREFACE TO THE PRESENT EDITION

ANNE CATHERINE EMMERICH was born on September 8th, 1774, at Flamske, near Koesfeld, Westphalia, West Germany, and became on November 13th, 1803, a nun of the Augustinian Order at the Convent of Agnetenberg at Dülmen (also in Westphalia). She died on February 9th, 1824. Although of simple education, she had perfect consciousness of her earliest days and could understand the liturgical Latin from her first time at Mass. During most of her later years she would vomit even the simplest food or drink, subsisting for long periods almost entirely on water and the Holy Eucharist. She was told in mystic vision that her gift of seeing past, present, and future was greater than that possessed by anyone else in history. From the year 1812 until her death she bore the stigmata of Our Lord, including a cross over her heart and wounds from the crown of thorns. An invalid confined to bed during her later years, her funeral was attended, nevertheless, by a greater concourse of mourners than any other remembered by the oldest inhabitants of Dülmen.

An explanatory note must be made about four basic works on the life and visions of Anne Catherine Emmerich: 1) *The Life of Christ and Biblical Revelations of Anna Catharina Emmerick,* Apostolate of Christian Action, Fresno, California, as recorded in the journals of Clemens Brentano and edited after his death in 1842 by Very Rev. Carl E. Schmöger, C.SS.R. This is a four-volume, 2,088-page book giving a day-by-day account of Our Lord's public life and the lives of His ancestors. 2) *The Dolorous Passion of Our Lord Jesus*

Christ, Christian Book Club of America, Hawthorne, California, a 320-page account of Our Lord's Passion and death, as recorded, compiled, and published by Clemens Brentano in 1835, but also containing Brentano's introductory fifty-five page biography of Sister Emmerich. 3) *The Life of the Blessed Virgin Mary,* TAN Books and Publishers, Rockford, Illinois, being an account of the ancestry and life of the Blessed Mother up to the public ministry of Our Lord, as well as from His death until her own. When he died in 1842, Brentano was well into this work, but it was carried along by his brother and finished by his brother's wife. 4) *The Life of Anna Catharina Emmerick,* by Very Rev. Carl E. Schmöger C.SS.R., Maria Regina Guild, Los Angeles, California. This is a two-volume, 1,297-page life of Sister Emmerich herself, including also many visions of the past, (her) present, and future, of saints' lives, and of many sacred subjects.

Much confusion exists about these books, but they are distinct in content and do not overlap, save that Sister Emmerich's life is briefly summarized in *The Dolorous Passion* and that *The Life of Christ* and *Dolorous Passion* both cover the passion of Our Lord. In the latter, however, the treatment is in greater detail and poignancy and *well* deserves the reader's attention!

The merit of the present volume is its expose of material otherwise unobtainable on Our Lady's ancestry, birth, childhood, education and betrothal, as well as on the Nativity, the early life of the Holy Family, and the final years of the Blessed Mother.

The reader will note two versions of Sister Emmerich's name. This is only the difference between the German and the English spelling.

"Long before her death," says Schmöger, "Sister Emmerich had uttered the following words: 'What the Pilgrim [Clemens Brentano] gleans, he will bear away, far, far away, for there is no disposition to make use of it here; but it will bring forth fruit in other lands, whence its effects will return and be felt even here.'"

May the republishing of this book contribute its share to fulfilling that beautiful prophecy.

August 20, 1970   Thomas A. Nelson

TRANSLATOR'S NOTE

I HAVE omitted some of Clemens Brentano's notes altogether and have translated only extracts of some of the others; but have included everything that seemed likely to interest the English reader.

EXTRACT FROM THE PREFACE TO THE GERMAN EDITION

MOST readers of *The Dolorous Passion of Our Lord Jesus Christ according to the visions of the devout Anne Catherine Emmerich* are no doubt aware that this book contains only a part of those visions. Clemens Brentano spent several years in Dülmen in the endeavour to reproduce with scrupulous care the visionary's utterances, which were sometimes fragmentary and sometimes formed a connected narrative. This was the origin of his diary, which was begun in January 1820 and contained a great variety of visions regarding the lives of the saints, the feasts of the Church and other events. Later, however, in the years 1821 and 1822, these visions became more and more concentrated on the life of Christ and of the holy persons about Him. The records of these visions, which still exist in their original form, were made by the late Clemens Brentano with almost documentary precision. He extracted from them everything relating to the life of Christ, and was thus able to present to the reader the public life of Our Lord day by day according to Catherine Emmerich's visions. The last portion of these records has been printed under the title of *The Dolorous Passion of Our Lord.*

Besides this large collection of accounts of the life of Christ, Clemens Brentano completed another smaller one relating to the life of the Blessed Virgin. After arranging the relevant extracts and choosing wood-cuts to illustrate them, he started printing them in 1841, and had finished a considerable part when a lingering illness put a stop to his work and finally caused his death on July 28th, 1842. After this sad event his papers, including those relating to Catherine Emmerich, came into the hands of his brother Christian Brentano in Aschaffenburg. The latter died on October 27th, 1851, without having carried out his intention of continuing to print the *Life of Our Lady;* but fortunately his widow was able, with the help of some learned friends, to complete the work.

In regard to its contents, we feel bound to repeat the declaration with which Clemens Brentano prefaced the first edition of the *Dolorous Passion*.

> Though the accounts of these visions, among many similar fruits of the contemplative love of Jesus, may appear in some degree remarkable, they solemnly reject the slightest claim to bear the character of historical truth. All that they wish to do is to associate themselves with the countless representations of the Passion by artists and pious writers, and to be regarded merely as a pious nun's Lenten meditations imperfectly comprehended and narrated and also very clumsily set down. She herself never attached to her visions anything more than a human and defective value, and therefore yielded to an inner admonition to communicate them only in obedience to the repeated commands of her spiritual directors and after a hard struggle with herself.

The same applies in essentials to the *Life of Mary* here presented, though with one difference. When the *Dolorous Passion* appeared, Catherine Emmerich's visions were known only to a few, though very distinguished men. In the meantime the voices of many thousands of readers have swelled the originally very modest applause. However the historical or theological character of the work may be judged, it is acknowledged to be a treasury of holy scenes and pictures which contribute to the edification and inspiration of the faithful. In this respect the *Life of Mary* is, we consider, a worthy companion to the *Dolorous Passion*. It does not, however, like the latter, present a complete and comprehensive narrative. The gaps which occur in it are to be explained by its close connection with the *Life of*

Christ. Since the latter necessarily often was concerned with the Virgin Mother, sections of the *Life of Mary* had to be omitted in order to avoid repetitions when the *Life of Christ* should be printed (as it was later). The latter work should therefore be read in conjunction with the *Life of Mary.*

OBSERVATIONS ON
THE SUPPLEMENTARY NOTES

THOSE who read or even merely look at this book must perforce ask themselves to what extent the statements of Anne Catherine Emmerich are consonant with what can be known of the persons, places, and events in question through the channels of inspired Scripture, reliable history, legitimate tradition, and established geography. Clemens Brentano set out to meet this inquiry as far as he could with the materials and evidence that were available to him at the time. His notes (as completed by his brother, cf. p. ix) have been preserved, and are here followed by his initials CB in parentheses. A further series of notes has been prepared for this edition, sometimes annotating the text directly, and sometimes elucidating the notes of Brentano. These are indicated by the initials SB in parentheses. Attention has been paid throughout to the witness of the four channels of information mentioned above, either to corroborate the statements or to indicate that there is no supporting evidence, or to suggest that there has been some confusion of facts, or occasionally to correct some detail (usually of a chronological, geographical, or philological nature) which appears to be mistaken.

These notes have not been concerned with the problem of the immediate provenance of the material and the relationship of the visionary to Brentano and any other sources which he may or may not have used. Nor are they concerned with the nature or origin of the visions. Their only object has been to test the accuracy of the material as it stands.

It is wise to be aware throughout of what Scripture relates about the events described, and to this end the Scriptural reference has been inserted in a note to each chapter-heading. Similarly, when a Biblical character or event appears, a reference is given except in the most obvious cases. Old Testament legislation is also referred to, when a point of ritual is raised, supplemented by Rabbinic rulings which were current at the time of Christ, and which are preserved in the *Mishnah*. In all these matters, it may be said at once that the statements of Anne Catherine Emmerich (always written AC in the Supplementary Notes) are never found to be counter to the Scriptures, nor mistaken about Jewish ritual at the time, as far as this is ascertainable, apart from a small point about the calendar. When AC's statements involve a particular interpretation of a Biblical text, this is noted, as in n. 1, p. 57 (on *Luke* 3:23), n. 1, p. 105 (on *John* 5:2), n. 2, p. 146 (on *Luke* 1:39), n. 1, p. 167, and n. 1, p. 301 (on *Matt.* 2:22-23), n. 2, p. 236 (on *Num.* 22:5), n. 1, p. 299 (on *Matt.* 2:13), n. 2, p. 319, and n. 1, p. 321 (on *Matt.* 2:16), n. 1, p. 337 (on *Job* 1:16, 17, 18), and n., 1, p. 340 (on *Gen.* 12:20). The Biblical references of Clemens Brentano (always referred to as CB) have all been checked, and they have always been found correct, though occasionally in need of supplement. His Rabbinic references, similarly, have sometimes required expansion.

The contemporary historian Josephus (A.D. 37–c. 100) is an indispensable source for the period. His main works, the *Antiquities of the Jews* and the *Jewish War (De Bello Judaico)*, are referred to by their usual abbreviations *Ant.* and *BJ.* The *Mishnah* is quoted by tractate and section. CB's references to other authors have also been checked, and sometimes more exact references have been provided. His philological observations have usually been simply supplemented by additional notes, confirming or correcting according to more recent studies. It may be said that CB's findings, especially in the field of Scripture and history, have in most cases been found reliable, and his annotations, especially in view of his confessed lack of training and equipment, deserve the highest commendation.

Many early Christian traditions were preserved in the so-called apocryphal gospels. These documents, while plainly composed not as serious histories but as edifying or even diverting imaginations, usually under the pseudonym of some Biblical person (being more like pious "historical novels" of the time), do in all probability enshrine many historical facts subsequently adorned with fancies of a later age. When a parallel can be traced between AC's statements and these traditional sources, the matter is duly noted, and it is interesting to observe how rarely AC's account shares the fanciful elaborations of the apocryphal material. Furthermore, her frequent descriptions of people's appearance and attire seem usually to be of an entirely independent nature. It is worth remembering in this connection that AC was at one time a professional seamstress, a fact which adds interest to her minute observation of clothes. Most of her intricate genealogical statements, so remarkably consistent throughout, find no parallels in the apocryphal literature. The documents referred to most frequently in the notes are the so-called *Protevangelion of James (Protev.), Pseudo-Matthew (Ps-Matt.)*, and the *Nativity of Mary (Nat. Mar.)*, with references to chapters. The editions used were *The Apocryphal New Testament*, translated by M. R. James (1924), and *The Apocryphal Gospels*, translated by J. Harris Cowper (1897). These editions made use of many texts hardly available to CB.

For exegetical work on the Bible, an invaluable aid has been the large *Catholic Commentary* published in 1953, where the general findings of modern scholarship have been made readily available and reliably presented. The references are to paragraphs.

The geographical side presented many problems, and here the same *Catholic Commentary* was of great assistance in the identification of Biblical sites, and the maps it includes are the result of the latest geographical surveys of the Holy Land.

For the conclusions of modern hagiography *The Book of Saints* (4th ed.), produced by the monks of Ramsgate in 1947, has been a handy work of reference. The *Catholic Encyclopedia* (1912) and the *Jewish Encyclopedia* (1905) have often given valuable assistance and guidance to sources.

Lastly, one cannot fail to mention the monumental work of Kaplan Helmut Fahsel, *Der Wandel Jesu in der Welt, nach den Visionen der Anna Katharina Emmerich,* Basel, 1942, which is by far the most elaborate work on the subject, and whose maps and genealogies have been consistently useful.

SEBASTIAN BULLOUGH, O.P.

Cambridge
In Festo SS. Nominis Mariae, 1953

CONTENTS

Chapter I

OUR LADY'S ANCESTORS

LAST night there came again before my soul everything that I had so often seen as a child concerning the life of the ancestors of the Blessed Virgin Mary. I saw it all in a series of pictures just as I did then. If only I could tell it all as I know it and have it before my eyes, it would certainly give great joy to the Pilgrim.[1] In my miserable state I was greatly revived by contemplating these pictures. As a child I was so certain of all I saw that if anyone told me any of the stories differently, I would say straight out: "No, this is how it is." And, indeed, I would have let myself be killed rather than deny that it was thus and not otherwise. Later on, life in the world confused me, and I kept silence. The inner certainty has, however, always remained with me, and last night I once more saw everything even to the smallest details.

When I was a child, my thoughts were always taken up with the Crib and the Child Jesus and with the Mother of God, and I often wondered very much why people told me nothing about the family of Our Lady. I could not understand at all why so little had been written down about her ancestors and relations. In the great longing which I had, I then received a multitude of visions of the Blessed Virgin's ancestors. I must have seen them back to the fourth or fifth generation. I saw

---

1. The "Pilgrim" is Clemens Brentano, who wrote down the visions at Catherine Emmerich's dictation. These were communicated by her to him on the morning of June 27th, 1819. (Tr.)

them always as wonderfully pious and simple people inspired by a quite extraordinary secret longing for the coming of the promised Messias. I saw them always living amongst other men who, compared to them, seemed to me rough and barbarous. They themselves, I saw, were so quiet, gentle and kindly, that I often said to myself in great anxiety about them: "Oh where can these good people find a refuge, how are they to escape from those rough, wicked men? I will seek them out and will be their servant, I will fly with them into a wood where they can hide themselves; I am sure I shall still be able to find them!" So clearly did I see them and believe in them, that I was always afraid and full of anxiety about them.

I always saw these people leading a life of great self-denial. I often saw that those among them who were married bound themselves mutually to observe continence for a time; and this gave me much joy, though why this was I could not clearly say. They practiced these separations chiefly when they were occupied with all kinds of religious ceremonies, accompanied by incense and prayers.[2] From these I perceived that there were priests among them. I often saw them moving from one place to another, leaving large homesteads and retiring to smaller ones, in order to lead their lives undisturbed by wicked people.

They were so devout and so full of longing towards God that I often saw them, alone in the field by day and by night too, running about and crying to God with such intense desire that, in the hunger of their hearts, they tore open their garments at their breasts, as if God were about to burn Himself into their hearts with the hot rays of the sun, or to quench with the moonlight and starlight their thirst for the fulfilment of the Promise.

Pictures like these came to me, I remember, when as

---

2. It is commonly stated that such separation was required of priests on duty, and this can be deduced from *Lev.* 15:18 (ceremonial uncleanness contracted) and *Lev.* 22: 3 (ceremonial cleanness required). (SB)

a child or as a young girl I was kneeling and praying to God, alone with the flock in the pastures, or at night on the high fields above our farm; or when, in Advent, I walked through the snow at midnight to the *Rorate* devotions in St. James' Church at Koesfeld, three-quarters of an hour away from our cottage at Flamske. The evening before, and in the night too, I prayed much for the poor souls in Purgatory. I thought that in their lives they had perhaps not been eager enough for grace; perhaps they had given way to other desires for the creatures and goods of the world, had fallen into many faults, and were now yearning to be released. So I offered up my prayer and my longing to God our Saviour for them, trying as it were to pay their debt for them. I got a little benefit, too, for myself, for I knew that the kind Holy Souls, in gratitude to me and because of their constant desire for help by prayers, would wake me at the right time and would not let me oversleep. And so they did; they floated round my bed like little flames, little dim, quiet flames, and woke me just in time for me to be able to offer up my morning prayer for them. Then I sprinkled myself and them with holy water, put on my clothes, and started on my way. I saw the poor little lights accompanying me in a regular procession; and on the way I sang with true heart's desire: "Drop down dew, ye heavens, from above, and let the clouds rain the Just One." And as I sang, I saw here and there in the wilderness and in the fields the beloved ancestors of Our Blessed Lady running about and crying for the Messias; and I did as they did, and came to Koesfeld always in time for the *Rorate*[3] Mass, even when the Holy Souls led me, as they sometimes did, a very long way round past all the Stations of the Cross.

Now, in my visions of these beloved ancestors of Our Lady praying so hard in their hunger for God, they seemed to me strange indeed in their dress and in their way of living, and yet so near and so clear to me, that

3. Mass of the Fourth Sunday in Advent.

I still know and have before my eyes all their features
and figures. And I kept asking myself: "What manner
of people are these? Everything is different from nowadays, yet there these people are, and all that I see has
really happened!" And so I always used to hope that I
might go to them.

In all they did and in all they said and in their religious services, these good people were very decided and
exact; and they made no lamentations except over the
sufferings of their neighbors.

THE ANCESTORS OF ST. ANNE[4]

I HAD a detailed vision of the ancestors of St. Anne, the
mother of the Blessed Virgin. They lived at Mara in
the region of Mount Horeb, and were connected spiri-
tually with a kind of very devout Israelites of whom I
have seen a great deal. I will relate as much as I can
recall about them. I was with these people almost the
whole of yesterday, and if I had not been oppressed by
so many visits, I should not have forgotten nearly all
of what I saw.

These devout Israelites who were connected with
the ancestors of St. Anne were called Essenes or
Essaees. They have, however, changed their name three
times, for they were first called Eskarenes, then Chasidaees, and finally Essenes. Their first name, Eskarenes,
came from the word Eskara or Azkara, which is the
name for the part of the sacrifice belonging to God,
and also for the sweet-smelling incense at the offering of wheaten flour.[5] The second name, Chasidaees,

---

4. Communicated in July and August 1821.
5. This was taken down in August 1821 by the writer from Catherine Emmerich's words.
In July 1840, when preparing the book for printing, he asked a language expert for
an explanation of the word Azkara, and was told that Azkarah meant commemora-
tion and is the name of the portion of the unbloody sacrifice, which was burnt on
the altar by the priest to the glory of God and to remind Him of His merciful promises.
The unbloody sacrifices generally consisted of the finest wheaten flour mixed with
oil and sprinkled with incense. The priest burnt as the Azkarah all the incense and
also a handful of flour and oil (baked or unbaked). In the case of the shew-bread
the incense alone was the Azkarah (*Lev.* 24:7). The Vulgate translates the word
Azkarah alternatively as "memoriale," "in memoriam," or "in monumentum." (CB)

means merciful.[6] I cannot remember what the name Essenes comes from.[7] The way of life of these devout people is an inheritance from the time of Moses and Aaron and in particular from the priests who carried the Ark of the Covenant; but it was not until the period between Isaias and Jeremias that their way of life was regularly established. At the beginning there were not many of them; later on, however, their settlements in the Promised Land occupied a space twenty-four hours' journey long and thirty-six hours' journey broad. They did not come to the region of the Jordan until later; they lived mostly on the slopes of Mount Horeb and Mount Carmel, the home of Elias.

In the lifetime of St. Anne's grandparents, the Essenes had a spiritual head who lived on Mount Horeb. He was an aged prophet called Archos or Arkas.[8] Their organization was very like that of a religious Order. All who wished to enter it had to undergo a year's tests, and the length of time for which they were accepted was decided by prophetic inspirations from above. The real members of the Order, who lived in a community, did not marry but lived in chastity; but there were others (who had formerly been in the Order or were attached to it) who married and carried out in their families,

---

Lev. 24:7, literally: "And thou shalt place upon the shew-bread pure incense, and it shall be for the bread as a memorial *(azkarah),* a burnt offering to the Lord." The other references to the word *azkarah* are in *Lev.* 2:2, 9:16, 5:12; 6:8; *Num.* 5:26 in connection with the burning of a meal-offering *(minhah).* The connection with the Essenes remains obscure. (SB)

6. *Hasid* (pl. *Hasidim),* originally meaning "merciful" (of God), came to mean "devout" of men, and was later in Maccabean times used to designate a specific group of devout and observant Jews who joined the Maccabean party in their fight for freedom *(1 Mac.* 2:42). These Hasideans (Gk. *Asidaioi),* as they were then called, are generally believed to be the forerunners of the Pharisees (cf. Lagrange, *Le Judaïsme avant Jésus-Christ,* 1931, pp. 56, 272), and probably of the Essenes (Bonsirven, *Le Judaïsme Palestinien,* 1935, I, pp. 43, 64), both sects being mentioned by Josephus in Maccabean times *(Ant.,* XIII, v, 9). (SB)

7. They were called *Essenoi* by Josephus, *Esseni* by Pliny, and *Essaioi* by Philo (and six times by Josephus). The origin of the name is uncertain (cf. Lagrange, *op. cit.,* p. 320). Their way of life, as described by AC, is for the most part fully attested by the contemporary historian Josephus *(BJ,* II, viii, 2-13), as well as by Philo *(Quod omnis probus liber sit,* 75-88). Pliny's remarks *(Hist. Nat.,* V, 17) attribute to the Essenes an antiquity of "thousands of years." There is no other evidence of an antiquity beyond Maccabean times. (Most texts in Lagrange, *op. cit.,* pp. 307-17.) Passing references by Josephus are in *Ant.,* XIII, v, 9 and XVIII, i, 5. (SB)

8. The spiritual head on Mount Horeb, Archos, is not mentioned in any of the documents. (SB)

and with their children and household, something similar in many ways to the traditional discipline of the real Essenes. Their relationship with these was like that between the lay members of a Catholic Third Order, or Tertiaries, and the professed priests of the Order. In all important matters, especially as to the marriages of their relations, these married Essenes always sought instruction and counsel from the aged prophet on Mount Horeb. St. Anne's grandparents belonged to this kind of married Essenes.

Later there arose a third kind of Essenes who exaggerated everything and fell into great errors, and I saw that the others would have no dealings with them.

The real Essenes were specially concerned with prophetic matters, and their head on Mount Horeb was often vouchsafed divine revelations in the cave of Elias respecting the coming of the Messias. He had knowledge of the family from which the mother of the Messias was to come, and at the time that he gave prophetic advice to the grandparents of St. Anne in matters of marriage, he saw that the day of the Lord was approaching. He did not, however, know how long the birth of the Saviour's mother might still be prevented or delayed by sin, and so he was always preaching penance, mortification, prayer, and inner sacrifice for this intention —pious exercises of which all Essenes had ever given the example.

Until Isaias assembled these people together and gave them a more regular organization, they were scattered about the land of Israel, leading lives of piety and intent on mortification. They wore their clothes without mending them till they fell off their bodies. They fought particularly against sexual immorality, and often by mutual consent lived in continence for long periods, living in huts far removed from their wives. When they lived together as husband and wife, it was only with the intention of producing a holy offspring which might bring nearer the coming of the Saviour. I saw them eating apart from their wives; the wife came to take her meal after the husband had left the table. There were ancestors of St. Anne and of other holy people among these early Essenes.

Jeremias too was connected with them, and the men called "Sons of the Prophet" came from them. They often lived in the desert and round Mount Horeb and Carmel, and later I saw many of them in Egypt. I also saw that for a time they were driven away from Mount Horeb by war and were reassembled by new leaders. The Maccabees also belonged to them. They had a great devotion to Moses, and possessed a sacred piece of his clothing given by him to Aaron, from whom it had come down to them. This was their most precious relic, and I had a vision of some fifteen of them being killed in defending it. Their prophet leaders had knowledge of the secret mysteries of the Ark of the Covenant.

The real Essenes who lived in chastity were indescribably pure and devout. They adopted children and brought them up to lead a very holy life. To be accepted as a member of the regular Order, a boy had to have reached the age of fourteen. Those who had been already tested had to undergo a year's novitiate, others two years. They did not carry on any form of trade, but exchanged the produce of their agriculture for whatever else they needed. If one of them had committed a grave sin, he was expelled from among them and excommunicated by their head. This excommunication had the force of that pronounced by Peter against Ananias, who was struck dead by it. Their head knew by prophetic inspiration who had committed sin. I also saw some Essenes undergoing penitential punishment; they were obliged to stand in a stiff robe with their arms extended immovably in sleeves lined with thorns.

Mount Horeb was full of little caves, which formed the cells where they lived. An assembly hall of light wattlework had been built on to the mouth of one of the large caves. Here they came together at eleven o'clock in the morning and ate. Each had a small loaf of bread in front of him with a goblet. The head went from place to place and blessed each one's bread. After the meal they returned to their separate cells. In this assembly-hall there was an altar on which stood little blessed loaves covered up; they were in some way sacred, and were, I think, distributed among the poor.

The Essenes had a great number of doves, which were tame and ate out of their hands. They ate doves, but also used them in their ritual ceremonies. They said something over them and let them fly away. I saw, too, that they released lambs in the desert after saying something over them, as if they were to take their sins on them.[9]

I saw them go three times a year to the Temple in Jerusalem. They had also priests among them whose special duty was the care of the sacred vestments; they cleaned them, contributed money for them, and also made new ones. I saw them engaged in cattle-breeding and agriculture, but specially in gardening. Mount Horeb was full of gardens and fruit-trees in the spaces between their huts. I saw many of them weaving and plaiting, and also embroidering priests' vestments. I did not see them producing silk; that came in bundles to be sold to them, and they exchanged other produce for it.

In Jerusalem they had a quarter of their own to live in and a separate place in the Temple as well. The other Jews rather disliked them because of their austerity. I saw, too, that they sent presents to the Temple; for example, great bunches of grapes, carried by two people on a pole. They also sent lambs, but not to be slaughtered; I think they just let them run into a garden. I did not see the real Essenes offering bloody sacrifices in these later times. I saw that before they journeyed to the Temple they made a very rigorous preparation by prayer, fasting, and penance, including even scourgings. If one laden with sins went to the

---

9. It is well known that the Essenes refused to sacrifice animals, but the ritual of releasing them (as described by AC) is one of the few matters that is not documented. In *Lev.* 14:53 the Law prescribed the freeing of a bird after purification from leprosy, and in 16:22 the ritual of the scapegoat, which was to "carry away all their iniquities into an uninhabited land." (SB)

Temple and to the Holy of Holies without having made atonement by penance, he usually died on the spot. If on their journey, or in Jerusalem itself, they found anyone who was ill or in any way helpless, they did not go to the Temple until they had given him all the aid in their power.

I saw that, in general, they employed themselves in healing. They gathered herbs and prepared potions. I saw also that those holy people whom I had seen some time before laying sick folk down on a bed of healing plants were Essenes.[10] I saw, too, that the Essenes healed the sick by the laying-on of hands, or by stretching

10. The little daughter of Catherine Emmerich's brother, who came from the farm of Flamske near Koesfeld to visit her at Dülmen in the winter of 1820, was seized with violent convulsions occurring every evening at the same time and beginning with distressing choking. These convulsions often lasted until midnight, and Catherine Emmerich, knowing as she did the cause and significance of this and indeed of most other illnesses, was greatly affected by her niece's sufferings. She prayed many times to be told of a cure for them, and at last was able to describe a certain little flower known to her which she had seen St. Luke pick and use to cure epilepsy. As a result of her minute description of the little flower and of the places where it grew, her physician, Dr. Wesener (the district doctor of Dülmen), found it; she recognized the plant which he brought her as the one she had seen, which she called "star-flower", and he identified it as *Cerastium arvense linnaei* or *Holosteum caryophylleum veterum* (Field Mouse-ear Chickweed). It is remarkable that the old herbal *Tabernamontani* also refers to the use of this plant for epilepsy. On the afternoon of May 22nd, 1821, Catherine Emmerich said in her sleep: "Rue [which she had used before] and star-flower sprinkled with holy water should be pressed, and the juice given to the child, surely that could do no harm? I have already been told three times to squeeze it myself and give it to her." The writer, in the hope that she might communicate something more definite about this cure, had, unknown to her, wrapped up at home some blossoms of this plant in paper like a relic and pinned the little packet to her dress in the evening. She woke up and said at once: "That is not a relic, it is the star-flower." She kept the little flower pinned to her dress during the night, and on the morning of May 23rd, 1821, she said: "I had no idea why I was lying last night in a field amongst nothing but star-flowers. I saw, too, all kinds of ways in which these flowers were used, and it was said to me, 'If men knew the healing power of this plant, it would not grow so plentifully around you.' I saw pictures of it being used in very distant ages. I saw St. Luke wandering about picking these flowers. I saw, too, in a place like the one where Christ fed the 5,000, many sick folk lying on these flowers in the open air, protected by a light shelter above them. The plants were spread out like litter for them to lie on; and arranged with the flowers in the center under their bodies, and the stalks and leaves pointing outwards. They were suffering from gout, convulsions, and swellings, and had under them round cushions filled with the flowers. I saw their swollen feet being wrapped round with these flowers, and I saw the sick people eating the flowers and drinking water which had been poured on them. The flowers were larger than those here. It was a picture of a long time ago; the people and the doctors wore long white woollen robes with girdles. I saw that the plants were always blessed before use. I saw also a plant of the same family but more succulent and with rounder, juicier, smoother leaves and pale blue blossoms of the same shape, which is very efficacious in children's convulsions. It grows in better soil and is not so common. I think it is called eyebright. I found it once near Dernekamp. It is stronger than the other." She then gave the child three flowers to begin with; the second time she was to have five.

themselves on them with arms extended. I saw them also healing at a distance in a wonderful way, for the sick who could not come themselves sent a representative to whom everything was done as it would have been to the sick person. The time was noted, and the distant sick person was cured at that very hour.

I saw that the Essenes on Horeb had in their caves recesses in the walls where bones, carefully wrapped in cotton and silk, were kept as sacred relics behind gratings. They were bones of prophets who had lived here, and also of the children of Israel who had died near here. There were little pots of green plants standing beside them. The Essenes used to light lamps and pray before the bones in veneration of them.

All the unmarried Essenes who lived together in communities on Mount Horeb and elsewhere observed the greatest cleanliness. They wore long white robes. The head of the Essenes on Horeb wore wonderful priestly vestments during solemn religious services, after the manner of the high priest in Jerusalem, only shorter and not so magnificent. When he prayed and prophesied in the cave of Elias on Mount Horeb, he always wore these sacred vestments, which consisted of about eight pieces. Amongst them was a very sacred relic, a sort of dalmatic or scapular, covering the breast and shoulders, which Moses had worn next to his body and had given to Aaron, from whom it had later descended to the Essenes. The prophet Archos, their head on Mount Horeb, always wore this dalmatic next his body when he was clothed in all his vestments and was praying for prophetic enlightenment. The lower part of his body was wrapped in a loin-cloth, while breast and shoulders were covered with this sacred garment, which I will describe as exactly as I can remember. It will probably be clearer if I cut out a sort of pattern of it in paper. [She then quickly cut the shape out of paper put together, saying:] This sacred scapulary had more or

---

She said: "I see the child's nature, but cannot rightly describe it; inside she is like a torn garment, which needs a new piece of stuff for each tear." (CB)

less this shape when spread out. Its stuff was woven as stiff as hair-cloth. On the middle of the breast and back was a triangular place of double thickness and as it were quilted. I cannot now say for certain what was between the layers. At the neck of the scapulary a triangular piece was cut out, and a ribbon or little strap ran across the top of the opening. Its lower point was still attached to the scapulary, and the triangle could be let down to hide completely another opening over the breast. The place of double thickness mentioned above was ribbed or quilted, and letters were fastened into it with little pins and on the inside with sharp little hooks sticking out and pricking the breast. On the cut-out triangle (which was also of double thickness) at the neck there was also something like letters. I do not now know what was inside these triangles. When the priest put on this sacred vestment, the upper triangle exactly covered the lower one. In the middle of the back there was another place where the stuff was quilted and of two thicknesses, and here, too, there were letters and sharp pins. Over his scapulary the head of the Essenes wore a grey woollen tunic, and on this again a large full tunic made of white twisted silk, girt with a broad belt inscribed with letters. He had a kind of stole round the neck, crossed over the breast, and it was held fast under the girdle and hung down below his knees. The stole was fastened with three straps above and below the place where it was crossed. On this he put a vestment not unlike a chasuble, which was also made of white twisted silk. [She cut out a pattern of this vestment as it looked when spread out.] The back was narrow and came down to the ground; it had two bells attached to the lower hem, which tinkled with the priest's movements and called the people to the service. The front was shorter and broader and open from the neck downwards. This front part had large openings on the breast and below it, through which the stole and undergarment could be seen. These openings were held together in places by fastenings

ornamented with letters and precious stones. The front
and back of this vestment were held together by strips
of stuff under the arms. [These were not shown in the
pattern which she cut out.] Round the neck was an
upright collar, hooked together in front. The priest's
beard, divided in the middle of the chin, fell down over
this collar. Over all this he finally put on a little cloak
of white twisted silk. It shimmered and shone and was
fastened in front with three clasps ornamented with
precious stones on which something was engraved. From
both shoulders of his cloak there were fringes, tassels,
and fruits hanging. Besides all this, he wore a short
maniple on one arm. The head-dress was, as far as I
can remember, also of white silk, twisted into a round
shape and padded, like a turban, yet resembling our
priests' birettas to a certain extent, for at the top it
had ridges like theirs and also a tuft of-silk. A little
plate of gold set with precious stones was fastened over
the forehead.

The Essenes were very austere and frugal in their
way of living. They generally ate only fruit, which they
often cultivated in their gardens. I saw that Archos
usually ate a bitter yellow fruit. About 200 years before
Christ's birth I saw near Jericho a very devout Essene
called Chariot.

Archos or Arkas, the old prophet on Mount Horeb,
ruled over the Essenes for ninety years. I saw how St.
Anne's grandmother questioned him about her own marriage. It is remarkable that it was always about female
children that these prophets made predictions, and that
Anna's ancestors and Anna herself had mostly daughters. It was as if the object of all their devotion and
prayers was to obtain from God a blessing on pious
mothers from whose descendants the Blessed Virgin,
the mother of the Saviour Himself, should spring, as
well as the families of His precursor and of His servants and disciples.

The place where the head of the Essenes on Mount
Horeb prayed and prophesied was the cave where Elias

had dwelt. Many steps led to it up the mountain-side, and one entered the cave through a small cramped opening and down a few steps. The prophet Archos went in alone. For the Essenes this was as if the high priest in the Temple went into the Sanctissimum, for here was their Holy of Holies. Within there were several mysterious holy things, difficult to describe. I will tell what I can remember of them. I saw Anna's grandmother seeking counsel from the prophet Archos.

Anna's grandmother came from Mara in the desert, where her family, which belonged to the married Essenes, owned property. Her name sounded to me like Moruni or Emorun. It was told me that this means something like "good mother" or "noble mother." [11] When the time came for her to be married, she had several suitors, and I saw her go to the prophet Archos on Horeb for him to decide whom she was to accept. She went into a separate part of the large assembly-hall and spoke to Archos, who was in the hall, through a grating, as if she were making her confession to him. It was only in this way that women approached the place. I then saw Archos put on his ceremonial vestments, and ascend thus arrayed the many steps to the top of Mount Horeb, where he entered the cave of Elias by the little door and down the steps. He shut the little door of the cave behind him, and opened a hole in the vaulting dimly illuminating the cave, the interior of which had been carefully hollowed out. Against the wall I saw a little altar carved out of the rock, and noticed, though not quite clearly, several sacred objects on it. On the altar were several pots with low-growing

---

11. These were Catherine Emmerich's words on August 16th, 1821. The names are here written down as the writer heard them pronounced by her lips, and also her explanation "noble mother." When the writer read this passage to a language expert in 1840, the latter said that it was indeed true that *Em romo* means a noble mother. (CB)

Em ramah could mean "noble mother," though the adjective *ram*, usually meaning materially "high" or else "proud," has no obvious parallel in a proper name, except perhaps in Amram (the father of Moses), which may mean "noble uncle." (SB)

bushes of herbs. They were the herbs which grow as high as the hem of Jesus' garment.[12] I know this herb, it grows with us but less vigorously. The plants gave Archos some sort of indication in his prophetic knowledge according to whether they faded or flourished. In the middle between these little bushes of herbs I saw something like a little tree, taller than them, with leaves that looked yellowish and were twisted like snail-shells. There seemed to me to be little figures on this tree. I cannot now say for certain whether this tree was living or was artificial, like the Tree of Jesse. [On the next day she said:] On this little tree with the twisted leaves could be seen, as on a tree of Jesse or genealogical table, how soon the coming of the Blessed Virgin was to be expected. It looked to me as if it were living and yet it seemed also to be a receptacle, for I saw that a blossoming branch was kept inside it. I think it was Aaron's rod, which had once been in the Ark of the Covenant. When Archos prayed in the cave of Elias for a revelation on the occasion of a marriage among Our Lady's ancestors, he took this rod of Aaron into his hand. If the marriage was destined to take its place in Our Lady's ancestry, the rod put forth a bud which produced one or more flowers, among which single flowers were sometimes marked with the sign of the elect. Certain buds represented particular ancestors of Anna, and when these came to be married, Archos observed the buds in question and uttered his prophecies according to the manner in which they unfolded.

The Essenes of Mount Horeb had, however, another holy relic in the cave of Elias; nothing less than a part of the most holy mystery of the Ark of the Covenant which came into their possession when the Ark fell into the hands of enemies. [She spoke here uncertainly of

---

12. She unquestionably meant that these herbs were the same as those mentioned by Eusebius in his ecclesiastical history, Book VII, Chapter 18, which he says grew round the statue of Jesus Christ put up by the woman of Caesarea Philippi, who was cured of the issue of blood. The plants acquired the power of healing all kinds of sicknesses as soon as they had grown high enough to touch the hem of the statue's garment. Eusebius says that this plant is of an unknown species. Catherine Emmerich had spoken before of the statue and of these plants. (CB)

a quarrel and of a schism among the Levites.] This holy thing, concealed in the Ark of the Covenant in the fear of God, was known only to the holiest of the high priests and to a few prophets, but I think that I learnt that it is in some way mentioned in the little-known secret books of the old Jewish thinkers.[13] It was no longer complete in the new Ark of the Covenant in the Temple as restored by Herod. It was no work of man's hands, it was a mystery, a most holy secret of the divine blessing on the coming of the Blessed Virgin full of grace, in whom by the overshadowing of the Holy Ghost the Word became Flesh and God became Man. Before the Babylonian captivity this holy thing had been whole in the Ark of the Covenant; I now saw part of it here in the possession of the Essenes. It was kept in a chalice of shining brown, which seemed to me to be made of a precious stone. They prophesied, too, with the help of this holy thing, which seemed sometimes to put forth as it were little buds.

Archos, after entering the cave of Elias, shut the door and knelt down in prayer. He looked up to the opening in the vaulting and threw himself face downwards on the ground. I then saw the prophetic knowledge that was given to him. He saw that from under the heart of Emorun, who was seeking his counsel, there grew as it were a rose-tree with three branches, with a rose on each of them. The rose on the second branch was marked with a letter, I think an *M*. He saw still more. An angel

---

13. In July 1840, some twenty years after this communication, as this book was being prepared for the press, the writer learnt from a language expert that the cabalistic book Zohar contains several references to this matter. (CB)

   The Zohar is a rabbinic book, claiming descent from Rabbi Simeon ben Yohai (second century), in the form of a commentary on the Pentateuch, interpreting it throughout, in an enigmatic and esoteric style, according to a mystical sense. The Zohar first became known through the 13th-century Rabbi Moses de Leon, who has often been accused of fabricating the whole thing. Present-day opinion, however, suspends judgment, while emphasizing that the Zohar shows evidence of being a compilation of texts and fragments whose composition probably extended over many centuries, and which is likely to enshrine teaching of the greatest antiquity. The Zohar is one of the principal sources of spiritual interpretation among the Jews, and its main theme may be said to be the significance of every detail in sacred history, and the symbolic reflection in this world of the eternal realities of Heaven. With regard to its connection with the statements of AC, see further n. 33, p. 44. (SB)

wrote letters on the wall; I saw Archos rise up as if awaking and read these letters. I forget the details. He then went down from the cave, and announced to the maiden who was awaiting his answer that she was to marry and that her sixth suitor was to be her husband. She would bear a child, marked with a sign, who was chosen out as a vessel of election in preparation for the coming of the Saviour.

Hereupon Emorun married her sixth suitor, an Essene called Stolanus; he did not come from Mara, and as a result of his marriage and of his wife's possessions he was given another name, which I can no longer remember distinctly; it was pronounced in different ways and sounded like Garesha or Sarzirius.[14] Stolanus and Emorun had three daughters, called, I remember, Ismeria and Emerentia, and a younger one whose name, I think, was Enue. They did not remain long at Mara, but moved later to Ephron. I saw that their daughters Ismeria and Emerentia both married in accordance with the prophetic counsels of the prophet on Horeb. (I can

---

14. Catherine Emmerich pronounced these and all other name-sounds with her Low-German accent and often hesitatingly. Her pronunciation, she said, only resembled the real names, and it is impossible to be sure how correctly or incorrectly they have been written down. It is all the more astonishing to find elsewhere long afterwards similar names for the same persons. The following is an instance. Several years after Catherine Emmerich's death the writer found in the *Encomium trium Mariarum Bertaudi,* Petragorici, Paris, 1529, and in particular in the treatise *De cognatione divi Joannis Baptistae cum filiabus et nepotibus beatae Annae,* lib. III, f. lii, etc., attached to it, that St. Cyril, the third General of the Carmelite Order, who died in 1224, mentions in a work concerning the ancestors of St. Anne similar visions of branches, buds, and flowers seen by the prophet of whom counsel was sought. He further states that Stolanus was also called Agarim or Garizi, names which reproduce sounds recognizable in the above-mentioned Garesha or Sarziri. On the other hand, in this account it is a Carmelite on Mount Carmel instead of an Essene on Mount Horeb of whom counsel is sought. Seventeen years after the death of Catherine Emmerich the writer was reading, on the feast of Corpus Christi, 1840, the life of Our Lady's holy mother in the *Actis Sanctorum,* Tom. VI, Julii, where Joannes Eckius in his homily on St. Anne says that Stolanus is called by tradition Stolan, and that the Roman Breviary of 1536 and several Breviaries printed before the reign of Pius V mention a daughter Gaziri, while others call her Garzim. A philological friend who was kind enough to read my proofs, observed: "It is surprising that the names Gaziri, Garzi (the final m has been added), Garsha or Garesha (all three forms are correct, though formed from different verbs) all agree in meaning 'outcast,' and that Agari(m) in Arabic also conveys the idea of flight and banishment. Stolanus in Greek contains the idea of wandering. Sarssir means starling and thus also signifies a wandering bird."(CB)

The Hebrew root *g-r-sh* and the corresponding Arabic root *g-sh-r* convey the idea of banishment. The Hebrew *ger* (and its Arabic equivalent) means a "stranger". The Greek *stolos* means a "journey" (cf. *apostolos*). *Zurzûr* is the Arabic for a "starling," being derived apparently from the bird's noise. (SB)

never understand why I have so often heard that Emerentia was the mother of Anna, for I always saw that it was Ismeria.) I will tell in God's name what I still have in my mind about these daughters of Stolanus and Emorun.[15]

Emerentia married one Aphras or Ophras, a Levite. Of this marriage was born Elisabeth, the mother of John the Baptist. A second daughter was named Enue like her mother's sister. At the time of Mary's birth she was already a widow. There was a third daughter, Rhode, one of whose daughters was Mara, whom I saw present at the death of the Blessed Virgin.

Ismeria married Eliud. They lived after the manner of the married Essenes in the region of Nazareth. They had inherited from their parents the tradition of discipline and continence in married life. Anna was one of their children. The firstborn of Ismeria and Eliud was a daughter called Sobe. Because this child did not bear the sign of the promise, they were much distressed and again went to the prophet on Mount Horeb to seek counsel. Archos exhorted them to betake themselves to prayer and sacrifice, and promised them consolation. After Sobe's birth, Ismeria remained barren for some eighteen years. When she again became pregnant by

---

15. It is certainly true that the writers who follow tradition generally give Emerentia as the mother of St. Anne; but they give the wife of Stolanus as Emerentia, whereas Catherine Emmerich calls her Emorun. According to tradition, Emerentia, the wife of Stolanus, bore Ismeria, the mother of Elisabeth, and Anna, the mother of the Blessed Virgin. Yet according to Catherine Emmerich's account, Anna is the granddaughter, not the daughter, of Stolanus. If this is a mistake of hers, the reason for it may be that the humble visionary has confused her own visions with the account which she had heard from her childhood of the traditional descent of St. Anne. The name Emerentia is perhaps nothing more than the Latinized form of the name (heard by her) of Emorun. But being either ignorant or forgetful of this, and having always heard of the names Emerentia and Ismeria as being traditionally in close association with Stolanus as the nearest relations of Anna before her marriage, she may have described them as daughters of Stolanus. At the same time it is very noticeable that she never confused any of the countless names which came to her ears except in extreme illness and distress. We are, however, inclined to suppose that there must be some error here, for tradition in general mentions St. Elisabeth as being a niece of St. Anne's, whereas according to Catherine Emmerich's account Elisabeth is the niece of Anna's mother, which would seem to make Elisabeth almost older than Anna, who is called a late-born child. Since the writer cannot explain the error which may possibly have crept in, he begs the kind reader to accept it with patience and thus make amends for the writer's lack of that Christian virtue in his difficult and often interrupted task of compiling an account of these visions. (CB)

God's blessing, I saw that Ismeria was given a revelation at night. She saw an angel beside her bed writing a letter on the wall. It seems to me that it was again that letter *M*. Ismeria told her husband of it; he also had seen it in his sleep, but now, while awake, they both saw the sign on the wall. After three months Ismeria gave birth to St. Anne, who came into the world with that sign upon her body.

In her fifth year Anna was, like Our Lady, taken to the school in the Temple, where she remained twelve years. She was brought home again in her seventeenth year, to find two children there—her little sister Maraha, who had been born while she was away, and a little son of her elder sister Sobe called Eliud. A year after this Ismeria fell mortally ill. As she lay dying she spoke to all her relations and presented Anna to them as the future mistress of the house. Then she spoke once more with Anna alone, telling her that she was a chosen vessel of grace, that she must marry, and must seek counsel from the prophet on Mount Horeb. Then she died.

Sobe, Anna's elder sister, was married to Salomo. Besides her son Eliud she had a daughter, Mary Salome, who married Zebedee and was the mother of the Apostles James and John. Sobe had a second daughter who was an aunt of the bridegroom of Cana and the mother of three of Our Lord's disciples. Eliud, the son of Sobe and Salomo, was the second husband of the widow Maroni of Naim and the father of the boy raised by Jesus from the dead.

Maraha, Anna's younger sister, was given the homestead in Sephoris when her father Eliud moved to the valley of Zabulon. She married and had a daughter and two sons, Arastaria and Cocharia, who became disciples. Anna had yet a third sister who was very poor and was the wife of a shepherd on Anna's pastures. She was often in Anna's house.

Enue, the third daughter of Stolanus, married and lived between Bethlehem and Jericho. One of her descendants was with Jesus.

Anna's great-grandfather was a prophet. Eliud, her father, was of the tribe of Levi; her mother Ismeria was of the tribe of Benjamin.[16] Anna was born at Bethlehem, but afterwards her parents moved to Sephoris, four hours from Nazareth, where they had a house and land. They also owned land in the beautiful valley of Zabulon, one and a half hours from Sephoris and three hours from Nazareth. In the fine season of the year Anna's father was often with his family in the valley of Zabulon,[17] and after his wife's death he moved there altogether. This led to the connection with the parents of Joachim, whom Anna married. Joachim's father was called Matthat[18] and was the step-brother of Jacob (father of St. Joseph) and of Joses. Matthat had settled in the valley of Zabulon.

I saw Anna's ancestors helping to carry the Ark of the Covenant with great devotion and piety, and I saw also that they received from the holy thing therein rays of light which extended to their descendants, to Anna and the Blessed Virgin. Anna's parents were rich. This was clear to me because of their possessions; they had many oxen; but they kept nothing for themselves alone, they gave everything to the poor. I saw Anna as a child; she was not particularly beautiful, but yet more so than others. She was far less beautiful than Mary, but remarkably simple and childlike in her piety; I have always seen her like that, whether as girl, mother, or old, old woman. Indeed, whenever I saw a real childlike old peasant woman, it always made me think "she is like Anna." She had several other brothers and sisters, all married, but she did not wish to marry. She

---

16. The Apocryphal Gospels tell us nothing about the ancestors of Our Lady, except the names of Joachim and Anne, which are also attested by the liturgy and the calendar. *Nat. Mar.* I further states that Joachim was from Nazareth and Anne from Bethlehem, and *Ps-Matt.* I that Anne's father was called Achar. Apart from these, AC's statements are all independent. (SB)

17. Most of AC's geographical references are to features traceable on the map, even though some, such as the Valley of Zabulon here, are not specifically mentioned in the Bible. (SB)

18. Matthat, son of Levi, is named in Luke's genealogy (3:23), and see further n. 39, p. 57. (SB)

was particularly fond of her parents, and though she had at least six suitors, she rejected them all. After taking counsel, like her ancestors with the Essenes, she was directed to marry Joachim, whom she did not yet know, but who sought her in marriage when her father Eliud moved to the valley of Zabulon, the home of Joachim's father Matthat.

ST. ANNE AND ST. JOACHIM

JOACHIM was far from handsome. St. Joseph, though no longer young, was in comparison a very handsome man. Joachim was short and broad and at the same time thin, and though he was a wonderfully pious, holy man, I can't help laughing when I think of his appearance. Joachim was poor. He was related to St. Joseph in the following way: Joseph's grandfather was de-scended from David through Solomon and was called Mathan. He had two sons, Jacob and Joses. Jacob was the father of Joseph. When Mathan died, his widow married as her second husband Levi (descended from David through Nathan), and by him had Matthat, the father of Heli, also called Joachim.[19]

Wooing was in those days a very simple affair. The suitors were quite awkward and bashful, and when the young people spoke to each other, they accepted the idea of marriage as something that had to be. If the bride-to-be said yes, the parents were glad, but if she said no and had reason for it, they were just as satis-fied. If everything was settled between the parents, the betrothal followed in the synagogue of the place. The priest prayed at the holy place where the scrolls of the Law lay, the parents in their usual place. Meanwhile the betrothed couple went together into a room and discussed their plans and their marriage contract; if they were in agreement, they told their parents, and their parents told the priest, who came towards them and received their declaration. On the next day the

19. Cf. *infra*, n. 28, p. 34 and n. 39, p. 57.

wedding took place in the open air and with many ceremonies.

Joachim and Anna were married in a little place with only a small school. Only one priest was present. Anna was about nineteen years old. They lived with Eliud, Anna's father. His house belonged to the town of Sephoris, but was some distance away from it, among a group of houses of which it was the largest. Here I think they lived for several years. There was something very distinguished about both of them; they were completely Jewish, but there was in them, unknown to themselves, a wonderful seriousness. I seldom saw them laugh, but they were certainly not sad when they began their married life. They had a serene and even character, and even in their young days they seemed a little like sedate old people. Often in my youth I have seen similar sedate young couples, and even then I used to say to myself, they are just like Anna and Joachim.

Their parents were well-to-do, they had many flocks and herds, beautiful carpets and household things, and many manservants and maidservants. I never saw them cultivating the fields, but often saw them driving cattle out to pasture. They were very pious, devout, charitable, simple, and upright. They often divided their herds and everything else into three parts, and gave a third of the beasts to the Temple, driving them there themselves and handing them over to the Temple servants. The second part they gave to the poor or in answer to the requests of their relations, some of whom were generally there to drive the beasts away. The remainder, which was generally the worst, they kept for themselves. They lived very frugally and gave to all who asked. As a child I often used to think, "Giving brings plenty; he who gives, receives twice in return," for I saw that their third always increased and that soon everything was in such abundance that they were able to make the three divisions again. They had many relations who were assembled in their house on all festive occasions, but I never saw much feasting. I saw them giving food to the poor now and then, but I never saw them having real banquets. When the family were together I generally saw them lying on the ground in a circle, speaking of God in eager expectation. I often saw bad men from their neighbourhood watching them with ill-will and bitterness as they spoke together, looking up to Heaven so full of longing. They were kindly disposed towards these ill-wishers, however, and lost no opportunity of asking them to their house, where they gave them double shares of everything. I often saw these men violently and angrily demanding what the good people gave them in love and charity. There were poor people in their own family, and I often saw them being given a sheep or even several.

The first child born to Anna in her father's house was a daughter, but she was not the child of promise. The signs which had been predicted were not present at her birth, which was attended by some trouble. I saw that Anna, when with child, was distressed about her servants. One of her maidservants had been led astray by a relation of Joachim. Anna, in great dismay at this infringement of the strict discipline of her house, reproached her somewhat severely for her fault, and the maidservant took her misfortune so to heart that she was delivered prematurely of a still-born child. Anna was inconsolable over this, fearing that it was her fault, with the result that her child was also born too soon. Her daughter, however, did not die. Since this child had not the signs of the promise and was born too early, Anna looked upon this as a punishment of God, and was greatly distressed at what she believed to be her own sin. She had, however, great joy in her new-born little daughter, who was called Maria. She was a dear, good, gentle child, and I always saw her growing up rather strong and fat. Her parents were very fond of her, but they felt some uneasiness and distress because they realized that she was not the expected holy fruit of their union. They therefore did penance and lived in continence for a long time. Afterwards Anna remained

barren,[20] which she looked upon as the result of her
having sinned, and so redoubled all her good works. I
saw her often by herself in earnest prayer; I saw, too,
how they often lived apart from each other, gave alms
and sent sacrifices to the Temple.

Anna and Joachim had lived with Anna's father Eliud
for some seven years (as I could see by the age of their
first child), when they decided to separate from their
parents and settle in a house with land in the neighborhood of Nazareth that had come to them from
Joachim's parents. There they intended in seclusion to
begin their married life anew, and to bring down God's
blessing on their union by a way of life more pleasing
to Him. I saw this decision being taken in the family,
and I saw Anna's parents making the arrangements
for their children's new home. They divided their flocks
and herds, setting apart for their children oxen, asses,
and sheep, all much bigger than we have at home. All
the household goods, crockery, and clothes were packed
upon asses and oxen standing before the door. All the
good people were so clever at packing the things up,
and the beasts so intelligent in the way they took their
loads and carried them off. We are not nearly so clever
in packing things into carts as these people were in
loading them onto beasts. They had beautiful household things; all the vessels were more delicate than
nowadays, as if each had been made by the craftsman
with special love and intention. I watched them packing the fragile jugs, decorated with beautiful ornamentation; they filled them with moss, wrapped more moss
round them, and made them fast to both ends of a
strap, so that they hung over the animal's backs, which
were covered with bundles of colored rugs and garments. I saw them, too, packing up costly rugs heavily
embroidered with gold; and the parents gave their
departing children a heavy little lump in a pouch, no

---

20. The Apocryphal Gospels *(Protev.* 2, *Ps-Matt.* I, *Nat. Mar.* I) represent Anna as
childless until the conception of Mary. *Protev.* 2 also relates an incident (though
of a different nature) with a handmaid. (SB)

doubt a piece of precious metal.

When everything was ready, the manservants and maidservants joined the procession, and drove the flocks and herds and the beasts of burden before them to the new home, which was some five or six hours' journey distant. I think it had belonged to Joachim's parents. After Anna and Joachim had taken leave of all friends and servants, with thanks and admonitions, they left their former home with much emotion and with good resolutions. Anna's mother was no longer alive, but I saw that the parents accompanied the couple to their new home. Perhaps Eliud had married again, or perhaps it was only Joachim's parents who were there. Maria Heli, Anna's elder daughter, who was about six or seven years old, was also of the party.

Their new home lay in a pleasant hilly country; it was surrounded by meadows and trees, and was one and a half hours, or a good hour, to the west of Nazareth, on a height between the valley of Nazareth and the valley of Zabulon. A ravine with an avenue of terebinth trees led from the house in the direction of Nazareth. In front of the house was an enclosed courtyard, the floor of which looked to me like bare rock. It was surrounded by a low wall of rocks or rough stones, with a wattle hedge growing either on it or behind it. On one side of this court there were small, not very solid buildings for the workpeople and for storing tools of various kinds; also an open shed had been put up there for cattle and beasts of burden. There were several gardens, and in one near the house was a great tree of a strange kind. Its branches hung down to the ground, took root there and threw up other trees, which did the same until it was encircled by a whole series of arbors. There was a door opening on hinges in the center of the rather large house. The inside of the house was about as big as a moderate-sized village church, and was divided into different rooms by more or less movable wickerwork screens which did not reach to the ceiling. The door opened into the first part of the house, a big ante-room running the whole breadth of the building and used for banquets, or, if necessary, it could be divided up by light movable screens to make small bedrooms when there were many guests. Opposite the house-door was a less solid door in the middle of the back wall of this ante-room, leading to the middle part of the house through a passage with four bedrooms on each side of it. These rooms were partitioned off by light wickerwork screens of a man's height and ending at the top in open trellis-work. From here this passage led into the third or back part of the house, which was not rectangular, as it ended in a semicircular curve like the apse of a church. In the middle of this room, opposite the entrance, the wall of the fireplace rose up to the smoke-opening in the roof of the house; at the foot of this wall was the hearth where cooking was done. A five-branched lamp hung from the ceiling in front of this fireplace. At the side of it and behind it were several rather large rooms divided off by light screens. Behind the hearth, divided off by screens of rugs, were the rooms used by the family—the sleeping-places, the prayer alcove, the eating and working rooms.

Beyond the beautiful orchards round the house were fields, then a wood with a hill behind it.

When the travellers arrived in the house they found everything already in order and in its place, for the old people had sent the things on ahead and had them arranged. The menservants and maidservants had unpacked and settled all the things just as beautifully and neatly as when they were packed up, for they were so helpful and worked so quietly and intelligently by themselves that one did not have to be giving them orders all the time about every single thing as one must do today. Thus everything was soon settled and quiet, and the parents, having brought their children into their new home, blessed and embraced them in farewell, and set off on their journey home, accompanied by their little granddaughter, who went back with them. I never saw feasting going on during such visits and on similar occasions; they often lay in a circle and had a few little bowls and jugs on the carpet before them, but their talk was generally of divine things and holy expectations.

I now saw the holy couple beginning an entirely new life here. It was their intention to offer to God all that was past and to behave as though their marriage had only then taken place, endeavoring to live in a manner pleasing to God, and thus to bring down upon them His blessing which they so earnestly desired beyond all else. I saw both of them going amongst their flocks and herds and following the example of their parents (as I have described above) in dividing them into three portions between the Temple, the poor, and themselves. The best and choicest portion was driven off to the Temple; the poor were given the next best one, and the least good they kept for themselves. This they did with all their possessions. Their house was quite spacious; they lived and slept in separate little rooms, where I saw them very often praying by themselves with great devotion. I saw them living in this way for a long time, giving generous alms, and each time they divided their herds and goods I saw that everything quickly increased again. They lived very abstemiously, observing periods of self-denial and continence. I saw them praying in penitential garments, and I often saw Joachim kneeling in supplication to God when he was with his herds far away in the pastures.

For nineteen years after the birth of their first child they lived thus devoutly before God in constant yearning for the gift of fruitfulness and with an increasing distress. I saw ill-disposed neighbors coming to them and speaking ill of them, saying that they must be bad people since no children were born to them, that the little girl with Anna's parents was not really her daughter, but had been adopted by her because of her barrenness, otherwise she would have had her at home, and so forth. Each time they heard such words, the distress of the good couple was renewed.

Anna's steadfast faith was supported by an inmost certainty that the coming of the Messias was near, and that she herself was among His human relations. She prayed for the fulfillment of the Promise with loud supplications, and both she and Joachim were always striving after more perfect purity of life. The shame of her unfruitfulness distressed her deeply. She could hardly appear in the synagogue without affront. Joachim, though short and thin, was robust, and I often saw him going to Jerusalem with the beasts for sacrifice. Anna was not tall either, and very delicately formed. Her grief so consumed her that her cheeks, though still slightly tinged with red, were quite hollow. They continued to give portions of their herds to the Temple and to the poor, while the portion they kept for themselves grew ever smaller and smaller.

After having besought God's blessing on their marriage for so many years in vain, I saw that Joachim was minded to offer another sacrifice at the Temple. He and Anna prepared themselves for this by penitential devotions. I saw them lying on the hard earth in prayer during the night, girt in penitential garments; after which Joachim went at sunrise across the country to where his herds were pasturing, while Anna remained at home by herself. Soon after this I saw Anna sending him doves, other birds and many different things in cages and baskets. They were all taken to him by menservants to be offered up in the Temple. He took two donkeys from the pasture, and loaded them with these baskets and with others into which he put, I think, three very lively little white creatures with long necks. I cannot remember whether they were lambs or kids. He had with him a staff with a light on the top of it, which looked as if it were shining inside a hollow gourd. I saw him arriving with his menservants and beasts of burden at a beautiful green field between Bethany and Jerusalem, a place where later I often saw Jesus stay. They journeyed on to the Temple, and stabled the donkeys at the same Temple inn, near the cattle-market, where Joachim and Anna afterwards lodged at Mary's Presentation. They then took the sacrificial offerings up the steps, and passed through the dwellings of the Temple servants as before.[21] Here Joachim's servants went back after handing over the offerings.

Joachim himself entered the hall, where stood the basin of water in which all the sacrifices were washed. He then went through a long passage into a hall on the left of the place in which were the altar of incense, the table of the shew-breads and the seven-branched candlestick.[22] There were several others assembled there to make sacrifices, and it was here that Joachim had to bear his hardest trial. I saw that one of the priests, Reuben[23] by name, disdained his offerings, and did not put them with the others on the right-hand of the hall, where they could be seen behind the bars, but thrust them on one side. He reproached the unfortunate Joachim loudly and before the others for his unfruitfulness, refused to admit him and sent him, in disgrace, to an alcove enclosed with gratings. I saw that upon this Joachim left the Temple in the greatest distress and betook himself to an assembly-house of the Essenes near Machaerus, passing Bethany on the way. Here he sought counsel and consolation. (In this same house, and earlier in a similar one near Bethlehem, lived the prophet Manachem,[24] who prophesied to the young Herod about his kingdom and his crimes.) From here Joachim betook himself to his most distant herds on

---

21. The reader must not be disconcerted by Catherine Emmerich's references (here and subsequently) to events which may not yet have been mentioned in her account. It must be remembered that the visions from the story of the Blessed Virgin, here given in chronological order, were vouchsafed to Catherine Emmerich year by year on the various church festivals with which these visions were connected; so that now when relating in July and August 1821, at the time of the feasts of St. Anne and St. Joachim, her visions of the life of Our Lady's parents, she is referring (in order to make herself more comprehensible) to something which she had already seen in previous years in November on the occasion of the feast of Our Lady's Presentation at the Temple. (CB)

22. Cf. *3 Kings* 7:48, 49. (SB)

23. The priest Reuben appears in *Protev.* I, *Ps-Matt.* 2, and in *Nat. Mar.* 2 is named Issachar. (SB)

24. This Manachem appears in no document. (SB)

Mount Hermon. His way led him across the Jordan through the desert of Gaddi. Mount Hermon is a long narrow mountain, beautifully green and rich with fruit-trees on the sunny side, but covered with snow on the other.

Joachim was so grieved and ashamed at having been rejected with scorn at the Temple that he did not even send to tell Anna whither he had betaken himself. She heard, however, of the humiliation he had suffered from others who had witnessed it, and her distress was indescribable. I saw her often lying weeping with her face to the earth, because she had no knowledge of where Joachim was. I believe that he remained hidden among his flocks on Mount Hermon for as long as five months. During the end of that time Anna's distress was much increased by the rudeness of one of her maidservants, who kept reproaching her for her misfortunes. Once, however, when this maidservant asked to be allowed to go away for the Feast of Tabernacles (which was just beginning), Anna, remembering how her former maidservant had been led astray, refused permission out of vigilant care for her household. Whereupon this maidservant attacked her so violently, declaring that her barrenness and Joachim's desertion of her was God's punishment for her severity, that Anna could not bear to have her in her house anymore. She sent her back to her parents with presents and accompanied by two menservants, with the request that they would take back their daughter who had been entrusted to her, as she could not keep her in her house any longer. After sending away this maid, Anna went sadly into her room to pray. Towards evening she threw a large shawl over her head, wrapping herself in it completely, and went with a shaded light to the great tree in the courtyard which I have described before as forming an arbor. Here she lit a lamp hanging on this tree in a sort of box, and prayed from a scroll. This tree was a very large one, there were arbors and seats arranged under it, for its branches reached over the wall to the ground, where they took root and shot up and again sank to the ground and took root, so that a whole series of arbors encircled it. This tree was like the tree in the Garden of Eden which bore the forbidden fruit. Its fruits hung from the ends of the branches generally in bunches of five. They are pear-shaped, and their flesh has blood-colored streaks; there is a hollow in the center, round which are the seeds embedded in the flesh. The leaves are very large, resembling, I think, those with which Adam and Eve covered themselves in the Garden of Eden. The Jews used these leaves specially for the Feast of Tabernacles. They decorated the walls with them, because they could be fitted together beautifully one behind the other like fishes' scales. Anna remained under this tree for a long time, crying to God and begging that even though He made her barren, yet He might not keep her pious companion Joachim far from her. And lo, there appeared to her an angel of God, he seemed to step down before her from the top of the tree, and spoke to her, telling her to be of good heart, for the Lord had heard her prayer;[25] she was to journey next day to the Temple with two maidservants, taking with her doves as a sacrifice. Joachim's prayer, too, he said, had been heard, and he was on his way to the Temple with his offerings; she would meet him under the Golden Gate. Joachim's sacrifice would be accepted, and they would be blessed and made fruitful; soon she would learn the name by which their child was to be called. He told her, too, that he had given a like message to her husband. Then he disappeared.

Anna, full of joy, thanked God for His mercies. She then went back into the house and gave her maidservants the necessary orders for their journey to the Temple next morning. I saw her afterwards lying down to sleep after praying. Her bed was a narrow blanket with a pillow under her head. (In the morning her blan-

---

25. The story of Anna's consolation by the angel, and the appointment of a rendezvous at the Golden Gate is found in *Protev.* 4, *Ps-Matt.* 3, *Nat. Mar.* 3. (SB)

ket was rolled up.) She took off her upper garments, wrapped herself from head to foot in an ample covering and lay down at full length on her right side, with her face to the wall against which was the bed. After she had slept for a short time, I saw a brightness pouring down towards her from above, which on approaching her bed was transformed into the figure of a shining youth. It was the angel of the Lord, who told her that she would conceive a holy child; stretching his hand over her, he wrote great shining letters on the wall which formed the name MARY. Thereupon the angel dissolved into light and disappeared. During this time Anna seemed to be wrapped in a secret, joyful dream. She rose half-waking from her couch, prayed with great intensity, and then fell asleep again without having completely recovered consciousness. After midnight she awoke joyfully, as if by an inner inspiration, and now she saw, with alarm mixed with joy, the writing on the wall. This seemed to be of shining golden-red letters, large and few in number; she gazed at them with unspeakable joy and contrite humility until day came, when they faded away. She saw the writing so clearly, and her joy thereat became so great, that when she got up she appeared quite young again. In the moment when the light of the angel had enveloped Anna in grace, I saw a radiance under her heart and recognized in her the chosen Mother, the illuminated vessel of the grace that was at hand. What I saw in her I can only describe by saying that I recognized in her the cradle and tabernacle of the holy child she was to conceive and preserve; a mother blessed indeed. I saw that by God's grace Anna was able to bear fruit. I cannot describe the wonderful manner in which I recognized this. I saw Anna as the cradle of all mankind's salvation, and at the same time as a sacred altar-vessel, opened, yet hidden behind a curtain. I recognized this after a natural manner, and all this knowledge of mine was one and was natural and sacred at the same time. (Anna was at that time, I think, forty-three years old.) She now got up, lit the lamp, prayed, and then started on her journey to Jerusalem with her offerings. All the members of her household were full of strange joyfulness that morning, though none but Anna knew of the coming of the angel.

At the same time I saw Joachim among his flocks on Mount Hermon beyond the Jordan constantly praying God to grant his supplications. As he watched the young lambs bleating and frolicking round their mothers, he felt sorely distressed at having no children, but did not tell his shepherds why he was so sad. It was near the time of the Feast of Tabernacles, and he and his shepherds were beginning to put up the tabernacles. Remembering his humiliation at the Temple, he had abandoned the idea of going up as usual to Jerusalem for the feast and offering sacrifices, but as he was praying I saw an angel appear to him, telling him to be of good courage and to journey to the Temple, for his sacrifice would be accepted and his prayers granted. He would meet his wife under the Golden Gate. Thereupon I saw Joachim joyfully dividing his flocks and herds once more into three portions—and what numbers of fine beasts he had! The least good he kept for himself, the next best he sent to the Essenes, and the best of all he drove to the Temple with his herdsmen. He arrived in Jerusalem on the fourth day of the feast, and stayed in his usual lodgings near the Temple. Anna arrived in Jerusalem also on the fourth day of the feast and stayed with Zacharias' relations by the fish-market. She did not meet Joachim until the end of the feast.

Although on the previous occasion it was by a sign from above that Joachim's offerings were rejected, I saw that the priest who had treated him so harshly instead of comforting and consoling him was in some way (I cannot remember how) punished by God. Now, however, the priests had received a divine warning to accept his offerings, and I saw that some of them, on being told of his approach with the sacrificial beasts, went out of the Temple to meet him and accepted his gifts. The cattle which he had brought as a gift to the Temple were not his actual offering. The sacrifice he brought to be slaughtered consisted of two lambs and three lively little animals, kids, I think. I saw, too, that many of his acquaintances congratulated him on his sacrifice being accepted. I saw that because of the feast the whole Temple was open and decorated with garlands of fruit and greenery, and that in one place a Tabernacle had been set up on eight detached pillars. Joachim went from place to place in the Temple exactly as he did before. His sacrifice was slaughtered and burnt at the usual place. Some part of it was, however, burnt at another place, to the right, I think, of the entrance hall with the great teaching pulpit.[26] I saw the priests making a sacrifice of incense in the Holy Place. Lamps, too, were lighted and lights burned on the seven-branched candlestick, but not on all seven branches at once. I often saw that on different occasions different branches of it were lighted. As the smoke arose from the offering, I saw as it were a beam of light falling upon the officiating priest in the Holy Place and at the same time on Joachim without in the hall. There came a sudden pause in what was going on, it seemed from astonishment and the realization of something supernatural. Thereupon I saw that two priests went out into the hall to Joachim as though by God's command, and led him through the side rooms up to the golden altar of incense in the Holy Place. The priest then laid something on the altar. This was not, I could see, separate grains of incense; it looked like a solid lump, but I cannot remember what it was.[27]

26. This statement is confirmed by the following: According to Jewish tradition a portion of the burnt offering had to be burnt, not on the altar, but near it and to the east, on the so-called ash-heap. This portion was the sinew of the thigh, which in Jacob's wrestling with the Angel withered up on being touched by the latter ("forthwith it shrank," *Gen.* 32:25). See also *Gen.* 32:32. (CB)

   Gen. 32:32 states that the Israelites "eat not of the sinew which shrank," but there is no available subsequent legislation about this matter. (SB)

27. It was doubtless a mixture, melted together, of the ingredients required by Jewish tradition for the daily incense-offering, namely myrrh, cassia, spikenard, saffron, sweet-scented reed, cinnamon, costus, sea-lavender, thrift, galbanum, and incense, mixed with pure salt. (CB)

   Exod. 30:34-38 prescribed four elements in the preparation of incense. Later rabbinic tradition increased these (as CB notes), and by the time of Christ thirteen elements were used, as Josephus relates *(BJ,* V, v, 5). (SB)

This lump gave out a powerful and sweet smell of incense as it was burnt upon the altar of incense before the veil of the Holy of Holies. Then I saw the priest going away, leaving Joachim alone in the Holy Place. While the incense-offering was being consumed I saw Joachim in a state of ecstasy, kneeling with outstretched arms. I saw approaching him a shining figure of an angel, such as later appeared to Zacharias when he received the promise of the Baptist's birth. The angel spoke to Joachim, and gave him a scroll on which I recognized, written in shining letters, the three names Helia, Hanna, Miriam.[28] Beside the last of these names I saw the picture of a little Ark of the Covenant or tabernacle. Joachim fastened this scroll to his breast under his garment. The angel told him that his unfruitfulness was no disgrace for him, but on the contrary, an honor, for the child his wife was to conceive was to be the immaculate fruit of God's blessing upon him and the crowning point of the blessing of Abraham. Joachim, being unable to grasp this, was led by the angel behind the veil hanging in front of the Holy of Holies. Between this veil and the bars of the screen before the Holy of Holies was a space large enough to stand in. I saw the angel approach the Ark of the Covenant, and it seemed to me as if he took something out of it, for I saw him hold towards Joachim a shining globe or circle of light, bidding him breathe upon it and look into it. (When he held the circle of light so near his face, it made me think of a custom at our country weddings where the sacristan gives

---

28. The writer was at the time unaware that these three names were only other forms of Joachim, Anna, and Mary. His later discovery of this proof of the accuracy of Catherine Emmerich's version of the names was a striking testimony to the authenticity of her visions. (CB)

See *infra*, n. 39, p. 57, on the identification of Joachim and Heli. The name Joachim *(Yehoyaqim)* means "The Lord shall make to stand (or rise)" (e.g. *4 Kings* 23:34). The name Helia (presumably *Heli-yah)* would mean "My strength is the Lord," but does not occur in the Bible. It is, however, maintained in *Cath. Enc.,* art. "Virgin Mary," p. 464, E d, that Elia (Helia) is but an abbreviation of the name Eliacim *(Elyaqim),* which, using the other divine name, means "God shall make to stand (or rise)", and, indeed, in *4 Kings* 23:34 the name of King Eliacim was changed by Pharaoh to Joakim *(Yoyaqim).* (SB)

one a little board to kiss with a head painted on it, and makes one pay three halfpence for doing so.) Then I saw as if all kinds of pictures appeared in the circle of light when Joachim breathed on it and that these were visible to him. His breath had in no way dimmed the circle of light, and the angel told him that the conception of Anna's child would be as untarnished as this globe, which had remained shining in spite of his having breathed on it. Thereupon I saw as if the angel lifted the globe until it stood like an encircling halo in the air, in which I saw, as through an opening in it, a series of pictures starting with the Fall and ending with the Redemption of mankind. The whole course of the world passed before my eyes as one picture merged into another. I knew and understood it all, but I cannot reproduce the details. Above, at the very summit, I saw the Blessed Trinity, and below and on one side of the Trinity I saw the Garden of Eden, with Adam and Eve, the Fall, the promise of Redemption and all its prototypes—Noah, the Flood, the Ark, the receiving of the blessing through Abraham, its handing on to his firstborn Isaac, from Isaac to Jacob, how it was taken from Jacob by the angel with whom he struggled, how the blessing came to Joseph in Egypt and increased in glory in him and in his wife. I saw how the sacred presence of the blessing was removed by Moses from Egypt with relics of Joseph and his wife Aseneth, and became the Holy of Holies of the Ark of the Covenant, the presence of the living God among His people. Then I saw the reverence paid by God's people to this sacred thing and their ceremonies respecting it; I saw the relationships and marriages which formed the sacred genealogy of Our Lady's ancestry, as well as all the prototypes and symbols of her and of Our Saviour in history and in the prophets. All this I saw in encircling symbols and also rising from the lower part of the ring of light. I saw pictures of great cities, towers, palaces, thrones, gates, gardens, and flowers, all strangely woven together as it were by bridges of light; and all were being attacked and assaulted by

fierce beasts and other figures of might. These pictures
all signified how Our Blessed Lady's ancestral family,
from which God was to take Flesh and be made Man,
had been led, like all that is holy, by God's grace through
many assaults and struggles. I remember, too, having
seen at a certain point in this series of pictures a garden surrounded by a thick hedge of thorns, which a host
of serpents and other loathsome creatures attempted in
vain to penetrate. I also saw a strong tower assaulted
on all sides by men-at-arms, who were falling down from
it. I saw many pictures of this kind, relating to the history of the ancestry of Our Lady; and the bridges and
passages which joined all together signified the victory
over all attempts to disturb, hinder, or interrupt the
work of salvation. It was as if by God's compassion there
had been poured into mankind, as into a muddy stream,
a pure flesh and a pure blood, and as if this had with
great toil and difficulty to reconstitute itself out of its
scattered elements, the whole stream striving the while
to draw it into its troubled waters; and then as if by
the countless mercies of God and the faithful cooperation of mankind, it had at last issued forth, after many
pollutions and many cleansings, in an unfailing stream
out of which rose the Blessed Virgin, from whom the
Word was made Flesh and dwelt among us.

Among the pictures that I saw in the globe of light
there were many which occur in the litany of Our Lady.
Whenever I say that litany, I see them and recognize
them and venerate them with great devotion. The pictures in the globe unfolded themselves still further till
they reached the fulfilment of all God's compassion
towards mankind, so divided and dispersed in its fallen
state, and ended, on the side opposite the Garden of
Eden, with the heavenly Jerusalem at the foot of the
Throne of God. After I had seen all these pictures, the
globe (which was really a series of pictures passing in
and out of a circle of light) disappeared. I think that
all this was a communication to Joachim of a vision
revealed to him by the angel and also seen by me.

Whenever I receive such a communication, it appears in a circle of light like a globe.

I saw now that the angel touched or anointed Joachim's forehead with the tip of his thumb and forefinger, and that he gave him a shining morsel to eat and a luminous liquid to drink from a gleaming little chalice which he held between two fingers. It was of the shape of the chalice at the Last Supper, but without a foot. It seemed to me, too, that this food which he put in his mouth took the form of a little shining ear of corn and a little shining cluster of grapes, and I understood that thereafter every impurity and every sinful desire left Joachim. Thereupon I saw that the angel imparted to Joachim the highest and holiest fruit of the blessing given by God to Abraham, and culminating, through Joseph, in the holy thing within the Ark of the Covenant, in the presence of God among His people. He gave Joachim this blessing in the same form as I had been shown before, except that while the angel of benediction gave Abraham the blessing from himself, out of his bosom as it were, he seemed to give it to Joachim from out of the Holy of Holies.[29]

The blessing of Abraham was as it were the beginning of God's grace given in blessing to the father of His future people so that from him might proceed the stones for the building of His Temple. But when Joachim received the blessing, it was as though the angel were taking the holy benediction from the tabernacle of this Temple and delivering it to a priest, in order that from him might be formed the holy vessel in which the Word was to be made Flesh. All this cannot be expressed in

---

29. Catherine Emmerich, who in communicating her many and various visions from the Old Testament often spoke in great detail of the Ark of the Covenant, never said that after the Babylonian captivity the first Ark of the Covenant with all its contents was placed in the rebuilt Temple or later in the Temple restored by Herod. She did, however, state that there was a restored Ark in the Holy of Holies of the Temple, in which were still preserved a few remains of the sacred contents of the first Ark of the Covenant, some of which she saw in the possession of the Essenes and venerated by them.

Josephus (BJ, V, v, 5) plainly states that there was "nothing at all" in the Holy of Holies in Herod's Temple. (SB)

words, for I speak of that Holy of Holies inviolate, yet violated in man when he sinned and fell. From my earliest youth I have very often, in my visions from the Old Testament, seen into the Ark of the Covenant, and have always had the impression of a complete church, but more solemn and awe-inspiring. I saw therein not only the Tables of the Law as the written Word of God, but also a sacramental presence of the Living God,[30] like the roots of the wine and wheat and of the flesh and blood of the future Sacrifice of our redemption.

The grace given by this blessed presence produced, with the cooperation of God-fearing men under the Law, that holy tree whose final blossoming was the pure flower in which the Word became flesh and God became Man, thus giving us in the New Covenant His humanity and His divinity by instituting the Sacrament of His Body and Blood, without which we cannot attain eternal life. I have never known the Ark of the Covenant without the sacramental presence of God except when it had fallen into the hands of the enemy, at which times the holy presence was safe in the hands of the High Priest or of one of the prophets. When only the Tables of the Law were present in the Ark of the Covenant, without the holy treasure, it seemed to me like the Temple of the Samaritans on Mount Garizim or like a church of our own time which is without the Blessed Sacrament and, instead of the Tables of the Law written by God's hand, contains only the books of Holy Scripture imperfectly understood by mankind.

In the Ark of the Covenant made by Moses, which stood in the Temple and Tabernacle of Solomon, I saw this most Holy Thing of the Old Covenant in the form of a shining circle crossed by two smaller rays of light intersecting each other; but now, when the angel imparted the blessing to Joachim, I saw this blessing

---

30. The reader need not be scandalized by the expression "sacramental presence of God," for Holy Writ clearly declares that God was present above the Ark of the Covenant in a mysterious and visible manner. (CB)

being given to him in the form as it were of something
shining, like a shining seed or bean in shape, which he
laid in the open breast of Joachim's garment. When the
blessing was imparted to Abraham, I saw grace being
conveyed to him in the same manner, and its virtue and
efficacy remaining with him in the degree ordained by
God until he handed it over to his firstborn son Isaac,
from whom it passed to Jacob and from him, through
the angel, to Joseph, and from Joseph and his wife, with
increased virtue, to the Ark of the Covenant. I perceived
that the angel bound Joachim to secrecy, and I understood why it was that later Zacharias, the Baptist's
father, had become dumb after he had received the
blessing and the promise of Elisabeth's fruitfulness from
the Angel Gabriel at the Altar of Incense. [*Luke* 1:9-
22.] It was revealed to me, that with this blessing
Joachim received the highest fruit and the true fulfillment of Abraham's blessing, namely the blessing for
the immaculate conception of the most Holy Virgin who
was to bruise the head of the serpent. The angel then
led Joachim back into the Holy Place and disappeared,
upon which Joachim sank to the ground in an ecstasy
as though paralyzed. The priests who re-entered the
Holy Place found him radiant with joy. They lifted him
up reverently, and placed him outside in a seat generally used only by priests. Here they washed his face,
held some strong-smelling substance to his nostrils,
gave him to drink and in general treated him as one
does someone who has fainted. When he had recovered,
he looked young and strong, and was beaming with joy.

It was a warning from on high that had led Joachim
into the Holy Place, and it was by a similar inspiration
that he was brought into a subterranean passage which
belonged to the consecrated part of the Temple and ran
under it and under the Golden Gate. I have been told
what was the meaning and origin of this passage when
the Temple was built, and also what it was used for,
but I have no clear recollection of this. Some religious
observance relating to the blessing and reconciliation

of the unfruitful was, I think, connected with this passage. In certain circumstances people were brought into it for rites of purification, expiation, absolution, and the like.[31] Joachim was led by priests near the slaughtering-place through a little door into this passage. The priests turned back, but Joachim continued along the passage, which gradually sloped downwards. Anna had also come to the Temple with her maidservant, who was carrying the doves for sacrifice in wicker baskets. She had handed over her offering and had revealed to a priest that she had been bidden by an angel to meet her husband under the Golden Gate. I now saw that she was led by priests, accompanied by some venerable women (among whom I think was the prophetess Anna), through an entrance on the other side into the consecrated passage, where her companions left her. I had a very wonderful view of what this passage was like. Joachim went through a little door; the passage sloped downwards, and was at first narrow but became broader afterwards. The walls were of glistening gold and green, and a reddish light shone in from above. I saw beautiful pillars like twisted trees and vines. After passing through about a third of the passage Joachim came to a place in the midst of which stood a pillar in the form of a palm-tree with hanging leaves and fruits. Here he was met by Anna, radiant with happiness. They embraced each other with holy joy, and each told the other their good tidings. They were in a state of ecstasy and enveloped in a cloud of light. I saw this light issuing from a great host of angels, who were carrying the appearance of a high shining tower and hovering above the heads of Anna and Joachim. The form of this tower was the same as I see in pictures, from the litany of Our Lady, of the Tower of David, the Tower

---

31. The matter of the tunnel is one that has long puzzled students. Josephus *(Ant.,* XV, xi, 5) certainly mentions an eastern gate where the "pure" could enter, and (ib., 7) a tunnel that led from the eastern gate into the central enclosure, adding that this was built specially for the king (Herod). Then the Mishnah, *Middoth*, I, 9, mentions a tunnel leading under the Temple to a bath-house within the enclosure, where ceremonial cleansing could be performed. Whether these refer to the same tunnel is uncertain. See further, n. 43, p. 62. (SB)

of Ivory, and so forth. I saw that this tower seemed to disappear between Anna and Joachim, who were enveloped in a glory of brightness. I understood, that as a result of the grace here given, the conception of Mary was as pure as all conceptions would have been but for the Fall. I had at the same time an indescribable vision. The heavens opened above them, and I saw the joy of the Holy Trinity and of the angels, and their participation in the mysterious blessing here bestowed on Mary's parents. Anna and Joachim returned, praising God, to the exit under the Golden Gate: towards the end the passage sloped upwards. They came into a kind of chapel under a beautiful and high arch, where many lights were burning. Here they were received by priests who led them away. The part of the Temple above which was the hall of the Sanhedrin lay over the middle of the subterranean passage; above this end of it were, I think, dwellings of priests whose duty it was to look after the vestments. Joachim and Anna now came to a kind of bay at the outermost edge of the Temple hill, overlooking the valley of Josaphat, where the path could no longer go straight on but branched to right and left. After they had visited another priest's house, I saw Joachim and Anna and their servants starting on their journey home. On their arrival at Nazareth, Joachim, after a joyful meal, gave food to many poor people and distributed generous alms. I saw how full he and Anna were of joy and fervor and gratitude to God when they thought of His compassion towards them; I often saw them praying together with tears.

It was explained to me here that the Blessed Virgin was begotten by her parents in holy obedience and complete purity of heart, and that thereafter they lived together in continence in the greatest devoutness and fear of God. I was at the same time clearly instructed how immeasurably the holiness of children was encouraged by the purity, chastity, and continence of their parents and by their resistance to all unclean temptations;

and how continence after conception preserves the fruit of the womb from many sinful impulses. In general, I was given an overflowing abundance of knowledge about the roots of deformity and sin.

THE CONCEPTION OF THE BLESSED VIRGIN

[Here follow various visions which Catherine Emmerich communicated at different times in the course of her yearly meditations during the octave of the feast of the Immaculate Conception. Though they do not directly continue the story of Our Lady's life, yet they throw a remarkable light on the mystery of her election, preparation, and veneration as the vessel of grace. As these visions were related by Catherine Emmerich in the midst of much suffering and many interruptions, it is not surprising if they are somewhat fragmentary in character.]

I SAW in a wonderful picture that God showed the angels how it was His Will to restore mankind after the Fall. At first sight I did not understand this picture, but soon it became quite clear to me. I saw the Throne of God and the Holy Trinity, and at the same time a movement within that Trinity. I saw the nine choirs of angels, and how God announced to them in what manner it was His Will to restore the fallen human race. I saw an inexpressible joy among the angels over this. I was now shown in a number of symbolic pictures the unfolding of God's designs for the salvation of mankind. I saw these pictures appearing among the nine choirs of angels and following each other in a kind of historical sequence. I saw the angels helping to make these pictures, protecting and defending them. I cannot now remember for certain the order in which they appeared, but will tell in God's name what I can still recollect. I saw a mountain as of precious stones appear before the Throne of God; it grew and spread. It was in terraces, like a throne; then it changed into the shape of a tower—a tower which enshrined every treasure of the spirit and every gift of grace and was surrounded by the nine choirs of angels. At one side of this tower vine tendrils and ears of corn, intertwined like the fingers of folded hands, seemed to be streaming down from the edge of a golden cloud. I cannot remember at what exact moment in the whole picture I saw this. I saw in the sky a figure like a virgin which passed into the tower and as it were melted into it. The tower was very broad and was flat at the top; it seemed to have an opening at the back through which the virgin passed into it. This was not the Blessed Virgin as she is in time, but as she is in eternity, in God. I saw the appearance of her being formed before the face of the Holy Trinity, just as when one breathes, a little cloud is formed before one's mouth.[32] I also saw something going forth from the Holy Trinity towards the tower. At this moment of the picture I saw a vessel like a ciborium being formed among the choirs of angels. The angels all joined in giving this vessel the form of a tower surrounded by many pictures full of significance. Beside it stood two figures joining hands behind it. This spiritual vessel went on increasing in size, beauty, and richness. Then I saw something proceed from God and pass through all nine choirs of angels; it seemed to me like a little shining holy cloud which became more and more distinct as it approached the sacramental vessel which it finally entered. But in order that I should recognize this to be a real and essential blessing of God conferring the grace of a pure and sinless line from generation to generation (like the cultivation of some plant in all its purity), I finally saw this blessing in the shape

---

32. See the Little Chapter in the Vespers of the Office of the Blessed Virgin Mary from *Ecclus.* 24:14. "From the beginning, and before the world, was I created, and unto the world to come I shall not cease to be" (*"Ab initio et ante saecula creata sum et usque ad futura saecula non desinam"*). Compare also the passage of Holy Writ which has long been applied by the Church to Mary: "I came out of the mouth of the Most High, the firstborn before all creatures. I made that in the heavens there should rise light that never faileth. . . . My throne is in a pillar of cloud" (*"Ego ex ore Altissimi prodivi primogenita ante omnem creaturam, ego feci in coelis, ut orietur lumen indeficiens. Thronus meus in columna nubis"*. (*Ecclus.* 24:5). (CB)

of a shining bean, enter the ciborium, which then passed into the tower.[33] I saw the angels actively taking part in the showing forth of these visions. There rose, however, from the depths below a series of what seemed to be false visions, for I saw the angels combating these and thrusting them aside. Many of these false visions I have forgotten, but here is what I still remember about them.

I saw a church rise up from below, almost in the same form in which the holy universal Church always

---

33. In the course of her many visions, some historical and some symbolical, from the Old and New Testaments, Catherine Emmerich referred to this blessing in many different connections, some of which we will here enumerate in their chronological order. "This was the same blessing by means of which Eve was brought forth from the right side of Adam. I saw this blessing withdrawn by God's merciful providence from Adam when he was about to acquiesce in sin; but it was restored to Abraham by the angel after the institution of circumcision, with the promise of Isaac's birth. Abraham handed it on, with solemn sacramental ceremony, to his firstborn Isaac, from whom it descended to Jacob. It was taken away from Jacob by the angel that strove with him and handed on to Joseph in Egypt. Finally it was taken by Moses, together with the bones of Joseph, in the night before the flight out of Egypt, and became the Israelites' sacred treasure in the Ark of the Covenant."

We had just prepared these disclosures for the press, but with considerable doubt and hesitation, when we learnt that the book Zohar (ascribed to Simon Bar Jochai in the second century of our era) reproduces almost word for word these and other statements of Catherine Emmerich about this mystery of the Jewish Covenant. Anyone able to read late Chaldaean can convince himself of this by referring to the following passages: *Zohar Par. Tol'doth,* pp. 340 and 345 (edit. Sulzbach), *Bereshith,* p. 135, *Terumah,* pp. 251, etc. (CB)

It would seem that CB was slightly misled in regard to the Zohar, and it is unlikely that he was in a position to examine it himself, since qualified Hebraists and Aramaic scholars admit its great difficulty. The Zohar does not appear to contain any notably close parallels with statements of AC, either about the "mystery of the Ark" (p. 15), or the "holy thing" within it (pp. 37-38), or about the blessing handed down through the Patriarchs to Moses (p. 35 and CB's note above).

The references given by CB above are to the Hebrew (and Aramaic) text published at Sulzbach in 1684, and refer to columns in the commentaries on Genesis and Exodus. We are adding here the standard modern references (to folios of the Mantua edition of 1588), which are also inserted in the English translation by Sperling and Simon (London, 1931-1934).

Bereshith (Genesis), col. 135 in Sulzbach (=f. 48b-49a, standard), contains no relevant reference; but f. 55b (Sulzbach, col. 171), commenting on "This is the book" (*Gen.* 5:1), takes that phrase literally and refers it to the story of the book containing sacred wisdom, which was given by God through an angel to Adam, and then handed down through the patriarchs and finally to Abraham.

Toledoth (Genesis), *col.* 340 in Sulzbach (=f. 146a, b, standard), recounts the many occasions on which Jacob received a blessing. The next reference, to col. 345 (=f. 148a, standard), belongs in fact to the next section *Wayyese,* and discusses the mystical meaning of the stones picked up by Jacob in Gen. 28:11.

Terumah (Exodus), col. 251 in Sulzbach (=f. 153b, 154a, standard), though commenting on the construction of the ark (*Exod.* 25), has no reference to the "mystery" or the "holy thing." A little earlier, however, f. 145b (Sulzbach, col. 238) has a passing reference to the heavenly mystery of the Holy of Holies.

It seems therefore legitimate to say that the Zohar, interesting though it is in itself, throws very little light on the matter in hand. (SB)

appears to me when I see it not as a particular building but as the Holy Catholic Church in general. There was, however, this difference, that the latter has a tower over the entrance and the church rising from the depths had not. It was a very large church but a false one. The angels thrust it aside so that it stood all crooked. I also saw a great bowl, with a lip on one side; which tried to enter the false church but was also thrust aside. I then saw the angels preparing a chalice, of the shape of the Chalice of the Last Supper, which passed into the tower entered by the virgin. I also saw a lower tower or building appear, with many doors, through which I saw crowds of people passing, among them figures like Abraham and the Children of Israel. I think this had reference to the slavery in Egypt. I saw a round terraced tower arise, which also had reference to Egypt. This was thrust back and made to stand crooked. I also saw an Egyptian temple arise, like the one on the ceiling of which I had seen the Egyptian priests, idolaters, fastening the image of a winged virgin after receiving from Elias' messenger communications of a prophetic vision of Our Lady. I will speak of his vision later; it was seen by the prophet on Mount Carmel. This temple, too, was thrust back and made to stand crooked.

I then saw between the choirs of angels, to the right of the holy tower, a branch which put forth buds, making a whole ancestral tree of little male and female figures holding each other's hands. This family tree ended with the appearance of a little crib with a little child in it. The crib was of the same shape as the one I had seen exposed in the temple of the Three Kings.[34] Then I saw a beautiful great church appear.

---

34. In Catherine Emmerich's visions of the public ministry of Our Lord, which she daily recounted in chronological order for three years, she saw Our Lord, after the raising of Lazarus (which happened on Oct. 7th of His third year of teaching), withdraw Himself beyond the Jordan in order to escape the persecutions of the Pharisees. From here He dismissed the Apostles and disciples to their homes, and Himself went on with three young men named Eliud, Silas, and Erimen-Sear. (These were descended from the companions of the Three Kings who, when the

The way in which all these pictures were united with each other and yet melted one into the other was very wonderful. The whole vision was indescribably rich and full of significance. Even the hateful, evil, false appearances of towers, chalices, and churches, which were thrust aside, were made to assist in the unfolding of the scheme of salvation.

[When recounting these scattered visions, she came back again and again to the unspeakable joy of the angels. There was no real conclusion to these fragmentary visions, which seem to have been a series of symbolic pictures of the history of our salvation. She added: "First of all I saw the emblems of the work of redemption among the choirs of angels, and then a series of

---

latter went away, had remained behind in the Holy Land and intermarried with the families of the shepherds of Bethlehem.) With these Our Lord journeyed to the place where the Three Kings were then settled, returning afterwards to the Promised Land by way of Egypt. On the first day of the January which preceded His death, He reentered Judaea, and on the evening of Monday, Jan. 8th, He again met the Apostles at Jacob's well, thereafter teaching and healing in Sichar, Ephron, round Jericho, in Capharnaum, and in Nazareth. Towards February He came again to Bethany and the surrounding country, teaching and healing in Bethabara, Ephraim, and round Jericho. From the middle of February till His Passion on March 30th, He was in Bethany and Jerusalem by turns. The Evangelists are silent about the whole period between the raising of Lazarus and Palm Sunday, except for St. John, who says (11:53, 54): "From that day therefore they devised to put him to death, wherefore Jesus walked no more openly among the Jews, but he went into a country near the desert, unto a city that is called Ephrem. And there he abode with his disciples." Catherine Emmerich mentions the presence of Our Lord in Ephraim near Jericho on Jan. 14th, 15th, and 16th, and again between Feb. 6th and 12th, without giving the exact date. We must, however, return to what gave rise to this note. From Dec. 1st to the 15th of the third year of His ministry, Catherine Emmerich saw and daily described the sojourn of Our Lord and His three companions in a town of tents inhabited by the three Holy Kings of Arabia, where they had established themselves shortly after their return from Bethlehem. Two of these chieftains were still alive. She describes in most remarkable detail their way of life and their religious practices and the festivities with which they received Jesus. Amongst many other things she recounted from Dec. 4th to 6th how these star-worshippers brought Our Lord into their temple (which she described as a square flattened pyramid surrounded with terraced wooden steps), from the top of which they observed the stars and inside which they performed their religious ceremonies. They showed Him in it the image of the Child Jesus in the crib, which they had made and placed therein immediately after their return from Bethlehem; this was made in the exact shape of the one they had seen in the star before they set out on their journey to Bethlehem. Catherine Emmerich describes it in the following words: "The whole representation was in gold and surrounded by a star-shaped sheet of gold. The golden child lay on a red blanket in a crib like the one at Bethlehem; his little hands were crossed on his breast and he was wrapped in swaddling-bands from breast to feet. They had even included the hay of the crib, it could be seen behind the child's head like a little white wreath; I cannot remember what it was made of. They showed Jesus this image; they had no other in their temple." This is her description of the image of the crib to which she refers above in the text. (CB)

pictures from Adam down to the Babylonian captivity."]

I saw something happening in Egypt very long ago which had a symbolic application to Our Lady. It must have been long before the days of Elias. I also saw something in Egypt, in his lifetime, which I will tell later.

I saw a place in Egypt, much farther away from the Promised Land than On or Heliopolis, where on an island in the river an idol stood. This idol had a head which was something between that of a man and of an ox, with three horns, one in the middle of the forehead. The figure was hollow, and had openings in its body in which sacrifices were burnt as in an oven. Its feet were like claws, and in one hand it held a plant like a lily which grows out of the water and opens and shuts with the sun. In the other hand the idol held a plant like ears of corn with quite thick grains; I think it grows out of the water too, but am not quite sure of this. After a great victory a temple had been built in honor of this idol, which was now to be consecrated, and all preparations had been made for the sacrifice. But as the people were on their way to the island I saw something wonderful happen. Near the idol I saw a dark and dreadful apparition, and then I saw a great angel descending upon it from Heaven like the one who appeared to St. John the Evangelist in the Apocalypse. This angel struck the dark figure in the back with his staff. The demon, writhing, was forced to speak out of the mouth of the idol, warning the people to consecrate the temple, not in honor of it but of a virgin who was to appear upon earth and to whom thanks for their victory were due. I cannot remember the exact circumstances, but I saw that the people set up in the new temple the image of a winged virgin, which was fixed to the wall. The virgin as she flew was bending down over a little ship in which lay a child in swaddling-clothes. The ship stood on a little pillar, with a leafy top like a tree. One of her outstretched hands had a balance hanging from it, and I saw two figures beside her on the wall who were putting something into each scale of the balance. The little ship in which the child lay was like that in which Moses lay on the Nile, but it was uncovered, whereas Moses' one was entirely closed in except for a small opening at the top.

I saw the whole Promised Land withered and parched with drought, and I saw Elias ascending Mount Carmel with two servants to beseech God to give rain. First they climbed over a high ridge, then up steps of rock to a terrace, then up many more rock-steps, and so reached a great open space with a hill of rocks in its midst in which was a cave. Elias climbed up steps to the top of this rocky hill. He left the servants at the edge of the open space and bade one of them look towards the Sea of Galilee, which had, however, a terrible aspect, for it was quite dried up and was full of hollows and caverns with rotting bodies of animals in the swampy ground. Elias crouched down on the ground with his head sunk between his knees, and covering himself in his mantle prayed fervently to God and cried seven times to his servant to know whether he did not see a cloud rising out of the lake. At his seventh call I saw the cloud rise up, and saw the servant announce it to Elias, who sent him to King Achab. I saw a white eddy form itself in the middle of the lake; out of this eddy rose a little black cloud like a fist, which opened and spread itself out. In this little cloud I saw from the first a little shining figure like a virgin. I saw, too, that Elias perceived this figure in the spreading cloud. The head of this virgin was encircled with rays, she stretched her arms out in the form of a cross, and had a triumphal wreath hanging from one hand. Her long robe seemed to be tied beneath her feet. She appeared as if hovering above the whole Promised Land in the cloud as it spread ever farther. I saw how this cloud divided into different parts and fell in eddying showers of crystal dew on certain holy and consecrated places inhabited by devout men and those who were praying for salvation. I saw these showers edged with the colors of the rainbow and the blessing taking shape in their midst like a pearl in its shell. It was explained to me that this was a symbolic picture, and that the favoured places watered by the showers from the cloud were in fact those which had had their share in contributing to the coming of the Blessed Virgin.

I saw as well a prophetic vision of how Elias, while the cloud was rising, discerned four mysteries relating to the Blessed Virgin. Unfortunately I have forgotten the details, and much else, as a result of disturbances and interruptions. Elias discerned in the cloud, among other things, that Mary would be born in the seventh age of the world; hence his sevenfold call to his servant. He saw, too, from what family she was to come. On one side of the country he saw a low but very broad family tree, and on the other a very high one, broad at the base but tapering towards its top, which bent down into the first tree. He understood all this, and discerned in this way four mysteries relating to the future mother of the Saviour. Hereupon I had a vision of how Elias enlarged the cave above which he had prayed and how he made the Sons of the Prophets into a more regular organization. Some of these were always praying in this cave for the coming of the Blessed Virgin and paying her honor in anticipation of her future birth. I saw that this devotion to Our Lady continued here uninterrupted, that the Essenes carried it on during Mary's earthly life, and that subsequently it was perpetuated up to our time by hermits and the Carmelite Order which eventually succeeded them.[35]

[When Catherine Emmerich communicated later her visions of the time of John the Baptist, she saw the same vision of Elias with reference to the state of the country and of mankind which prevailed in St. John's time. We therefore reproduce from this what follows as explanatory of what she has said above.]

---

35. This is the general tradition about the origins of the Carmelite Order. It is briefly recounted in the Breviary Lessons for the Feast of Our Lady of Mount Carmel (July 16th), where mention is also made of the tradition that the cloud seen by Elias (3 *Kings* 18:42-45) is a symbol of Our Lady. (SB)

I saw a great commotion in the Temple at Jerusalem, much consultation, much writing with reed pens, and messengers being sent about the country. Rain was besought from God with cries and supplications, and search was made everywhere for Elias. I saw Elias receiving food and drink in the wilderness from the angel, who held a vessel like a little shining barrel with white and red diagonal stripes. I saw all Elias' dealings with Achab, the sacrifice on Mount Carmel, the slaughter of the priests of Baal, Elias' prayer for rain and the gathering of the clouds. I saw as well as the dryness of the earth, a great dryness and failing of good fruit amongst men. I saw that by his prayer Elias called forth the blessing of which the cloud was the form, and that he guided and distributed its showers in accordance with inner visions; otherwise it might perhaps have become a destroying deluge. He asked his servant seven times for news of the cloud; this signifies the seven generations or ages of the world which must go by before the real blessing (of which this cloud of blessing was but a symbol) took root in Israel. Elias himself saw in the ascending cloud an image of the Blessed Virgin, and discerned several mysteries relating to her birth and descent.[36]

I saw that Elias' prayer called down the blessing at first in the form of dew. Layers of cloud sank down which formed themselves into eddies with rainbow edges; these finally dissolved into falling drops. I saw therein an association with the manna in the desert, but the manna lay thick and crisp on the ground in the morning like fleeces, and could be rolled up and taken away. I saw this whirling eddy of dew floating along the banks of the Jordan, but dropping down only at certain notable places, not everywhere. In particular at Ainon, opposite Salem, and at the places where Baptisms took place later, I clearly saw these shining

---

36. In the Office for the Immaculate Conception and in other liturgical books there occurs the following verse: "As a cloud I covered all the earth" (*Ecclus.* 24:6), which is in complete harmony with this prophetic vision of the Mother of God. (CB)

eddies floating downwards. I asked what the colored edges of these dew-eddies portended, and was given as an explanation the example of the mother-of-pearl shells in the sea which also bore edges of shining color; they expose themselves to the sun, absorbing the light and cleansing it of color until the pure white pearls take form in their centers. It was shown to me, too, that this dew and the rain that followed it was something much more than the ordinary refreshing of the earth by moisture. I was given clearly to understand that without this dew the coming of the Blessed Virgin would have been delayed by more than a hundred years; whereas, after this softening and blessing of the earth, nourishment and refreshment were imparted to the human beings who lived on the fruits of the soil; the blessing communicated itself to their bodies and ennobled them. This fructifying dew was associated with the coming of the Messias, for I saw its rays penetrating generation after generation until they reached the substance of the body of the Blessed Virgin. I cannot describe this. Sometimes, on the colored edge that I have mentioned I saw emerge one or more pearls having the likeness of a human figure which disappeared in a breath to unite itself with others of these pearls. The picture of the pearl-shell was a symbol of Mary and Jesus.

I saw, too, that just as the earth and mankind were parched and panting for rain, so, at a later time, was the spirit of man thirsting for the baptism of John; so that the whole picture was not only a prophecy of the coming of the Blessed Virgin, but also of the state of the people at the time of the Baptist. In the first instance there was the alarm of the people, their longing for rain and their search for Elias, followed, nevertheless, by their persecution of him; and later there was a like yearning of the people for baptism and penance, and again the lack of comprehension by the synagogue and its messages to John.

In Egypt I saw the message of salvation being

announced in the following manner. I saw that by God's command Elias sent messages to summon devout families scattered about in three regions to the east, north, and south. For this purpose he sent forth three of the sons of the prophets, but only after asking a sign from God that he had decided rightly, for it was a difficult and dangerous mission, and he had to choose messengers whose prudence would lessen the danger of their being murdered. One travelled northwards, one eastwards, and the third southwards. This last one had to pass through a considerable part of Egyptian territory, where the Israelites were in particular danger of being killed. This messenger took the way followed by the Holy Family on their flight into Egypt. I think, too, that he passed near On, where the Child Jesus took refuge. I saw him come to an idolatrous temple on a great plain; in this temple, which was surrounded by a meadow and by many other buildings, they adored a living bull. They had an image of a bull and many other idols in their temple; their sacrifices were gruesome and they slaughtered deformed children. They seized the son of the prophet and brought him before the priests. Fortunately the latter were very inquisitive, otherwise they might easily have murdered him. They questioned him as to whence he came and what brought him there, and he answered without hesitation, telling them how a virgin would be born from whom the salvation of the world was to come, and that then all their idols would fall in pieces.[37]

---

37. Epiphanius, in his work on the life of the Prophet, says of Jeremias: "This prophet gave the Egyptian priests a sign and told them that all their idols would fall in pieces, when a virgin mother should set foot in Egypt with her Divine Child. And so it befell. Therefore do they to this day adore a Virgin Mother and a Child lying in the crib. When King Ptolemy questioned them as to the reason therefor, they answered, 'This is a secret which we received from our ancestors to whom it was announced by a holy prophet, and we await its fulfilment.'" *(Epiphan.,* Vol. II, p. 240). The above-mentioned son of the prophet sent to Egypt by Elias cannot, however, be taken to be Jeremias, for the latter lived some three centuries later. (CB)

This is presumably the Greek Father, St. Epiphanius of Salamis, † 403, but an examination of various editions, old and new, has so far failed to identify the passage. The quotation may be linked with Jeremias' prophecy (43:13) of the shattering of the idols of Egypt after his warning to the Jews who had assassinated Godolias and were preparing to flee to Egypt *(Jer.* 41-43). (SB)

They were amazed at his announcement, seemed greatly moved thereby and let him go unharmed. I saw them taking counsel together thereafter, and having the image of a virgin constructed and fixed in the middle of the temple-roof. This image, represented as floating downwards at full length, had a head-dress like the idols, so many of which lie in rows there, half like a woman, half like a lion. On the top of the head was something like a little high vessel or bushel of fruit; the elbows were close to the body, while the forearms were held out in a gesture as it were of withdrawal and repulse. In her hands were ears of corn. She had three breasts; a large one in the middle, with two smaller ones on each side of it but lower down. The lower part of the body was clothed in a long dress, and from the feet, which were comparatively small and pointed, hung tassels or something of the sort. She had as it were wings on her arms both above and below the elbows; these wings seemed to be made of delicate feathers spreading out on each side like rays and intertwined with each other. Feathers ran crosswise down both thighs and over the middle of the body to the feet. The dress had no folds. They venerated this image and sacrificed to it, begging it not to destroy their god Apis and their other gods. At the same time they continued their gruesome idolatry as before, except that they always began by invoking this virgin. In making this image they had, I believe, followed the indications given them by the son of the prophet in his account of the vision which Elias had seen.

I saw also that by the great mercy of God it was announced to certain God-fearing heathens that the Messias was to be born from a virgin in Judaea. The ancestors of the three holy kings, the star-worshippers of Chaldaea, received this message by the appearance of a picture in a star or in the sky, by which they made prophecies. I saw traces of these prophetic images of Our Lady in the pictures in their temple, which I have described in my account of Jesus' visit to them after

the raising of Lazarus in the last quarter of the third
year of His ministry.

[On the feast of the Archangel Michael in September 1821, Catherine Emmerich recounted, amongst
other fragments of a vision of the holy angels, the following fragment of the story of Tobias, whom she had
seen with the Archangel Raphael as his guide.]

I saw many things from the life of Tobias, which is
an allegory of the history of the coming of salvation in
Israel; not an imaginative allegory, but one which actually happened and was lived. It was shown to me that
Sara, the wife of the young Tobias, was a prototype of
St. Anne. I will relate as much as I can remember of
the many things that happened, but shall not be able
to reproduce them in their right order. The elder Tobias
was an emblem of the God-fearing branch of the Jewish race, those who were hoping for the Messias. The
swallow, the messenger of spring, indicated the near
approach of salvation. The blindness of old Tobias signified that he was to beget no more children, and was
to devote himself entirely to prayer and meditation; it
signified also the faithful, though dim, longing and waiting for the light of salvation and the uncertainty as to
whence it was to come. Tobias' quarrelsome wife represented the empty and harassing forms into which the
Pharisees had converted the Law. The kid which she
had brought home in lieu of wages had, as Tobias warned
her, really been stolen, and had for that reason been
handed on to her in return for very little. Tobias knew
the people concerned and all about it, but his wife only
mocked him. This mockery also indicated the contempt
of the Pharisees and formalists for the devout Jews
and Essenes and the relationship between the two
groups, but I cannot now remember how this was.

The Archangel Raphael was not telling an untruth
when he said that he was Azarias, the son of Ananias,
for the general meaning of these words is: "The help
of the Lord out of the cloud of the Lord."[38] This angel,

38. This interpretation, alluded to but not definitely established by earlier commen-

the companion of young Tobias, represented God's watchfulness over Our Lady's descent through her ancestors and His preservation and guidance of the Blessing through the generations which preceded her conception. In the prayer of the Elder Tobias, and of Sara, the daughter of Raguel (I saw both these prayers being brought by the angels at one and the same time before the Throne of God and there granted), I recognized the supplications of the God-fearing Israelites and of the Daughters of Sion for the coming of salvation, as well as the simultaneous prayers of Joachim and Anna, separated from each other, for the promised offspring. The blindness of the elder Tobias and his wife's mockery of him also symbolized Joachim's childlessness and the rejection of his sacrifice at the Temple. The seven husbands of Sara, the daughter of Raguel, who were destroyed by Satan, came to their end through sensuality; for Sara had made a vow to give herself only to a chaste and God-fearing man. These seven men symbolized those whose entry into Our Lord's ancestry according to the flesh would have hindered the coming of the Blessed Virgin, and thus the advent of salvation. There was also a reference to certain unblest periods in the history of salvation and to the suitors whom Anna had to reject that she might be united to Joachim, the father of Mary. The maidservant's reviling of Sara (*Tob.* 3:7) symbolized the reviling by the heathen and by the godless and unbelieving among the Jews against the expectation of the Messias, for whose coming all God-fearing Jews were, like Sara, inspired to pray with ever-increasing fervor. It was also an image of the reviling of Anna by her maidservant, whereafter that holy mother prayed with such fervor that her prayer was granted. The fish which was about to swallow young Tobias symbolized the powers of darkness, heathendom

---

tators, is shown by Biblical philology to be perfectly correct. (CB)

The names Azarias and Ananias both occur in Neh. 3:23, where Ananias is in Hebrew *Ananyah,* which may mean "the cloud of the Lord," but the much commoner name is *Hananyah,* "the Lord is merciful." *Azaryah* means "the help of the Lord." (SB)

and sin striving against the coming of salvation, and also Anna's long barrenness. The killing of the fish, the removal of its heart, liver, and gall, and the burning of this by Tobias and Sara to make smoke—all these symbolized the victory over the demon of fleshly lusts who had strangled Sara's seven husbands, as well as the good works and continence of Joachim and Anna, by which they had obtained the blessing of holy fruitfulness. I also saw therein a deep significance relating to the Blessed Sacrament, but can no longer explain this. The gall of the fish, which restored the sight of Tobias' father, symbolized the bitterness of the suffering through which the chosen ones among the Jews came to know and share in salvation; it indicated also the entry of the light into the darkness brought about by Jesus' bitter sufferings from His birth onwards.

I received many explanations of this kind, and saw many details of the history of Tobias. I think the descendants of young Tobias were among the ancestors of Joachim and Anna. The elder Tobias had other children who were not godly. Sara had three daughters and four sons. Her first child was a daughter. The elder Tobias lived to see his grandchildren.

I saw the line of the descent of the Messias proceeding from David and dividing into two branches. The right-hand one went through Solomon down to Jacob, the father of St. Joseph. I saw the figures of all St. Joseph's ancestors named in the Gospel on this right-hand branch of the descent from David through Solomon. This branch has the greater significance of the two; I saw the line of descent issuing from the mouths of the separate figures in streams of white colorless light. The figures were taller and looked more spiritual than those of the left-hand line. Each one held a long flower-stem with hanging leaves like those of palms: this stem was crowned with a great bell-shaped flower shaped like a lily and having five stamens, yellow at the top, from which a fine yellow dust was scattered. These flowers differed in size, vigor, and beauty. The flower borne by Joseph, the foster-father of Jesus, was the most beautiful and purest of all, with fresh and abundant petals. Halfway down this ancestral tree were three rejected shoots, blackened and withered. In this line through Solomon there were several gaps separating its fruits more widely from each other. The right-hand and left-hand branches met several times, and they crossed each other at a point a few generations before the end. I was given an explanation about the higher significance of the line of descent through Solomon. It had in it more of the spirit and less of the flesh, and had some of the significance belonging to Solomon himself. I cannot express this.

The left-hand line of descent went from David through Nathan down to Heli, which is the real name of Joachim, Mary's father, for he did not receive the name of Joachim till later, just as Abram was not called Abraham until later. I forget the reason, but it will perhaps come back to me. In my visions I often hear Jesus called after the flesh a son of Heli.[39]

I saw this whole line from David through Nathan flowing at a lower level: it generally issued from the navels of the separate figures. I saw it colored red, yellow, or white, but never blue. Here and there were stains; then the stream became clear again. The figures upon it were smaller than those of the line through Solomon.

39. Many ancient and modern commentators of the Greek text have suggested the following version of the passage in St. Luke (3:23): "He was supposed to be the son of Joseph, but was in truth descended from Heli," instead of "being as it was supposed the son of Joseph, who was of Heli". The absence of any mention of Mary (whose line of descent is, however, given by St. Luke) is explained by the basic principle of the Jewish genealogists: "The father's race is called a race, the mother's race is not called a race" (Talmud Baba Bathra, f. 110). The father of Mary was, according to this rule, the first of Our Lord's forebears according to the flesh who could be named in His line of descent. Christ, who had no earthly father, may be as truly called, according to the flesh, the son of Heli as Laban (*Gen.* 29:5) could be called the son of Nachor, and Zacharias (*1 Esdras* 5:1) could be called the son of Addo, for these were both great-grandchildren. (CB)

The emphasis on Our Lord's Davidic descent (*Luke* 1:32, 69) shows that Our Lady must also have been of the Davidic line (see Fr. R. Ginns, O.P., in *Cath. Comm.,* 1953, 748b). The interpretation proposed by CB requires a fresh punctuation of Luke 3:23 (literal translation from the Greek): "Jesus . . . being the son (as it was supposed of Joseph) of Heli." This rendering, though according to Fr. Ginns (*ib.,* 750g) "rejected by the majority of scholars," is a tenable reading of the Greek. It involves the interpretation of "son" as "grandson" through the mother, as CB explains; and the identification of Heli with Joachim (cf. *supra,* n. 28 p. 34). The more usual reconciliation of the genealogies in Luke and Matthew is by the supposition of a second marriage of Joseph's mother. (SB)

They carried smaller branches which hung down sideways and had little yellow-green leaves with serrated edges; their branches were crowned with reddish buds of the color of wild roses. These were always closed; they were not flower-buds but the beginnings of fruits. A double row of little twigs hung down on the same side as the serrated leaves. At a point three or four generations above Heli or Joachim, the two lines crossed each other and rose up, ending with the Blessed Virgin.[40] At the point of crossing I think I already saw the blood of Our Lady beginning to shine in the stream of descent.

St. Anne descended on her father's side from Levi, and on her mother's side from Benjamin. I saw in a vision the Ark of the Covenant being borne by her ancestors with great piety and devotion; I saw them receiving rays of blessing from it which extended to their descendants, to Anna and to Mary. I always saw many priests in the house of Anna's parents, and also in Joachim's house; this was the result of the relationship with Zacharias and Elisabeth.

[On the afternoon of July 26th, 1819, Sister Emmerich, after relating many things about Anna, Our Lady's holy mother, fell asleep as she was praying. After a while she sneezed three times and exclaimed impatiently, but still half asleep, "Oh, why must I wake up?" Then she woke up completely and said with a smile: "I was in a much better place, I was much better off than here. I was being much comforted, and then all of a sudden I was woken by my sneeze and someone said to me, 'You must wake up,' but I did not want to, I was so happy there and was annoyed at having to go away, then I had to sneeze, and I woke up."

---

40. Catherine Emmerich no doubt meant by this the connection between the line of David through Nathan and that through Solomon (see p. 56). In the third generation upwards from Joachim, St. Joseph's grandmother (who had married as her first husband Matthan, of the line of Solomon, and had by him two sons, one of whom was Jacob, the father of St. Joseph) took as her second husband Levi, of the line of Nathan, and had by him Matthat, the father of Heli or Joachim. Thus Joachim and Joseph were related to each other. It is remarkable that Raymundus Martini, in his *Pugio fidei* (p. 745, ed. Carp), also states that St. Joseph's grandmother after the death of Matthan married a second husband, from whom Joachim was descended. (CB)

[Next day she told me:] I had just fallen asleep last night after saying my prayers when someone whom I recognized as a young girl I had often seen before came to my bed. She said to me rather shortly: "You have been speaking a great deal about me today, you shall now have a sight of me, so that you may make no mistakes." So I asked her: "Have I perhaps talked too much?" She answered abruptly "No!" and disappeared. She was still a girl, slim and attractive, her head was covered with a white hood, drawn together at the back of her neck and ending there in a hanging knot as if her hair were inside it. Her long dress, which completely covered her, was of whitish wool, the sleeves of it seemed to be rather full at the elbows. Over this she wore a long cloak of brownish wool, like camel's hair.

Hardly had I had time to feel touched and pleased by this vision, when suddenly I saw by my bed an aged woman in similar dress with her head more bent and very hollow cheeks—a Jewess of some fifty years, thin but handsome. "Why," I thought, "does this old Jewess come to me?" Then she said: "You need not be afraid; I only want to show you how I was when I bore the mother of the Lord, so that you may make no mistakes." I asked at once: "Oh, where is the dear little child Mary?" and she replied: "I have not got her with me now." Then I asked again: "How old is she now?" And she answered: "Four years old." I asked her once more: "But have I spoken rightly?" and she said shortly, "Yes." I asked her: "Oh, please do not let me say too much!" She did not answer and disappeared.

Then I woke up, and thought over everything that I had seen of Anna and of the childhood of the Blessed Virgin, and everything became clear to me and I felt blissfully happy. Next morning, when I was again asleep, I had a new and very beautiful vision. I thought I could not forget it, but the next day brought with it so many interruptions and sufferings that nothing of it remains in my mind.

VISION OF THE FEAST OF THE IMMACULATE CONCEPTION[41]

DURING the whole night I saw a terrible, horrifying picture of the sins of the whole world; but towards morning I fell asleep again and was transported to the place in Jerusalem where the Temple had stood, and then on to the region of Nazareth, where the house of Joachim and Anna used to stand. I recognized the country round. Here I saw a slender column of light rising out of the earth like the stem of a flower. This column was crowned with the appearance of a shining octagonal church, which grew forth from the stem like the calyx of a flower or the seed-vessel of a poppy.[42] The column grew up within this church like a little tree, with symmetrical branches bearing the figures of those among Our Lady's family who were the objects of veneration on this feast. It was as if they were standing on the stamens of a flower. I saw Our Lady's holy mother St. Anne, standing between Joachim and another man, her father perhaps. Beneath St. Anne's breast I saw a space filled with light, somewhat in the shape of a chalice, and in this I saw the figure of a shining child growing and developing. Its little hands were crossed on its breast and its little head was bent, and countless rays of light issued from it towards one part of the world. (I thought it strange that they did not shine in all directions.) On others of the surrounding branches were many figures turned towards the center in veneration, and all round

---

41. Related on December 8th, 1819.
42. Catherine Emmerich had visions of all the feasts of the Church being celebrated by the Church Triumphant, even when they were no longer celebrated on earth by the Church Militant. She saw these feasts being celebrated in a shining transparent church, the shape of which she generally described as octagonal. She saw a mysterious gathering of all the saints who were particularly associated with the feast in question, sharing in the celebrations. She usually saw this church floating in the air; but it is noteworthy that in all the feasts having so to speak a blood-relationship with Jesus Christ or with the mysteries of His life, she saw this church not floating in the air but appearing as the crown of a pillar or of a stem thrusting itself up like a flower or fruit growing out of the earth. What, however, surprised the writer in particular was that on all feasts of saints who had received the stigmata (for instance, St. Francis of Assisi or St. Catherine of Siena), she saw the church not floating in the air but on the stem growing out of the earth. She never made any reflection on this point, probably from humility, though it might well have been edifying had she done so. (CB)

within the church I saw orders and choirs of saints, countless in number, all turning in prayer towards that holy mother. This celebration, in the sweetness of its harmony and devotion, can only be compared to a meadow of innumerable flowers, stirred by a gentle wind and lifting their heads to offer their scents and their colors to the sun from which they have received life itself and all they have to offer. Above this symbolical picture of the Feast of the Immaculate Conception the tree of light sent up another shoot, and in this second crown I saw a further moment of the feast being celebrated. Mary and Joseph were kneeling here, and a little lower St. Anne, all in adoration of the child Jesus, whom I saw above them in the top of the tree, holding in His hand the orb or globe and surrounded by an infinite glory of light. Around this scene, and bowing in adoration before it, were, nearest of all, the three holy kings, the shepherds, and the Apostles and disciples; farther away other saints joined in the choirs of worshippers. In the light from above I saw indistinct figures of Powers and Principalities, and still higher I saw as it were a half-sun, its light streaming down through the dome of the church. This second picture seemed to indicate the approach of the Feast of the Nativity after the Feast of the Immaculate Conception. When the picture first appeared, I seemed to be standing outside the church, looking outwards from under the pillar; later I saw into the inside of the church as I have described it. I saw, too, the little child Mary developing in the space of light under St. Anne's heart, and received at the same moment an inexpressible conviction of the Immaculate Conception. I read it as clearly as in a book, and understood it. It was shown to me, that a church to the glory of God had once stood here, but had been given over to destruction in consequence of unworthy disputes about this holy mystery; that the Church Triumphant, however, still celebrated this feast on this spot.

[During her visions of Our Lord's ministry Catherine Emmerich related the following on December 16th, 1822.]

I often hear the Blessed Virgin telling the women
who were her close intimates (for instance, Joanna Chusa
and Susanna of Jerusalem) various secrets about herself and about Our Lord, which she knows partly from
inner knowledge and partly from what her holy mother
Anna told her. Thus today I heard her telling Susanna
and Martha that during the time when she was bearing Our Lord within her she never felt the slightest
discomfort, nothing but infinite inner joy and beatitude.
She told them, too, that Joachim and Anna had met in
the hall under the Golden Gate in a golden hour; and
that God's grace had been granted to them here in such
abundance as to make it possible for her alone, from
her parents' holy obedience and pure love of God, to
have been conceived in her mother's womb without any
stain of sin. She also explained to them that but for
the Fall the conception of all men would have been as
pure. She spoke, too, of her beloved elder sister Mary
Heli, that her parents had realized that she was not
the promised fruit and how, in their longing for that
fruit, they had long practiced continence. It was a joy
to me to hear now from the Blessed Virgin herself what
I have always seen about her elder sister. I saw now
the whole sequence of grace received by Mary's parents
just as I have always described it, from the appearance
of the angel to Anna and Joachim down to their meeting under the Golden Gate; that is to say, in the subterranean hall under the Golden Gate. I saw Joachim
and Anna encompassed by a host of angels with heavenly light. They themselves shone and were as pure as
spirits in a supernatural state, as no human couple had
ever been before them. I think that the Golden Gate
itself was the scene of the examination and absolution
of women accused of adultery, and that other ceremonies
of reconciliation took place here.[43] There were five of
these subterranean passages under the Temple, and one

---

43. Catherine Emmerich's remarks are here in agreement with the accounts of the
    most ancient Jewish literature. Thus, for instance, Mishnah, tract. *Tamid,* c. 5,
    and *Sotah,* c. I. (CB)

also under the part where the virgins lived. These were used for certain ceremonies of atonement. I do not know whether others before Joachim and Anna had gone there, but I think the place was very seldom visited. I cannot at present recall whether it was in general connected with sacrifices offered by the unfruitful, but the priests had been given some order about it.

[On December 8th, 1820, on the Feast of the Immaculate Conception of Mary, the soul of Catherine Emmerich was transported in an active state of prayer and meditation over a great part of the earth. The whole of this visionary journey will be described in its proper place, but in the meantime we will reproduce the following extracts from it in order to give some idea of these journeyings of her soul.

[She came to Rome, was with the Holy Father, visited a much-loved and devout nun in Sardinia, reached Palestine after a short visit to Palermo, went to India, and thence to what she calls the mountain of the Prophet.[44] Thence she journeyed to Abyssinia, where

---

Mishnah, *Tamid,* V, 7, states that the ceremonially unclean were to wait at the eastern gate, but the tractate *Sotah,* I, 5, dealing with adultery, directs that the woman be taken to the "eastern or Nicanor's gate," where also lepers and mothers awaiting "purification" were to go. The "Golden Gate" was probably an eastern gate. An eastern gate is also mentioned in *Middoth,* I, 9, in connection with ceremonial cleansing (see *supra,* n. 33. p. 40). *John* 8:2 mentions that Our Lord was teaching in the Temple when He spoke with the woman taken in adultery. (SB)

44. "Mountain of the Prophet" is the name given by Catherine Emmerich to a place high above all the mountains of the world to which she was taken for the first time on Dec. 10th, 1819, in her ecstatic state of dream-journeying, and again several times later. There she saw the books of prophetic revelation of all ages and all peoples preserved in a tent and examined and superintended by someone who reminded her partly of St. John the Evangelist and partly of Elias—particularly of the latter, since she perceived the chariot which had transported that prophet from the earth standing here on the heights near the tent and overgrown with green plants. This person then told her that he compared with a great book lying before him all the books of prophetic knowledge that had ever been given (often in a very confused state) or would in future be given to mankind; and that much of these he crossed out or destroyed in the fire burning at his side. Mankind, he said, was not yet capable of receiving these gifts, another must first come, and so forth. She saw all this on a green island in a lake of clear water. On the island were many towers of different shapes, surrounded by gardens. She had the impression that these towers were treasuries and reservoirs of the wisdom of different peoples, and that under the island, which was full of murmuring streams, lay the source of rivers held to be sacred (the Ganges amongst them) whose waters issued forth at the foot of the mountain range. The direction in which she was led to this mountain of the Prophet was always (taking into account the starting-point of her journey) towards the highest part of Central Asia. She described places,

she came to a strange Jewish city on a high mountain-rock and visited its ruler Judith,[45] with whom she spoke of the Messias, of that day's feast of the Conception of His Mother, of the holy Advent time, and of the approaching Feast of His Birth. During the whole of this journey she did all that a conscientious missionary would have done on a similar journey to carry out his task and make use of his opportunities; she prayed, taught, helped, comforted, and learnt. But in order to make plain to the reader, in her own words, what she perceived on this journey regarding the Feast of the Immaculate Conception, we must refer him to the note on pages 45-46, in which that part of Our Lord's ministry to which she here alludes is described in detail.]

When in my great dream-journey I came into the Promised Land, I saw all those things which I have

---

natural scenery, human beings, animals, and plants of the region which she traversed before being carried up through a lonely and desolate space, as if through clouds, to the place mentioned above. Her detailed description of this place, with all that she experienced there, will be set down in its proper place with an account of her whole visionary journey. On her return journey she was carried down through the region of clouds once more, and then again traversed lands rich in luxuriant vegetation and full of animals and birds, until she reached the Ganges and saw the religious ceremonies of the Indians beside this river.

The geographical situation of this place and Catherine Emmerich's statement that she had seen everything up there overgrown with living green, reminded someone who read her account twenty years later of traditions about a place of this kind (sometimes with a similar inhabitant) in the religions of several Asiatic peoples. The Prophet Elias is known to the Musulmans (under the name of Chiser, i.e. the Green One) as a wonderful half-angelic being, who dwells in the north on a mountain known as Kaf, celebrated in many religious and poetical writings, and there watches over secrets at the source of the river of life. The Indians called their holy mountain Meru, while to the Chinese it was Kuen-lun, both connected with representations of a state of paradise and both situated on the heights of Central Asia, where Catherine Emmerich saw the Mountain of the Prophet. The ancient Persians also believed in such a place and called it Elbors or Albordsch. According to Isa. 14:13 ("I will sit in the mountain of the covenant, in the sides of the north"), the Babylonians would seem to have held a similar belief. That they, like the Persians and Moslems, placed this mountain in the north is explained by their geographical position as regards the mountains of Central Asia. (CB)

45. When the writer copied down the very detailed account of her dealings with this Judith and her description of the place, he only knew (from the direction taken by her journey) that she was in Abyssinia; several years after her death he found in the journeys of Bruce and Salt an account of a Jewish settlement on the high mountains of Samen in Abyssinia. The ruler of this settlement was always called Gideon and, if it was a woman, Judith—the name which Catherine Emmerich herself mentioned. (CB)

James Bruce, *Travels and Adventures in Abyssinia*. He was one of the first Europeans to go there, and his journey was in 1769. Henry Salt, *A Voyage to Abyssinia*. An account of a journey made on behalf of His Majesty's Government in 1809-1810. (SB)

related about the Conception of the Blessed Virgin. Thereupon I entered into the daily visions of Our Lord's ministry and had today reached the 8th of December of the third year of His teaching. I found Jesus not in the Promised Land, but was brought by my guide eastwards over the Jordan to Arabia, where the Lord, accompanied by three young men, was in a tent-city of the three holy kings in which they had settled after their return from Bethlehem.

I saw that the two holy kings who were still alive were celebrating with their tribe a three-day feast starting from today, December 8th. On this night, fifteen years before Christ's birth, they had seen for the first time the star promised by Balaam rise in the sky [*Num.* 24:17: "A star shall rise out of Jacob"]—the star for which they and their forefathers had waited so long, scanning the heavens in patient watchfulness. They discerned in it the picture of a virgin, bearing in one hand a sceptre and in the other a balance. The scales were held even by a perfect ear of wheat in the one and by a cluster of grapes in the other. Therefore every year since their return from Bethlehem they kept a three-day feast beginning with this day. I saw, too, that as a result of this vision on the day of the conception of Mary, fifteen years before the birth of Christ, these star-worshippers did away with a terrible religious custom of theirs—a cruel sacrifice of children, long practiced among them as the result of revelations which had been misunderstood by them and confused by evil influences. They had carried out at different times and in different manners sacrifices of both children and grown people. I saw that before Mary's conception they had the following custom. They took a child of one of the purest and most devout mothers amongst the followers of their religion, and she esteemed herself very fortunate to offer up her child in this way. The child was flayed and strewn with flour to absorb the blood. They ate this blood-soaked flour as a holy repast, and continued strewing the flour and eating until there was no blood left in the child's body. Finally the child's flesh was cut up into small pieces, which were distributed among them and eaten.[46] I saw them performing this gruesome ceremony with the greatest simplicity and devoutness, and I was told that they had adopted this dreadful practice as a result of misunderstanding and distorting certain prophetic and symbolical indications which they had received regarding the Holy Eucharist. I saw that this terrible sacrifice was carried on in Chaldaea, in the country of Mensor, one of the three holy kings, until he put an end to its horrors on receiving enlightenment in a vision from Heaven on the day of Mary's conception. I saw him on a high wooden pyramidal edifice, engaged in studying the stars, as his people had done for centuries in accordance with their ancient traditions. I saw King Mensor lying in an ecstasy as he contemplated the stars; his limbs were rigid and he had lost consciousness. His companions came to him and brought him back to himself, but at first he seemed not to know them at all. He had seen the picture in the star with the Virgin, the scales, the ear of corn, and the cluster of grapes, and had received an inner admonition, after which that cruel ceremony was abolished.

---

46. In this connection it seems remarkable that among the writers of the first centuries of the Christian era who reproduce the accusations made by the heathens against the Christians, Minutius Felix mentions this reproach among others; that when the Christians initiated anyone into their religion, they laid before him a child completely covered with flour, so as to hide the murder which they were about to make him commit. He was then obliged to stab the child over and over again with a knife. They greedily sucked up the streaming blood, cut the child into small pieces and devoured them all. This crime, committed in common, was a mutual pledge of silence and secrecy in regard to other shameful excesses with which they ended their assemblies.

Should the origin of this accusation perhaps be sought in the above-mentioned sacrifice of children by the star-worshippers, who were among the first followers of Christianity? In any case, it may well be supposed that ideas of this kind (which, as we see in the case of the Magi, arise from superstition and from misinterpretation of messages of salvation) may be the hidden cause lying at the root of the murder of Christian children by Jews. If this be so, these dark and cruel deeds must be added to the many motives for which we have to pity the unfortunate people of Israel rather than to despise them; for it conceals a distorted longing for the Saviour. This constantly recurring phenomenon has so far as we know never been thoroughly investigated and elucidated in a completely unprejudiced spirit. Of late years it has generally been treated (like all historical riddles whose source is obscure) in a complacent and condescending manner as being nothing but a fanatical accusation. (CB)

Minutius Felix, *Octavius,* IX, 5, and cf. XXX, I. (SB)

After seeing at night in my sleep the fearful picture of the murdered child on my right hand, I turned over in horror in my bed, but saw it again on my left hand. I begged God most earnestly to free me from this dreadful sight. I woke up and heard the clock strike. My heavenly Bridegroom said to me, pointing round Him as He spoke: "See far more evil that befalls Me every day at the hands of many throughout the whole world." And as I looked about me into the distance, many things came before my soul which were indeed still more dreadful than that sacrifice of children; for I saw Jesus Himself cruelly sacrificed on the Altar by unworthy and sinful celebrations of the Holy Mysteries. I saw how the blessed Host lay on the altar before unworthy degenerate priests like a living Child Jesus, whom they cut and terribly mutilated with the paten. Their sacrifice, though an efficacious celebration of the Holy Mysteries, appeared like a cruel murder.[47]

The same cruelty was shown to me in the heartless treatment of the members of Christ, His followers, and God's adopted children. I saw at the present time countless good, unhappy men being everywhere oppressed, tormented and persecuted; and I always saw that it was Jesus who suffered this ill-treatment. The times are terrible; a refuge is no longer anywhere to be found; a dense cloud of sin lies over the whole world, and I see men giving way to the worst crimes with complete indifference and unconcern. I saw all this in many visions while my soul was being led through many lands over the whole earth. At last I came back to the visions of the Feast of Our Lady's Conception.

I am quite unable to tell in what a wonderful way I journeyed last night in dream. I was in the most different parts of the world and in the most different ages, and very often saw the Feast of Mary's Conception being

---

47. Just as the sacrifice on Calvary was accomplished by the cruelty of ungodly priests and by the bloodthirsty hands of brutal executioners, so is the Sacrifice of the Mass, even when unworthily celebrated, a true Sacrifice; but the guilty and unworthy priest who celebrates it plays the part not only of the Jewish priests who condemned Our Lord but also of the soldiers who crucified Him. (CB)

celebrated in the most different places. I was in Ephesus, and saw this feast being celebrated in the house of the Mother of God, which was still standing there as a church. It must have been at a very early time, for I saw the Way of the Cross set up by Mary herself still in perfect preservation. [The second Way of the Cross was set up in Jerusalem and the third in Rome.]

The Greeks kept this feast long before the schism. I still remember something of this, but am not quite sure what led up to it. I saw how a saint, Sabbas, I think, had a vision relating to the Immaculate Conception. He saw the picture of the Blessed Virgin on the globe, crushing the head of the serpent under her feet, and recognized that the Blessed Virgin alone was conceived unwounded and unstained by the serpent.[48] I saw, too, that one of the Greek churches or one of the Greek bishops refused to accept this truth unless the picture came to them across the sea. Then I saw the appearance of the picture float over the sea to their church and appear on the altar, whereupon they began to keep the feast. That church possessed a life-size picture of Our Lady painted by St. Luke just as she was in her earthly life, in a white robe and veil. (I have an idea that this picture had been sent from Rome, where they have only a half-length portrait.) They had placed the picture above the altar in the place where the vision of the Immaculate Conception had appeared. I think it was in Constantinople, or perhaps I have seen it venerated there in earlier times.

I was in England, too, and saw the feast being introduced and celebrated there in olden times. In this con-

---

48. On July 5th, 1835, the writer discovered from Cardinal Baronius' notes on the *Martyrologium Romanum* of December 8th that in the Sforza Library there is a Codex (No. 65) containing a speech by the Emperor Leo, who ascended the throne in 886, about this feast in Constantinople. It appears from this speech that the celebration of the feast was much anterior to this date. According to Canisius *(De beatissima virgine Maria,* lib. I, c. 7) and Galatinus *(De arcanis catholicae veritatis,* lib. 7, c. 5), the feast is included in the Martyrology of St. John Damascene *(d.* A.D. 749). St. Sabbas, Abbot, mentioned by Catherine Emmerich, is known for his devotion to Our Lady. He died *c.* A.D. 500. (CB)

The year of the death of St. Sabbas is given in Ramsgate's *Book of Saints* (1947) as A.D. 532. (SB)

nection I saw the day before yesterday, on the Feast of St. Nicholas, the following miracle. I saw an abbot, coming from England, in great danger in a ship in a storm. They prayed very fervently for the protection of the Mother of God, and I saw an apparition of the holy bishop Nicholas of Myra floating over the sea to the ship and telling the abbot that he had been sent by Mary to announce to him that he was to cause the Feast of the Immaculate Conception to be kept in England on December 8th, and that then the ship would arrive safely. In reply to the abbot's question as to what prayers should be used for this feast, he answered, the same as those for Our Lady's nativity. The name of Anselm[49] was also associated with the introduction of this feast, but I have forgotten the details.

I also saw the introduction of this feast into France, and how St. Bernard wrote in opposition to it because its introduction had not come from Rome.[50]

NOTE BY THE WRITER

ALL that has so far been recorded of the blessing given to Joachim and Anna is compiled from visions and

---

49. It is remarkable that Catherine Emmerich does not give the name of Anselm to the abbot who had the vision, since Petrus de Natal in *Catal. Sanct.*, lib. I, c. 42, does so, as the writer discovered in July 1835. Her account seems to be supported by Baronius in his notes to the Roman Martyrology for Dec. 4th, where he states that the announcement was made, not to Anselm, but at an earlier date in 1070 in exactly similar circumstances to Elsinus or Elpinus, a Benedictine abbot. This is said to be stated also in J. Carthagena in his homilies *De Arcanis Deiparae*, tom. I, lib. I, hom. 19, on the authority of a letter from St. Anselm to the bishops of England. It was this holy Bishop of Canterbury who first introduced the feast into England. (CB)

Petrus de Natalibus' *Catalogus Sanctorum* was published in Venice in 1506. As the subsequent work of Baronius (1586, 1589) shows, AC is right in not attributing the event to Anselm. The source of the Helsin legend, a letter ascribed to Anselm, is now, however, considered to be spurious, though this need not impugn the truth of the legend itself. The Anselm mentioned by AC (with no title) is wrongly identified by CB with the Archbishop of Canterbury († 1109). It was his nephew, also called Anselm, who introduced the feast into England when he became Abbot of Bury St. Edmund's in 1121, having doubtless become acquainted with the feast as observed at the Greek abbey of St. Sabbas in Rome, where he was abbot 1109-1121. Cf. *Cath. Encyc.*, art. "Immaculate" (Holweck), pp. 677b-678a. (SB)

50. It was introduced in 1245 by the Chapter of the Cathedral of Lyons, to which Bernard wrote to oppose it. (CB)

The date should read 1140-1145. The reference is to St. Bernard's letter, "To the Canons of the Church of Lyons," traditionally numbered 174, and numbered

reminiscences of Catherine Emmerich during the feast of the Immaculate Conception on December 8th. She explained, however, on that day in the year 1821 that the meeting of Joachim and Anna under the Golden Gate did not occur in December but in the autumn, at the end of the Feast of Tabernacles (which lasted from the 15th to 23rd of the month Tishri, i.e. in September or October).[51] Thus she saw Joachim building tabernacles with his shepherds (see p. 32) before going to the Temple, and Anna receiving the promise of fruitfulness while she was praying under a tree which formed a tabernacle. In the previous year, 1820, she had, however, stated that she remembered Joachim having gone up to Jerusalem with his offerings on the occasion of a dedication festival. This cannot be the usual Jewish dedication feast in the winter (the 25th day of the month, Kislev, but must doubtless be a memorial festival of Solomon's dedication of the Temple. According to Catherine Emmerich's daily accounts of the three years of Jesus' ministry, Our Lord was in Aruma (a few hours' distant from Salem) at the close of the Feast of Tabernacles in the second year of His ministry, and taught there about the approaching destruction of the Temple.

This feast is, it is true, not mentioned in the works about Jewish antiquities which we commonly consult, but its existence cannot, I think, be doubted, apart from Catherine Emmerich's statements, if it is remembered that Solomon celebrated the consecration of his Temple in connection with the Feast of Tabernacles (*3 Kgs.* 8:2-66, and *2 Par.* 7:10), and that the Masora on *3 Kgs.*

---

chronologically 215 (between 1140 and 1145) by Fr. Bruno Scott-James in his recent (1953) translation. (SB)

51. The Feast of Tabernacles was celebrated, according to *Lev.* 23:34-36, for the seven days 15th to 21st Tishri, with an eighth day of festival on the 22nd. The Hebrew lunar months do not correspond exactly to our months, and Tishri falls in Sept./Oct. CB quite correctly distinguishes the Dedication Feast of Solomon's Temple in the month Tishri, celebrated in connection with the Feast of Tabernacles (*3 Kings* 8:2-66; *2 Par.* 7:10), from the Dedication Feast on the 25th Kislev, which commemorated the cleansing of the Temple by Judas Maccabaeus in 164 B.C. (*1 Mach.* 4:52). This feast was also called *Hanukkah* and the "Feast of Lights" by Josephus (*Ant.* XII, vii, 7), and *Encaenia* or "Dedication" in the Gospel. (*John* 10:22). (SB)

8:2 and 54 appoints the account of the consecration of Solomon's Temple as festival lessons for the second and eighth days of the Feast of Tabernacles. Although Catherine Emmerich saw the meeting of Joachim and Anna happening at the close of the Feast of Tabernacles, and thus two months earlier than the Church's celebration of Mary's conception, it was always on the occasion of that feast on December 8th that she was impelled to communicate visions about Our Lady's conception. She said, too, that it was on that day, not at the time of the Feast of Tabernacles in the autumn, that the remembrance of this grace-bringing event was already being celebrated by the three holy kings when Christ visited them in Arabia after the raising of Lazarus.

Here end the additional communications by Catherine Emmerich about the conception of Mary: the story of Our Lady's life is now resumed.

II

MORE ABOUT THE IMMACULATE
CONCEPTION: THE BIRTH OF OUR LADY

I HAD a vision of the creation of Mary's most holy soul and of its being united to her most pure body. In the glory by which the Most Holy Trinity is usually represented in my visions I saw a movement like a great shining mountain, and yet also like a human figure; and I saw something rise out of the midst of this figure towards its mouth and go forth from it like a shining brightness. Then I saw this brightness standing separate before the Face of God, turning and shaping itself—or rather being shaped, for I saw that while this brightness took human form, yet it was by the Will of God that it received a form so unspeakably beautiful. I saw, too, that God showed the beauty of this soul to the angels, and that they had unspeakable joy in its beauty. I am unable to describe in words all that I saw and understood.

When seventeen weeks and five days after the conception of the Blessed Virgin had gone by (that is to say, five days before Anna's pregnancy was half accomplished), I saw Our Lady's holy mother lying asleep in her bed in her house near Nazareth. Then there came a shining light above her, and a ray from this light fell upon the middle of her side, and the light passed into her in the shape of a little shining human figure. In the same instant I saw Our Lady's holy mother raise herself on her couch surrounded by light. She was in ecstasy, and had a vision of her womb opening like a tabernacle to enclose a shining little virgin from whom man's whole salvation was to spring. I saw that this was the instant in which for the first time the child moved within her. Anna then rose from her couch, dressed herself, and announced her joy to the holy Joachim. They both thanked God, and I saw them praying under the tree in the garden where the angel had comforted Anna. It was made known to me that the Blessed Virgin's soul was united to her body five days earlier than with other children, and that her birth was twelve days earlier.

Several days before Our Lady's birth Anna had told Joachim that the time was approaching for her to be delivered. She sent messengers to Sephoris, where her younger sister Maraha lived; to the widow Enue (sister of Elisabeth) in the valley of Zabulon; and to her niece Mary Salome at Bethsaida, asking these three women to come to her. I saw them on their journeys. The widow Enue had a serving-lad with her; the other two women were accompanied by their husbands who, however, went back on approaching Nazareth. I saw that on the day before Anna was delivered Joachim sent his many manservants out to the herds, and among Anna's new maidservants he kept in the house only those who were needed. He, too, went out into his nearest pasture. I saw that Anna's firstborn daughter, Mary Heli, looked after the house. She was then about nineteen years old and was married to Cleophas, one of Joachim's chief shepherds, by whom she had a little daughter, Mary Cleophas, now about four years old. After praying, Joachim chose out his finest lambs, kids, and cattle, sending shepherds to take them to the Temple as a thank-offering. He did not return home until nightfall.

I saw the three cousins arriving at Anna's house in the evening. They went to her in her room behind the hearth and embraced her. After Anna had told them that the time was near for her to be delivered, they stood up and sang a hymn together: "Praise the Lord God; He has shown mercy to His people and has redeemed Israel and has fulfilled the promise which He gave to Adam in Paradise that the seed of the woman should crush the head of the serpent," and so on. I can no longer recite it all by heart. Anna prayed as though in ecstasy. She introduced into the hymn all the prophetic symbols of Mary. She said: "The seed given by God to Abraham has ripened in me." She spoke of the promise to Sara of Isaac's birth and said: "The blossoming of Aaron's rod is perfected in me." At that moment I saw her as though suffused with light; I saw the room full of radiance, and Jacob's ladder appearing above it. The women were overcome with astonishment and joy, and I think that they also saw the vision. When the prayer of welcome was over, the travellers were refreshed with a slight meal of bread and fruit, and water mixed with balsam. They ate and drank standing up, and then lay down till midnight to rest from their journey. Anna did not go to bed, but prayed, and at midnight woke the other women to pray with her. They followed her to her praying-place behind a curtain.

Anna opened the doors of a little cupboard in the wall which contained a casket with holy objects. On each side were lights—perhaps lamps, but I am not sure. They had to be pushed up in their holders, and then little bits of shavings put underneath to prevent them from sinking down. After this the lights were lit. There was a cushioned stool at the foot of this sort of little altar. The casket contained some of Sara's hair (Anna had a great veneration for her), some of Joseph's bones (brought by Moses from Egypt), and something belonging to Tobias, I think a relic of his clothing; also the little shining, white, pear-shaped goblet from which Abraham had drunk when blessed by the angel. (This had been given to Joachim from the Ark of the Covenant when he was blessed in the Temple. I now know that this blessing took the form of wine and bread and was a strengthening and sacramental food.)

Anna knelt before the little cupboard with one of the women on each side and the third behind her. She recited another hymn; I think it mentioned the burning bush of Moses. Then I saw the room filled with supernatural light which became more intense as it wove itself round Anna. The women sank to the ground as though stunned. The light round Anna took the exact form of the burning bush of Moses on Horeb, and I could no longer see her. The whole flame streamed inwards; and then I suddenly saw that Anna received the shining child Mary in her hands, wrapped her in her mantle, pressed her to her heart, and laid her naked on the stool in front of the holy relics, still continuing her prayer. Then I heard the child cry, and saw that Anna brought out wrappings from under the great veil which enveloped her. She wrapped the child first in grey and then in red swaddling-bands up to her arms; her breast, arms, and head were bare. The appearance of the burning bush around Anna had now vanished.

The women stood up and received the newborn child in their arms with great astonishment. They shed tears of joy. They all joined in a hymn of praise, and Anna lifted her child up on high as though making an offering. I saw at that moment the room full of light, and beheld several angels singing *Gloria* and *Alleluia*. I heard all their words. They announced that on the twentieth day the child was to be called Mary.

Anna now went into her bedroom and lay down on her couch. The women in the meantime unwrapped the child, bathed it, and wrapped it up again, and then laid it beside its mother. There was a little woven wicker basket which could be fastened beside the bed or against the wall or at the foot of the bed, whichever was wanted, so that the child could always have its place near its mother and yet separate.

The women now called Joachim, the father. He came to Anna's couch and knelt down weeping, his tears falling on the child; then he lifted it up in his arms and uttered his song of praise, like Zacharias at John's birth. He spoke in this hymn of the holy seed, implanted by God in Abraham, which had continued amongst God's people by means of the covenant ratified by circumcision, but had now reached its highest blossoming in this child and was, in the flesh, completed. I also heard how this song of praise declared that now was fulfilled the word of the prophet: "There shall come forth a rod out of the root of Jesse." He said, too, in great humility and devoutness, that he would now gladly die.

It was only then that I noticed that Mary Heli, Anna's elder daughter, did not have sight of the child until later. Although she had become the mother of Mary Cleophas several years before, she was not present at Our Lady's birth—perhaps because, according to Jewish rules, it was not considered seemly for a daughter to be with her mother at such a time.

Next morning I saw the serving men and maids and many people from nearby gathered round the house. They were allowed to enter in groups, and the child was shown by the women to them all. Many were greatly moved, and some led better lives thereafter. The neighbors had come because they had seen in the night a glowing light above the house, and because the birth of Anna's child after long unfruitfulness was looked upon as a great favor from Heaven.

In the moment when the newborn child lay in the arms of her holy mother Anna, I saw that at the same time the child was presented in Heaven in the sight of the Most Holy Trinity, and greeted with unspeakable joy by all the heavenly host. Then I understood, that there was made known to her in a supernatural manner her whole future with all her joys and sorrows. Mary was taught infinite mysteries, and yet was and remained a child. This knowledge of hers we cannot understand, because our knowledge grows on the tree of good and evil. She knew everything in the same way as a child knows its mother's breast and that it is to drink from it. As the vision faded in which I saw the child Mary being thus taught in Heaven through grace,

I heard her weep for the first time.

I often see pictures like this, but for me they are inexpressible and probably for most people not quite comprehensible; therefore I do not relate them.

In the moment of Mary's birth I saw the tidings brought to the patriarchs in Limbo. I saw them all, especially Adam and Eve, filled with inexpressible joy at the fulfillment of the promise given in Paradise. I also perceived that the patriarchs advanced in their state of grace, that the place of their sojourn became brighter and more spacious, and that it was given to them to have more influence on earth. It was as if all their labor and penance, all the struggling, crying and yearning of their lives had matured into its destined fruit.

At the time of Mary's birth I saw a great and joyful agitation in nature, in the animal world, in the hearts of all good men, and I heard the sound of sweet singing. Sinners, however, were overwhelmed by fear and sorrow. I saw, specially near Nazareth, but also in the rest of the Promised Land, many who were possessed break out at that time into violent ravings. They were hurled from side to side with loud cries, and the devils shrieked from within them, "We must surrender, we must go out!"

In Jerusalem I saw how the aged priest Simeon, who lived in the Temple, was startled at the moment of Mary's birth by loud shrieks coming from the madmen and those possessed of the devil, of whom many were shut up in a building in one of the streets on the Temple Hill. Simeon lived near them and was partly responsible for looking after them. About midnight I saw him go to the open space before the house of those possessed and inquire of one of them who lived nearest as to the cause of the loud cries with which everyone had been roused from their sleep. The man cried still louder that he must go out. Simeon opened the door, the possessed one rushed out, and Satan cried from within him: "I must go out, we must all go out! A virgin has been born! There are so many angels on earth who torment us! We must now go out and may nevermore enter into men!" I saw Simeon praying fervently; the wretched man was flung back and forth on the open space, and I saw the devil go out of him. It gave me great pleasure to see the aged Simeon. I also saw the prophetess Anna and Noemi wakened and informed by visions of the birth of a chosen child. [Noemi was the sister of Lazarus' mother; she was in the Temple and later became Mary's teacher.] They met and told each other of what they had seen. I think they knew Anna, Our Lady's mother.

In the night of Mary's birth I saw in a city of the Chaldaeans that five sibyls, or virgin prophetesses, were granted visions. I saw them hastening to the priests, who then made known in many places that these prophetesses had seen that a virgin had been born and that many gods had come down to earth to greet her, while other spirits fled before her lamenting. I saw, too, that the picture of a Virgin holding scales evenly balanced with corn and grapes, which the watchers of the stars had seen since Mary's conception, was no longer visible to them. In the hour of Mary's birth it seemed to move out of the star, in which it left a gap, and to sink down and away from it in one particular direction. They now made and set up in their temple the great idol which I saw there in my visions of the life of Our Lord; it had some connection with the Blessed Virgin.[1]

---

1. On Dec. 7th of the third year of Our Lord's ministry she saw a temple of the Chaldaeans about which she related the following: "On a neighbouring hill they had a terraced pyramid with galleries, from which they zealously watched the stars. They prophesied from the manner in which animals moved and they interpreted dreams. They sacrificed animals, but had a horror of the blood and always let it run away into the earth. In their religious observances they had holy fire and holy water, holy juice from a plant and little holy loaves of bread. Their temple, oval in shape, was full of images very delicately wrought in metal. They had a strong presentiment about the Mother of God. The principal object in the Temple was a three-cornered pillar ending in a point. On one side of this was an image with many arms and with animals' feet. It held in its hands, among other things, a globe, a diadem, a bunch of herbs, and a big ribbed apple held by its stalk. Its face was like a sun with rays, it was many-breasted, and represented the productive and preservative powers of nature. Its name sounded like Miter or Mitras. On the other side of the pillar was the figure of an animal with a horn. It was a unicorn, and its name sounded like Asphas or Aspax. It was thrusting with its horn against another evil beast which was on the third side. This had a head like an owl; it had a curved

Later they set up in their temple another symbolic image of the Blessed Virgin, the closed garden. I saw live animals lying in this temple and being cared for. I am not sure whether they were dogs. They were fed with the flesh of other animals. Within the temple of the three holy kings I had till now always seen a wonderful illumination at night. It was as if one looked up into a starry sky set with all the constellations. They used to make alterations in this artificial sky in their temple according to the visions they saw in the heavens. Thus after the birth of Mary the illumination which had previously come from outside now came from within.

When the Blessed Virgin was born, I saw cast into the sea, from its place in the temple on an island in a river, that image of a winged woman with a balance in her hand, bending down over a child in a little ship lying in the top of a tree—the image which I had seen placed there long ago, before the time of Elias, in accordance with the forced utterance of an idol. The little tree on which lay the child in the ship, remained in its place. A church was built there later.

At the moment of Mary's birth I saw falling from

---

beak, four legs with claws, two wings, and a tail ending like a scorpion's. I have forgotten its name; indeed, I find it very difficult to remember such outlandish names and often mix them up. I can only say that they sounded something like this or that. Over the two fighting beasts there was an image standing on the corner of the pillar which was intended to represent the mother of all the gods. Its name sounded like the Lady Aloa or Aloas. They also called her 'corn granary.' A cluster of high ears of corn grew out of its body: its head was pressed down on to its shoulders and bent forward, for on the nape of its neck it bore a vessel containing wine or about to do so. They had a saying: 'The Corn shall become bread, the grape shall become wine, for the refreshment of all mankind.' Over this image was a sort of crown, and there were two letters on the pillar which looked to me like O and W [perhaps Alpha and Omega]. What, however, surprised me most in this temple was a little round garden, covered over with gold network and standing on a bronze altar. Above it was the picture of a virgin. In the middle of this garden was a fountain with several sealed basins one above the other, in front of which was a green vine with a beautiful red cluster of grapes which hung down into a dark-colored wine-press. Its form reminded me vividly of the Holy Cross, but it was a wine-press. Above in a hollow trunk was fixed a wide funnel with a bag hanging from its spout. Two movable arms, fixed to each side of the hollow trunk, were used as levers to press the grapes that were in the bag so that the juice ran out of the trunk through openings made in it lower down. The little round garden, which was about five to six feet in diameter, was full of delicate green shrubs, flowers, fruits and little trees which were all, like the vine, very life-like and had the same significance as it." (See *Canticle of Canticles* 4:12.) (CB)

the temple-ceiling pieces of that winged female figure with three breasts which I had seen fixed to the ceiling of a temple when a messenger from Elias announced his master's prophecy of a coming Virgin. The face, the three breasts, and the lower part of the body all fell down and were broken to pieces. The bushel-shaped crown, the arms with the ears of corn, the upper part of the body and the wings did not fall down.

On the 9th of September, the day after Mary's birth, I saw in the house several other relations from the neighborhood. I heard many names but have forgotten them again. I also saw many of Joachim's menservants arriving from the more distant pastures. All were shown the newborn child, and all were filled with great joy. The meal in the house was accompanied by much rejoicing.

On the 10th and 11th of September, I again saw many visiting the child Mary. Among them were relations of Joachim's from the valley of Zabulon. On these occasions the child was brought into the front part of the house in its little cradle and put on a high stand (like a sawing-bench) to be shown to the people. The child was wrapped in red, covered with transparent white stuff, up to its bare arms, and had a transparent little veil round its neck. The cradle was covered with red and white stuff.

I saw Mary Cleophas (the two- or three-year-old child of Anna's elder daughter and of Cleophas) playing with the child Mary and caressing her. Mary Cleophas was a fat, sturdy child, and wore a sleeveless white dress, with a red hem hung with red buttons like tiny apples. Round her bare arms she wore little white wreaths, which seemed to be made of feathers, silk, or wool.

[September 22nd-23rd] Today I saw great preparations for a feast in Anna's house. All the furniture was moved aside, and in the front part of the house the dividing screens had been taken away to make one large hall instead of a number of small rooms. Along each side of this hall I saw a long, low table set out for a meal with many things that I had not noticed before. Fragile vases with openwork tops like baskets stood on the table; they may have been for flowers. On a side-table I saw many little white sticks, apparently made of bone, and spoons shaped like deep shells, with handles ending in a ring. There were also little curved tubes, perhaps for sucking up liquid.

In the center of the hall a kind of altar-table had been set up, covered in red and white. On it lay a little, trough-shaped, basket-cradle, of red and white wicker-work, covered with a sky-blue cloth. Beside this altar stood a lectern draped in a cloth on which lay parchment prayer-scrolls. Five priests from Nazareth stood before the altar, one of them wearing grander vestments than the others; Joachim stood near them. In the background near the altar were several men and women belonging to the families of Anna and Joachim, all in festal attire. I remember seeing Anna's sister Maraha from Sephoris, and Anna's elder daughter and others. Anna herself, though no longer in bed, remained in her room behind the hearth and did not appear at the ceremony.

Enue, Elisabeth's sister, brought out the child Mary, wrapped to the arms in red swaddling-clothes covered with transparent white stuff, and laid her in Joachim's arms. The priests approached the altar where the scrolls lay and prayed aloud. Two of them held up the train of the principal one. Joachim then laid the child in the hands of the high priest, who, lifting her up in offering as he prayed, laid her in the cradle on the altar. He then took a pair of scissors which, like our snuffers, had a little box at the end to hold what was cut off. With this he cut off three little tufts of hair from the child's head (one from each side and one from the top) and burnt them in a brazier. Then he took a vase of oil and anointed the child's five senses, touching with his thumb her ears, eyes, nose, mouth, and breast. He also wrote the name Mary on a parchment and laid it on the child's breast. She was then returned to Joachim, who gave her to Enue to be taken back to Anna. Hymns were sung and after that the meal began, but I saw no more.

[On the evening of September 7th, the vigil of the Feast of Our Lady's Nativity, Catherine Emmerich was unwontedly—as she said, supernaturally—gay, although she felt ill at the same time. She was in an unusually lively and confidential mood. She spoke of extraordinary joy in all nature because of Mary's approaching birth, and said that she felt as if a great joy was awaiting her next day, if only this did not turn to sorrow.[2]] There is such jubilation in nature: I hear birds singing, I see lambs and kids frolicking, and where Anna's house once stood the doves are flying about in great flocks as if drunk with joy. Of the house and its surroundings nothing now remains; it is now a wilderness. I saw some pilgrims, holding long staffs and their garments girt about them, with cloths wrapped round their heads like caps. They are going through this part of the country on their way to Mount Carmel. A few hermits from Mount Carmel live here, and the pilgrims asked them in amazement what was the meaning of this joy in nature. They were told that it was ever thus in that country on the eve of Mary's birth, and that it was probably there that Anna's house had stood. A pilgrim who had passed that way before had, they said, told them that this was first noticed a long time ago by a devout man, and that this had led to the celebration of the feast of Our Lady's Nativity.

I now saw this institution of the feast myself.[3] Two

---

2. In a vision of the Blessed Virgin she had received the promise that on the next day, Sept. 8th (which was also her own birthday), she would be granted the favor of sitting up in bed for several weeks, leaving the bed and walking about the room several times, which she had been unable to do for some ten years. The fulfillment of this promise was attended by all the spiritual and bodily sufferings which had been announced to her at the time, as will be recounted in its proper place. (CB)

3. The main feature of the story, the holy man who heard music in the air and, on asking what it was, received a revelation about Mary's birthday, which then led to its general observance, is found in the *Legenda Aurea* of B. James of Voragine, O.P. (c. 1255) for Sept. 8th. The oldest documentary evidence for the feast is from the sixth century, and its general acceptance not until the eighth or ninth (*Cath. Encyc.*, art. "Nativity" [Holweck], p. 712d). (SB)

hundred and fifty years after the death of the Blessed
Virgin I saw a very devout man journeying through the
Holy Land in order to seek out and venerate all the
places connected with the life of Jesus upon earth. I
saw that this holy man was given guidance from above,
and often remained for several days in prayer and contemplation at different places, enjoying many visions
and full of interior delight. He had for many years felt,
in the night of the 7th to the 8th of September, a great
joyfulness in nature and heard a lovely singing in the
air; and at last, in answer to his earnest prayer, he was
told by an angel in a dream that this was the birth-
night of the Blessed Virgin Mary. He received this revelation on his journey to Mount Sinai or Horeb. It was
told him at the same time that in a cave of the Prophet
Elias on that mountain was a walled-up chapel in honor
of the Mother of the Messias, and that he was to inform
the hermits living there of both these things. Thereupon
I saw him arriving at Mount Sinai. The place where the
monastery now stands was already at that time inhabited by isolated hermits, and just as precipitous on the
side facing the valley as it is now, when people have to
be hoisted up by means of a pulley. I saw now that
upon his announcement the Feast of the Nativity of
the Blessed Virgin was first celebrated here by the hermits on September 8th about A.D. 250, and that its celebration spread later to the Universal Church. I saw,
too, how he and the hermits looked for the cave of Elias
and the chapel in honor of the Blessed Virgin. These
were, however, very difficult to find among the many
caves of the Essenes and of other hermits. I saw many
deserted gardens here and there near these caves, with
magnificent fruit-trees in them. After praying, the
devout man was inspired to take a Jew with them when
they visited these caves, and was told that they might
recognize as the cave of Elias the one that he was
unable to enter. I saw thereupon how they sent an aged
Jew into the caves, and how he felt himself thrust out
of the narrow entrance of one of them, however much

he tried to force his way in. In this way they recognized it as the cave of Elias. They found in it a second cave, walled-up, which they opened; and this was the place where Elias had prayed in veneration of the future mother of the Saviour. The big, beautifully patterned stones which made the wall were used later for building the church. They also found in the cave many holy bones of Patriarchs and Prophets, as well as many woven screens and objects of earlier worship. All these were preserved in the church. I saw much of Mount Horeb on this occasion, but have forgotten it again. I still remember that the place where Moses saw the burning bush is called in the language of the place "The Shadow of God," and that one may walk on it only with bare feet. I also saw a mountain there entirely of red sand, on which, however, very fine fruit-trees grew.

I saw much of St. Bridget, and was given much knowledge of what had been revealed to this saint about Mary's conception and birth. I remember that the Blessed Virgin said to her that if women with child celebrated the vigil of her Nativity by fasting and by the pious recitation of nine Ave Marias in honor of her nine-months' sojourn in her Mother's womb; and if they renewed this devotion frequently during their pregnancy and the day before they expected their confinement, at the same time receiving with devotion the Holy Sacrament, she would bring their prayer before God and beg for a happy delivery even in difficult and dangerous conditions.

I myself had today a vision of Our Lady who came to me and told me, among other things, that whoever recited with love and devotion on the afternoon of this day nine Ave Marias in honor of her nine months' sojourn in her mother's womb and of her birth, continuing this devotion for nine days, would give the angels nine flowers each day for a bouquet which they would receive in Heaven and present to the Blessed Trinity, to obtain favor for the suppliant. Later I felt myself transported to a height between heaven and earth. The earth lay below, dark and troubled; above in Heaven I saw the Blessed Virgin before the Throne of God, between the choirs of angels and the ordered hosts of the saints. I saw, built for her out of devotions and prayers on earth, two portals or thrones of honor which grew at last into palaces like churches, and even into whole cities. It was strange to see how these buildings were made entirely of herbs, flowers, and garlands all intertwined, their different species expressing the different kinds and different merits of the prayers of individual human beings and of whole communities. I saw all being taken by angels or saints from the hands of the suppliants and being carried up to Heaven.

PURIFICATION OF ST. ANNE

SOME weeks after Mary's birth I saw Joachim and Anna journeying to the Temple with the child to make sacrifice. They presented the child here in the Temple in devotion and gratitude to God, who had taken from them their long unfruitfulness, just as later the Blessed Virgin according to the Law offered and ransomed the Child Jesus in the Temple. (*Lev.* 12). The day after their arrival they made sacrifice, and already then made a vow to dedicate their child completely to the Temple in a few years' time. Then they travelled back to Nazareth with the child.

III

THE PRESENTATION OF THE BLESSED VIRGIN IN THE TEMPLE[1]

[ON October 28th, 1821, Catherine Emmerich described in these words what she was at that moment seeing in a waking vision:] The child Mary will, I think, soon be brought to the Temple in Jerusalem. Already some days ago I saw the three-year-old child Mary standing before Anna in a room in her house and being instructed in her prayers, as the priests were soon to come to examine the child in preparation for her reception in the Temple. Today a feast in preparation for this event is taking place in Anna's house, and guests are gathering there—relations, men, women, and children. There are also three priests, one from Sephoris (a nephew of Anna's father), one from Nazareth, and a third from a place on a mountain some four hours from Nazareth. The name of this place begins with the syllable Ma.[2] These priests have come partly to examine the child Mary to see whether she is fitted for dedication to the Temple, and partly to give directions about her clothing, which has to comply with a prescribed ecclesiastical pattern. There were three sets of garments, each consisting of a kind of petticoat, a bodice, and a robe of different colors. There were also two wreaths of silk and wool, and an arched crown. One of the priests him-

---

1. The story of the Presentation of Our Lady in the Temple at the age of three years appears in the Apocryphal Gospels: *Protev.* 7, *Ps-Matt.* 6, *Nat. Mar.* 6, *Hist. Jos.* 3; and is attested by the liturgical feast on Nov. 21st. (SB)
2. There is a place called Madin about twelve miles northeast of Nazareth on the high ground above the Lake of Galilee. Cf. *Jos.* 11.1. (SB)

self cut out some pieces of these garments and arranged everything as it should be.

[A few days later] (on November 2nd) Catherine Emmerich continued: Today I saw great festivities in the house of Mary's parents. (I am not sure whether this actually happened then or whether it was a repetition of an earlier vision, for I had seen something like it before during the last three days, but because of much suffering and many interruptions it escaped my mind.) The three priests were still there, and besides them there were several relations of the family with their little daughters; for instance, Mary Heli and her seven-year-old child Mary Cleophas, who is much stouter and sturdier than the child Mary. Mary is very delicately formed, and has reddish-fair hair, smooth, but curly at the ends. She can already read, and all are astonished at the wise answers she gives. Maraha, Anna's sister from Sephoris, is also there with a little daughter, and so are other relations with their little girls.

The garments, which had been partly cut out by the priests, had now been finished by the women. During the ceremony the child was dressed in them several times and asked various questions. It was all very solemn and serious, and though the old priests sometimes smiled gently during the proceedings, they were greatly impressed by Mary's wise answers and by her parents' tears of joy. The ceremony took place in a square room near the eating-room. It was lit by an opening in the roof covered with gauze. A red carpet was spread on the floor, and on this stood an altar-table with a red cloth and a white one over it. Above this table was a picture in some sort of embroidery or needlework which hung like a curtain in front of a kind of little cupboard containing scrolls of writings and prayers. (It was a picture of a man, I think of Moses. He was dressed in a flowing praying-mantle like the one he wore when he went up the mountain to ask something of God. In the picture he was not holding the Tables of the Law in his hand; they were hanging at his side or on his arm. Moses was very tall and broad-shouldered. He had red hair. His head was very long and pointed, like a sugar-loaf, and he had a big hooked nose. On his broad forehead he had two protuberances like horns, turned inwards towards each other. They were not hard like animals' horns, but had soft skin, as it were ribbed or streaked, and only projected slightly from the forehead like two small lumps, brownish and wrinkled. He already had them as a child, but then they were little warts. This gave him a very strange appearance, which I never liked because it reminded me involuntarily of pictures of Satan. I have several times seen protuberances like these on the foreheads of old prophets and of some old hermits. Some of these had only one, in the middle of the forehead.) On the altar lay Mary's three sets of ceremonial garments as well as many other stuffs presented by her relations on the occasion of the child's entry into the Temple. There was a sort of little throne raised on steps in front of the altar. Joachim and Anna and the other relations were gathered round, the women standing at the back and the little girls beside Mary. The priests entered bare-footed. There were five of them, but only three took part in the ceremony in their vestments. One of the priests took the garments from the altar, explained their significance and handed them to Anna's sister from Sephoris, who dressed the child in them. First of all she put on her a little yellow knitted dress, and over it a colored scapulary or bodice decorated at the breast with cords. It was put over her head and tied round her. Over this she wore a brownish robe with arm-holes, over which hung pieces of the stuff. This robe was open at the neck, but closed from the breast downwards. Mary wore brown sandals with thick green soles. Her reddish-fair hair, curling at the ends, had been combed smooth, and she wore a wreath of white wool or silk ornamented at intervals with striped feathers, of a finger's breadth and curving inwards. I know the bird in that country from which these feathers come. A big square cloth, ash-grey in color, was then thrown over the child's head like a cloak. It could be drawn together under the arms, which rested in its folds as in slings. It seemed to be a penitential or praying garment or a travelling cloak.

As Mary stood there in this dress, the priests put to her all manner of questions which had to do with the way of life of the virgins of the Temple. Among other things they said to her: "When your parents dedicated you to the Temple, they made a vow on your behalf that you should never taste wine, vinegar, grapes, or figs; what will you yourself now add to this? You may reflect on this during the meal." Now the Jews, and especially the Jewish girls, were very fond of drinking vinegar, and so was Mary. After more of such questions, the first set of garments was removed and the second put on. First a sky-blue dress, then a bodice more ornamented than the first one, a bluish-white robe, and a white veil shimmering like silk, with folds at the back of the neck like a nun's head-dress and fastened round the head by a wreath of silk flower-buds with little green leaves. Then the priests put a white veil over her face, drawn together above so as to cover her head like a hood. It was held by three clasps which enabled the veil to be thrown back to uncover either a third, a half, or the whole of the face. She was instructed in the use of this veil, how it was to be lifted and then dropped at meals and when she had to give answers to questions and so forth. She was also instructed in many other rules of behavior during the meal of which the whole party partook in the next room. Mary's place at table was between two priests, with another facing her. The women and little girls were at one end of the table, separate from the men. During the meal the child was examined several times by question and answer in the use of the veil. They also said to her: "You are still allowed to eat any kind of food," and handed her various dishes in order to test her power of self-denial. But Mary partook of only few dishes and but little of each, and filled her hearers with great amazement by the childlike wisdom of her answers. I saw that during the meal and during the whole examination there were angels beside her, helping and guiding her.

When the meal was over, all went once more into the other room and stood before the altar, where the child was again undressed and then clothed in ceremonial garments. This time she wore a violet-blue dress woven with a pattern of yellow flowers; over this was a bodice or corset embroidered in different colors ending in a point and fastening under the arms, where it gathered and held the fullness of the dress. Above this was a violet-blue robe, fuller and grander than the other ones, and ending in a short, rounded train. Down each side of the front of this robe were embroidered three silver stripes with what seemed to be little gold rosebuds strewn between them; the robe was fastened across the breast by a band which ran through and was held by a clasp on the bodice. The robe was open down to the lower edge of the bodice, and formed two pockets at the sides in which the arms rested. Below the bodice the robe was fastened with buttons or hooks, but showed five stripes of the silver embroidery running down to the hem. The hem itself was also embroidered. The back of this robe fell in ample folds, projecting beyond the arms on either side. Over this was thrown a great gleaming veil shot with colors, white and violet-blue. The crown which was now put on her head was a broad band of thin metal, wider above than below, its upper edge surmounted by points with knobs. Over the top of the crown five metal bands met in a central knob. These bands were covered with strands of silk, and the outside of the broad metal band was ornamented with little silk roses and five pearls or precious stones. The inside of the band shone like gold. Mary, dressed in these ceremonial garments, the significance of each of which had been explained to her by the priest, was led up the steps and placed before the altar. The little girls stood beside her. She then declared what she would bind herself to give up when in the Temple. She said that she would eat neither meat nor fish and would drink no milk, but only a drink made out of the pith of a reed and water, such as poor people drink in the Promised Land, like rice-water or barley-water with us; sometimes she would put a little terebinth juice into the water. This is like a white treacly oil, very refreshing but not so delicate as balsam. She gave up all spices, and said that she would eat no fruit except a kind of yellow berry that grows in clusters. I know it well; in that country it is eaten only by children and poor people. She said that she would sleep on the bare earth and would rise three times in the night to pray. The other temple-maidens rose only once.

Mary's parents were deeply moved by her words. Joachim, taking the child in his arms, said, weeping: "Oh, my dear child, that is too hard, your old father will never see you again if you mean to live so austerely." It was very touching to hear. The priests, however, told her that she was to rise only once in the night, like the others, and they made the other conditions milder; for example, on great feast-days she was to eat fish. (There was a great fish-market in Jerusalem in the lower part of the town supplied with water from the pool of Bethesda. Once when it dried up, Herod wanted to make an aqueduct and fountain,[3] and to meet the expense by selling sacred vessels and vestments from the Temple. This caused a real uproar. The Essenes came from all parts of the country to Jerusalem to resist it, for, as I have just remembered, it was the Essenes who had charge of the priestly vestments.)

The priests also said to the child Mary: "Many of those virgins who are accepted by the Temple without payment or outfit are obliged, with the consent of their parents, to wash, as soon as they are strong enough, the blood-stained garments of the priests and other rough woollen cloths. This is hard work and often means

3. Pilate, not Herod, proposed to make an aqueduct with Temple funds, and thereby caused a riot of 10,000 Jews, according to Josephus (*Ant.*, XVIII, iii. 2). (SB)

bloody hands. But this you need not do, seeing that your parents are paying for your sojourn in the Temple." Mary declared at once without hesitation that she would gladly undertake this work if she were considered worthy. While these questions and answers were being made, the clothing ceremony came to an end. During these holy proceedings I often saw Mary appear so tall among the priests that she stood high above them, whereby I was given a picture of her wisdom and grace. The priests were filled with joyful astonishment. At the end of the ceremony I saw Mary being blessed by the first among the priests. She stood on a little elevated throne between two priests, and the one who blessed her stood facing her, with others behind him. The priests prayed from scrolls, answering each other, and the first one held his hands over her as he blessed her. At this moment I was granted a wonderful insight into the inner being of the holy child Mary. I saw her as if transfused with light by the priest's blessing, and under her heart in an indescribable glory of light I saw the same appearance as I had seen in contemplating the Holy of Holies in the Ark of the Covenant. In a shining space shaped like Melchisedech's chalice I saw indescribable figures of the blessing in the form of light. It was as though corn and wine, flesh and blood, were striving to unite with each other. I saw at one and the same time how, above this appearance, her heart opened like a temple door; and how this mystery, surrounded by a kind of canopy of symbolic jewels, passed into her opened heart. It was as though I saw the Ark of the Covenant entering the Holy of Holies in the Temple. Thenceforth, the highest good then on earth was enshrined in her heart. Then I saw only the holy child Mary filled with a glow of burning devotion. I saw her as though transfigured and hovering above the ground. During this vision I perceived that one of the priests (I think it was Zacharias) had been inspired with an inner conviction that Mary was the chosen vessel of the mystery of salvation; for I saw him receive, a ray from the blessing which in my vision had entered into her.

The priests now led the child, blessed and arrayed in her finest ceremonial garments, up to her parents, who were much moved. Anna lifted Mary up to her breast and gave her an affectionate but solemn kiss. Joachim, with deep emotion, gave her his hand seriously and reverently. Mary's elder sister embraced the blessed child in her beautiful dress in a much more lively manner than Anna, who did everything with reflection and moderation. Mary Cleophas, Mary's niece, threw her arms joyfully round her neck like any child. After Mary had been saluted by all present, her ceremonial garments were taken off, and she appeared once more in her ordinary ones. Towards evening several of the guests, including some of the priests, went away to their homes. I saw them standing up to take a light meal; there were fruits and rolls of bread in bowls and dishes on a low table. They all drank out of one goblet. The women ate separately.

HER DEPARTURE FOR THE TEMPLE

I CAME into the house of Mary's parents at night-time, and saw several of their relations asleep there. The family themselves were busy with preparations for departure. The hanging lamp with many branches was burning before the hearth. Little by little I saw the whole house astir.

Joachim had sent menservants the morning before to the Temple with beasts for sacrifice; five of each kind, the best he had. They made a very fine herd. I saw him now busy loading the luggage on a pack-animal standing before the house. Mary's clothes were neatly arranged in separate packages and tied on to the animal, together with presents for the priests. It made quite a heavy load. A broad package was arranged to make a comfortable seat in the middle of the animal's back. Anna and the other women had packed everything in bundles which were easy to load. I also saw several kinds of baskets hanging at the donkey's sides. In one of these baskets, rounded like the tureens that rich people have for their soup, with a lid opening in the middle, there were birds of the size of partridges. Other baskets, like the ones used for carrying grapes, contained different kinds of fruit. When the loading was quite finished, a big cover with heavy hanging tassels was put over everything. In the house I saw all the stir and agitation of departure. I saw a young woman, Mary's elder sister, moving about with a lamp. I saw her daughter Mary Cleophas following her about most of the time. I noticed yet another woman whom I took to be a maidservant. I also now saw two priests there. One was a very old man wearing a hood which hung down in a point on his forehead and had flaps over his ears. His upper garment was shorter than the under one and had straps like a stole hanging on it. It was he who had taken the chief part in Mary's examination yesterday and blessed her. I saw him continuing to talk to the child and teaching her different things. Mary was a little more than three years old, very delicately and finely made, and was as developed as a child of five with us. She had reddish-fair hair, smooth, but curly at the ends; it was longer than the seven-year old Mary Cleophas' fair hair, which was short and curly. Most of the children and grown-up people wore long robes of brownish undyed wool.

I was particularly struck by two boys among this company who did not seem to belong to the family at all and held no converse with any of them. It seemed as if no one even saw them, though they spoke to me, and were very charming and attractive with their fair curly hair. They had books which seemed to be for learning from. (Little Mary had no book, though she could read already.) Their books were not like ours, but strips some two feet wide rolled round a stick with a projecting knob at each end. The taller of the two boys opened his scroll and came up to me, and read something out of it which he explained to me. The golden letters, each one of which stood alone, were quite strange to me; they were written the wrong way round, and each letter seemed to signify a whole word. The language was completely strange to my ears, yet I understood it. Unfortunately I have now forgotten what he explained to me, but I think it had to do with Moses; perhaps it will come back to me. The younger of the boys held his scroll in his hands as if it were a toy; he jumped about like a child and played with his scroll, swinging it in the air. I cannot at all express how much I was attracted by these children; they were different from all the people there, who seemed not to notice them at all.

[Catherine Emmerich spoke for a long time with childlike delight of these two boys, but could not clearly say who they really were. After, however, having eaten and then slept for a few minutes, she recollected herself and said:] It was the spiritual meaning of these boys that I saw; their presence there was not a natural one. They were only the symbolic representations of prophets. The taller of the two, the one who carried his scroll so solemnly, showed me in it the passage in the third chapter of the book of Exodus where Moses sees the Lord in the burning bush and is told to put off his shoes from his feet. He explained this to me; as the bush was on fire without being burnt, so now the fire of the Holy Spirit was burning in the child Mary, who, all unconscious of it, was bearing this holy flame within her.[4] This passage also, he said, foreshadowed the union, now approaching, of the Godhead with humanity. The fire signified God, the thorn-bush mankind. The boy also explained to me the meaning of the putting off of the shoes, but I have no clear recollection of what he said; I think it signified the removal of the outer covering to disclose the reality within; and foreshadowed the fulfillment of the law and the coming of One greater than Moses and the prophets. The other boy carried

---

4. For the burning bush (*Ex.* 3:2) as a type of Our Lady, cf. the second antiphon at Lauds on Jan. 1st. (SB)

his scroll at the end of a thin stick, blowing in the wind like a flag; this signified the joyous entry of Mary on the path which was leading her to her destiny as the Mother of the Redeemer. The childish behavior of this boy as he played with his scroll showed how Mary, though overshadowed by so great a Promise and called to so holy a destiny, kept all the innocent playfulness of a child. Actually these boys explained to me seven passages out of their scrolls, but in the interruptions and troubles of daily life I have forgotten everything except what I have now told. O my God [she here exclaimed], all that I see is so beautiful and so deep, so simple and so clear, and yet I cannot tell it properly and cannot help forgetting so much because of the miserable, detestable happenings of this wretched earthly life.[5]

[A year earlier, in the middle of November 1820, Catherine Emmerich, while communicating her visions of the Presentation, referred to the appearance of these boy-prophets in the following connection. On the evening of November 16th a penitential girdle was brought near Catherine Emmerich when she was asleep. It had been made by a man who was striving to mortify himself but was without any spiritual advice or direction. He had made it with much exaggerated austerity out of leather straps pierced with nails, but he had been able to wear it for hardly an hour. Though it was two feet away from her, the sleeping Catherine Emmerich quickly drew her hands away from this girdle, saying:] Oh that is quite impossible and senseless! I, too, once wore a girdle like this for a long time, in

---

5. One may well be alarmed by the power of the world over fallen mankind when one considers how earthly things brought forgetfulness upon this favored soul who was not at all attached to them.

Every year about this time she saw this picture of Mary's departure for the Temple, and each time the appearance of the two prophets as boys was in some way interwoven with it. She sees them appear as boys and not at their real age, because they were not personally present at the proceeding but accompany her only as emblems. Painters, when making historical pictures, are in the habit of representing not in their real form, but as youths, genii, or angels, those persons who are intended to illustrate some truth or other. Thus we may see that this manner of representation is not a result of their poetical imagination, but lies in the nature of all visionary appearances. (CB)

accordance with an inner warning. It was a means of mortification and self-conquest, but was made of quite short spikes of brass wire set close together. This is a really murderous girdle; the man has taken great pains in making it, but could only wear it for a few minutes. One should never do anything like this without the approval of a wise director of souls: he did not know that, of course, because he had no director at hand. Such exaggeration does more harm than good!

[Next morning she recounted the visions of the night in the form of a dream-journey. She said, among other things:]

Hereupon I came to Jerusalem, at what period I am not sure, but it was in the time of the old Jewish kings. I have forgotten what I saw. Then I was made to go towards Nazareth to the house of Anna, Our Lady's holy mother. Before the city of Jerusalem two boys joined me who were going the same way; one held a scroll very solemnly in his hand, while the younger had tied his scroll to a little stick and was merrily playing with it in the wind as if it were a little flag. They spoke to me joyfully about the fulfillment of the time in their prophecies, for they were figures of prophets. I had with me that man's exaggerated penitential girdle which had been brought me, and showed it, by I know not what impulse, to the prophet boy who was Elias. He said to me, "That is a belt of torture not allowed to be worn. But on Mount Carmel I made and wore a girdle and have bequeathed it to all the children of my order, the Carmelites. That man should wear this girdle, it will profit him far more." Thereupon he showed me a girdle of a hand's breadth on which all kinds of letters and lines were inscribed, signifying various conquests and struggles, and he indicated various parts of it, saying, "That man could wear this for eight days and this for one day," and so on. Oh, how I wish the good man could know that!

When we came near to Anna's house and I wanted to go in, I could not do so, and my leader, my guardian angel, said to me: "You must first of all lay much aside, you must be nine years old." I did not know how this was to be done, but he helped me, I cannot remember how. Three years of my life had to disappear altogether, those three years when I was so vain about my clothes and always wanted to be a smart young girl. Well, I was suddenly nine years old, and now I was able to go into the house with the prophet boys. As I did so, the three-year-old child Mary came up to me and measured herself against me; she was just the same height as me when she stood up by me. How kind and friendly she was, and at the same time so serious!

Immediately after I was standing in the house beside the boy-prophets. Nobody seemed to notice us, and we got in nobody's way. Though they had been old men hundreds of years ago, they were not at all surprised at being present there as young boys: and I, though a nun over forty years old, was not at all surprised either at being now a poor peasant child of nine years. When one is with these holy people, one is surprised at nothing, except at the blindness and sinfulness of mankind.

I saw the travellers starting on their journey to Jerusalem at daybreak. The child Mary came running out of the house to the pack-animals, so eager was she to go to the Temple. The boy-prophets and I stood at the door following her with our eyes. They again showed me passages in their scrolls, one of which spoke of the glory of the Temple, but added that even greater glory was contained within it. The travellers had two pack-animals with them. One of the donkeys which was heavily loaded was led by a servant and was always a little ahead of the party. On the other donkey, which stood loaded before the house, a seat had been prepared, and Mary was placed on this. She wore the little yellow dress from the first set of garments, and was wrapped in the big cloak, which was drawn round her so that her arms rested in its folds. Joachim, who led this donkey, carried a tall staff like a pilgrim's with a big round knob at the top. Anna walked a short way ahead with little Mary Cleophas. A maid-

servant accompanied them on the whole journey, and
some of the women and children went part of the way
with them. They were relations, and turned off to their
homes where the roads parted. One of the priests also
accompanied the party for a little time.

They had a light with them, but it disappeared completely in the light which in my visions of night journeys always illuminates the road about the Holy Family
and other holy persons, though they themselves never
seem to see it. At first it seemed to me that I was walking with the boy-prophets behind the child Mary, and
afterwards, when she was on foot, at her side. I sometimes heard the boys singing the 44th Psalm *(Eructavit cor meum verbum bonum)* and the 49th *(Deus
deorum Dominus locutus est),* and they told me that
these Psalms would be sung by two choirs at the reception of the child in the Temple, as I should see when
they arrived.

I saw the road going downhill at first and later rising again. When it was morning and full day, I saw the
travellers resting beside a spring from which ran a
brook; there was a meadow there, and they rested beside
a hedge of balsam shrubs. These shrubs always had
stone basins under them to catch the balsam that
dripped from them, thus providing the passers-by with
a refreshing drink, with which they could also fill their
jugs. In the hedges there were berries which they picked
and ate. They also had little rolls of bread to eat. The
boy-prophets had by now disappeared. One of them was
Elias, the other I think was Moses. I am sure that the
child Mary saw them, but she said nothing about it.
She saw them just as when one is a child one often
sees holy children appearing to one (or when one is
grown-up one sees holy virgins or youths) without saying anything of it to others, because in such moments
one is in a state of quiet contemplation.

Later I saw the travellers stop at a house standing
by itself, where they were made welcome and were
given food. The people who lived there seemed to be

relations. Little Mary Cleophas was sent back from here. During the day I had several glimpses of their journey, a rather difficult one. They had to pass over hill and dale, and in the valleys there were often cold mists and much dew, though here and there I saw sunny patches where flowers were showing. Before reaching their resting-place for the night they crossed a little stream. They spent the night at an inn at the foot of a hill on which there is a town. Unfortunately I can no longer say for certain what was the name of this place. I saw it on other journeys of the Holy Family, and can easily be mistaken about its name.[6] I can only say this much, but not with certainty; they travelled in the same direction that Jesus followed in the September of His thirtieth year, when He went from Nazareth to Bethany and thence to be baptized by John. The Holy Family took the same way on their flight from Nazareth to Egypt. On that flight their first shelter was at Nazara, a small place between Massaloth and a hill-town, but nearer the latter. I see so many places around me and hear so many names that I may very easily mix them up. This town stretches up the hillside and is divided into several different parts, though all belonging to each other. There is a great lack of water there, and it has to be drawn up from below with ropes. There are several old towers in ruins, and on the top of the hill is a sort of watchtower with a structure of beams and ropes for hauling things up from the town below. The many ropes make it look rather like the masts of a ship. It must be an hour's climb to the top of the hill. (The travellers stopped at an inn down below.) There is a very extensive view from this hill. Part of this town is inhab-

---

6. From the situation of this town and from the mention of its having some heathen inhabitants, and of Jesus having travelled in this direction in His thirtieth year on His way to His Baptism, we may conclude that it was Endor. For in her daily visions of the ministry of Our Lord, Catherine Emmerich saw Him celebrating the Sabbath in a small place near Endor in the middle of September of the first year of His ministry on His way to His Baptism. Also in this rather deserted hill-town she saw Him teaching the Canaanites settled here since the defeat of Sisera, in whose army their ancestors had served. (CB)

Endor lies northeast of the Plain of Esdraelon, where the battle was fought in which Sisera was defeated (*Jgs.* 4). (SB)

ited by heathen people who were treated by the Jews as slaves and forced to do hard labor; for instance, they were made to work at the Temple and other buildings.

[On November 4th, 1821, she said:] This evening I saw Joachim and Anna with the child Mary and a maidservant arrive at an inn twelve hours distant from Jerusalem. They were accompanied by a manservant who often went ahead with the heavily loaded donkey. Here they caught up with the herd of their beasts on the way to the Temple to be sacrificed; these, however, continued at once on their road. Joachim must have been very well known here, for he was as if in his own house. His beasts for sacrifice always used to stop here. He also came here when he returned to Nazareth from his hidden life among the shepherds. I saw the child Mary asleep here beside her mother. (I have had so much to do these days with the Holy Souls that I think it has made me forget part of the journey to the Temple.)

[On November 5th, 1821, she related:] This evening I saw the child Mary with her parents arrive in a town to the northwest of Jerusalem, barely six hours' journey from it. This town is called Bethoron and lies at the foot of a hill. On the way they crossed a stream flowing westwards into the sea near Joppa, where Peter taught after the coming of the Holy Ghost. Great battles were once fought near Bethoron. I saw them, but have forgotten them again.[7] (See *Joshua* 10:11). It was about two hours' journey from here to a place on a high-road from where one could see Jerusalem. I heard the name of this road or place, but cannot distinctly recall it.[8]

Bethoron is a large town, inhabited by Levites. Very

---

7. Upper Bethoron is on the hill and Lower Bethoron at the foot of the hill. *Jos.* 10:11 mentions the battle "in the descent of Beth-horon"; and a big battle took place here as recorded in *1 Mach.* 3:16-24. (SB)
8. She remembered that the name sounded like Marion (possibly "Marom," i.e. "the height"). It is known that a road ran from Jerusalem past Bethoron to Nicopolis and Lydda. Catherine Emmerich gave all kinds of other details about the hills and valleys on the journey up to this point, but as she sees more distinctly than she can describe, it is impossible to reproduce these details, particularly as the topographical position from which she sees them cannot be determined. (CB)

fine, big grapes grow here, and many other fruits as well. The Holy Family stayed with friends in a well-kept house. The man was a school-teacher; it was a Levite school, and there were a number of children in the house. I was much surprised to see here several women related to Anna, with their little daughters, who were, I had thought, on the way to their own homes. However, as I now saw, they had taken a shorter road and had arrived here first, I suppose in order to welcome the travellers. These women and children were from Nazareth, Sephoris, Zabulon, and thereabouts; some of them had already been in Anna's house during the examination; for instance, Mary's elder sister and her little daughter Mary Cleophas, and Anna's sister from Sephoris with her daughters. The stay here was made the occasion of great rejoicing over the child Mary. She was led into a big room accompanied by the other children, and was placed on a raised seat with a canopy, arranged for her like a little throne. The school-teacher and others again asked her all manner of questions, putting wreaths on her head. All were astonished by the wisdom of her answers. I also heard about the cleverness of another girl who had passed through here a short time ago on her way home from the Temple school. Her name was Susanna, and later she followed Jesus with the holy women. It was her place that Mary was to take in the Temple, for there was a limited number of such places. Susanna was fifteen years old when she left the Temple, and thus about eleven years older than Mary. Anna, too, had been educated in the Temple, but did not go there till she was five years old. The child Mary was exceedingly joyful at being so near the Temple; I saw Joachim pressing her to his heart in tears, and saying: "O my child, I fear I shall not see you again."

A meal was now prepared, and while all were reclining at table I saw Mary running about full of loving gaiety, sometimes nestling against her mother or standing behind her and throwing her little arms round her neck.

[On November 6th, 1821:] Today very early I saw the travellers leaving Bethoron for Jerusalem. All their relations, the children, and the people of the inn went with them. They took with them presents of clothing and fruit for the child. It looks to me as if there were going to be great festivities in Jerusalem. I learnt for certain that Mary was three years and three months old, but she was like a little girl of five or six in our country. Their journey did not take them through either Ussen Scheera or Gophna, though they were known in those places; but they must have passed near them.

ARRIVAL IN JERUSALEM

[IN the evening of November 6th, 1821, Catherine Emmerich said:] Today at midday I saw the arrival in Jerusalem of the child Mary with those accompanying her. Jerusalem is a strange city; one must not picture it with crowded streets like, for instance, Paris. In Jerusalem are many valleys, steep ways winding behind city walls. No doors or windows are to be seen, for the houses, which stand on high ground, face away from the walls. New quarters have been added one by one, each enclosing a fresh ridge of hill, but leaving the old town-walls standing between them. These valleys are often spanned by solid stone bridges. The living-rooms of the houses usually face on to inner courts; on the street side only the door is to be seen, or perhaps a terrace high up on the top of the wall. The houses are very much shut up; unless the inhabitants have business in the markets or are visiting the Temple, they spend most of their time in the inner rooms and court-yards. In general the streets of Jerusalem are rather quiet, except near the markets and palaces, where crowds of travellers and soldiers and people going in and out of the houses fill the streets with life and movement. Rome is much more pleasantly situated; its streets are not so steep and narrow and are much more lively.

When all the people of Jerusalem are assembled in the Temple, many of the districts of the city seem quite dead. (It was because of the seclusion of the inhabitants within their houses and of the number of deserted valley-paths that Jesus was so often able to go about the city with His disciples undisturbed.) Water is scarce in Jerusalem, and one often sees great structures of arches with channels to carry it in different directions, also towers to the top of which it is driven or pumped. In the Temple, where a great deal of water is needed for washing and cleansing the vessels, it is used very carefully. It is brought up from below by means of large pumping works. There are a great many dealers in the city: they usually group themselves with others of the same trade, and set up lightly-made huts in open places and markets surrounded by porticoes. There are, for instance, not far from the Sheep Gate many dealers in every kind of metal-work, gold, and precious stones. They have light round huts, brown, as if smeared with pitch or resin. Although light, these huts are quite strong; they are used as dwellings, and awnings are stretched from one to another under which the wares are set out.

The gentler slope of the hill on which the Temple lies is terraced with several streets of houses, built one above the other behind thick walls. These are inhabitated partly by priests and partly by inferior temple-servants charged with menial duties, such as cleaning out the trenches into which is cast all the refuse from animals slaughtered in the Temple. On one side [she means the northern one][9] the Temple hill falls very steeply into a black gully. Little gardens belonging to the priests make a green strip round the top of the hill. Work on the Temple never ceased: even in Christ's lifetime building was going on in different parts of it. There was a quantity of ore in the Temple hill, which

---

9. It is the eastern side of the Temple hill that falls steeply into the Valley of Kedron. (SB)

was dug out in the course of building and made use of. There are many vaults and smelting-furnaces under the Temple. I never found a good place in the Temple to pray in: it is all so extraordinarily solid, heavy and high, and the little courts are themselves so narrow and dark and so encumbered with seats and other things, that when there are great multitudes, the narrow spaces and the crowds between the thick high walls and pillars have a really terrifying effect. The perpetual slaughtering and all the blood filled me, too, with horror, though all is performed with incredible order and cleanliness. It is a long time, I think, since I saw so clearly as I do today all the buildings, inside and out; but there is so much to describe that I shall never be able to do so properly.

The travellers, with the child Mary, approached Jerusalem from the north, but did not enter it on that side; as soon as they reached the outlying gardens and palaces, they skirted the town, turning east through part of the valley of Josaphat, leaving the Mount of Olives and the road to Bethany on their left, and entered the city by the Sheep Gate, which leads to the cattle-market. By this gate is a pool, in which the sheep destined for sacrifice are washed for the first time to remove the heavy dirt. But this is not the Pool of Bethesda.[10] The little company soon turned again to the right between walls as though going to another quarter of the town. On their way they passed through a long valley, on one side of which rose the towering walls of one of the upper parts of the city. They went towards the western side of Jerusalem, to the neighborhood of the

fish-market, where the ancestral house of Zacharias of

---

10. *John* 5:2, usually rendered, "There is at Jerusalem a pond Probatica (=sheep), which in Hebrew is named Bethsaida (or Bethesda or Bezatha)," seems to identify the sheep-pool and Bethsaida, which AC states are distinct. But the most probable rendering of the Greek is "There is at Jerusalem by the Probatica (i.e. sheep gate) a swimming-pool called in Hebrew Bezatha," and excavations have revealed traces of a swimming-pool "with five porches" (*John*, ib.) (cf. *Cath. Comm.*, 791c). This is evidently not the same as the sheep-dipping pool mentioned by AC. (SB)

Hebron stood. In it was a very old man, I think he was a brother of Zacharias' father. Zacharias always stayed here when he performed his service at the Temple. He was in the city now; his time of service had just come to an end, but he had remained a few days longer in Jerusalem on purpose to be present at Mary's reception in the Temple. He was not in his house when the company arrived. There were yet other relations in the house, from the neighborhood of Bethlehem and Hebron, with their children, amongst them two little nieces of Elisabeth, who was not there herself. These all went out with many young girls, carrying little garlands and branches, to meet the travellers, who were still a quarter of an hour away on the valley path. They gave them a joyful welcome, and led them to Zacharias' house, where great rejoicings took place. They were given some refreshment, and then preparations were made to conduct the whole company to a ceremonial inn in the neighborhood of the Temple. Joachim's beasts for sacrifice had already been brought from near the cattle-market to stables near this special inn. Zacharias now came to lead the company from his house to the inn. The child Mary was dressed in the second set of ceremonial garments with the sky-blue dress. A procession was formed, headed by Zacharias with Joachim and Anna. Mary followed, surrounded by four girls dressed in white, and behind them came the other children and relations. They went along several streets, passing the palace of Herod and the house where, later, Pilate lived. Their way led them towards the northeastern corner of the Temple hill; behind them was the fortress Antonia, a big high building on the northwestern side of the Temple. They had to climb a high wall by a flight of many steps. They wanted to take the child Mary by the hand, but to everyone's surprise she ran up swiftly and joyfully by herself.

The house they were going to was a ceremonial inn not far from the cattle-market. There were four of these inns round the Temple, and this one had been hired

for them by Zacharias. It was a large building, with a
big courtyard surrounded by a kind of cloister with
sleeping-places and long, low tables. There was also a
large room with a hearth for cooking. The place to
which Joachim's sacrificial beasts had been taken was
near by. On each side of it were the dwellings of the
Temple servants who had charge of the animals for
sacrifice.

When the company entered the inn, their feet were
washed, as is the custom with new arrivals; the men's
feet were washed by men, the women's by women. Then
they went into a room where a big many-branched lamp
hung from the middle of the ceiling over a large metal
basin with handles, full of water, in which they washed
their hands and faces. Joachim's pack-donkey was
unloaded and led by the manservant to the stable.
Joachim, who had given notice of his intention to sacrifice, followed the Temple servants to the near-by stables, where they inspected his beasts.

Joachim and Anna then made their way with the
child Mary to a priest's house higher up the hill. Here,
too, the child ran up the steps with surprising energy
as though upheld and urged by a spiritual force. The
two priests in this house, one very old and one younger,
gave them a friendly welcome; both had been present
at Mary's examination in Nazareth and were expecting her. After they had spoken of the journey and of
the approaching presentation ceremony, they summoned
one of the Temple women, an aged widow who was to
have charge of the child. (She lived near the Temple
with other women who, like her, were occupied in various feminine employments and in the training of young
girls. Their dwelling was farther away from the Temple than the rooms in which were the oratories of the
women and of the maidens dedicated to the Temple.
These rooms were built directly on to it, and from them
one could look down unseen into the holy place below.)
The woman who now came in was so muffled up that
only a little of her face could be seen. The child Mary

was introduced to her as her future foster-child by the priests and by her parents. She was grave but friendly, and the child was serious, humble, and respectful. They told her of Mary's disposition and character, and discussed various matters connected with the ceremony of her presentation. This elderly woman accompanied them to the inn and was given a package of the child's belongings, which she took back with her to arrange in Mary's new home. Those who had accompanied the party from Zacharias' house returned there, and only the relations who had come with the Holy Family remained in the inn hired by Zacharias. The women of the party settled themselves there and made preparations for a banquet on the following day.

[On November 7th Catherine Emmerich said:] I spent the whole of today watching the preparations for Joachim's sacrifice and for Mary's reception in the Temple. Early in the morning Joachim and some other men drove the sacrificial animals to the Temple, where they underwent another inspection by the priests; some of them were rejected, and these were at once driven to the cattle-market in the city. Those which were accepted were driven into the slaughtering-place, where I saw many things happening, but can no longer say in what order. I remember that Joachim laid his hand on the head of each animal before it was sacrificed. He had to catch the blood in a vessel, and had also to receive certain portions of the animal. There were all kinds of pillars, tables, and vessels there, where everything was cut up, distributed, and arranged in order. The bloody froth was taken away, while the fat, spleen, and liver were set apart. Everything was sprinkled with salt. The intestines of the lambs were cleansed and, after being filled with something, were put back into the body to make it seem whole again. The legs of all the animals were tied together crosswise. Some of the meat was taken into another court and given to the Temple virgins, who had to do something with it—perhaps to prepare it for their own or for the priests' food. All was done with incredible orderliness. The priests and Levites moved about always two by two, and the most difficult and complicated tasks were accomplished as if by clockwork. The pieces of meat were not actually offered up till the following day; in the meantime they lay in salt.

There were great rejoicings in the inn today, and a banquet; there must have been a hundred people there, counting the children. There were present at least twenty-four girls of varying ages; among them I saw Seraphia, who after Jesus' death was known as Veronica. She was tall, and might have been ten or twelve years old. They were making wreaths and garlands for Mary and her companions, and decorating seven candles or torches. The candlesticks, which were without pedestals, were shaped like sceptres; I cannot remember what fed the flame at the top, whether it was oil or wax or something else. During the festivities there were several priests and Levites going in and out of the inn, and these also took part in the banquet. When they expressed astonishment at the greatness of Joachim's sacrifice, he explained that he wished to show his gratitude to the best of his power; he could not forget how, by God's mercy, his shame in the Temple at the rejection of his sacrifice had been followed by the granting of his petitions. Today, too, I saw the child Mary going for a walk near the inn with the other little girls. Much else I have forgotten.

MARY'S ENTRY INTO THE TEMPLE AND PRESENTATION

[ON November 8th, 1821, Catherine Emmerich related:] Today Joachim went first to the Temple with Zacharias and the other men. Afterwards Mary was taken there by her mother Anna in a festal procession. First came Anna and her elder daughter Mary Heli, with the latter's little daughter Mary Cleophas; then the holy child Mary followed in her sky-blue dress and robe, with wreaths round her arms and neck; in her hand she held a candle or torch entwined with flowers. Decorated candles like this were also carried by three maidens who walked on each side of her, wearing white dresses embroidered with gold. They, too, wore pale-blue robes; they were wreathed round with garlands of flowers, and wore little wreaths round their necks and arms as well. Next came the other maidens and little girls, all in festal dress but each different. They all wore little robes. The other women came at the end of the procession. They could not go direct from the inn to the Temple, but had to make a detour through several streets. The beautiful procession gave pleasure to all who saw it, and at several houses honor was paid to it as it passed. There was something indescribably moving in the holiness apparent in the child. As the procession approached the Temple, I saw many of the Temple servants struggling with great efforts to open an immensely large and heavy door, shining like gold and ornamented with a multitude of sculptured heads, bunches of grapes, and sheaves of corn. This was the Golden Gate. The procession passed under this gate, to which fifteen steps led up, but whether in a single flight I cannot remember. Mary would not take the hands held out to her; to the admiration of all she ran eagerly and joyfully up the steps without stumbling. She was received in the gateway by Zacharias, Joachim, and several priests, and led under the gate (which was a long archway) to the right into some large halls or high rooms, in one of which a meal was being prepared. Here the procession dispersed. Several of the women and children went to the women's praying-place in the Temple, while Joachim and Zacharias proceeded to the sacrifice. In one of the halls the priest again examined the child Mary by putting questions to her. They were astonished at the wisdom of her answers, and left her to be dressed by Anna in the third and most magnificent violet-blue ceremonial garment, with the robe, veil, and crown which I have already described at the ceremony in Anna's house.

In the meantime Joachim had gone with the priests to the sacrifice. He was given fire from the appointed place, and then stood between two priests at the altar. I am at present too ill and upset to describe all the circumstances of the sacrifice, but will tell what is still present to my mind.

The altar could be approached from three sides only. The meat prepared for the sacrifice was not put all together, but was divided into separate portions placed round the altar. Flat shelves could be drawn out of the three sides of the altar, and on these the offerings were laid to be pushed to the center of it; for the altar was too large for the officiating priest to be able to reach the center with his arm. At the four corners of the altar there stood little hollow columns of metal, crowned with chimneys or something similar—wide funnels made of thin copper, ending in pipes curving outwards like horns, which carried away the smoke above the heads of the officiating priests. When Joachim's sacrifice started to burn, Anna went, with the child Mary in her ceremonial dress and with her companions, into the outer court of the women, which is the place in the Temple set apart for women. This court was separated from the court of the altar of sacrifice by a wall surmounted by a grille; there was, however, a door in the center of this dividing wall. The women's court slants upwards from the wall, so that a view of the altar of sacrifice cannot be had by all, but only by those standing at the back. When, however, the door in the dividing wall was opened, a number of the women were able to see the altar through it. Mary and the other little girls stood in front of Anna, and the other women of the family remained near the door. In a separate place there were a number of Temple boys dressed in white and playing flutes and harps. After the sacrifice, there was set up in the doorway leading from the court of sacrifice to the women's court a portable decorated altar[11] or sacrificial table, with several steps leading up to it.

Zacharias and Joachim came out of the court of sacrifice and went up to this altar with a priest, in front of whom stood another priest and two Levites with scrolls and writing materials. Anna led the child Mary up to them; the maidens who had accompanied Mary stood a little behind. Mary knelt on the steps, and Joachim and Anna laid their hands on her head. The priest cut off a few of her hairs and burnt them in a brazier. Her parents also said a few words, offering up their child; these were written down by two Levites. Meanwhile the maidens sang the 44th Psalm *(Eructavit cor meum verbum bonum)* and the priests the 49th Psalm *(Deus, deorum Dominus, locutus est)* accompanied by the boys with their instruments.

I then saw Mary being led by the hand by two priests up many steps to a raised place in the wall dividing the outer court of the Holy Place from the other court. They placed the child in a sort of niche in the middle of this wall, so that she could see into the Temple, where there were many men standing in ranks; they seemed to me to be also dedicated to the Temple. Two priests stood beside her, and still others on the steps below, singing and reading aloud from their scrolls. On the other side of the dividing wall there was an old high priest standing at an altar of incense, so high up that one could see half of his figure. I saw him offering incense and the smoke from it enveloping the child Mary.

During these ceremonies I saw a symbolic vision round the Blessed Virgin which eventually filled and dimmed the whole Temple. I saw a glory of light under Mary's heart, and understood that this glory encompassed the Promise, the most holy blessing of God. I saw this glory appear as if surrounded by the Ark of Noah, so that the Blessed Virgin's head projected above

---

11. This altar-table was set up in this doorway because women were not permitted to go farther. When the meeting of Joachim and Anna took place, Joachim had gone through this door into the subterranean passage, while Anna had come from the opposite direction. (CB)

it. Then I saw the shape of the Ark about the glory change into the shape of the Ark of the Covenant, which in its turn changed into the shape of the Temple. Then I saw these shapes disappear, and out of the glory there rose before Our Lady's breast a shape like the Chalice of the Last Supper, and above this, before her mouth, a bread marked with a cross. On each side of her there streamed out manifold rays of light at the ends of which appeared in pictures many mysteries and symbols of the Blessed Virgin, as for example all the titles in the Litany of Our Lady. Behind her shoulders two branches of olive and cypress or cedar and cypress stretched crosswise above a slender palm-tree, which I saw appear just behind her with a little leafy shrub. In the spaces between this arrangement of green branches I saw all the instruments of Our Lord's Passion. The Holy Ghost hovered over the picture in human rather than dove-like form, winged with rays of light: and above I saw the heavens open and disclose, floating in the air above Our Lady, the heavenly Jerusalem, the City of God, with all its palaces and gardens and the mansions of future saints. All were filled with angels, and the whole glory, which now surrounded the Blessed Virgin, was filled with angels' faces.

How can this be expressed? Its variations, its unfoldings, and its transformations were so innumerable that I have forgotten a very great deal. The whole significance of the Blessed Virgin in the Covenant of the Old and New Testaments and to all eternity was set forth therein. I can compare this vision with the smaller one which I had a short time ago of the holy Rosary in all its glory. (Seemingly clever people who speak slightingly of the Rosary are much less sensible than poor unimportant folk who pray with it in all simplicity, for these adorn it with the beauty of obedience and humble devotion, trusting in the Church's recommendation of it to the faithful.)

With this vision before me, all the splendor and magnificence of the Temple and the beautifully decorated wall behind the Blessed Virgin seemed quite dim and dingy, even the Temple itself seemed to be no longer there, so full was everything of Mary and her glory. As the whole significance of the Blessed Virgin unfolded itself before my eyes in these visions I saw her no longer as the child Mary, but as the Blessed Virgin, hovering tall above me. I saw the priests and the smoke of the offering and everything through the picture; it was as if the priests behind her were uttering prophecies and admonishing the people to thank God and to pray that this child should be magnified. All those who were present in the Temple were hushed and filled with solemn awe, though they did not see the picture that I saw. It disappeared again little by little just as I had seen it come. At last I saw nothing but the glory under Mary's heart, with the Blessing of the Promise shining within it. Then this disappeared, too, and I saw the holy dedicated child in her ceremonial dress standing alone once more between the priests. The priests took the wreaths from off the child's arms and the torch from her hand and gave them to her companions. They placed a brown veil or hood on her head, and led her down the steps through a door into another hall, where she was met by six other (but older) Temple virgins who strewed flowers before her. Behind her stood her teachers: Noemi, the sister of Lazarus' mother, the Prophetess Anna, and still a third woman; the priests gave the child Mary over to them and withdrew. Her parents and near relations now approached; the singing was over, and Mary said farewell. Joachim's emotion was particularly deep; he lifted Mary up, pressed her to his heart, and said to her with tears, "Remember my soul before God!" Thereupon Mary with her teachers and several maidens went into the women's dwelling on the north side of the Temple itself. They lived in rooms built in the thickness of the Temple walls. Passages and winding stairs led up to little praying cells near the Holy Place and Holy of Holies.

Mary's parents and relations went back to the hall

by the Golden Gate where they had first waited, and partook of a meal there with the priests. The women ate in a separate hall. I have forgotten much of what I saw and heard, amongst other things the exact reason why the ceremony was so rich and solemn; but I do recollect that it was so as a result of a revelation of the Divine Will.

(Mary's parents were really well off; it was only as mortification and for almsgiving that they lived so poorly. I forget for how long Anna ate nothing but cold food; but their servants were well fed and provided for.) I saw many people praying in the Temple, and many had followed the procession to its gates. Some of those present must have had some idea of the destiny of Our Lady, for I remember Anna speaking with enthusiastic joy to various women and saying to them, "Now the Ark of the Covenant, the Vessel of the Promise, is entering the Temple." Mary's parents and other relations reached Bethoron the same day on their journey home.

I now saw a festival among the Temple virgins. Mary had to ask the teachers and each of the young girls whether they would suffer her to be among them. This was the custom. Then they had a meal, and afterwards they danced amongst themselves. They stood opposite each other in pairs, and danced in various figures and crossings. There was no hopping, it was like a minuet. Sometimes there was a swaying, circular motion of the body, like the movements of the Jews when they pray. Some of the young girls accompanied the dancing with flutes, triangles, and bells. There was another instrument which sounded particularly strange and delightful. It was played by plucking the strings stretched on the steeply sloping sides of a sort of little box. In the middle of the box were bellows which when pressed up and down sent the air through several pipes, some straight and some crooked, and so made an accompaniment to the strings. The instrument was held on the player's knees.

In the evening I saw the teacher Noemi lead the

Blessed Virgin to her little room, which looked into the Temple. It was not quite square, and the walls were inlaid with triangular shapes in different colors. There was a stool in it and a little table, and in the corners were stands with shelves for putting things on. Before this room was a sleeping-place and a room for dresses, as well as Noemi's room. Mary spoke to her again about rising often to pray in the night, but Noemi did not yet allow this.

The Temple women wore long, full, white robes with girdles and very wide sleeves, which they rolled up when working. They were veiled.

I never remember seeing that Herod entirely rebuilt the Temple: I only saw various alterations being made in it during his reign. Now, when Mary came to the Temple, eleven years before Christ's birth, nothing was being built in the Temple itself, but (as always) in the outer portions of it: here the work never stopped.

[On November 21st Catherine Emmerich said:] Today I had a view of Mary's dwelling in the Temple. On the northern side of the Temple hall, towards the Holy Place, there were several rooms high up which were connected with the women's dwellings. Mary's room was one of the outermost of these towards the Holy of Holies. From the passage one passed through a curtain into a sort of antechamber, which was divided off from the room itself by a partition, semi-circular or forming an angle. In the corners to the right and left were shelves for keeping clothes and other things. Opposite the door in this partition steps led to an opening high up in the wall which looked down into the Temple. This opening had a carpet hanging before it and was curtained with gauze. Against the wall in the left-hand side of the room there was a rolled-up carpet, which, when spread out, made the bed on which Mary slept. A bracket-lamp was fixed in a niche in the wall, and today I saw the child standing on a stool and praying by its light from a parchment roll with red knobs. It was a very touching sight. The child was wearing a little blue-and-white striped dress woven with yellow flowers. There was a low round table in the room. I saw Anna come in and place on the table a dish with fruits of the size of beans and a little jug. Mary was skillful beyond her years: I saw her already working at little white cloths for the service of the Temple.

[Catherine Emmerich generally communicated the above visions about the time of the feast of the Presentation of Our Lady. Besides these, however, she related at different times the following accounts of Mary's eleven-year sojourn in the Temple:]

I saw the Blessed Virgin in the Temple, ever progressing in learning, prayer, and work. Sometimes I saw her in the women's dwelling with the other young girls, sometimes alone in her little room. She worked, wove, and knitted narrow strips of stuff on long rods for the service of the Temple. She washed the cloths and cleansed the pots and pans. I often saw her in prayer and meditation. I never saw her chastising or mortifying her body, she did not need it. Like all very holy people she ate only to live, and took no other food except that which she had vowed to eat. Besides the prescribed Temple-prayers, Mary's devotions consisted of an unceasing longing for redemption, a perpetual state of inner prayer, quietly and secretly performed. In the stillness of the night she rose from her bed and prayed to God. I often saw her weeping at her prayers and surrounded by radiance. As she grew up, I always saw that she wore a dress of a glistening blue color. She was veiled while at prayer, and also wore a veil when she spoke with priests or went down to a room by the Temple to be given work or to hand over what she had done. There were rooms like this on three sides of the Temple; they always looked to me like sacristies. All sorts of things were kept there which it was the duty of the Temple maidens to look after, repair, and replace.

I saw the Blessed Virgin living in the Temple in a

perpetual ecstasy of prayer. Her soul did not seem to be on the earth, and she often received consolation and comfort from Heaven. She had an endless longing for the fulfillment of the Promise, and in her humility hardly ventured on the wish to be the lowliest maidservant of the Mother of the Redeemer. Mary's teacher and nurse in the Temple was called Noemi, she was a sister of Lazarus' mother and was fifty years old. She and the other Temple women belonged to the Essenes. Mary learnt from her how to knit and helped her when she washed the blood of the sacrifices from the vessels and instruments, or when she cut up and prepared certain parts of the flesh for the Temple women and priests; for this formed part of their food. Later on Mary took a still more active part in these duties. When Zacharias did his service in the Temple he used to visit her, and Simeon was also acquainted with her.

The Blessed Virgin's significance cannot have been quite unknown to the priests. Her whole being, the abundance of grace in her, and her wisdom were so remarkable from her childhood in the Temple onwards that they could not be entirely concealed in spite of her great humility. I saw aged holy priests filling great scrolls with writing about her, and I have been shown these scrolls, lying with other writings, though I cannot remember at what period.

IV

THE EARLY LIFE OF ST. JOSEPH

[We here break off Catherine Emmerich's somewhat disconnected description of the Blessed Virgin's sojourn in the Temple to give the following accounts of St. Joseph's youth.]

AMONG many things which I saw today of the youth of St. Joseph I remember what follows.

Joseph, whose father was called Jacob, was the third of six brothers. His parents lived in a large house outside Bethlehem, once the ancestral home of David, whose father Isai or Jesse had owned it. By Joseph's time there was, however, little remaining of the old building except the main walls. The situation was very airy, and water was abundant there. I know my way about there better than in our own little village of Flamske.

In front of the house was an outer court (as in the houses of ancient Rome), surrounded by a covered colonnade like a cloister. I saw sculptures in this colonnade like the heads of old men. On one side of the court was a fountain under a stone canopy. The water issued from animals' heads in stone. There were no windows to be seen in the lower story of the dwelling-house itself, but high up there were circular openings. I saw one door. A broad gallery ran round the upper part of the house, with little towers at each of its four corners, like short, thick pillars, ending in big balls or domes on which little flags were fastened. Stairs led up through these little towers from below, and from openings in the domes one had a view all round without being seen oneself. There were little towers like this on David's palace in Jerusalem, and it was from the dome of one of these that he saw Bethsabee at her bath. This gallery ran round a low upper story with a flat roof on which was another building with another little tower. Joseph and his brothers lived in the upper story, and their teacher, an aged Jew, lived in the topmost building. They all slept in a circle in one room, in the middle of the story which was surrounded by the gallery. Their sleeping-places were carpets, rolled up against the wall in the daytime and separated by removable screens. I have often seen them playing up there in their rooms. They had toys in the shape of animals, like little pugs. [Catherine Emmerich uses this word indiscriminately for any creatures she does not know.] I also saw how their teacher gave them all kinds of strange lessons which I did not rightly understand. I saw him making all kinds of figures on the ground with sticks, and the boys had to walk on these figures; then I saw the boys walking on other figures and pushing the sticks apart, placing them differently and rearranging them and making various measurements at the same time. I saw their parents, too; they did not trouble much about their children and had little to do with them. They seemed to me to be neither good nor bad.

Joseph, whom I saw in this vision at about the age of eight, was very different in character from his brothers. He was very gifted and was a very good scholar, but he was simple, quiet, devout, and not at all ambitious. His brothers knocked him about and played all kinds of tricks on him. The boys had separate little gardens, at the entrance of which stood figures like babies in swaddling-clothes on pillars, but sheltered a little (in niches perhaps?). I have often seen figures like these, and there were some on the curtain which hung by the praying-place of St. Anne and also of the Blessed Virgin, but on Mary's curtain this figure held something in its arms that reminded me of a chalice with something wriggling out of it. Here in St. Joseph's house the figures were like babies in swaddling-clothes with round faces surrounded by rays. In still earlier times I noticed many figures of this kind, particularly in Jerusalem. They appeared, too, in the Temple decorations. I saw them in Egypt as well, where they sometimes had little caps on their heads. Amongst the figures which Rachel carried off from her father Laban there were some like these, but smaller, as well as other different ones. I have also seen these figures lying in little boxes or baskets in Jewish houses. I think perhaps that they represented the child Moses floating on the Nile, and that the swaddling-bands perhaps symbolized the tightly binding character of the Law. I often used to think that this little figure was for them what the Christ Child is for us.

I saw herbs, bushes, and little trees in the boys' gardens; and I saw how Joseph's brothers often went in secret to his garden and trampled or uprooted something in it. They made him very unhappy. I often saw him under the colonnade in the outer court kneeling down with his face to the wall, praying with outstretched arms, and I saw his brothers creep up and kick him. I once saw him kneeling like this, when one of them hit him on the back, and as he did not seem to notice it, he repeated his attack with such violence that poor Joseph fell forward onto the hard stone floor. From this I realized that he was not in a waking condition, but had been in an ecstasy of prayer. When he came to himself, he did not lose his temper or take revenge, but found a hidden corner where he continued his prayer.

I saw some small dwellings built against the outer walls of the house, inhabited by a few middle-aged women. They went about veiled, as I often saw women doing who lived near schools in the country. They seemed to form part of the household, for I often saw them going in and out of the house on various errands. They carried water in, washed and swept, closed the gratings in front of the windows, rolled up the beds against the walls and placed wickerwork screens in front of them. I saw Joseph's brothers sometimes talking to these maid-servants or helping them with their work and joking with them, too. Joseph did not do this; he was serious and solitary. It seemed to me that there were also daughters in the house. The lower living-rooms were arranged rather like those in Anna's house, but everything was more spacious. Joseph's parents were not very well satisfied with him; they wanted him to use his talents in some worldly profession, but he had no inclination for that. He was too simple and unpretentious for them; his only inclination was towards prayer and quiet work at some handicraft. When he was about twelve years old, I often saw him go to the other side of Bethlehem to escape from his brothers' perpetual teasing. Not far from the future cave of the Nativity there was a little community of pious women belonging to the Essenes, who dwelt in a series of rock-chambers in a hollowed-out part of the hill on which Bethlehem stood. They tended little gardens near their dwellings and taught the children of other Essenes. Little Joseph went to visit these women, and I often used to see him escaping from his brothers' teasing to go to them and join in their prayers, which they read by the light of a lamp in their cave from a scroll hanging on the wall. I also saw him visiting the caves of which one was afterwards the birth-place of Our Lord. He prayed there quite alone, or made all kinds of little things out of wood; for there was an old carpenter who had his workshop near these Essenes with whom Joseph spent much of his time. He helped him with his work and so little by little learnt his craft. The art of measuring which he had practiced at home under his master's tuition was here of great use to him. His brothers' hostility at last made it impossible for him to remain any longer in his parents' house; I saw that a friend from Bethlehem (which was separated from his home by a little stream) gave him clothes in which to disguise himself. In these he left the house at night in order to earn his living in another place by his carpentry. He might have been eighteen to twenty years old at that time. To begin with, I saw him working with a carpenter at Libonah.[1] This was the place where he first really learnt his craft.

His master had his dwelling against some ancient walls which ran from the town along a narrow ledge of hill, like a road leading up to some ruined castle. Several poor people lived in the walls. I saw Joseph making long stakes in a place between high walls with openings above to let in light. These stakes were frames for wicker-screens. His master was a poor man, and made mostly only such common things as these rough wicker-screens. Joseph was very devout, good, and simple-minded, everybody loved him. I saw him helping his master very humbly in all sorts of ways— picking up shavings, collecting wood, and carrying it back on his shoulders. In later days he passed by here with the Blessed Virgin on one of their journeys, and I think he visited his former workshop with her.

His parents thought at first that he had been carried off by robbers; but I saw that he was discovered at last by his brothers and severely taken to task, for they were ashamed of his low way of life. He was, however, too humble to give it up; though he left that place and worked afterwards at Thanath,[2] near

---

1. It appears from various communications of Catherine Emmerich's about the ministry of Our Lord that the town in which St. Joseph first worked was not the Libnah which is in the tribe of Juda some hours to the west of Bethlehem, but Libonah on the south side of Mount Garizim. According to the Book of *Judges* 21:19, it is to be found north of Silo. (CB)
2. Thanath or Thaanath (see *Jos.* 16:6) lies, according to Eusebius, ten miles to the east of Nablus in the direction of the Jordan, whereas the place here mentioned by Catherine Emmerich must, by her account, lie northwest of Nablus. She must therefore no doubt have meant Thaanath instead of Thanath, and have been misunderstood by the writer, who at the time had no knowledge whatever of the geography of Palestine and no means of supplying it. Such misunderstanding was all the more likely to occur because Catherine Emmerich when ill or in a state of ecstasy often pronounced the names somewhat unclearly in her low-German Münster dialect and sometimes mixed them up. A further convincing proof that she here meant Thaanach may be found in the daily account which she gave in 1823 of the third year of Our Lord's ministry. She saw in her visions that Jesus taught on the 25th and 26th of the month Siva in Thaanach, a town of the Levites near Megiddo, and that He visited there the former carpenter's shop of His foster-father Joseph. (CB)

Megiddo, by a small river called Kishon which runs
into the sea. (This place is not far from Apheke,[3] the
home of the Apostle Thomas.) Joseph lived here with
a well-to-do master, and the carpenter's work which
they did was of a higher quality. Later still I saw him
working in Tiberias for a master-carpenter. He might
have been as much as thirty-three years old at that
time. His parents in Bethlehem had been dead for some
time. Two of his brothers still lived in Bethlehem, the
others were dispersed. The parental home had passed
into other hands, and the whole family had come down
in the world very rapidly. Joseph was very devout and
prayed fervently for the coming of the Messias. He was
just engaged in building beside his dwelling a more
retired room for prayer, when an angel appeared to
him and told him not to do this, for, as once the patriarch Joseph at about this time had, by God's Will, been
made overseer of all the corn of Egypt, so he, the second Joseph, should now be entrusted with the care of
the granary of salvation.[4] Joseph in his humility did
not understand this, and gave himself up to continual
prayer, till he received the call to betake himself to
Jerusalem to become by divine decree the spouse of
the Blessed Virgin. I never saw that he was married
before; he was very retiring and avoided women.

[Later in Catherine Emmerich's visions we shall come
across various other allusions to the family history of
Joseph and in particular of his brothers. These allusions are, however, too scattered and interwoven in the
great mass of her communications for the writer to collect them all together in this place with certainty and
clarity. Since, however, an opportunity occurs here
unsought, we will mention an elder brother of Joseph's
who lived in Galilee.

[When we were looking up in our diaries the passage where Catherine Emmerich explained on August

---

3. Aphek is about twenty-five miles north of Thaanach. (SB)
4. The same idea is found in St. Bernard's *Homilia* 2 *super Missus est,* recited in the
Breviary on St. Joseph's feast. (SB)

24th, 1821, the relationship between Joseph and Joachim (see p. 20), we found a detailed account given by her on the same day (being the feast of St. Bartholomew) of a story from the life of that Apostle. This vision had presented itself very vividly to her in connection with a relic of the Saint. In the course of it she stated that the father of Bartholomew of Gessur had for some long time frequented the healing waters near Bethulia and had afterwards settled permanently in the region, chiefly on account of his friendship with an elder brother of Joseph. She added:]

He went to a valley near Dabbeseth which was the home of Zadok, a devout man and an elder brother of Joseph. The devout father of Bartholomew had become much attached to him during his sojourn at Bethulia. Zadok had two sons and two daughters, and these children were on friendly terms with the Holy Family. When the twelve-year-old Jesus remained behind in the Temple and His parents missed Him, this was one of the families in which they sought for Him. I saw the sons amongst Jesus' playmates when He was a boy.

V

A SON IS PROMISED TO ZACHARIAS

I SAW Zacharias talking with Elisabeth of his grief; it was near the time for his turn of service in the Temple, and it was always with sorrow that he went, for he was looked on with contempt there because of his unfruitfulness. Zacharias had to perform his service in the Temple twice a year.

They lived not in Hebron itself, but in Jutta, about an hour's distance from it. There were many remains of walls between Jutta[1] and Hebron, as if these two places had once been connected with each other. On the other sides of Hebron were also many scattered buildings and groups of houses, the remains, it seemed, of the former city of Hebron, which must once have been as large as Jerusalem. Priests of lower rank lived at Hebron, while those of higher rank lived at Jutta. Zacharias was a kind of superior of the latter. He and Elisabeth were held in great honor there for their virtue and their unbroken descent from Aaron.

I then saw how Zacharias and several other priests of the neighborhood met together on a small farm which he owned near Jutta. There was a garden with various arbors and a little house. Zacharias prayed here with his companions and taught them. It was a kind of preparation for the forthcoming service at the Temple. I also heard him speak of his heaviness of heart,

---

1. Jutta, the modern *Yattah,* lies about five miles south of Hebron. See also n. 2, p. 148. (SB)

and how he had a presentiment that something was about to befall him.

I then saw him go with these people to Jerusalem; he had to wait four days more before it was his turn to sacrifice. In the meantime he prayed in the Temple. When it was his turn to kindle the incense-offering, I saw him go into the Holy Place, where the golden altar of incense stood in front of the entrance to the Holy of Holies. The ceiling above it had been opened so that one could see the sky. One could not see the sacrificing priest from outside, but one could see the smoke rising up. When Zacharias had entered, another priest said something to him and then went away.[2]

Now that Zacharias was alone, I saw him go through a curtain into a place where it was dark. He brought something out from there which he placed on the altar, and kindled fire to make smoke. Then I saw a radiance descending upon him from the right side of the altar, and within it a shining figure approaching him, and I saw how he sank down towards the right-hand side of the altar in alarm and at the same time rigid in ecstasy. The angel lifted him up and spoke with him for a long time, and Joachim answered him. I saw the heavens opening above Zacharias, and two angels descending and ascending as if on a ladder. His girdle was loosened and his robe was open, and it appeared to me as if one of the angels took something from him and as if the other put into his side as it were a little shining substance. That was what happened also when Joachim received the blessing of the angel for the conception of the Blessed Virgin. It was usual for the priests to leave the Holy Place as soon as they had kindled the incense-offering, so when Zacharias was so long in coming out, those praying outside became anxious. He had become dumb, and I saw him writing on a tablet before coming out. When he emerged from the Temple

---

2. Probably he had said to him, as was the custom, "Kindle the incense-offering." See Mishnah, tract. *Tamid*, 6, §3, edit. Surenh, p. 305. (CB)

The tractate *Tamid*, IV-VII, describes the whole course of the daily sacrifice. This passage is in tome V, p. 305, in the edition of Surenhusius. (SB)

and came into the outer court, a crowd gathered round him and asked why he had stayed so long. But he could not speak; he waved his hands and pointed to his mouth and to the tablet, which he at once sent to Elisabeth at Jutta, to tell her of the merciful promise of God and of his own dumbness. After a short time he returned there himself; Elisabeth had also been given a revelation, but I can no longer remember what it was.

[This rather incomplete account is all that Catherine Emmerich, who was ill at the time, related on this subject; see *Luke* 1:5-25.]

VI

MARRIAGE OF THE BLESSED VIRGIN TO JOSEPH

THE Blessed Virgin lived with other virgins in the Temple under the care of pious matrons. The maidens employed themselves with embroidery and other forms of decoration of carpets and vestments, and also with the cleaning of these vestments and of the vessels used in the Temple. They had little cells, from which they could see into the Temple, and here they prayed and meditated. When these maidens were grown up, they were given in marriage. Their parents in dedicating them to the Temple had offered them entirely to God, and the devout and more spiritual Israelites had for a long time had a secret presentiment that the marriage of one of these virgins would one day contribute to the coming of the promised Messias.[1]

---

1. Although in general late Jewish writers contest the statement that women or virgins were engaged in the service of the Temple, we find confirmation that this was so partly on the authority of the Church (which celebrates the Feast of Our Lady's Presentation on Nov. 21st) and partly in the Bible and in ancient writings. Already in the time of Moses (see *Exod.* 38:8), and again in the last days of the Judges (*1 Kgs.* 2:22), we find women or virgins employed in the service of the Temple; and in the description in *Ps.* 67 of the bringing of the Ark of the Covenant to Mount Sion, there is an allusion in v. 26 to "young damsels playing on timbrels." The statement that virgins were dedicated to the Temple and brought up there is confirmed by Evodius, a pupil of the Apostles and successor of St. Peter at Antioch (it is true that this is in a letter first appearing in Nicephor, II, c. 3), who expressly refers to Our Blessed Lady in this connection. Gregory of Nyssa and John Damascene, amongst others, also mention this, while Rabbi Asarja states in his work *Imre Binah*, c. 60, that virgins devoted to God's service lived in community in the Temple. We are thus able to quote a Jewish authority for the existence of these Temple maidens. (CB)

Nicephor is the fourteenth-century Byzantine historian Nicephorus Callistus, who wrote *Ecclesiasticae Historiae*, libri XVIII. Rabbi Azariah ben Moses de'Rossi

When the Blessed Virgin had reached the age of fourteen and was to be dismissed from the Temple with seven other maidens to be married, I saw that her mother Anna had come to visit her there. Joachim was no longer alive and Anna had by God's command married again. When Our Lady was told that she must now leave the Temple and be married, I saw her explaining to the priests in great distress of heart that it was her desire never to leave the Temple, that she had betrothed herself to God alone and did not wish to be married. She was, however, told that it must be so.[2]

Hereupon I saw the Blessed Virgin supplicating God with great fervor in her praying cell. I also remember that I saw Mary, who was parched with thirst as she prayed, going down with a little jug to draw water from a fountain or cistern, and that she there heard a voice (unaccompanied by any visible appearance) and received a revelation which comforted her and gave her strength to consent to her marriage. This was not the Annunciation, for I saw that happen later in Nazareth. I must, however, once have thought that I saw the appearance of an angel here too, for in my youth I often confused this vision with the Annunciation and thought that I saw the latter happening in the Temple.[3]

(1513/4-1578) was an Italian Jew. The treatise *Imre Bina* ("words of understanding") forms a part of his chief work, *Meor Enayim* ("light of the eyes"), published at Mantua in 1574. Both are therefore very late authorities. (SB)

2. In the Old Testament the state of virginity was, at least in general, not considered as meritorious. Among the countless forms of vows, which according to the Mishnah were usual amongst the Jews of old, we find no trace of any vow of chastity. As long as the coming of the Redeemer was in expectation only, a marriage rich in children was the height of blessedness and godliness on earth. See *Ps.* 126:3: "The inheritance of the Lord are children; the reward, the fruit of the womb": and, for one of God's early blessings, see *Deut.* 7:14: "Blessed shalt thou be among all people. No one shall be barren among you of either sex." This explains why the priests did not yield to Mary's wish, even though instances of persons vowed to chastity, especially among the Essenes, were by no means unknown. (CB)

3. It is remarkable that the apocryphal "Protevangelium of James," which the Church has pronounced not to be genuine, states among other things that Mary journeyed from the Temple to Nazareth accompanied by several maidens. These had been given by the Temple various threads to spin, of which the scarlet and purple ones had fallen to Mary's lot. Taking a jug, she went out to draw water, and lo, a voice said to her, "Hail, Mary," etc. Mary looked to right and left, to discover whence this voice came, and went into the house in alarm. She put down the jug, took the purple thread and laid it on her chair to work, and lo, the angel of the Lord stood before her face and said, "Fear not, Mary," etc. Thus here, too, there is an allusion to a voice while Our Lady was fetching water, but all happens in Nazareth and is

I saw, too, that a very aged priest, who could no longer walk (it was doubtless the high priest), was carried on a chair by others before the Holy of Holies, and that while the incense-offering was being kindled, he read prayers from a parchment scroll lying on a stand in front of him. I saw that he was in a spiritual ecstasy and saw a vision, and that the forefinger of his hand was laid upon the passage of Isaias in the scroll: "And there shall come forth a rod out of the root of Jesse; and a flower shall rise up out of his root." [*Is.* 11:1.] When the old priest came to himself again, he read this passage and apprehended something from it.

Then I saw that messengers were sent throughout the land and all unmarried men of the line of David summoned to the Temple. When these were assembled in large numbers at the Temple in festal garments, the Blessed Virgin was presented to them. Among them I saw a very devout youth from the region of Bethlehem; he had always prayed with great fervor for the fulfillment of the Promise, and I discerned in his heart an ardent longing to become Mary's husband. She, however, withdrew again into her cell in tears, unable to bear the thought that she should not remain a virgin.

I now saw that the high priest, in accordance with the inner instruction he had received, handed a branch to each of the men present, and commanded each to inscribe his branch with his name and to hold it in his hands during the prayer and sacrifice.

After they had done this, their branches were

---

connected with the Annunciation. This event is similarly described in the apocryphal "History of Joachim and Anna and of the birth of Mary the blessed Mother of God ever virgin and of the Childhood of the Redeemer," printed by Thilo from a Latin MS. in the Paris library; except that in this case an interval of three days elapses between the voice at the fountain and the appearance of the angel in salutation. (CB)

CB's note needs clarifying. AC distinguishes two angelic visits, the first here at the well, at Jerusalem, with no apparition and no recorded voice (not in the Gospel), and the second, later at Nazareth, after the wedding, the Annunciation proper (*Luke* 1:26-38). St. Luke simply follows St. Luke (one visit at Nazareth), while *Ps-Matt.* 9 gives the two visits, at the well and the Annunciation, at one day's interval, but with no exact indication of place, and *Protev.* II (as given here by CB) combines the episode at the well and the Annunciation, and places it all at Nazareth. J. C. Thilo published a collection of apocryphal texts at Leipzig in 1832. (SB)

collected and laid upon an altar before the Holy of
Holies, and they were told that the one among them
whose branch blossomed was destined by the Lord to
be married to the maiden Mary of Nazareth. While the
branches lay before the Holy of Holies the sacrifice and
prayer were continued, and meanwhile I saw that youth,
whose name will perhaps come back to me,[4] in a hall
of the Temple crying passionately to God with outstretched arms. I saw him burst into tears when after
the appointed interval their branches were given back
to them with the announcement that none had blossomed, and therefore none of them was the bridegroom
destined by God for this maiden. The men were now
sent home, but that youth betook himself to Mount
Carmel, to the sons of the prophets who had lived there
as hermits ever since the time of Elias. From then on
he spent his time in continual prayer for the fulfillment of the Promise.

I then saw the priests in the Temple making a fresh
search in the ancestral tables to see whether there was
any descendant of David's who had been overlooked.
As they found that of six brothers registered at Bethlehem one was missing and unknown, they made search
for his dwelling-place, and found Joseph not far from
Samaria in a place beside a little stream, where he
lived alone by the water and worked for another master. On the command of the high priest, Joseph now
came, dressed in his best, to the Temple at Jerusalem.
He, too, had to hold a branch in his hand during the
prayer and sacrifice, and as he was about to lay this
on the altar before the Holy of Holies, a white flower
like a lily blossomed out of the top of it, and I saw over
him an appearance of light like the Holy Ghost.[5] Joseph
was now recognized as appointed by God to be the

---

4. He is by tradition called Agabus, and in Raphael's representation of the Betrothal
of Our Lady (generally called "Sposalizio") he is pictured as a youth breaking his
staff over his knee. (CB)
5. The miracle of Joseph's rod (with the dove issuing from the rod) appears in *Protev.* 9, *Ps-Matt.* 8, and (with the dove alighting on the rod) in *Nat. Mar.* 8. The name
Agabus for the unsuccessful suitor is not found elsewhere. (SB)

bridegroom of the Blessed Virgin, and was presented to her by the priests in the presence of her mother. Mary, submissive to the Will of God, accepted him meekly as her bridegroom, for she knew that all things were possible with God, who had accepted her vow to belong to Him alone, body and soul.

THE WEDDING

[In the course of her continuous visions of Our Lord's daily ministry, Catherine Emmerich (on September 24th, 1821) saw Jesus teaching in the synagogue at Gophna, four days before His baptism. He was dwelling with the family of a head of the synagogue related to Joachim. On this occasion she heard two widows, his daughters, exchanging remembrances of the wedding of Our Lord's Mother and foster-father, at which they had been present in their youth with other relations. Of this she told what follows.]

WHILE the two widows were recalling the wedding of Mary and Joseph as they talked together, I saw a picture of this wedding and in particular of the beautiful wedding garments of the Blessed Virgin, of which these good women could not say enough. I will tell you what I can still remember.

The wedding of Mary and Joseph, which lasted for seven or eight days, was celebrated on Mount Sion in Jerusalem in a house which was often hired out for festivities of this kind. Besides Mary's teachers and schoolfellows from the Temple school many relations of Anna and Joachim were present, amongst others a family from Gophna with two daughters. The wedding was very ceremonious and elaborate. Many lambs were slaughtered and sacrificed. The Blessed Virgin's wedding garments were so remarkably beautiful and splendid that the women who were present used to enjoy speaking about them even in their old age. In my vision I heard their conversation and saw the following:

I saw Mary in her wedding-dress very distinctly. She wore a white woollen undergarment without sleeves: her arms were wrapped round with strips of the same stuff, for at that time these took the place of closed sleeves. Next she put on a collar reaching from above the breast to her throat. It was encrusted with pearls and white embroidery, and was shaped like the under-collar worn by Archos the Essene, the pattern of which I cut out not long ago [see pp. 11-12]. Over this she wore an ample robe, open in front. It fell to her feet and was as full as a mantle and had wide sleeves. This robe had a blue ground covered with an embroidered or woven pattern of red, white, and yellow roses interspersed with green leaves, like rich and ancient chasubles. The lower hem ended in fringes and tassels, while the upper edge joined the white neck-covering. After this robe had been arranged to fall in long straight folds, a kind of scapulary was put on over it, such as some religious wear, for instance the Carmelites. This was made of white silk with gold flowers: it was half a yard wide, and was set with pearls and shining jewels at the breast. It hung in a single width down to the edge of the dress, of which it covered the opening in front. The lower edge was ornamented with fringes and beads. A similar width hung down the back, while shorter and narrower strips of the silk hung over the shoulders and arms; these four pieces, spread out round the neck, made the shape of a cross. The front and back pieces of this scapulary were held together under the arms by gold laces or little chains; the fullness of the robe was thus gathered together in front and the jewelled breastpiece pressed against it; the flowered material of the robe was a little puffed out in the openings between the laces. The full sleeves, over which the shoulder-pieces of the scapulary projected, were lightly held together by bracelets above and below the elbow. These bracelets, which were about two fingers in breadth and engraved with letters, had twisted edges. They caused the full sleeves to puff out at the shoulders, elbows, and wrists. The sleeves ended in a white frill of silk or wool, I think. Over all this she wore a sky-blue mantle, shaped like a big cloak, which in its turn was covered by a sort of mourning cloak with sleeves made after a traditional fashion. These cloaks were worn by Jewish women at certain religious or domestic ceremonies. Mary's cloak was fastened at the breast, under her neck, with a brooch, above which, round her neck, was a white frill of what looked like feathers or floss silk. This cloak fell back over the shoulders, came forward again at the sides, and ended at the back in a pointed train. Its edge was embroidered with gold flowers.

The adornment of her hair was indescribably beautiful. It was parted in the middle of her head and divided into a number of little plaits. These, interwoven with white silk and pearls, formed a great net falling over her shoulders and ending in a point half-way down her back. The ends of the plaits were curled inwards, and this whole net of hair was edged with a decorated border of fringes and pearls, whose weight held it down and kept it in place. Her hair was encircled by a wreath of white unspun silk or wool, three strips of the same material meeting in a tuft on the top of her head and holding it in place. On this wreath rested a crown of about a hand's-breadth, decorated with jewels and surmounted by three bands of metal crowned by a knob. This crown was ornamented in front with three pearls, one above the other, and with one pearl on each side.

In her left hand she carried a little silken wreath of red and white roses, and in her right hand, like a sceptre, a beautiful gilded torch in the shape of a candlestick without a foot. Its stem (thicker in the middle than at the ends) was decorated with knobs above and below where it was held. It was surmounted by a flat cup in which a white flame was burning.

The shoes had soles two fingers thick heightened at toe and heel. These soles were made entirely of green material, so that the foot seemed to rest on grass. Two white-and-gold straps held them fast over the instep of the bare foot, and the toes were covered by a little flap which was attached to the sole and was always worn by well-dressed women.

It was the Temple maidens who plaited Mary's beautiful hair arrangement; I saw it being done, several of them were busy with it and it went quicker than one would think. Anna had brought the beautiful clothes which Mary in her humility was unwilling to wear. After the wedding the network of hair was thrown up over her head; the crown was removed, and a milk-white veil put on her which hung down to her elbows. The crown was then put on again over this veil.

The Blessed Virgin had very abundant hair, reddish-gold in color. Her high, delicately traced eyebrows were black; she had a very high forehead, large downcast eyes with long black lashes, a rather long straight nose, delicately shaped, a noble and lovely mouth, and a pointed chin. She was of middle height, and moved about in her rich dress very gently and with great modesty and seriousness. At her wedding she afterwards put on another dress of striped stuff, less grand, a piece of which I possess among my relics. She wore this striped dress also at Cana and on other holy occasions. She wore her wedding-dress again in the Temple several times.

Very rich people used to change their dresses three or four times at weddings. Mary in her grand garments looked like the great ladies of much later times; for instance, the Empress Helena, or even Cunegunde, although the manner in which Jewish women muffled themselves up on ordinary occasions was very different and was more after the fashion of Roman women. (In connection with these clothes I observed that very many weavers lived near the Cenacle on Mount Sion, who made many kinds of beautiful materials.)

Joseph wore a long full coat of pale blue, fastened down the front from breast to hem with laces and bosses or buttons. His wide sleeves were also fastened at the sides with laces; they were much turned up and seemed to have pockets inside. Round his neck he wore a kind of brown collar or rather a broad stole, and two white strips hung over his breast, like the bands worn by our priests, only much longer.

I saw the whole course of the marriage of Joseph and Mary and the wedding banquet and all the festivities, but I saw so many other things at the same time, and am so ill and so disturbed in many ways, that I do not venture to say more about it for fear of confusing my account.

OUR LADY'S WEDDING-RING

[On July 29th, 1821, Catherine Emmerich had a vision of the separate grave-clothes of Our Lord Jesus and of images of Our Lord which had been miraculously imprinted on cloths. Her visions led her through various places in which these holy relics were sometimes preserved with great honor and sometimes forgotten by men and venerated only by the angels and by devout souls. In the course of these visions she thought that she saw the Blessed Virgin's wedding-ring preserved in one of these places, and spoke of it as follows:]

I SAW the Blessed Virgin's wedding-ring; it is neither of silver nor of gold, nor of any other metal; it is dark in color and iridescent; it is not a thin narrow ring, but rather thick and at least a finger broad. I saw it smooth and yet as if covered with little regular triangles in which were letters. On the inside was a flat surface. The ring is engraved with something. I saw it kept behind many locks in a beautiful church. Devout people about to be married take their wedding-rings to touch it.

[On August 3rd, 1821, she said:] In the last few days I have seen much of the story of Mary's wedding-ring, but as the result of disturbances and pain I can no longer give a connected account of it. Today I saw a festival in a church in Italy where the wedding-ring is

to be found. It seemed to me to be hung up in a kind
of monstrance which stood above the Tabernacle. There
was a large altar there, magnificently decorated, one
saw deep into it through much silverwork. I saw many
rings being held against the monstrance. During the
festival I saw Mary and Joseph appearing in their wedding garments on each side of the ring, as if Joseph
were placing the ring on the Blessed Virgin's finger. At
the same time I saw the ring shining and as if in movement.[6]

To the right and left of this altar I saw two other
altars, which were probably not in the same church,
but were only shown to me in my vision as being
together. In the altar to the right was an *Ecce Homo*
picture of Our Lord, which a devout Roman senator, a
friend of St. Peter's, had received in a miraculous manner. In the altar to the left was one of the grave-clothes
of Our Lord.

When the wedding festivities were over, Anna went
back to Nazareth with her relations, and Mary also
went there, accompanied by several of her playmates
who had been discharged from the Temple at the same
time as her. They left the city in a festal procession. I
do not know how far the maidens accompanied her.
They once more spent the first night in the Levites'
school at Bethoron. Mary made the return journey on
foot.

Joseph went to Bethlehem after the wedding in order
to settle some family affairs there. He did not come to
Nazareth until later.

---

6. When the writer copied down these words of Catherine Emmerich on Aug. 4th,
1821, he could not think of any reason why she should have seen this picture on
Aug. 3rd. He was therefore greatly surprised at reading, several years after Catherine Emmerich's death, in a Latin document about the Blessed Virgin's wedding-
ring (which is preserved in Perugia), that it is shown to the public on Aug. 3rd (III
nonas Augusti). Of this probably neither of us knew anything. (CB)

   Our Lady's wedding-ring is preserved at the Cathedral of Perugia in a chapel,
which also has a fine tabernacle (mentioned by AC) by Cesarino del Roscetto, of
1519. Cf. *Baedeker.* (SB)

FROM MARY'S RETURN HOME TO THE ANNUNCIATION

[Catherine Emmerich always had these visions of the story of the Holy Family on the days appointed by the Church for their celebration; nevertheless, the date on which she saw some of these events sometimes differed from the ecclesiastical feast-days. For instance, she saw the real historical date of the birth of Christ a whole month earlier, on November 25th, which according to her visions coincided with the tenth day of the month Kislev in that year. Fifteen days later she saw Joseph keeping for several days the Feast of the Dedication of the Temple, or the Feast of Lights (which began on the 25th day of the month Kislev) by burning lights in the cave of the Crib. From this it follows that she saw the Feast of the Annunciation also a month earlier, i.e. on February 25th. It was in the year 1821 that Catherine Emmerich first gave an account of this event. She was seriously ill at that time, and her statement was therefore somewhat fragmentary to begin with.

[She had stated earlier that Joseph did not go to Nazareth immediately after the wedding, but had journeyed to Bethlehem to arrange certain family affairs. Anna and her second husband and the Blessed Virgin with some of her playmates went back to Galilee to Anna's home, which was about an hour's distance from Nazareth. Anna arranged for the Holy Family the little house in Nazareth, which also belonged to her, the Blessed Virgin still living with her in the meantime during Joseph's absence. Before communicating her vision of the Annunciation, Catherine Emmerich recounted two fragments of earlier visions, whose significance we can only conjecture. Some time after the marriage of the Blessed Virgin to Joseph she recounted, still in a very weak state after a serious illness:]

I HAD sight of a festival in Anna's house. I noticed her second husband, some six guests besides the ordinary household, and some children collected with Joseph and Mary round a table on which stood goblets. The Blessed Virgin was wearing a colored cloak, woven with red, blue, and white flowers like ancient chasubles. She had a transparent veil and over it a black one. This festival seemed to be a continuation of the wedding festival.

[She related no more about this, and one may suppose that it was the meal taken when the Blessed Virgin left her mother after Joseph's arrival and moved into the house in Nazareth with him. Next day she related:] Last night in my vision I was looking for the Blessed Virgin, and my guide brought me into the house of her mother Anna, which I recognized in all its details. I no longer found Joseph and Mary there. I saw Anna preparing to go to the near-by Nazareth, where the Holy Family now lived. She had a bundle under her arm to take to Mary. She went over a plain and through a thicket to Nazareth, which lies in front of a hill. I went there, too. Joseph's house was not far from the gate; it was not so large as Anna's house. A quadrangular fountain to which several steps led down was nearby, and there was a small square court before the house. I saw Anna visiting the Blessed Virgin and giving her what she had brought. I saw, too, that Mary shed many tears and accompanied her mother, when she returned home, for part of the way. I noticed St. Joseph in the front part of the house in a separate room.

VII

THE ANNUNCIATION

[ON March 25th, 1821, Sister Emmerich said:] Last night I saw the Annunciation as a Feast of the Church, and was once more definitely informed that at this moment the Blessed Virgin had already been with child for four weeks. This was expressly told me because I had already seen the Annunciation on the 25th of February, but had rejected the vision and had not related it. Today I again saw the exterior circumstances of the whole event.

Soon after the Blessed Virgin's marriage I saw her in Joseph's house in Nazareth, where I was taken by my guide. Joseph had gone away with two donkeys, I think to fetch either his tools or something that he had inherited. He seemed to me to be on his way home. Anna's second husband and some other men had been at the house in the morning, but had gone away again. Besides the Blessed Virgin and two girls of her own age (I think they were playfellows from the Temple), I saw in the house Anna and her widowed cousin, who worked for her as serving-maid and later went with her to Bethlehem after Christ's birth. The whole house had been newly fitted out by Anna. I saw these four women going busily about the house and then walking at leisure together in the courtyard. Towards evening I saw them come back into the house and stand praying at a little round table. Then, after eating some vegetables set before them, they separated.

Anna went to and fro in the house for some time still, busying herself with household matters. The two girls went to their separate room, and Mary, too, went into her bedchamber.

The Blessed Virgin's bedchamber was in the back part of the house, near the hearth, which was here placed, not in the center as in Anna's house, but rather on one side. The entrance to the bedchamber was beside the kitchen. Three steps, not level but sloping, led up to it, for the floor of this part of the house rested on a raised ledge of rock. The wall of the room facing the door was rounded, and in this rounded part (which was shut off by a high wicker screen) was the Blessed Virgin's bed, rolled up. The walls of the room were covered up to a certain height with wickerwork, rather more roughly woven than the light movable screens. Different-colored woods had been used to make a little checkered pattern on them. The ceiling was formed by intersecting beams, the spaces between being filled with wickerwork decorated with star-patterns.

I was brought into this room by the shining youth who always accompanies me, and I will relate what I saw as well as such a poor miserable creature is able.

The Blessed Virgin came in and went behind the screen before her bed, where she put on a long white woollen praying-robe with a broad girdle, and covered her head with a yellowish white veil. Meanwhile the maid came in with a little lamp, lit a many-branched lamp hanging from the ceiling, and went away again. The Blessed Virgin then took a little low table which was leaning folded up against the wall and placed it in the middle of the room. As it leant against the wall it was just a movable table-leaf hanging straight down in front of two supports. Mary lifted up this leaf and pulled forward half of one of the supports (which was divided), so that the little table now stood on three legs. The table-leaf supported by this third leg was rounded. This little table was covered with a blue-and-red cloth, finished with a hanging fringe along the straight edge of the table. In the middle of the cloth there was a design, embroidered or quilted; I cannot remember whether it was a letter or an ornament. On the round side of the table was a white cloth rolled up, and a scroll of writing also lay on the table.

Our Lady put up this little table in the middle of the room, between her sleeping-place and the door, rather to the left, in a place where the floor was covered by a carpet. Then she put in front of it a little round cushion and knelt down with both hands resting on the table. The door of the room was facing her on the right, and she had her back to her sleeping-place.

Mary let the veil fall over her face and crossed her hands (but not her fingers) before her breast. I saw her fervently praying thus for a long time, with her face raised to Heaven. She was imploring God for redemption, for the promised King, and beseeching Him that her prayer might have some share in sending Him. She knelt long in an ecstasy of prayer; then she bowed her head on to her breast.

But now at her right hand there poured down such a mass of light in a slanting line from the ceiling of the room that I felt myself pressed back by it against the wall near the door. I saw in this light a shining white youth, with flowing yellow hair, floating down before her. It was the Angel Gabriel. He gently moved his arms away from his body as he spoke to her. I saw the words issuing from his mouth like shining letters; I read them and I heard them. Mary turned her veiled head slightly towards the right, but she was shy and did not look up. But the angel went on speaking, and as if at his command Mary turned her face a little towards him, raised her veil slightly, and answered. The angel again spoke and Mary lifted her veil, looked at him and answered with the holy words: "Behold the handmaid of the Lord, be it done unto me according to thy word."

The Blessed Virgin was wrapped in ecstasy. The room

was filled with light;[1] I no longer saw the glimmer of the burning lamp, I no longer saw the ceiling of the room. Heaven seemed to open, a path of light made me look up above the angel, and at the source of this stream of light I saw a figure of the Holy Trinity in the form of a triangular radiance streaming in upon itself. In this I recognized—what can only be adored and never expressed—Almighty God, Father, Son and Holy Ghost, and yet only God Almighty.

As soon as the Blessed Virgin had spoken the words, "Be it done unto me according to thy word," I saw the Holy Ghost in the appearance of a winged figure, but not in the form of a dove as usually represented. The head was like the face of a man, and light was spread like wings beside the figure, from whose breast and hands I saw three streams of light pouring down towards the right side of the Blessed Virgin and meeting as they reached her. This light streaming in upon her right side caused the Blessed Virgin to become completely transfused with radiance and as though transparent; all that was opaque seemed to vanish like darkness before this light. In this moment she was so penetrated with light that nothing dark or concealing remained in her; her whole form was shining and transfused with light. After this penetrating radiance I saw the angel disappear, with the path of light out of which he had come. It was as if the stream of light had been drawn back into Heaven, and I saw how there fell from it on to Our Lady, as it was drawn back, a shower of white rose-buds each with its little green leaf.

While I was seeing all this in Mary's chamber, I had a strange personal sensation. I was in a state of constant fear, as if I was being pursued, and I suddenly saw a hideous serpent crawling through the house and up the steps to the door by which I was standing. The horrible creature had made its way as far as the third step when the light poured down on

---

1. The tradition about the light at the Annunciation is preserved in the liturgy (Mar. 25th, Resp. ii): *"Et expavescit Virgo de lumine."* (SB)

the Blessed Virgin. The serpent was three or four feet long, had a broad flat head and under its breast were two short skinny paws, clawed like bat's wings, on which it pushed itself forward. It was spotted with all kinds of hideous colors, and reminded me of the serpent in the Garden of Eden, only fearfully deformed. When the angel disappeared from Our Lady's room, he trod on this monster's head as it lay before the door, and it screamed in so ghastly a way that I shuddered. Then I saw three spirits appear who drove the monster out in front of the house with blows and kicks.

After the angel had disappeared, I saw the Blessed Virgin wrapped in the deepest ecstasy. I saw that she recognized the Incarnation of the promised Redeemer within herself in the form of a tiny human figure of light, perfectly formed in all its parts down to its tiny fingers.

Here in Nazareth it is otherwise than in Jerusalem, where the women must remain in the outer court and may not enter the Temple, where only the priests may go into the Holy Place. Here in Nazareth, here in this church, a virgin is herself the Temple, and the Most Holy is within her, and the high priest is within her, and she alone is with Him. Oh, how lovely and wonderful that is, and yet so simple and natural! The words of David in the 45th Psalm were fulfilled: "The Most High hath sanctified His own tabernacle; God is in the midst thereof, it shall not be moved."

It was at midnight that I saw this mystery happen. After a little while Anna with the other women came into Mary's room. They had been wakened by a strange commotion in nature. A cloud of light had appeared above the house. When they saw the Blessed Virgin kneeling under the lamp in an ecstasy of prayer, they respectfully withdrew. After some time I saw the Blessed Virgin rise from her knees and go to her little altar against the wall. She unrolled the picture hanging on the wall which represented a veiled human form—the same picture that I had seen in Anna's house when she was making ready for Our Lady's journey to the Temple [see pp. 87-88]. She lit the lamp on the wall and stood praying before it. Scrolls lay before her on a high desk. Towards morning I saw her go to bed.

My guide now led me away; but when I came into the little court before the house, I was seized with terror, for that fearful snake was lurking there in hiding. It crept towards me and tried to shelter in the folds of my dress. I was in dreadful fear; but my guide snatched me hurriedly away, and those three spirits reappeared and smote the monster. I still seem to hear with a shudder its appalling shrieks.

That night, as I contemplated the Mystery of the Incarnation, I was taught many things. Anna was given the grace of interior knowledge. The Blessed Virgin knew that she had conceived the Messias, the Son of the Most High. All that was within her was open to the eyes of her spirit. But she did not then know that the Throne of David His father, which was to be given Him by the Lord God, was a supernatural one; nor did she then know that the House of Jacob, over which He was, as Gabriel declared, to rule for all eternity, was the Church, the congregation of regenerated mankind. She thought that the Redeemer would be a holy king, who would purify His people and give them victory over Hell. She did not then know that this King, in order to redeem mankind, must suffer a bitter death.

It was made known to me why the Redeemer deigned to remain nine months in His Mother's womb and to be born as a little child, and why it was not His Will to appear as perfect and beautiful as the newly-created Adam; but I can no longer explain this clearly. I can, however, remember this much—that it was His Will to reconsecrate man's conception and birth which had been so sadly degraded by the Fall. The reason why Mary became His Mother and why He did not come sooner was that she alone, and no creature before her or after her, was the pure Vessel of Grace, promised by God to mankind as the Mother of the Incarnate Word, by the merits of whose Passion mankind was to be redeemed from its guilt. The Blessed Virgin was the one and only pure blossom of the human race, flowering in the fullness of time. All the children of God from the beginning of time who have striven after salvation contributed to her coming. She was the only pure gold of the whole earth. She alone was the pure immaculate flesh and blood of the whole human race, prepared and purified and ordained and consecrated through all the generations of her ancestors; guided, guarded, and fortified by the Law until she came forth as the fullness of Grace. She was pre-ordained in eternity and passed through time as the Mother of the Eternal. [See *Prov.* 8:22-35.]

At the Incarnation of Christ the Blessed Virgin was a little over fourteen years old. Christ reached the age of thirty-three years and three times six weeks. I say three times *six*, because that figure was in that moment shown to me three times one after the other.

VIII

THE VISITATION[1]

SOME days after the Annunciation St. Joseph returned to Nazareth and made further arrangements for working at his craft in the house; he had never lived in Nazareth before and had not spent more than a few days there. Joseph knew nothing of the Incarnation; Mary was the Mother of the Lord, but also the handmaid of the Lord, and she kept His secret in all humility. When the Blessed Virgin felt that the Word was made Flesh in her, she was conscious of a great desire to pay an immediate visit to her cousin Elisabeth at Jutta near Hebron, whom the angel had told her was now six months with child. As the time was now drawing near when Joseph wished to go up to Jerusalem for the Passover, Our Lady decided to accompany him in order to help Elisabeth in her pregnancy. Joseph therefore started with the Blessed Virgin on the journey to Jutta.[2]

[Catherine Emmerich described the following single scenes from the journey of Joseph and Mary to Elisabeth; but it must be understood that owing to her illness and to various interruptions very many gaps occur in her account. She gave no description of their departure, but only a few pictures from successive days of their journey, which we here transcribe.]

They travelled in a southerly direction and had a

---

1. The Visitation: *Luke* 1:39-56. St. Joseph's worries: *Matt.* 1:18-25. (SB)
2. Jutta near Hebron; *Luke* 1:39 says: "Into the hill country . . . into a city of Juda." It has been suggested that "Juda" was written by mistake for "Jutta." (SB)

donkey with them, on which Mary rode from time to time. Some baggage was packed on to it, amongst which was a striped sack of Joseph's (it seemed to me to be knitted) in which was a long brownish garment of Mary's with a sort of hood. This garment was fastened in front with ribbons. Mary put it on when she went into the Temple or into a synagogue. On the journey she wore a brown woollen undergarment, and over this a grey dress with a girdle. Her head-covering was yellowish in color. They made the long journey rather quickly. I saw them, after they had crossed the plain of Esdraelon in a southerly direction, entering the house of a friend of Joseph's father in the town of Dothan, on a hill. He was a well-to-do man and came from Bethlehem. His father was called brother by Joseph's father, though he was not really his brother, but he came of David's line through a man who was, I think, also a king and was called Ela, Eldoa, or Eldad, I cannot remember clearly which it was.[3] There was much trading in this place.

Once I saw them spending the night in a shed; and one evening, when they were still twelve hours distant from Zacharias' dwelling, I saw them in a wood, going into a hut of wattle-work, on which green leaves and beautiful white flowers were growing. This hut was meant for travellers: beside the roads in that country

---

3. Catherine Emmerich saw Jesus at Dothan in this house on Nov. 2nd (the 12th day of the month Marcheswan) of the thirty-first year of His life. He was healing the dropsy of Issachar, the fifty-year-old husband of the daughter of this family, whose name was Salome. On that occasion Issachar spoke of the visit of Joseph and Mary here mentioned. The descendant of David whose name is given uncertainly by Catherine Emmerich as Eldoa or Eldad, and whom she describes as being the link between Joseph's and Salome's families, might perhaps have been Elioda or Eliada, a son of David's, mentioned in *2 Kgs*. 5:16, and in *1 Par.* 3:8. Although it may seem natural that Catherine Emmerich should confuse various name-sounds, such confusion should not necessarily always be assumed. Hebrew proper names have a very definite signification; but since the same signification can be conveyed in speaking by several different expressions, one person may often bear different names. Thus we find a son of David's sometimes called Elishua ("God helpeth") and sometimes Elishama ("God heareth"); and Eldea or Eldaa may mean "God cometh" just as much as Eliada. The uncertain mention of this descendant of David's as being also a king need not surprise us, for there can be no doubt that David's sons or descendants administered the government in the vassal states. (CB)

The Vulgate forms of the name of David's son are Elisua in *2 Kgs*. (Sam.) 5:15, and Elisama in *1 Par.* 3:6. In Hebrew, Elishua ("God saveth") and *Elishama* ("God heareth"). The name of the son Elioda or Eliada is in both places *Elyada,* which with its by-forms means "God knoweth." (SB)

are many open arbors like this, and even solid buildings. Travellers can spend the night in them, or shelter from the heat and prepare the food which they have
brought with them. Some of these shelters are looked
after by a family living near at hand who are ready to
supply any needs in return for a small payment.

[Here there seems to be a gap in the account. Probably the Blessed Virgin was present with Joseph at the
Passover in Jerusalem, and did not go to Elisabeth until
after that; for while Joseph's journey to the Feast is
mentioned above, we are told later that Zacharias
reached home, after attending the Passover, the day
before the Visitation.]

They did not go direct from Jerusalem to Jutta, but
made a detour to the east in order to avoid the crowds.
They passed near a little town two hours distant from
Emmaus, and took roads which Jesus often travelled
in the years of His ministry. They still had two hills to
pass. Between these two hills I once saw them sitting
and resting. They were eating bread and mixing in their
drinking water drops of balsam which they had collected on their way. It was very hilly here. They passed
over-hanging rocks with great caves in which were all
kinds of strange stones. The valleys were very fertile.
Then their path led them through wood, moorland, meadows, and fields. Towards the end of their journey I particularly noticed a plant with little delicate green leaves
and with flower-clusters of nine little pale-red, closed
bells or vessels. There was something in these with
which I had to do but what it was I cannot remember.[4]

[The following visions were communicated by Catherine Emmerich partly at the time of the Feast of the
Visitation in July 1820 and partly at a time when she

---

4. A learned friend tells me that this flower is probably the cypress-cluster (*Lawso-
nia spinosa inermis, Linn.*) mentioned in the Canticle of Canticles, 1:13: "A cluster
of cypress my love is to me in the vineyards of Engaddi." Mariti, in his journey
through Syria and Palestine, mentions this shrub and its flowers in the region here
traversed by the Blessed Virgin. He describes the leaves as smaller and more delicate than those of the myrtle; the flowers are, he says, rose-red and the flower-
cluster shaped like a bunch of grapes. This agrees with the general description
given by Catherine Emmerich. (CB)

had heard the words of Eliud, an aged Essene from Nazareth. Eliud accompanied Jesus on His journey to His Baptism by John in September of the first year of His ministry, and told Him many things about the history of His parents and of His earliest childhood, for Eliud was intimate with the Holy Family.]

Zacharias' house was on the top of a hill by itself. Other houses stood in groups round about. Not far off a biggish stream flowed down from the mountain. It seemed to me to be the moment when Zacharias was returning home from the Passover at Jerusalem. I saw Elisabeth, moved by great longing, going out of her house for a considerable distance on the way to Jerusalem; and I saw how alarmed Zacharias was, as he made his way home, to meet Elisabeth on the road so far from home in her condition. She told him that she was so agitated in her heart because she could not help thinking all the time that her cousin Mary of Nazareth was coming to her. Zacharias tried to remove this impression from her mind and explained to her, by signs and by writing on a tablet, how unlikely it was that a newly married woman should undertake so long a journey just then. They went back to the house together. Elisabeth was, however, unable to abandon her expectation, for she had learnt in a dream that one of her family had become the mother of the promised Messias. She had at once thought of Mary, had longed to see her, and had in spirit perceived her in the distance on her way to her. She had made ready a little room to the right of the entrance and had placed seats in it. On the following day she sat there for a long time waiting and gazing out of the house, watching for the coming visitor. Then she got up and went a long way on the road to meet her.

Elisabeth was a tall aged woman with a small, delicate face. Her head was wrapped in a veil. She only knew the Blessed Virgin by hearsay. Mary saw her from far off and recognized her at once. She ran to meet her, while Joseph discreetly remained behind. Mary was already among the neighbors' houses, whose inhabitants, moved by her marvellous beauty and struck by a supernatural dignity in her whole being, withdrew shyly as she and Elisabeth met. They greeted each other warmly with outstretched hands, and at that moment I saw a shining brightness in the Blessed Virgin and as it were a ray of light passing from her to Elisabeth, filling the latter with wonderful joy. They did not stay near the people in the houses, but went, holding each other by the arm, through the outer court towards the house. At the door Elisabeth once more made Mary welcome, and they then went in. Joseph, who came into the court leading the donkey, handed it over to a manservant and went to Zacharias in an open hall at the side of the house. He greeted the venerable old priest with great humility. Zacharias embraced him warmly and spoke with him by writing on his tablet, for he was dumb since the angel had appeared to him in the Temple. Mary and Elisabeth, after passing through the house-door, came into a hall which, it seemed to me, was also the kitchen. Here they took each other by both arms, Mary greeted Elisabeth very warmly and each pressed her cheek against the other's. Again I saw a radiance stream from Mary into Elisabeth, whereby the latter was transfused with light. Her heart was filled with holy joy. She stepped back, her hand raised, and exclaimed full of humility, joy and exaltation: "Blessed art thou among women and blessed is the fruit of thy womb. And whence is this to me that the mother of my Lord should come to me? For behold as the voice of thy salutation sounded in my ears, the infant in my womb leaped for joy. And blessed art thou that hast believed, because those things shall be accomplished that were spoken to thee by the Lord."

As she said the last words she led Mary into the little room which she had prepared, so that she might sit down and rest after her journey. It was only a few paces away. Mary let go Elisabeth's arm, which she had clasped, crossed her hands over her breast and uttered the *Magnificat* with exaltation.

(When the aged Essene Eliud conversed with Jesus, as mentioned above, about this event, I heard him expounding the whole of Mary's song of praise in a wonderful manner. I feel myself, however, incapable of repeating this explanation.)

I saw that Elisabeth followed in prayer the whole of the *Magnificat* in a similar state of exaltation; afterwards they sat down on quite low seats with a table before them, also low, on which stood a little goblet. Oh, I was so blissfully happy, I prayed with them the whole time, and then I sat down near at hand: oh, I was so happy! [Catherine Emmerich recounted this in the morning as if it had happened on the previous day. In the afternoon she said in her sleep:] Joseph and Zacharias are now together and are talking about the nearness of the Messias according to the fulfillment of the prophecies. Zacharias is a tall handsome old man, dressed as a priest; he answers always with signs or by writing on a tablet. They are sitting in an open hall at the side of the house, looking on to the garden. Mary and Elisabeth are sitting in the garden on a carpet under a big spreading tree; behind it is a fountain from which water streams if one pulls at a tap. I see grass and flowers round them, and trees with little yellow plums. They are both eating little fruits and little loaves from Joseph's knapsack; what touching simplicity and frugality! There are two maidservants and two menservants in the house; I see them moving about here and there. They are preparing a table with food under a tree. Zacharias and Joseph come and eat a little. Joseph wanted to go back to Nazareth at once; but I think he is going to stay a week. He knows nothing of Our Lady being with child. Mary and Elisabeth were silent about it; in the depths of their being, there was a secret understanding between them. Several times in the day, and especially before meals when they were all together, the two holy women said a kind of litany. Joseph prayed with them, and I saw then a cross appear in the midst between the two women (although as yet there was no cross); it was indeed as though two crosses visited each other.

[On July 3rd she related as follows:] Yesterday evening they ate all together. They sat under a tree in the garden by the light of a lamp till nearly midnight. Then I saw Joseph and Zacharias alone in a place of prayer. I saw Mary and Elisabeth in their little room. They stood opposite each other, as if wrapt in ecstasy, and said the *Magnificat* in prayer together. Besides the clothes already described the Blessed Virgin wore a transparent black veil as well, which she lowered when speaking with men. Today Zacharias took St. Joseph to another garden at some distance from the house. Zacharias is very orderly and precise in all he does. This garden is rich in beautiful trees and abundant fruit and is very well kept. A shady alley leads through the middle of it. At the end of the garden there is a little hidden summer-house with a door at the side. In the top of this little house are window openings closed by sliding shutters. In it is a wicker couch cushioned with moss or other delicate plants. I also saw two white statues in it, of the size of children. I do not quite know how they came to be there or what they signified, but they seemed very like Zacharias and Elisabeth, only very much younger.

This afternoon I saw Mary and Elisabeth working together in the house. The Blessed Virgin took part in all the household work. She made preparations for the child that was expected. I saw them both working together, they were knitting a big coverlet for Elisabeth's lying-in. Jewish women used coverlets like these when in child-bed; an inner lining was fastened to the middle of it so that the mother could be wrapped up together in it with her child. It was as if she were in a little boat or in a big shoe, wrapped up herself like a child in swaddling-clothes. She was supported on pillows and could sit upright or lie down as she liked. The edges of the coverlet were sewn with flowers and texts.

Mary and Elisabeth prepared also many different things as presents for the poor when the child was born. (I see Anna often sending her maidservant to look after everything in the house at Nazareth during the absence of the Holy Family. I saw her there once herself.)

[On July 4th she said:] Zacharias has gone with Joseph for a walk in the fields. His house stands by itself on a hill, it is the best house in the neighborhood. Others lie scattered around. Mary is rather tired, she is alone with Elisabeth in the house.

[On July 5th she said:] I saw Zacharias and Joseph spending last night in the garden which is distant from the house, either sleeping in the summer-house, or praying out of doors in the garden. At dawn they returned to the house. I saw Elisabeth and the Blessed Virgin in the house. Every morning and evening they joined together in prayer and recited the *Magnificat,* which Mary had received from the Holy Ghost at Elisabeth's greeting of her. With the Angel's salutation the Blessed Virgin was consecrated as the Church. With the words "Behold the handmaid of the Lord, be it done to me according to thy word," the Word entered into her, saluted by the Church, by His maidservant. God was now in His Temple, Mary was now the Temple and the Ark of the New Covenant. Elisabeth's greeting and the movement of John beneath his mother's heart was the first act of worship of the community in the presence of this Holy Thing. When the Blessed Virgin uttered the *Magnificat,* the Church of the New Covenant, of the new Espousals, celebrated for the first time the fulfillment of the divine promises of the Old Covenant, of the old Espousals, and poured forth thanks with a *Te Deum laudamus.* Ah, who can express the wonder of seeing the devotion of the Church towards the Saviour even before His Birth!

Tonight, as I watched the two holy women at their prayers, I had many visions and explanations of the *Magnificat* and of the coming of the Blessed Sacrament in the present condition of the Blessed Virgin.

The illness from which I am now suffering and many disturbances have made me quite forget all that I saw. From the passage in the *Magnificat* "He hath shewed might in His arm" onwards there appeared to me all kinds of pictures from the Old Testament symbolic of the most holy Sacrament of the Altar. Amongst them was a picture of Abraham sacrificing Isaac and of Isaias announcing something to a wicked king who scorned it. I have forgotten this. I saw many things from Abraham to Isaias and from Isaias to the Blessed Virgin, and in everything I always saw the coming of the Blessed Sacrament to the Church of Jesus Christ, who was Himself still resting under His Mother's heart.[5]

[After Catherine Emmerich had said this, she recited the Litany of the Holy Ghost and the hymn *Veni Sancte Spiritus* and fell asleep smiling. After a while she said with great fervor:] I must do nothing more at all today and must allow nobody in, then I shall see again all that I have forgotten. If I can only have complete quiet, I shall be able to perceive and relate the holy mystery of the Ark of the Covenant and the holy Sacrament of the Old Covenant. I have seen that time of quiet, it is a beautiful time. I saw the writer beside me, and I am then to learn very many things. [As she spoke these words, her face glowed in her sleep like a child's: she drew from under the bed-covering her hands marked with the wounds of the stigmata and said:] It is very warm where Mary is in the Promised Land. They are now all going into the garden of the house, first Zacharias and Joseph and then Elisabeth and Mary. An awning like a tent is stretched under a tree. On one side stand low seats with backs to them.

[She then continued:] I am to rest and see again all that I have forgotten: that sweet prayer to the Holy Ghost has helped me, so sweet and gentle it is. [At five o'clock in the evening she accused herself, saying:] I weakly gave way and did not keep the command to

---

5. The Message of Isaias which she has forgotten is beyond doubt his prophecy to King Achaz: *Is.* 7:3-25. (CB)

allow nobody in. A woman of my acquaintance came and talked for a long time of hateful incidents which angered me. Then I fell asleep. God kept His word better than me, for He showed me again all that I had forgotten; but as a punishment most of it has again escaped me. [She then said what follows. Although some of it is repetition, we reproduce it, because we cannot express what she said otherwise than she herself did. She said:] I saw as usual the two holy women with child standing opposite one another in prayer and reciting the *Magnificat*. In the middle of the prayer I was shown Abraham sacrificing Isaac. Here followed a series of pictures symbolizing the coming of the Blessed Sacrament. I do not think I have ever perceived so clearly the holy mysteries of the Old Covenant.

[Next day she said:] As was promised to me, I perceived once more all that I had forgotten. I was full of joy at being able now to relate so many wonderful things about the Patriarchs and the Ark of the Covenant, but there must have been a lack of humility in my joy, for God ordained that I should no longer be able to set in order and communicate the innumerable things that I perceived.

[The cause of this new disturbance was a particular incident which renewed in her the sufferings of Our Lord's Passion, a phenomenon constantly recurring in her life. This rendered her even more incapable of consecutive narration. However, after her visions of the repeated recital of the *Magnificat* by the two holy women, she communicated at intervals much that she had learnt of the mysterious blessing in the Old Testament and of the Ark of the Covenant, though in a fragmentary and disconnected manner. We have tried therefore to compile them in chronological order; but, that we may not interrupt the life of the Blessed Virgin unduly, we shall add them in an appendix or keep them for some other appropriate place.]

In the evening of yesterday, Friday, July 6th, I saw Elisabeth and the Blessed Virgin going to Zacharias' distant garden. They were carrying fruit and little loaves of bread in a small basket and were going to spend the night there. When Joseph and Zacharias came there later, I saw the Blessed Virgin go towards them. Zacharias had his little writing-tablet with him, but it had grown too dark for writing, and I saw that Mary, by the interior bidding of the Holy Ghost, told him that he would speak that night. Then I saw that Zacharias put away his writing-tablet, and that he was able to speak with Joseph and pray with him throughout that night. I saw this, and when I shook my head in great surprise[6] and would not accept it, my guardian angel or spiritual guide, who is always with me, said to me, pointing in another direction, "You do not believe this, then turn your eyes hither!" But where he pointed I saw quite another picture from a much later time.

I saw the holy hermit St. Goar[7] in a place where corn was being reaped. Messengers from a bishop who was ill-disposed towards him were talking with him with evil intent. As he started off with them to go to that bishop, I saw him looking round for a hook on which to hang his cloak. He saw a ray of the sun shining through an opening in the wall, and in his simple faith he hung his cloak on it, and I saw that the cloak remained hanging firmly fixed in the air. I was amazed at this miracle of simple faith, and was no longer surprised at Zacharias being given the power of speech by the Blessed Virgin in whom God Himself dwelt. My guide then spoke to me about what we call miracles, and I remember distinctly that he said: A living child-like confidence in God in all simplicity makes everything real, makes everything substantial. What he said

---

6. AC expresses surprise at Zacharias' release from dumbness, but this was presumably temporary and by miraculous intervention—the lesson of the story of St. Goar—since at the birth of John the Baptist he was still dumb (*Luke* 1:62-64). AC has nothing about the birth of the child. (SB)

7. His feast is on July 6th (the day when Catherine Emmerich made this communication), a fact unknown at the time to the writer. When he learnt it later by a casual glance at the calendar, he received a fresh confirmation of the organic connection of all her visions with the festivals of the Church. (CB)

St. Goar, the hermit of Oberwesel on the Rhine, died *c.* 575 (Ramsgate, *Book of Saints,* 1947). (SB)

gave me a complete interior understanding about all miracles, but I cannot express it perfectly.

I saw the four holy people spend the night in the garden. They sat down and ate, or they walked two by two up and down, talking and praying, and took it in turns to rest in the little summer-house. I understood that when the Sabbath was over Joseph was to return to Nazareth, and that Zacharias was to accompany him for part of the way. It was moonlight and a clear starry sky. Round these holy people was indescribable peace and beauty.

Again, as the two holy women prayed, I saw a part of the mystery of the *Magnificat,* but am again to see all in the octave of the Feast before Saturday or Sunday and shall then perhaps be able to tell something of it. I am now only permitted to say: The *Magnificat* is a hymn of thanks for the fulfillment of the blessing given in the sacrament of the Old Covenant.

During Mary's prayer I saw a continuous succession of all her ancestors. In the course of time there followed each other three times fourteen marriages, in each of which the son succeeded directly to the father: and from each of these marriages I saw a ray of light projected towards Mary as she stood there in prayer. The whole vision grew before my eyes like a family tree made by branches of light becoming ever nobler and nobler, until at last, in a more clearly defined place in this tree of light, I saw shine forth more brightly the holy and immaculate flesh and blood of Mary, from which God was to become Man. I prayed to her in yearning and hope, as full of joy as a child who sees the Christmas tree towering above him. It was all a picture of the coming of Jesus Christ in the Flesh and of His most holy Sacrament. It was as though I saw the wheat ripening for the Bread of Life for which I hunger. It is not to be expressed, I can find no words to say how that Flesh was formed, in which the Word became Flesh. How can it be expressed by a poor mortal who is still in that flesh of which the Son of God and of Mary said

the flesh profiteth nothing, it is the spirit that quick-
eneth? He, who said that only those who ate His flesh
and drank His blood should have everlasting life and
be raised up by Him in the last day. Only His flesh and
blood were meat and drink indeed; only those who ate
and drank thereof abode in Him and He in them.

I saw, in an inexpressible way, from the beginning,
from generation to generation, the approach of the Incarnation, and with it the approach of the most holy Sacrament of the Altar. Then came a series of patriarchs,
followed by the institution of the priesthood to offer up
the living God among men as sacrifice and food until
His Second Coming—an institution conferred by the
Incarnate God, the new and redeeming Adam, upon His
Apostles and transmitted by them by the laying-on of
hands in an unbroken succession of generation after
generation of priests. In all this I clearly perceived how
the chanting of Our Lord's genealogy before the Blessed
Sacrament on the Feast of Corpus Christi contains a
great mystery. I also perceived that just as amongst
the ancestors of Christ according to the flesh there were
some who were not holy, and indeed were sinners, without however ceasing to be the rungs in Jacob's ladder
on which God descended to mankind; so even unworthy Bishops still have the power to consecrate the
Blessed Sacrament and to impart priestly Ordination
with all the powers accompanying it. When one sees
this one clearly understands why in old German spiritual books the Old Testament is called the Old Covenant
or the Old Espousals, and the New Testament the New
Covenant or the New Espousals. The highest flowering
of the Old Espousals was the Virgin of Virgins, the
Bride of the Holy Ghost, the most chaste Mother of the
Redeemer, the spiritual vessel of honor, the singular
vessel of devotion, in whom the Word became Flesh.
With this mystery begins the New Espousals, the New
Covenant. In the priesthood and in all those who follow the Lamb it bears the mark of virginity; in it marriage is a great Sacrament, that of Christ and His Bride,

the Church (*Eph.* 5:32).

In order to state as clearly as I can how the approach of the Incarnation, and with it the approach of the most Holy Sacrament of the Altar, was explained to me, I can only repeat how everything was set before my eyes in a great series of pictures; although it is impossible, owing to my present condition and to many interruptions from without, to bring what I saw into a detailed and comprehensible whole. I can only say in general: First I saw the Blessing of the Promise which God gave to the First Man in Paradise, and from that Blessing I saw a ray of light proceed to the Blessed Virgin as she stood there opposite St. Elisabeth, reciting the *Magnificat* in prayer. Then I saw Abraham, who had received this Blessing from God, and I again saw a ray of light proceeding from him to the Blessed Virgin. Then came the other Patriarchs who were the holders and bearers of that holy treasure, and from each of them a ray of light fell upon Mary. Then I saw the passage of this Blessing down the ages until it reached Joachim. He was endowed with the highest Blessing from the inmost sanctuary of the Temple so that he might become the father of the most holy Virgin Mary conceived without original sin. In her the Word became Flesh by the operation of the Holy Ghost and dwelt amongst us hidden for nine months in her, as the Ark of the Covenant of the New Testament, until in the fullness of time we saw His glory, born of the Virgin Mary, a glory as it were of the Only-begotten of the Father, full of grace and truth.

[On July 7th she said:] Last night I saw the Blessed Virgin in Elisabeth's house asleep in her little room, lying on her side with her head resting on her arm. She was wrapped from head to foot in a long white covering. Beneath her heart I saw a glory of light streaming out; it was pear-shaped and in the center of it was an indescribably bright little flame of light. In Elisabeth I saw a glory shining which was larger and rounder but not so bright, and the light within it was less bright.

[On July 8th (a Saturday) she said:] When the Sabbath began yesterday, Friday evening, I saw a lamp being lit and the Sabbath being celebrated in a room in Zacharias' house which I had not seen before. Zacharias, Joseph, and some six other men, probably from the neighborhood, were praying under the lamp. They were standing round a chest with scrolls lying on it. They were wearing cloths hanging down over their heads; they did not make as many contortions as the Jews of today, though they occasionally bowed their heads and raised their arms. Mary, Elisabeth, and a few other women stood apart behind a grating in an alcove from which they could see into the praying-place. All their heads were covered with praying-mantles. After the Sabbath meal I saw the Blessed Virgin in her little room with Elisabeth, standing and reciting the *Magnificat* in prayer. Her hands were crossed on her breast and her black veil lowered over her face; they stood opposite each other against the wall, praying as though in choir. I recited the *Magnificat* in prayer with them, and again, during the second part of it, which refers to the promises of God, I had many glimpses, near and distant, of single ancestors of Mary, from whom threads of light proceeded towards her, as she stood before me praying. These threads or rays of light came, I saw, always out of the mouth of her male ancestors, whereas those from the female ones came from under their hearts and ended in the glory within Mary.

Abraham must (at the time when his Blessing was brought to bear on the future of the Blessed Virgin) have lived near the place where Our Lady was now reciting the *Magnificat,* for I saw the ray of light from him streaming upon her from quite near, whereas I saw the rays from persons much nearer to her in time coming from a much greater distance.

After they had finished the *Magnificat,* which I always saw them reciting morning and evening since the Visitation, Elisabeth withdrew and I saw the Blessed Virgin going to bed. She took off her girdle and her upper garment, leaving only her long brown under-garment. She took a roll of stuff lying at the head of her low couch which I should otherwise have taken to be a bolster, but now saw was a rolled-up length of woollen material almost a yard wide. She held one end of it tight under one armpit, and then wrapped it round and round her body from head to foot and then upwards so that she was quite enveloped in it and could only make short steps. Her arms were free below the elbows and the face and throat were open. She wrapped herself up in this way standing beside her couch, which was slightly raised at the head, and then lay down straight on it, stretched out on her side, her cheek resting on her hand. I did not see men sleeping wrapped up in this way.

[On Sunday, July 9th, she said:] Yesterday, Saturday, I saw Zacharias during the whole of the Sabbath in the same dress that he put on at the beginning of it. He had a long white robe with not very full sleeves. He was girt about several times with a broad girdle inscribed with letters and with straps hanging from it. At the back of his robe was fastened a hood which fell in folds from his head down his back, like a veil gathered together at the back. When he had something to do in the course of the day on Saturday or had to go anywhere, he threw his robe over one shoulder and tucked it under his girdle below the other arm. Each leg was wrapped round with broad bands separately like trousers, and these wrappings were held fast by the straps with which his sandals were attached to his bare feet. Today he also showed Joseph his priest's mantle, which was very beautiful. It was an ample, heavy mantle, of shining material shot with purple and white, and was fastened at the breast with three jewelled clasps. It had no sleeves.

I did not see them eating again until Sunday evening when the Sabbath was over. They ate together under the tree in the garden by the house. They ate green leaves which they dipped into sauce and they sucked little green bundles also dipped in sauce. There were also on the table little bowls of some small fruit, and other bowls from which they ate something with transparent brown flat spoons. I think it was honey, which they ate with flat horn spoons. I also saw little loaves being brought to them to eat.

After this Joseph, accompanied by Zacharias, started on his journey home. It was a still moonlight night full of stars. They prayed beforehand all separately. Joseph again had his little bundle with him, in which were small loaves and a little jug, and his staff with a crook at the top. Zacharias had a long staff with a knob. They both wore their travelling mantles over their heads. Before they went, they embraced Mary and Elisabeth alternately by clasping them to their breasts. I did not see them kiss each other then. They went off gaily and quietly, and the two women accompanied them for a short while, after which they wandered off alone through the indescribably lovely night. Mary and Elisabeth then went back into the house, into Mary's room. A lamp was burning there on an arm projecting from the wall. This was always so when she prayed and when she went to bed. The two women again stood opposite to each other, veiled, and recited the *Magnificat* in prayer. On this occasion the promised vision, which I had forgotten, was repeated: but I have seen so much tonight that I can say but little of it. I only saw the handing down of the Blessing until it came to Joseph in Egypt.

[On July 11th she said:] Last night I had a vision of Mary and Elisabeth of which I only remember that they prayed the whole night long. I cannot recollect the cause. In the daytime I saw Mary doing all kinds of work, for instance, weaving coverlets. I saw Joseph and Zacharias still on their journey: they spent the night in a shed. They had made long detours and had, I believe, paid many visits. I think they spent three days on their journey. Except this I have forgotten almost everything.

[On July 13th she said:] I saw Joseph once more in

his house yesterday, Wednesday the 12th. He seems to have gone straight home without passing through Jerusalem. Anna's maidservant is looking after everything for him and keeps going to and fro between his house and Anna's. Otherwise Joseph was alone. I saw Zacharias coming home again. As always, I saw Mary and Elisabeth reciting the *Magnificat* in prayer and working together. Towards evening they walked in the garden, where there was a fountain, which is unusual here; they always had a little jug of juice with them. Towards evening, when it grew cool, they generally went for a walk in the country round, for Zacharias' house was isolated and surrounded by meadows. They usually went to bed at nine o'clock, but always got up before sunrise.

[This is all that Catherine Emmerich communicated of her visions of the Blessed Virgin's visit to Elisabeth. It should be noticed that she described this event on the occasion of the Feast of the Visitation at the beginning of July, but that the actual visit probably took place in March, since she saw the message of the Incarnation being given to the Blessed Virgin already on February 25th, and closely followed by Our Lady's journey to Elisabeth. That journey was, according to Catherine Emmerich, undertaken when Joseph went to attend the Passover, which began on the 14th of the month Nisan, corresponding to our month of March.

[On June 9th, 1821, Catherine Emmerich discovered near her a relic of Christ's disciple Parmenas, and amongst other visions having reference to this saint she communicated the following, which belongs to this portion of her narrative.]

After Our Lady's return from Jutta to Nazareth I saw her spending several days in the house of the parents of Parmenas, Our Lord's future disciple, who was not yet born.[8] I think I saw this at the same time of year as it actually happened. I had that impression

8. Parmenas was one of the seven deacons (*Acts* 6:5). Cf. following page. (SB)

during my vision. In that case the birth of John the Baptist would have happened at the end of May or the beginning of June. Mary stayed for three months with Elisabeth, until after the birth of John, but was not present on the occasion of his circumcision. [Owing to interruptions, Catherine Emmerich did not relate anything further about John's birth or circumcision, and we therefore refer the reader to the words of the Gospel (*Luke* 1:57-80).]

The Blessed Virgin returned home to Nazareth after John's birth and before his circumcision. Joseph came to meet her half-way. [Catherine Emmcrich was so ill and agitated that she did not tell who accompanied the Blessed Virgin till then, nor did she mention the place where she met Joseph. Perhaps this was Dothan, where they stayed on their journey to Elisabeth with the friend of Joseph's father. She was no doubt accompanied thither by relations of Zacharias or by friends from Nazareth who were undertaking the same journey. What follows may be taken as confirming this supposition.]

When Joseph travelled back with the Blessed Virgin during the second half of her journey from Jutta to Nazareth, he noticed from her figure that she was with child, and was sore beset by trouble and doubt, for he knew nothing of the Angel's annunciation to Our Lady. Immediately after his marriage, Joseph had gone to Bethlehem to arrange about some inheritance; in the meantime Mary had gone to Nazareth with her parents and some of her play-fellows. The angelic salutation happened before Joseph returned to Nazareth. Mary in shy humility had kept God's secret to herself. Joseph, though greatly disquieted by what he had perceived, said nothing, but struggled in silence with his doubts.[9] The Blessed Virgin, who had foreseen this trouble, became thoughtful and serious, which only increased St. Joseph's uneasiness. When they came to Nazareth,

---

9. AC's account of St. Joseph's worry in silence accords with *Matt.* 1:19-20, in strong contrast with the unseemly doubts fancied in the Apocryphal Gospels, especially in *Protev.* 13. (SB)

I saw that the Blessed Virgin did not at once go into Joseph's house with him, but spent a few days with relations. These were the parents of a son, Parmenas (not yet born), who became a disciple of Jesus and was one of the seven deacons in the first community of Christians in Jerusalem. These people were related to the Holy Family, for the mother was a sister of the third husband of Mary Cleophas, the father of Simeon, bishop of Jerusalem. They had a house and a garden of spices in Nazareth. They were also related to the Holy Family through Elisabeth. I saw that the Blessed Virgin stayed for several days with these people before she came to Joseph's house. Joseph's uneasiness increased, however, to such an extent that, now that Mary was preparing to return to him in his house, he made up his mind to leave her and to disappear in secret. While he was harboring this thought, an Angel appeared to him in a dream and reassured him.

IX

ADVENT[1]

THE actual date of Christ's Birth, as I always see it, is
four weeks earlier than its celebration by the Church;
it must have happened on St. Catherine's feast-day. I
always see the Annunciation as happening at the end
of February. Already at the end of October I saw it
being announced in the Promised Land that an enrollment and taxing of the people was to be made by decree
of the Emperor. After that I saw many people travelling up and down the country.

[Sunday, November 11th, 1821:] For several days in
succession I have seen the Blessed Virgin with her
mother Anna, whose house is about an hour's journey
away from Nazareth in the valley of Zabulon. The only
woman remaining in Our Lady's house at Nazareth is
Anna's maidservant, who looks after St. Joseph while
Mary is with Anna. In fact, as long as Anna was alive
they had no completely separate household, but always
received their provisions from her. For several weeks
already I have seen the Blessed Virgin busy with preparations for the Birth of Christ. She is sewing and knitting coverlets, cloths and swaddling-bands. There is more
than enough of everything.

Joachim is no longer alive; I see another man in the
house. Anna has married again. Her second husband
was employed in the Temple in connection with the

---

1. This chapter represents the journey of Mary and Joseph to Bethlehem for the enrollment: *Luke* 2:1-6. (SB)

beasts for sacrifice. I saw Anna sending him out food when he was with the flocks and herds; there were little loaves and fishes in a leathern wallet with several divisions in it. There is a rather tall little girl, about seven years old, in the house, who helps the Blessed Virgin and is taught by her. I think she might be a daughter of Mary Cleophas. Her name was Mary, too. Joseph is not at Nazareth, but must soon be coming, for he is on his way back from Jerusalem, where he has taken beasts for sacrifice.

I saw the Blessed Virgin in the house. She was far advanced in pregnancy, and sat in a room working with several other women. They were preparing coverlets and other things for Mary's confinement. Anna, who possessed pastures with flocks and herds, was well-to-do. She supplied the Blessed Virgin with plenty of everything that it was customary for a person in her rank of life to have. As she thought that Mary would be in her (Anna's) house for the birth of her child, and that all her relations would come to visit her there, she made all the preparations in a very lavish manner, with specially beautiful coverlets and rugs. I saw a coverlet of the kind that was in Elisabeth's house when John was born. It was embroidered with all kinds of texts and emblems, and had a kind of inner lining sewn into it in which the mother could wrap herself. She could fasten this lining round her with tapes and buttons, and be as it were in a little boat or like a baby in its swaddling-bands. She could recline comfortably in it, supported by cushions, when visited by friends, and the latter sat round her on the edge of the coverlet. All these things, as well as many swaddling-bands for the child itself, were prepared in Anna's house. I saw gold and silver threads being used. Not all the coverlets and other things were for Mary's own use; much was intended as presents for the poor, who were always remembered on happy occasions of this kind. I saw the Blessed Virgin and other women sitting on the floor round a big chest, knitting and working at a big coverlet lying in the chest between them. They used two little sticks on which colored threads were wound. Anna was very busy; she went hither and thither fetching and distributing wool and apportioning their tasks to her maidservants.

[November 12th:] Joseph will arrive back in Nazareth today. He was in Jerusalem, taking beasts there for sacrifice. He left them at the little inn a quarter of an hour on the road from Jerusalem to Bethlehem. The house was kept by a devout old childless couple. It was a suitable lodging for quiet people. Joseph went from there to Bethlehem, but did not visit his relations in that town. He only wanted to find out about an enrollment and taxation of the people which made it necessary for everyone to betake himself to his birthplace. He did not, however, have himself inscribed as yet, because he intended to journey with Mary to the Temple in Jerusalem after the days of her purification, and then to go to Bethlehem and settle there. I do not know for certain what were his reasons, but Joseph did not like being in Nazareth.[2] He therefore looked about him in Bethlehem and made inquiries about stones and timber, for he had it in his mind to build himself a house there. Having found out what he wanted, he returned to the inn near Jerusalem, took his sacrifice to the Temple, and hurried home again.

As he was crossing the field of Chimki,[3] six hours from Nazareth, at midnight last night, an angel appeared to him and warned him that he was to go to Bethlehem with Mary at once, for it was there that she was to bear her child. He also indicated everything that she was to take with her for her use, explaining that they were to be few and simple things, and in particular no

2. AC several times explains that Joseph only lived a short time at Nazareth in the house provided by Anna, and did not at first intend to remain there. This intention throws light on *Matt.* 2:23, from which it would appear that he deliberately chose Nazareth as a dwelling-place on his return from Egypt, the alternative being the plan (explained by AC) of settling at Bethlehem, his birthplace. This plan he deliberately rejected, since Bethlehem was in Judaea and "he was afraid to go thither" (*Matt.* 2:22) because of Archelaus. (SB)
3. The Field of Chimki is identified by AC (*infra,* p. 172) with Ginim; see next note. (SB)

embroidered coverlets. Also, besides the ass upon which Mary was to sit, he was to take with him a she-ass one year old that had not yet had a foal. He was to let her run free and was always to follow whatever path she took. This evening Anna went with the Blessed Virgin to Nazareth; no doubt they knew that Joseph was arriving. But they do not seem to know that Mary would journey to Bethlehem from Anna's house. They thought no doubt that Mary would bear her child in her own house in Nazareth, for I saw them taking there, packed in saddle-bags, many of the things they had prepared. I saw amongst them several shawls of blue material with hoods. I think they were meant for wrapping the child in. Joseph arrived at Nazareth in the evening.

[November 13th:] Today I saw the Blessed Virgin and her mother Anna in the house in Nazareth, where Joseph revealed to them what had been told him the previous night. Thereupon they returned to Anna's house, and I saw them preparing to leave immediately. Anna was distressed. The Blessed Virgin must have known that she was to bear her child in Bethlehem, but had been silent out of humility. She knew it from the writings of the Prophets about the birth of the Messias, all of which she treasured in her little cupboard at Nazareth. (She had been given them by her women-teachers in the Temple and had been instructed in them by these holy women. She used to read them very often and pray for their fulfillment. Her prayers were ever full of yearning for the coming of the Messias; she ever extolled as blessed her who should bear the holy child, and hoped only to be allowed to serve her as her lowest maid-servant. Never in her humility had she thought that she herself might be the chosen one.) Since she knew from those passages in the Prophets that the Saviour was to be born in Bethlehem, she yielded joyfully to the Divine Will and began the journey, which was difficult for her at that time of the year, when it was often decidedly cold in the valleys between the ranges of hills.

This evening I saw Joseph and the Blessed Virgin,

accompanied by Anna, Mary Cleophas, and some menservants, starting off from Anna's house. Mary sat on the comfortable side-saddle of a donkey, which also carried her baggage. Joseph led the donkey. A second donkey was taken for Anna to ride back on. Her husband was away in the fields when they started on their journey.

[November 14th:] This morning I saw the holy travellers arrive at an open field called Ginim,[4] six hours' journey from Nazareth, where the angel had appeared to Joseph two days before. Anna had a pasture here and the menservants were told to fetch the young she-ass which Joseph was to take with him. She sometimes ran in front of them and sometimes beside them. Anna and Mary Cleophas here took a tender farewell of the travellers and returned home with the menservants.

(This field Ginim is several miles long and is shaped like a pear. Another field, called Gimmi, lies nearer Nazareth not far from a shepherds' village high up in the hills called Gimmi or Gimchi, where Jesus taught shepherds from the 7th to the 9th of September before His Baptism. These shepherds had lepers hidden among them. He also healed here the dropsical woman of the house where He stayed, and was mocked by the Pharisees. Farther away from this place and to the southwest of Nazareth, beyond the river Kishon, is a settlement of lepers, consisting of scattered huts round a lake formed by the river. Jesus healed here on September 30th before His Baptism. The field Ginim, traversed today by the Holy Family, is separated from the other field Gimmi by a little river or river-bed. The names are so alike that I may easily have confused them.)

I saw the Holy Family going on their way and climbing Mount Gilboa.[5] They did not pass through any town;

---

4. The Field of Ginim, six hours from Nazareth, is presumably Engannim or Ginaea, the modern Jenin, eighteen miles south of Nazareth, near the corner of the Plain of Esdraelon. Engannim is mentioned in *Jos.* 15:34 and 19:19, and is probably to be identified with Beth-haggan (Douay "the garden house") of *4 Kings* 9:27. Cf. *Cath. Comm.,* 275i. (SB)

5. This would refer to the foothills to the west of Mt. Gilboa. (SB)

they followed the young she-ass, which always took lonely by-ways. I saw them stopping at a house in the hills belonging to Lazarus, not far from the town of Ginim and in the direction of Samaria. The steward, who knew them from other journeys, gave them a friendly welcome. Their family was on intimate terms with Lazarus. There are beautiful orchards and avenues here. The house stands high, so that one has a very wide view from the roof. Lazarus inherited it from his father; Our Lord Jesus often stayed here during His ministry and taught in the surrounding country. The steward and his wife conversed in a very friendly way with the Blessed Virgin. They were surprised that she should have been willing to undertake such a long journey in her condition, when she might have had every comfort at home with her mother Anna.

[Thursday to Friday night, November 15th-16th:] I saw the Holy Family some hours' journey beyond this last place, going at night towards a mountain through a very cold valley. It looked as if there was hoar-frost on the ground. The Blessed Virgin was suffering from the cold and said to Joseph: "We must rest, I can go no farther." Hardly had she spoken when the she-ass that was running with them stood still under a terebinth tree, very big and old, near which was a spring of water. They stopped under this tree; Joseph spread coverings for the Blessed Virgin to sit on, after helping her to alight from the donkey, and she sat down under the tree. Joseph hung a lighted lantern, which he carried with him, on the lower branches of the tree. (I often saw travellers in that country do this at night.) The Blessed Virgin prayed earnestly to God that He would not suffer her to take harm from the cold. At once she was filled with so great a warmth that she held out her hands to St. Joseph to warm his. They refreshed themselves here with fruit and little loaves of bread which they had with them, and drank water from the spring near by, mixing it with balsam which Joseph had brought with him in a little jug. Joseph spoke very comfortingly to the Blessed Virgin: he is so good, and so sorry that the journey is so difficult. When Our Lady complained of the cold, he spoke to her about the good lodging which he hoped to find for her in Bethlehem. He said he knew of a house with very good people where they would find a comfortable lodging at very little cost. It was, he said, better to pay something than to be taken in for nothing. He spoke highly of Bethlehem in general, and comforted Our Lady in every possible way. (This upset me, because I knew well that things would turn out quite differently. Even this holy man, you see, indulged in human hopes.)

So far they have crossed two little streams in the course of their journey: one of these they crossed on a high foot-way, while the two donkeys waded through the water. It was strange to see how the young she-ass, who was free to go where she would, kept running round the travellers. Where the path narrowed, as for instance between hills, and so could not be mistaken, she ran sometimes before and sometimes behind them, but where there was a parting of the ways she always appeared again and took the right path. Where they were to rest, she stood still, as here by the terebinth tree. I do not remember whether they spent the night under the tree, or whether they went on to another shelter.

This terebinth was a very old and sacred tree, of the grove of Moreh near Sichem. When Abraham was journeying into the land of Chanaan, he had here a vision of God, who promised him this land for his descendants. (*Gen.* 15.) He then built an altar under the terebinth. Before Jacob went to Bethel, to sacrifice to the Lord, he buried under this terebinth all the strange gods of Laban and the jewels which his family carried with him. (*Gen.* 35:4.) Under this tree Josue built the tabernacle for the Ark of the Covenant and made the people assembled there renounce their idols. (*Josue* 24:26.) It was here that Abimelech, the son of Gedeon, was hailed as king of the Sichemites. (*Jgs.* 9:6.)

[November 16th:] Today I saw the Holy Family arriving at a big farm, about two hours' journey south of the tree I have mentioned. The woman of the house was absent, and her husband turned St. Joseph away, saying that he could easily go on farther. After they had gone on for some distance, they found that the she-ass had run into an empty shed, which they also entered. Some shepherds, who were busy cleaning it out, showed them great friendliness, and gave them straw and little bundles of reeds and twigs to make a fire with. These shepherds went to the house where the Holy Family had been turned away and told the woman of the house, who had now come home, how kind and God-fearing Joseph was, and what a beautiful and wonderfully holy wife he had; whereupon she upbraided her husband for having turned away such good people. I saw, too, that the woman at once went to the place where the Holy Family was sheltering, but was too shy to go in, and went home again to fetch some food.

(The place where they were was on the north side of a hill somewhere between Samaria and Thebez. Almost to the east of it, beyond the Jordan, is Succoth; and somewhat more to the south, but also beyond Jordan, is Ainon, this side of Salem. It must be about twelve hours' journey from Nazareth.)[6]

After a time the woman, accompanied by two children, came to the Holy Family with some provisions. She apologized and was very friendly and sympathetic. After they had refreshed and rested themselves, the husband also came, and asked Joseph to forgive him for having sent him away. He advised him to continue uphill for an hour, where before the Sabbath began he would find a good inn in which he could spend the Sabbath. After this they started off again. After having

---

6. The geographical indications here are fairly correct according to the latest available maps (in *Cath. Comm.*, 1953). A place between Samaria and Thebez (about ten miles apart) would find Succoth about twenty miles east-southeast, but Aenon near Salim (the Ennon of *John* 3:23) would lie farther *north,* about fifteen miles north of Succoth, though another place nearer Succoth may be intended, and is so marked by Fahsel. (SB)

climbed for about an hour, they came to a rather considerable inn, which consisted of several buildings, surrounded by trees and pleasure-gardens, in which were shrubs of balsam on espaliers, though the inn was on the northern slope. The Blessed Virgin had alighted from her donkey, which Joseph was leading. They came up to the house, and when the innkeeper came out Joseph asked him for lodging. He excused himself, saying that his house was full. His wife also came out, and when the Blessed Virgin came up to her and begged so humbly and simply for shelter, she was deeply moved, and the innkeeper himself could not gainsay her. He made comfortable quarters for them in a nearby shed and put their pack-donkey in a stable. The young she-ass was not there, she was running free in the country round; she always went off when she was not needed to show the way. Joseph prepared his Sabbath lamp here, and kept the Sabbath praying beneath it with the Blessed Virgin with the most touching devotion. They ate a little, and then rested on mats spread out on the floor.

[November 17th:] I saw the Holy Family spending the whole day here and praying together. I saw the mistress of the house and her three children with the Blessed Virgin, and the farmer's wife of the day before also came with her two children and paid Our Lady a visit. There was real intimacy among them as they sat together, and the two women were greatly impressed by Mary's wisdom and modest behavior. They listened with great attention to Our Lady, who talked much with the children and taught them. The children had little parchment rolls, from which Mary made them read to her. She spoke to them in such a lovely way about what they read, that they could not take their eyes off her. It was sweet to see and sweeter still to hear. In the afternoon I saw St. Joseph walking about with the innkeeper in the country round, looking at the gardens and fields, and talking of holy things, as I saw was always the Sabbath practice of devout people in that land. They remained here for the following night as well.

[Sunday, November 18th:] The good people of this inn have become extremely fond of the Blessed Virgin, and have an intense sympathy with her and with her condition. They begged her in the most friendly way to stay and await her confinement here. They even showed her a comfortable room which they would make ready for her. The woman offered her, with all her heart, to care for her and look after her in every way. However, they started again on their journey early in the morning, and went down a valley on the southeastern side of the mountains. They went farther away from Samaria, towards which the first part of their journey seemed to be directed. As they descended the hill, they could see the temple on Mount Garizim, which is visible from a great distance. There are many figures of lions or other animals on the roof which gleam white in the sunshine. I saw them travelling about six hours today, and towards evening I saw them arrive at a large shepherd's house in a field, where they were well received. This was about an hour's journey to the southeast of Sichem.

The man of the house was a steward of the orchards and fields belonging to the neighboring town. The house was not right down in the plain, but on a slope. All the country here was better and more fertile than during the first part of their journey, for this was the sunny side, and in the Promised Land at this time of year that makes a considerable difference. Between here and Bethlehem lay many other shepherds' dwellings, scattered about in the intersecting valleys. The people here belonged to those shepherds whose daughters later married some of the followers of the three holy kings who remained behind when their masters left. From one of these marriages came a boy who was healed by Our Lord in this house at the Blessed Virgin's request in the second year of His ministry, on July 31st (the 7th day of the month Ab) after He had talked with the

Samaritan woman. Jesus took him with two other youths as companions on His journey to Arabia, after the raising of Lazarus, and afterwards he became a disciple. Jesus often stayed here and taught. There were children in the house, and Joseph blessed them before he went away.

[November 19th:] Today I saw them travelling in more level country. The Blessed Virgin sometimes goes on foot. They often stop to rest and refresh themselves. They have little loaves with them, and a drink which is both cooling and strengthening. This is contained in delicately made little jugs shining like bronze, with two ears. It is balsam, which they mix with water. They sometimes pick berries and fruits which may still be found hanging in sunny places on the trees and bushes. Mary's saddle on the donkey has a foot-rest hanging on each side, so that her feet do not hang down as is usual in our country. She sits sometimes to the right and sometimes to the left of the pack-donkey, which moves very quietly and evenly. Joseph's first action, whenever they rest by the way or stop for the night, is to make ready a comfortable place for the Blessed Virgin to sit and rest. He often washes his feet, and Mary does the same. They have the habit of washing often.

It was already dark when they came to a house standing by itself. Joseph knocked at the door and asked for lodging. The master of the house refused, however, to open, and when Joseph explained Mary's condition and said that she could go no farther, adding that he was not asking for lodging without payment, the hard-hearted man retorted angrily that his house was not an inn, and that he wanted to be left alone and not disturbed by knocking, which he could not bear. He told Joseph to go on his way, and was so relentless that he did not even open the door, but shouted his harsh words from behind it. So they went on a little way and turned into a shed where they found the she-ass standing. Joseph kindled a light and prepared a bed for the Blessed Virgin, with her help. He brought the pack-donkey in, too, and found some straw and fodder for him. They prayed, took some refreshment, and slept for a few hours. It must be about six hours' journey from the last inn to this place. They must be some twenty-six hours from Nazareth and ten from Jerusalem. Until now they have not taken any high-roads, but have cut across several trade-roads leading from the Jordan to Samaria and running into the highways which go from Syria to Egypt. The by-roads which they took are very small, and in the mountains sometimes so narrow that a man must pick his way very carefully so as not to stumble. The donkeys, however, are very sure-footed. Their shelter here was on level ground.

[November 20th:] The day had not yet broken when they left this place. Their way led uphill again. I think they were near the road leading from Gabara[7] to Jerusalem and that the frontier between Samaria and Judaea was here. They were again roughly refused admission at another house. When they were several hours northeast of Bethany, it happened that Mary was greatly in need of rest and refreshment; so Joseph turned off the road for about half an hour to a place where he knew there was a beautiful fig-tree, which as a rule was full of fruit. This tree had benches round it for people to rest on. Joseph knew it from a former journey. When, however, they got there, they found no fruit at all on the tree, which distressed them very much. I have a dim recollection that afterwards Jesus had something to do with this tree. It never bore fruit anymore, but was green, and I think that the Lord cursed it as He passed by when escaping from Jerusalem and that it withered away.[8] After this they came to a house where the man was at first very harsh to Joseph when he humbly asked him for lodging. He shone his light onto

---

7. Gabara is in Galilee, north of Nazareth. (SB)
8. Catherine Emmerich was so exceedingly ill from Nov. 19th to 21st that when she recounted these events on Nov. 22nd she could not give the exact situation of this tree, but could only say that it was somewhere near the path of the Holy Family. It is in any case *not* the cursed fig-tree mentioned in the Gospels. (CB)
   The barren fig-tree of *Matt.* 21:19 and *Mark* 11:13 stood between Bethany and Jerusalem. (SB)

the Blessed Virgin's face and scoffed at Joseph for taking so young a woman about with him; he was, he supposed, jealous. The woman of the house then came up
and took pity on the Blessed Virgin, showing her a
room in a side-building in a very friendly way, and
bringing little loaves of bread for them to eat. The man,
too, was sorry for his rudeness, and became very friendly
towards the holy travellers. After this they came to a
third house. It was inhabited by young people, but I
saw an old man with a stick walking about in it. Their
reception here was tolerably good but not particularly
friendly. Nobody took much trouble about them. The
people here were not real simple shepherds; they were
like rich peasants with us who are more or less entan-
gled in the world and in trade and so on. Jesus visited
one of these houses on October 20th (the first day of
the month Tishri) after His Baptism, and found the
resting-place of His parents decorated and used as a
praying-place. I am not sure whether it was the one
where the man had at first jeered at Joseph. I have a
dim remembrance that the people there had arranged
it like this immediately after the wonders accompanying His Birth. Towards the end of their road Joseph
made many halts, for the journey grew more and more
difficult for the Blessed Virgin. They followed the way
taken by the she-ass, and made a day and a half's
detour eastwards of Jerusalem. Joseph's father had
owned pastureland round here, so he knew the country very well. If they had travelled due south, across
the desert behind Bethany, they would probably have
reached Bethlehem in six hours, but that way was hilly
and at that time of year very difficult; so the she-ass
led them through valleys which brought them nearer
to the Jordan.

[November 21st:] Today I saw the holy travellers
entering a big shepherd's house while it was still full
day. This must be about three hours from John's baptizing place on the Jordan and about seven hours from
Bethlehem. It is the same house in which thirty years

later Jesus spent the night of October 11th before the
morning on which he passed near the Baptist for the
first time after His Baptism. Near the house, and apart
from it, was a shed in which were kept the agricul-
tural implements and the shepherd's things. In the
court was a fountain with baths round it, supplied with
water from the fountain by pipes. The master of the
house must have owned much land; it was a large
establishment. I saw many menservants coming and
going and having their meals there. The master of the
house received the travellers in a very friendly way
and was very ready to help. They were shown a comfortable room, and their pack-donkey was well looked
after. A manservant was told to wash Joseph's feet at
the fountain and to give him other clothes while his
own were cleaned from dust and smoothed out. A maid
did the same for the Blessed Virgin. They ate and slept
here. The mistress of the house was rather perverse
in character. She lived in a separate room and kept
herself apart. She had surreptitiously examined the
travellers, and as she was young and vain she was
vexed by the beauty of the Blessed Virgin: she was
also afraid that Mary might appeal to her to let her
stay and be confined there, so she kept away in a hostile spirit and insisted that they should leave the next
day. (This is the same woman whom Jesus found there
in this house, blind and crippled, thirty years later on
October 11th, after His Baptism. After reproaching her
for her inhospitality and vanity He healed her.) There
were also children in the house. The Holy Family spent
the night here.

[November 22nd:] I saw the Holy Family leaving their
place of shelter about midday. Some of the inmates of
the house accompanied them for part of their way. After
a short journey of about two hours westward they came
to a place where scattered houses, with gardens and
forecourts, stand in a long row on either side of a main
road. Some relations of Joseph's lived here. They were,
as far as I remember, sons by a second marriage of a

stepfather or stepmother. I saw the house, it had a good situation and was quite large. They went, however, right through this place, and then turned right for half an hour, in the direction of Jerusalem, until they reached a large inn, in the court of which there was a big fountain with many pipes. A large company was assembled here, attending a funeral. The interior of the house, in the center of which was the fireplace and its chimney, had been made into one large hall by the removal of the low wooden screens which at other times divided it into separate rooms. Black curtains hung behind the hearth, in front of which stood a veiled black object like a coffin. A large assembly of men were praying round it. They wore long black garments with short white ones over them, and some had black fringed maniples hanging on one arm. In another room women completely veiled were sitting on the floor in low boxes and mourning.

The owners of the inn themselves, who were busy with the funeral, welcomed the travellers only from a distance. The servants of the house, however, gave them a very friendly reception and showed them every attention. A separate lodging was prepared for them by letting down mats which had been rolled up to the ceiling, so that they were in a kind of tent. There were many beds in this house rolled up against the wall, and mats could be let down to make many separate cells. Afterwards I saw the people of the house visiting the Holy Family and conversing with them in a friendly manner. They no longer wore the white garments over their black ones. After Joseph and Mary had refreshed themselves and taken a little food, they prayed together and retired to rest.

[November 23rd:] Joseph and Mary left here for Bethlehem about midday. They still had some three hours' journey before them. The mistress of the house urged them to stay where they were, for, she said, it seemed to her that Mary might be delivered at any moment. Mary, however, dropping her veil, said that she had still thirty-six hours before her. (I am not sure that she did not say thirty-eight.) The woman was very anxious to keep her, not in the house itself, but in another building. As they left, I saw Joseph talking to the innkeeper about his donkeys. He spoke very highly of them, and said he had brought the she-ass with him in order to pawn her in case of necessity.

When the people of the house spoke of the difficulty of finding lodging in Bethlehem, Joseph said he had friends there and would certainly be well received. (It makes me always so sorry when he talks so certainly of being well received. He talked to Mary in that way, too, as they went along. One sees by this that even such holy people can be mistaken.)

The journey from the last inn to Bethlehem must have taken about three hours. They made a circuit round the north side of Bethlehem and approached the town from the west. They made a halt under a tree some little way off the road. Mary alighted from the donkey and arranged her clothing, after which Joseph went with her to a large building a few minutes outside Bethlehem, surrounded by courtyards and other small buildings. There were trees in front of it, and round about it were crowds encamped in tents. This was the old ancestral house of David and once Joseph's family home. Relations or acquaintances of Joseph's still lived there, but they treated him as a stranger and as a person whom they did not want to know. This house was now being used for the receipt of the money from the Roman taxation. Joseph, leading the donkey by the bridle, went at once to this house with the Blessed Virgin, because every new arrival had to report himself here and was given a paper, without which he could not be admitted into Bethlehem.

[After several pauses Catherine Emmerich spoke as follows in her visionary state:] The young she-ass that runs free has not gone with them here, she has run off round the outside of the town towards the south, where it is flatter and there is a sort of open valley. Joseph has gone into the house. Mary is with some women in a little house beside the courtyard: they are very friendly to her and are giving her some food. These women are cooking for the soldiers. They are Roman soldiers, with strips of leather hanging round their loins. The weather here is very pleasant and not at all cold. The hill between Jerusalem and Bethany is in full sunshine; one has a fine view of it from here. Joseph is in a big room with an uneven floor. They are asking him who he is and are referring to long scrolls of which a great many are hanging on the walls. They unroll them and read aloud to him his ancestry and also Mary's: he did not seem to know that she also descended so directly from David through Joachim; he himself descended from an earlier offspring of David's. The man asks him: "Where is your wife?" Owing to many disorders the people of the country have not been properly registered for seven years.[9] I see the figures V and II, making seven [she forms this figure with her fingers]. This taxation has been going on for several months. Some payments were made here and there during those seven years, but nothing regular. The people were made to pay twice over. Some of them stayed here for as long as three months. Joseph came rather late to the tax office, but was treated in quite a friendly way. He has not paid anything yet, but was asked about his means, and stated that he had no land and lived by his handicraft and from the assistance given him by his wife's mother.

There are a great number of scribes and high officials in many of the rooms. On the upper floors are Romans and many soldiers. There are also present Pharisees and Sadducees, priests, elders and every kind of official and scribe, both Jewish and Roman. There is no such commission in Jerusalem, but they are estab-

---

9. The question of the successive registrations in the Roman Province of Syria is very intricate, together with the identification of the one in the year of Christ's birth; but there is evidence for censuses in Egypt and Gaul earlier in the reign of Augustus (cf. *Cath. Comm.*, 749a). AC's reference *(infra,* p. 185) to the sharing of the revenue of the taxation remains entirely obscure. (SB)

lished in several other places, such as Magdala on the sea of Galilee, where the inhabitants of Galilee are taxed, and also those of Sidon, I think because of their commercial dealings. Only the people who are not resident anywhere and have no land on which they can be taxed have to present themselves at their birthplace. From now on the tax has to be paid in three months in three installments. Each of these three instalments goes to a different object. The first is shared by the Emperor Augustus, Herod, and another king who lives near Egypt. He has rendered some service in war and has a right to a district up in the north, so they have to apportion something to him. The second installment has to do with the building of the Temple; it seems as if it were used to pay off a debt. The third installment is intended for widows and poor people, who have had nothing for a long time, but of all this little reaches the right people, just as happens today. The money is meant for nothing but good causes, and yet remains in the hands of the great. All this business of writing made a terrible fuss and commotion.

Joseph was now allowed to go, and when he got downstairs the Blessed Virgin was called before the scribes in a passage, but they did not read anything aloud to her. They told Joseph that it was unnecessary for him to have brought his wife with him, and seemed to be bantering him on account of her youth. Joseph was ashamed of this being said before Mary; he was afraid she might think that he was not respected in his birthplace.

After this they went on into Bethlehem, the buildings of which were at some distance from each other. The entrance was through ruined walls as if the gate had been destroyed. Mary remained with the donkey at the very entrance of the street while Joseph sought a lodging in the nearest houses—in vain, for Bethlehem was full of strangers, all running from place to place. Joseph returned to Mary, saying that as no shelter was to be found there, they would go on far-

ther into the town. He led the donkey on by the bridle, and the Blessed Virgin walked beside him. When
they came to the beginning of another street, Mary
again stopped by the donkey, and Joseph again went
from house to house in vain seeking a lodging, and
again came sadly back. This happened several times,
and the Blessed Virgin often had long to wait. Everywhere the houses were filled with people, everywhere
he was turned away, so he said to Mary that they would
go to another part of Bethlehem where they would
surely find lodging. They went a little way back in the
direction in which they had come and then turned southwards. They went hesitatingly through the street, which
was more like a country road, for the houses were built
on slopes. Here, too, their search was fruitless. On the
other side of Bethlehem, where the houses lie farther
apart, they came to a lower-lying open space, like a
field, where it was more solitary. There was a sort of
shed here, and not far from it a great spreading tree,
with shady branches like a big lime-tree. The trunk
was smooth and the spreading branches made a kind
of roof. Joseph led the Blessed Virgin to this tree, and
made her a comfortable seat against its trunk with
their bundles, so that she might rest while he sought
for shelter in the houses near. The donkey stood with
its head turned towards the tree. At first Mary stood
upright, leaning against the tree. Her ample white
woollen dress had no girdle and hung round her in
folds: her head was covered with a white veil. Many
people passed by and looked at her, not knowing that
the Redeemer was so near to them. She was so patient,
so humble, so full of hopeful expectation. Ah, she had
to wait a long, long time; she sat down at last on the
rug, crossing her feet under her. She sat with her head
bent and her hands crossed below her breast.

Joseph came back to her in great distress; he had
found no shelter. His friends, of whom he had spoken
to the Blessed Virgin, would hardly recognize him. He
was in tears and Mary comforted him. He went once

more from one house to another; but as he gave the approaching confinement of his wife as his chief reason for his request, he met with even more decided refusals. Although the place was solitary, the passers-by at last began to stand still and look curiously at the Blessed Virgin from a distance, as one may well do if one sees somebody waiting in the dusk for a long time. I think some of them even spoke to her, asking her who she was. At last Joseph came back. He was so upset that he came up hesitatingly. He said he had had no success, but he knew of one place outside the town, belonging to the shepherds, who often went there when coming with their flocks to the town. There they would, in any case, find a shelter. He said that he knew the place from childhood; when his brothers had tormented him, he had often escaped there to hide from them and to say his prayers. Even if the shepherds did come there, he would easily come to an understanding with them; but at this time of year they were seldom there. As soon as he had settled her there in peace and quiet, he would look round again for something else. They then went outside Bethlehem to the east of the town by a lonely footpath, going to the left. It was like a path along the ruined walls, ditches, and banks of some little town. At first the path ascended slightly, and then descended after crossing a hill. On the east of the town, a few minutes outside it, they came to a hill or high bank, in front of which was an open space made pleasant by several trees. There were pine-trees (cedar or terebinth) and other trees with small leaves like our box-trees. The place was such as one might find right at the end of the old ramparts of some little town.

[In order to avoid continually interrupting the narrative, we will here describe as fully as possible the surroundings of this hill and the interior of the Cave of the Nativity according to the repeated accounts given by Catherine Emmerich.]

Among many other different grottoes or cave-dwellings there was, at the south end of this hill, round which the road wound its way to the Shepherd's Valley, the cave in which Joseph sought shelter for the Blessed Virgin. From the west the entrance led eastwards into the hill through a narrow passage into a larger chamber, half semicircular and half triangular. The walls of the cave were of the natural rock, and only on the south side, which was encircled by the road to the Shepherd's Valley, was it completed by a little rough masonry. On this south side was another entrance into the cave, but this was generally blocked up, and Joseph had to clear it before he could use it. If you came out of this entrance and turned to the left, you came upon a wider entrance into a lower vault, narrow and inconvenient, which stretched under the Cave of the Nativity. From the ordinary entrance to the cave, which faced westwards, one could see nothing but a few roofs and towers of Bethlehem. If you turned to the right on coming out of this entrance, you came to the entrance of a lower cave, which was dark and was at one time the hiding-place of the Blessed Virgin. In front of the main entrance, supported on posts, there was a light roof of reeds, extending round the south of the cave to the entrance on that side, so that one could sit in front of the cave in shade. On the south side there were, high up, three openings for light and air, closed by gratings fixed in masonry. There was a similar opening in the roof of the cave. This roof, which was covered with turf, formed the extremity of the ridge on which Bethlehem stood.

[According to Catherine Emmerich's repeated descriptions the interior of the cave was arranged as follows:] From the west one came through a light wickerwork door into a moderately broad passage opening into a chamber which was partly angular and partly semicircular. Towards the south it broadened out considerably, so that the ground-plan of the whole can be compared to a head resting on its neck. As you came out of the neck of the cave, whose roof was lower, into the higher part of the cave with its natural vaulting, you stepped down to a lower level. The floor of the whole cave was, however, higher at the sides, round which ran a low stone bench of varying breadth. The walls of the cave as nature had made them were, though not quite smooth, clean and pleasant and had something attractive about them. I liked them better than the rough, clumsy masonry which had been added on, for instance on the upper part of the south wall of the entrance, where three openings for light and air had been made. In the center of the roof of the cave there was another opening, and, if I remember rightly, I saw besides this three slanting holes piercing the upper part of the cave at intervals from south to east. From the north side of the passage an entrance led into a smaller side-cave. Passing this entrance you came upon the place where Joseph lit his fire; after that the wall turned northeast into the higher and bigger cave, and it was here that Joseph's pack-donkey stood, by the broad part of the stone bench which ran round its walls. Behind this, in the thickness of the rock wall to the north, was a small chamber just big enough to hold the donkey and containing fodder. The wall of the cave then turned southeast, encircling the chamber (which grew broader towards the south) and finally turned north to end at the main entrance.

The Blessed Virgin was in the eastern part of this cave, exactly opposite the entrance, when she gave birth to the Light of the World. The crib in which the child Jesus was laid stood on the west side of the southern and more roomy part of the cave. This crib was a hollowed-out stone trough lying on the ground and used for cattle to drink from; over it stood a longish rectangular manger or rack, narrower below and broader above, made of wooden lattice-work and raised on four feet so that the beasts could comfortably eat the hay or grass in the rack and lower their heads to drink the water in the trough beneath. When the three holy kings presented their gifts, the Blessed Virgin was sitting with the child Jesus opposite the crib on the eastern side of this part of the cave. If you go from the place where the crib is out of the cave in a westerly direction into the so-called neck of the cave, you come first of all, following the southern wall, to the southern entrance mentioned above and later opened by Joseph, and then arrive at St. Joseph's own room, which he later partitioned off on the south side by wicker screens in this passage. On this side there was a hollow in the wall where he put away all kinds of things.

The road to the Shepherds' Valley ran past the south side of the cave. Here and there were little houses standing on hills, and scattered about in the fields were sheds thatched with reeds on four, six, or eight posts, with wicker walls. Towards the east of the cave the ground fell into a closed valley shut off on the north side and about a quarter of an hour's journey wide. Its slopes were covered with bushes, trees, and gardens. If one walked through the tall luxuriant grass in the meadow, watered by a spring, and through the trees planted in rows, one came to the eastern ridge of this valley. By following this very pleasant path in a south-easterly direction from the Cave of the Nativity, one came to a projecting spur of the ridge containing the rock-tomb of Maraha,[10] the nurse of Abraham, which was called the Milk Cave or the Sucklings' Cave. The Blessed Virgin came here several times with the child Jesus. Above this cave was a great tree with seats in it, and from here one had a much better view of Bethlehem than from the Cave of the Nativity.

I was told much that had happened in the Cave of the Nativity of symbolical and prophetical significance in Old Testament times, but can only remember that Seth, the child of promise, was here conceived and born by Eve after a seven years' penance. She was told here by an angel that this seed was given by God in place of Abel. Seth was hidden and suckled by his mother in

---

10. Maraha, Abraham's nurse, is not known in any available document. (SB)

this cave and in Maraha's cave, for his brothers were hostile to him just as Jacob's sons were to Joseph. In these caves, inhabited by men in earlier times, I have often seen places hollowed out by them in the rock in which they and their children could sleep in comfort on skins or grass. So perhaps the hollow in the stone bench beneath the crib may have been a sleeping-place of Seth's or of a later inmate. But I cannot say this for certain now.

I also remember from my visions of the ministry of Jesus that the Lord on October 6th, after His Baptism, was keeping the Sabbath in the Cave of the Nativity, which had been made into a place of prayer by the shepherds; and that He told the shepherds that His Heavenly Father had appointed this as the place of His Birth as soon as Mary had conceived.

Abraham had a nurse, Maraha, whom he greatly revered; she lived to a great age and he always took her on his journeys, riding on a camel. She lived with him for a long time in Succoth. Afterwards, towards the end of her life, she was here in the Shepherds' Valley, where he had his tents near to this cave. When she was more than a hundred years old and her death was at hand, she asked Abraham to bury her in this cave, prophesying about it and naming it the Cave of Milk or the Cave of the Sucklings. Some miracle, which I have forgotten, happened here, and a spring of water burst forth. The cave was then a high narrow passage of a white and not very hard substance. A mound of this blocked up part of the passage but did not reach to the roof. If one climbed over this mound, one came to the entrances of other caves higher up. There were also several deep passages running into the hill under the cave. Later it was enlarged. Abraham made Maraha's tomb out of the mound lying in the passage. Below was a massive block of stone on which rested a kind of heavy stone trough on short thick feet. The trough had a jagged top. One could see between the trough and the block under it. I was surprised to see nothing of it at the time of Jesus' Birth.

This cave with the nurse's tomb was symbolically prophetic of the Mother of the Saviour giving suck to her child while pursued by enemies; for in Abraham's youth a symbolically prophetic persecution took place, and his nurse saved his life by hiding him in a cave. As far as I can remember, the king in Abraham's country had a dream or was told by prophecy about a child to be born who would become a danger to him. The king took measures to prevent this. Abraham's mother concealed her pregnancy and gave birth to him in secret in a cave. Maraha, the nurse, suckled him in secret. She lived as though she were a poor slave, and worked in a wilderness near the cave in which she suckled the child Abraham. Afterwards his parents took him back, and on account of his being unusually big he was thought to have been born before that prophecy. However, when he was a boy, he was again in danger as the result of some supernatural utterances, and the nurse again saved him by hiding him away. I saw her carrying him off in secret, tied to her waist under her big cloak. Many children of his size were murdered at that time.

This cave had been a place of devotion since Abraham's time, particularly for mothers and their babies. This was prophetic, for the reverence paid to Abraham's nurse was symbolic of that paid to the Blessed Virgin. In the same way Elias had seen Our Lady in the rain-bearing cloud, and had made a place of prayer in her honor on Mount Carmel [see p. 49]. Maraha had contributed to the coming of the Messias by nourishing with her milk the ancestor of the Blessed Virgin. I cannot, alas, explain it rightly, but it was like a deep spring of water running through the whole of life and always being replenished, until there burst forth from it the clear stream of Our Blessed Lady. [This was the expression used by Catherine Emmerich in her state of ecstatic sleep.]

The tree which stood beside this cave was like a great lime-tree, with big shady branches. It was a tere-

binth, pointed at the top and broad below. It had white
seeds, which were oily and could be eaten. Abraham
met Melchisedech under this tree, but I cannot remember
on what occasion. Joseph enlarged the cave still
more and closed the passages leading downwards from
it. The tree stands on a hill; beneath it is a door, set
at a slant, leading into a passage or kind of vestibule
where another door, set straight, opens into the tomb-
cave itself. The latter is round rather than square. The
shepherds often used the passage to shelter in. This
big old tree cast a wide shadow. It was regarded as
sacred by the shepherds and others in the neighborhood, and also by devout travellers. It was the custom
to rest and pray there. I do not remember the history
of the tree, but it had some connection with Abraham:
he may perhaps have planted it. Near it was a fireplace which could be covered over, and there was also
a spring in front of the tree, from which the shepherds
used at certain times to draw water supposed to have
a special healing property. On each side of the tree
there were open huts to sleep in. It was all surrounded
by a fence.

[While Catherine Emmerich was recounting this, she
was in great pain; and when the writer said to her, "So
this was a terebinth tree?" she answered in sudden
absence of mind: "Tenebrae, not Terebinth, under the
shadow of Thy Wings, that is a wing—Tenebrae—under
Thy Shadow will I rejoice." The writer did not understand the significance of these words, perhaps she was
applying the words of the Psalm to the tree. She spoke
with great intensity of feeling and seemed to be comforting herself with these words.]

St. Helena built a church here and Mass has been
said here: I think it seemed to be in a chapel dedicated
to St. Nicholas.

[November 23rd:] The sun was already low when
they reached the entrance of the cave. The young she-
ass, which had left them at Joseph's ancestral house
to run round the outside of the town, met them as soon

as they arrived here and gambolled joyfully round them. "Look," said the Blessed Virgin to Joseph, "it is certainly the will of God that we should go in here." Joseph was, however, very distressed and secretly ashamed at having spoken so often of their good reception in Bethlehem. He put the pack-donkey under the shelter by the entrance of the cave and prepared a place for Our Lady to rest there while he kindled a light, opened the wicker-work door of the cave and went into it. The passage into the cave was narrow, for it was full of bundles of straw like rushes, stacked against the walls with brown mats hanging over them. Behind, the cave itself was encumbered with a quantity of things. Joseph cleared out as much as was necessary to make a comfortable resting-place for the Blessed Virgin at the eastern end of the cave. Then he fastened a burning lamp in the wall of the dark cave and led the Blessed Virgin in. She sat down on the couch of rugs and bundles which he had prepared. He apologized most humbly for the poorness of the shelter, but Mary was joyful and contented in her inmost spirit. As she rested there, Joseph hurried with a skin which he had brought with him into the valley-meadow behind the hill, where there was a tiny brook. He fastened the skin with two pegs under the spring so that the water had to run into it, and then brought it back to the cave. Then he went to the town and fetched little bowls, some fruit, and bundles of twigs. The Sabbath was approaching, and because of the many strangers in the town, who were in urgent need of all kinds of things, tables had been set up at the street corners where indispensable necessities could be bought at reduced prices. Those who sold were menservants or people who were not Jews. I cannot quite remember about this. Joseph came back bringing burning coals in a sort of closed metal basket with a handle like a stalk under it. He emptied these out by the entrance to the cave on the northern side and made a little fire. He had the fire-basket and other small utensils with him on the journey. The bundle of wood was of thin sticks neatly tied together with broad rushes. Joseph then prepared a meal: it consisted of a kind of porridge made from yellow grains and a cooked fruit, thick, and when opened for eating, full of seeds. There were also little flat loaves of bread. After they had eaten and prayed, Joseph prepared a sleeping-place for the Blessed Virgin. He first made a mattress of rushes, and then spread on it a coverlet of the kind I have described as having been prepared in Anna's house. At the head he put a rolled-up rug. After bringing in the pack-donkey and tying him up out of the way, he closed the openings in the roof to keep out the draught, and then prepared his own sleeping-place in the entrance. As the Sabbath had now begun, he stood with the Blessed Virgin under the lamp, reciting the Sabbath prayers with her, after which they ate their little meal in a spirit of great piety. Joseph then left the cave and went into the town, while Mary wrapped herself up to lie down to rest. During Joseph's absence I saw for the first time the Blessed Virgin kneeling in prayer. She knelt on her couch, and then lay down on the coverlet on her side. Her head rested on her arm, which lay on the pillow. Joseph did not come back till late. He was distressed and I think he wept. He prayed and then lay down meekly on his couch at the entrance of the cave.

[Sunday, November 24th:] Catherine Emmerich was very ill today and could communicate only the little that follows:]

The Blessed Virgin spent the Sabbath in the Cave of the Nativity in prayer and meditation and in great spiritual fervor. Joseph went out several times, probably to the synagogue in Bethlehem. I saw them sharing the food which had been prepared the day before, and praying together. In the afternoon of the Sabbath, when it is the Jewish custom to go for a walk, Joseph took the Blessed Virgin through the valley behind the cave to the tomb of Maraha, Abraham's nurse. They spent some time in this cave, which was roomier than the Cave of the Nativity, and in which Joseph had prepared a place for Our Lady to sit. The rest of the time they spent under the sacred tree near it, in prayer and meditation, until some time after the close of the Sabbath, when Joseph took her back again.

Mary had told St. Joseph that tonight at midnight would be the hour of the Child's birth, for then the nine months since the Annunciation would have been completed. She begged him to do all that was possible on his part so that they might show as much honor as they could to the Child promised by God and supernaturally conceived. She asked him, too, to join with her in praying for the hard-hearted people who had refused to give them shelter. Joseph suggested to the Blessed Virgin that he should summon to her assistance some pious women whom he knew in Bethlehem. She declined, however, saying that she needed no human help. Just before the close of the Sabbath Joseph went into Bethlehem, and as soon as the sun had set, he quickly bought a few necessary things—a stool, a little low table, a few little bowls, and some dried fruit and grapes. With them he hurried back to the cave and then to the tomb of Maraha, and took the Blessed Virgin back to the Cave of the Nativity, where she lay down on her couch in the easternmost corner. Joseph prepared some more food, and they ate and prayed together. He then completely divided off his sleeping-place from the rest of the cave by surrounding it with posts and hanging on them mats which he had found in the cave. He fed the donkey, which was standing to the left of the entrance against the wall of the cave; then he filled the manger above the crib with rushes and fine grass or moss, and spread a covering over it which hung down over the edge.

On the Blessed Virgin telling him that her time was drawing near and that he was to retire into his room and pray, he hung up some more burning lamps in the cave and went out, as he had heard a noise outside. Here he found the young she-ass, who until now had been wandering about loose in the valley of the shepherds. She came joyfully running up and gambolled round him. He tied her up under the shelter before the cave and strewed fodder before her.

When Joseph came back into the cave and stood at the entrance to his sleeping-place looking towards the Blessed Virgin, he saw her with her face turned towards the east, kneeling on the bed facing away from him. He saw her as it were surrounded by flames, the whole cave was as if filled with supernatural light. He gazed at her like Moses when he saw the burning bush; then he went into his little cell in holy awe and threw himself on his face in prayer.

X

THE BIRTH OF OUR LORD[1]

I SAW the radiance round the Blessed Virgin ever growing greater. The light of the lamps which Joseph had
lit was no longer visible. Our Lady knelt on her rug in
an ample ungirt robe spread out round her, her face
turned towards the east. At midnight she was wrapt
in an ecstasy of prayer. I saw her lifted from the earth,
so that I saw the ground beneath her. Her hands were
crossed on her breast. The radiance about her increased;
everything, even things without life, were in a joyful
inner motion, the stones of the roof, of the walls, and
of the floor of the cave became as it were alive in the
light. Then I no longer saw the roof of the cave; a
pathway of light opened above Mary, rising with ever-
increasing glory towards the height of Heaven. In this
pathway of light there was a wonderful movement of
glories interpenetrating each other, and, as they
approached, appearing more clearly in the form of choirs
of heavenly spirits. Meanwhile the Blessed Virgin, borne
up in ecstasy, was now gazing downwards, adoring her
God, whose Mother she had become and who lay on
the earth before her in the form of a helpless newborn
child.[2] I saw our Redeemer as a tiny Child, shining
with a light that overpowered all the surrounding radiance, and lying on the carpet at the Blessed Virgin's

---

1. *Matt.* 2:1; Birth, Adoration of the Shepherds, Circumcision: *Luke* 2:7-21. (SB)
2. AC's delicate description of the painless, miraculous birth of Christ finds parallels
   (especially in the cave being filled with light) in *Protev.* 19 and *Ps-Matt.* 13, though
   both these apocryphal sources introduce a midwife, whose services are not required.
   (SB)

knees. It seemed to me as if He were at first quite small and then grew before my eyes. But the movement of the intense radiance was such that I cannot say for certain how I saw it.

The Blessed Virgin remained for some time rapt in ecstasy. I saw her laying a cloth over the Child, but at first she did not touch Him or take Him up. After some time I saw the Child Jesus move and heard Him cry. Then Mary seemed to come to herself, and she took the Child up from the carpet, wrapping Him in the cloth which covered Him, and held Him in her arms to her breast. She sat there enveloping herself and the Child completely in her veil, and I think Mary suckled the Redeemer. I saw angels round her in human forms, lying on their faces and adoring the Child. It might have been an hour after His birth when Mary called St. Joseph, who was still lying in prayer. When he came near, he threw himself down on his face in devout joy and humility. It was only when Mary begged him to take to his heart, in joy and thankfulness, the holy present of the Most High God, that he stood up, took the Child Jesus in his arms, and praised God with tears of joy.

The Blessed Virgin then wrapped the Child Jesus in swaddling-bands. I cannot now remember how these bands were wound round; I only know that the Child was wrapped to His armpits first in red and then white bands, and that His head and shoulders were wrapped in another little cloth. Mary had only four sets of swaddling-bands with her. Then I saw Mary and Joseph sitting side by side on the bare earth with their feet under them. They did not speak, and seemed both to be sunk in meditation. On the carpet before Mary lay the newborn Jesus in swaddling-clothes, a little Child, beautiful and radiant as lightning. Ah, I thought, this place enshrines the salvation of the whole world, and no one guesses it. Then they laid the Child in the manger, which was filled with rushes and delicate plants and covered with a cloth hanging over the sides. It stood

above the stone trough lying on the ground, to the right
of the entrance, where the cave makes a big curve towards the south. This part of the cave was at a lower
level than the place where Our Lord was born: the floor
slanted downwards in a step-like formation. After laying the Child in the crib, they both stood beside Him
giving praise to God with tears of joy. Joseph then
arranged the Blessed Virgin's resting-place and her seat
beside the crib. Both before and after the Birth of Jesus,
I saw her dressed in white and veiled. I saw her there
in the first days after the Nativity, sitting, kneeling,
standing, and sleeping on her side, wrapped up but in
no way ill or exhausted. When people came to see her,
she wrapped herself up more closely and sat upright
on her lying-in coverlet.

In these pictures of Christ's birth, which I see as an
historical event and not as a Feast of the Church, I do
not see such radiant and ecstatic joy in nature as I do
on Christmas night when the vision that I see expresses
an interior significance. Yet I saw in this vision an
unwonted joy and an extraordinary movement at midnight in many places even to the uttermost parts of
the earth. I saw the hearts of many good men filled
with joyful yearning, while all the wicked were overcome by great fear. I saw many animals filled with joy;
in some places I saw flowers, herbs, and shrubs shoot-
ing up, and trees drinking in refreshment and scattering sweet scents. I saw many springs of water gush
forth and increase. In the night of the Saviour's Birth,
an abundant spring welled up in the cave in the hill
to the north of the Cave of the Nativity. Next day St.
Joseph captured it and made an outlet for it. The sky
was dull over Bethlehem and had a dull reddish glow;
but over the Cave of the Nativity and over the valley
by Maraha's tomb and the Shepherd's Valley lay a shining mist of dew. In the Shepherd's Valley there was a
hill about an hour and a half's journey from the Cave
of the Nativity, where the vineyards begin which stretch
from there towards Gaza. On this hill were the huts of

three shepherds who were the rulers of the shepherds' families in this region just as the three holy kings were rulers of the tribes belonging to them. About twice as far away from the Cave of the Nativity as this hill was the so-called Shepherds' Tower. This was a very high pyramid-shaped erection of wooden beams, built among green trees on a base of big stones on a hill in the midst of the fields. It was surrounded by stairs and galleries, and in places there were little covered stands like watch-towers. It was all hung with mats. It resembled those tower-like edifices which were used in the land of the three holy kings to observe the stars at night; from the distance it looked like a tall many-masted ship under sail. One had from it a very wide view of the whole region; one saw Jerusalem, and also the Mount of Temptation in the desert of Jericho. The shepherds stationed men up there to watch the flocks as they moved about and to give warning of danger by blowing horns if they saw in the distance robbers or armed bands. The families of the various shepherds lived round the tower within a circle of some five hours in circumference; their farms were separate and surrounded by fields and gardens. The tower was their general meeting-place, as it was also for the watchers, who kept their belongings here and got their food from here. There were huts built on the slopes of the hill on which the tower stood, and separate from these there was a large shed, divided into many partitions, where the wives of the watchers lived and prepared food for them. Here by the tower I saw tonight some of the flocks and herds out in the open, but by the hill of the three shepherds I saw them in a shed. When Jesus was born, I saw the three shepherds standing together before their hut, marvelling at the wonderful night. They looked about them, and were astonished to see a wonderful radiance over the place where the Cave of the Nativity was. I also saw the shepherds at the more distant tower in great commotion. I saw some of them climbing the tower and gazing at the strange radiance over the cave. As the three shepherds thus gazed up into the sky, I saw a cloud of light sinking down towards them. As it drew near, I perceived a movement in it, a changing and transformation into figures and forms, and I heard a song which gradually grew louder. It was sweet and gentle and yet clear and joyful. The shepherds were at first afraid, but forthwith an angel stood before them and spoke to them: "Fear not," he said, "for behold, I bring you good tidings of great joy that shall be to all the people; for this day is born to you a Saviour, who is Christ the Lord, in the city of David. And this shall be a sign unto you. You shall find the infant wrapped in swaddling-clothes and laid in a manger." While the angel was announcing this, the radiance round him increased, and I now saw five or seven beautiful great shining forms of angels standing before the shepherds. They were holding in their hands a long scroll on which was written something in letters as big as one's hand, and I heard them praising God and singing "Glory be to God in the highest: and on earth peace to men of good will." The shepherds at the tower saw the same vision, but somewhat later. The angels also appeared to a third party of shepherds near a spring three hours from Bethlehem and to the east of the Shepherd's Tower. I did not see the shepherds hasten at once to the Cave of the Nativity, which was about an hour and a half distant from the three shepherds and twice as far from the tower; but I saw them at once consulting together as to what they should bring as a present to the newborn Child, and getting their gifts together with all speed. They did not arrive at the Crib until early in the morning.

At the time that the Child Jesus was born my soul made countless journeys to all parts of the world, to see the wonderful happenings at the birth of Our Saviour. As, however, I was very ill and tired, it often seemed to me as if the pictures came to me instead of I to them. I have seen countless events, but have forgotten most of them because of much suffering and many disturbances; all that I can remember are the following fragments.

I saw last night that Noemi, the teacher of the Blessed Virgin, and the prophetess Anna, and the aged Simeon in the Temple, and Our Lady's mother, Anna, in Nazareth, and Elisabeth in Jutta, all had visions and revelations about the birth of the Saviour. I saw the child John, in Elisabeth's house, moved by wonderful joy. Though they all saw and recognized Mary in these visions, they did not know where the miracle had taken place, not even Elisabeth. Anna alone knew that Bethlehem was the place of salvation.

Last night I saw a wonderful happening in the Temple. All the written scrolls of the Sadducees were several times hurled out of their shelves and strewn about the floor. This caused great alarm; they ascribed it to sorcery and paid much money to keep it secret.

[She here recounted some obscure story about two sons of Herod's who were Sadducees and had been placed in the Temple by him;[3] and how he was always engaged in some dispute or other with the Pharisees and was always trying by underhand means to obtain more power in the Temple.]

I saw much in Rome last night, but of all the pictures I saw I have forgotten many and may easily have confused some of them. I will tell them as I remember them.

When Jesus was born, I saw that in Rome, on the other side of the river, where many Jews lived [she here described not very clearly a place like a hill surrounded by water, forming a kind of peninsula], a spring as of oil burst forth and caused general astonishment. A magnificent idol of Jupiter also broke in pieces in a temple of which the whole roof fell in. They made sacrifices in great alarm, and asked another idol—of Venus, I think—what this signified, and received the answer (which must have been spoken by the devil out of the

---

3. Herod's two sons, placed in the Temple, are mentioned by AC (*infra.,* p. 216) as natural sons. History is, however, silent in their regard. (SB)

mouth of the idol): "This befell because a virgin without a husband conceived a son and has now given birth to him." This idol spoke also of the fountain of oil that had sprung forth. Where it sprang forth, there now stands a church dedicated to the Mother of God.[4]

I saw the heathen priests consulting their records in great alarm. Seventy years before, when that idol was being magnificently adorned with gold and precious stones, and was being honored with solemn sacrifices, there lived in Rome a very good and pious woman (I am not sure whether she was a Jewess or not) whose name sounded like Serena or Cyrena. She had enough money to live on, saw visions, and was impelled to prophesy. I have forgotten a great deal about her, but I think she used often to tell people the cause of their unfruitfulness. This woman had openly proclaimed that such costly honors should not be paid to the idol, for one day it would burst asunder. The priests called her to account because of this declaration, and demanded that she should say when this would happen; and as she could not at once reply, she was imprisoned and tortured until she obtained by her prayers to God the reply that the idol would break in pieces when a pure virgin should bear a son. This announcement was received with derision, and she was released as being out of her senses. Now, when the collapse of the temple did indeed shatter the idol, they recognized that she had prophesied truly, and were

4. The tradition about strange portents in Rome at the birth of Christ is very ancient. Its first appearance in a document seems to be in the *Universal History* of Orosius (A.D. 418), the friend of St. Augustine. We find here the fountain of oil, the idol speaking, the vision of Augustus, and so forth. The story was elaborated by the time of the fourteenth-century Byzantine historian Nicephorus Callistus. The matter is fully studied in Graf, *Roma nella memoria e nelle immaginazioni del medio evo*, Turin, 1882, Vol. I, pp. 308-331, where the texts are reproduced.

The Church of Our Lady in question is *Santa Maria in Ara Coeli*, on the Capitol Hill, where Augustus is said to have put up a new altar *(infra, p. 205)*.

The mention *(infra, p. 205)* of the consul Lentulus need not be associated with the fictitious letter of Lentulus (a supposed Roman official in Judaea) about the appearance of Christ. But there was a consul Lucius Lentulus after the death of Julius Caesar (44 B.C.), mentioned by Josephus *(Ant., XIV, x, 13)*. Lentulus the friend of Peter in Rome is unknown, and is not likely to be Lentulus Getulicus who was involved in a plot against Caligula in A.D. 41 and was executed, since Peter probably did not come to Rome until A.D. 42. The priest Moses was one of the first martyrs under Decius, and died in 251. (Ramsgate *Book of Saints*). (SB)

astonished at her having fixed a time for this event. They knew of course nothing of Christ having been born of the Blessed Virgin.

I saw that both the Roman consuls called for reports about this event and about the appearance of the fountain of oil. One of the consuls was called Lentulus and was an ancestor of the martyred priest Moses and of the Lentulus who was a friend of St. Peter in Rome.

I also saw something connected with the Emperor Augustus, but can no longer remember it distinctly. I saw the Emperor with some other men on a hill in Rome, on the other side of which was the temple that had fallen in. There were steps leading up the hill, which had a golden gate on it. Business matters were settled there. When the Emperor descended the hill, he saw on the right-hand side, over the top of the hill, an apparition in the sky. It was a vision of a virgin above a rainbow, a child was soaring up from her. I think that only he saw it. He asked for an explanation of this apparition from an oracle that had long been dumb, and it gave an answer about a newborn child before whom all must give way. Thereupon he caused an altar to be set up on the hill over which he had seen the appearance, and dedicated it with many sacrifices to the Firstborn of God. I have forgotten much of all this.

I saw also in Egypt an event which proclaimed the birth of Christ. Far away in the country beyond Matarea, Heliopolis and Memphis, a great idol, which until then had uttered oracles of many kinds, fell suddenly silent. The king then ordered that great sacrifices should be offered throughout the country in order that the idol might explain its silence. The idol was thereupon obliged by God to say that it was silent and must give way because a virgin had given birth to a son, to whom a temple would here be erected. On hearing this, the king of that country decided to build a temple in his honor near the temple of the idol. I cannot clearly remember what happened, but I know that the idol was taken away and a temple was built here in honor of the virgin with the Child whom it had proclaimed, and that she was there honored after their heathen fashion.

At the hour when the Child Jesus was born I saw a wonderful vision which appeared to the three holy kings. These kings were star-worshippers and had a tower shaped like a pyramid with steps. It was made partly of timber and was on the top of a hill; one of them was always there, with several priests, to observe the stars. They always wrote down what they saw and communicated it to each other. On this night I think I saw two of the kings on this tower. The third, who lived to the east of the Caspian Sea, was not with them. They always observed one particular star, in which they saw various changes; they also saw visions in the sky. Last night I saw the picture which appeared to them; there were several variations of it. They did not see it in one star, but in a figure composed of several stars, and these stars were in motion. They saw a beautiful rainbow over the moon, which was in one of its quarters. Upon the rainbow a Virgin was enthroned; her right foot was resting on the moon. To the left of the Virgin, on the rainbow, was a vine, and on the right a sheaf of wheat. In front of the Virgin I saw the form of a chalice, shaped like the one used by Our Lord at the institution of the Blessed Sacrament. It seemed to rise up or to issue more clearly out of the radiance surrounding it. I saw a little child coming forth out of this chalice, and above the child a transparent disc, like an empty monstrance, from which rays like ears of wheat proceeded. It made me think of the Blessed Sacrament. On the right-hand side of the child issuing from the chalice a branch grew forth on which an octagonal church blossomed like a flower. It had a great golden gate and two small side-doors. The Virgin moved the chalice, the child, and the host with her right hand, guiding them into the church before her. I saw into it, and as I did so it seemed to become quite big. I saw an appearance of the Holy Trinity in the back of the church. The tower of the church rose above this appearance, which at last turned into a city radiant with light, like the heavenly Jerusalem. In this picture I saw many things developing out of each other as I looked into this church; but I can no longer remember in what order I saw them, nor can I recollect in what manner the kings were informed that the Child had been born in Judaea. The third king who lived farther away saw the same picture in his own home in the same hour. The kings were filled with inexpressible joy at this vision, and immediately gathered together their treasures and presents and began their journey. It was only after several days that all three met. Already in the days just before the birth of Christ I noticed that they were in a state of great activity on their observatory tower and saw visions of many kinds.

How great was God's compassion towards the heathen! Shall I tell you from whence this prophecy came to the kings? I will recount now only just the end of it, for at this moment I cannot remember the whole. The ancestors of the three kings, from whom they descended in an unbroken line from father to son, lived as long ago as five hundred years before Christ's birth. (Elias[5] must have lived eight hundred years before Christ.) Their ancestors were richer and more powerful than the three kings, for their possessions and inheritances had not been so much divided up as later on. Even in those times they lived in cities of tents—except the ancestor to the east of the Caspian Sea, whose city I now see; its foundations are of stone and the tents are set up on these, for it lies beside the sea, which often overflows. (Here on the mountains one is so high up; I see a sea to my right and one to my left; it is like looking into a black hole.) These chieftains were already at that time star-worshippers; but besides that they practised dreadfully evil ceremonies; they sacrificed old men and cripples and slaughtered children as well. The most cruel of all their practices was to put the children,

---

5. Elias makes his appearance in *3 Kgs.* 17:1 in the reign of King Achab, 874-853 B.C. (SB)

dressed in white, into cauldrons, and to boil them alive. But at last all this was changed for the better, and in spite of it God allowed these blind heathens to know of the birth of the Redeemer so long beforehand. In those days three daughters of these early chieftains were living at the same time. They were learned in the science of the stars, and all received at the same time the spirit of prophecy.

They all three saw at the same time in a vision that a star should rise out of Jacob and that a virgin should give birth to the Saviour without knowing man. They wore long cloaks, and went about the whole country preaching amendment of life and announcing that the messengers of the Redeemer would one day come to them and bring them the ceremonies of the true religion. They also prophesied many things about our own and even later times. The fathers of these three virgins then built a temple in honor of the future Mother of God to the south of the sea, where their three countries met, and made sacrifices to her—some of them in that cruel manner of which I have spoken. The prophecies of the three virgins included something definite about a picture in the stars and various transformations in it: whereupon they began to look for this picture from a hill near the temple to the future Mother of God. They took note of everything and according to what they observed they kept on making various alterations on and in their temples, in their ceremonies and in their decorations. They varied the color of the tent-roof of the temple, which was sometimes blue, sometimes red, and sometimes yellow or still another color. They transferred (and this seemed to me remarkable) their weekly feast-day to the Sabbath. Before it used to be Thursday, and I still remember its name. [Here she stammered something which sounded like Tanna or Tanada, but was not clearly audible.][6]

6. Here her story was interrupted by so strange and sudden an occurrence that we feel bound to communicate it, so characteristic is it of her condition. It was about six o'clock in the evening of Nov. 27th, 1821, when she spoke these last words in her sleep. It must be remembered that for many years her feet had been paralyzed;

[In the course of her visions of Christmas night Catherine Emmerich saw much that indicated the exact date of Christ's birth, but she forgot a great deal of it owing to illness and the disturbance of receiving visitors on the following day, which was her name-day, the feast of St. Catherine. That evening, however, shortly after these visits, she repeatedly gave utterance, in a state of trance, to the following fragments of these visions. It should be noted that she sees all dates written in Roman figures, i.e. with letters; and finds some difficulty in reading them; though she nearly always

she could not walk, and could with difficulty raise herself to a sitting position, so that she was, as always, lying stretched out on her couch. The door stood open between her room and the room adjoining it in which her confessor was at that moment sitting by the lamp reading his Breviary. She had just said these words with such truth of expression that it was impossible to doubt that she was seeing it all actually happening before her eyes. Hardly, however, had she stammered out the word "Tanada" than the enfeebled and paralyzed sleeper suddenly sprang up from her couch with lightning speed, hurried into the adjoining room, and rushed to the window, striking out with hands and feet as if she were attacking and warding off something. Then, turning to her confessor, she said, "That was a great big brute, but I gave him a kick and sent him off." After these words she sank down as if fainting, and lay very quietly and calmly on the floor of the room before the window. The priest at his Breviary was, like the writer, staggered by this highly surprising incident, but without wasting words he said to her, "Sister Emmerich, under obedience, go back to your bed"; whereupon she at once got up, returned to her room, and lay down again on her bed.

When the writer asked her, "What was that strange incident?" she told him the following. She was wide awake and in full consciousness, and though she was tired, she was in the cheerful state of mind of someone who has won a victory. "Yes, it was indeed odd. I was so far, far away in the land of the three kings. I was standing on the high mountain ridge between the two seas, looking down into their tent-cities (just as one looks out of the window here into the poultry-yard), when I suddenly felt myself called home by my guardian angel. I turned round and saw here in Dülmen, passing in front of our little house, a poor old woman whom I knew. She had come out of a little grocer's shop. She was in a very bad and evil-tempered mood, and was grumbling and cursing to herself in a quite abominable way. Then I saw that her guardian angel abandoned her and that a great black devil-shape laid itself across her path in the dark, to make her stumble over him and break her neck and so die in her sins. When I saw that, I let the three kings be (*'liess ich drei Könige drei Könige sein'*), prayed earnestly to God to help the poor woman, and was back here in my room. Then I saw that the devil was beating against the window in dreadful fury and was trying to break into the room; I saw that he had a whole bundle of nooses and knotted strings in his claws. He was trying, out of revenge, to start a great complication and annoyance here with all these; so I rushed at him and gave him a kick which made him stagger back. That will have given him something to remember! And then I lay down before the window across his path, to prevent him from coming in."

It is indeed strange that while she is looking down from the Caucasus and seeing and recounting things that happened five hundred years before Christ's birth as though they were before her eyes, she should at the same moment see the danger surrounding a poor little old woman close to her house at home and should hurry energetically to help her. It was an amazing spectacle to see her rushing in like a living skeleton and fighting with such violence, whereas in her waking state, she can, since Sept. 8th, hardly move forward a few steps on her crutches without fainting. (CB)

makes herself clear by repeating them several times
in the order in which they appear or by showing them
on her fingers. Today she did both. This is what she
said:]

Now, you can read this: look, there it is: Christ was
born when the year of the world 3997 was not yet
quite completed. Afterwards people forgot the period
of three years and a portion of a year which inter-
vened between His birth and the year 4000, and then
reckoned our new era as beginning four years later,
so that Christ was born seven years and a portion of
a year earlier than according to our reckoning.[7] One
of the consuls in Rome at that time was called Lentulus; he was an ancestor of the priest and martyr Moses,
of whom I possess a relic here, and who lived at the
time of St. Cyprian. The Lentulus who was a friend
of St. Peter in Rome also descended from him. Christ
was born in the forty-fifth year of the Emperor Augustus. Herod reigned forty years in all until his death.[8]
He was, it is true, only a vassal-king for seven years,
but harassed the country grievously and committed
many cruelties. He died about the time of Christ's sixth
year. I think that his death was kept a secret for some
time. His end was dreadful, and in the last days of his
life he was responsible for many murders and much
misery. I saw him crawling about in a room padded
with cushions. He had a spear, and stabbed at anyone
who came near him. Jesus must have been born about
the thirty-fourth year of Herod's reign. Two years before

---

7. The date of Christ's birth is usually fixed by modern scholars in 8 B.C. (e.g. Fr. T.
Corbishley, S.J., in *Cath. Comm.*, 676a), or at latest 6-4 B.C. (*ib.*, 749a), but the
argument is from contemporary history (such as the death of Herod in 4 B.C.), and
not, as AC suggests, from the computation of the Annus Mundi. Yet it is interesting that AC's date 7 B.C. is so near the conclusions of present-day studies. (SB)

8. The chronological data are fairly exact by modern conclusions. The forty-fifth year
of Augustus is reckoned (as was the custom among the older historians, e.g. Mura-
tori in 1744-1749) from his assumption of power as a triumvir in 44 B.C., and cor-
responds therefore to A.D. 1 (though AC had just said that Christ was born in 7
B.C.). Herod reigned 40-4 B.C. (thirty-six years—AC says forty), and AC gives his
thirty-fourth year for the birth of Christ, i.e. 6 B.C. There is therefore some confusion in the correlation of the data.

For Herod's madness, cf. Josephus *Ant.*, XVII, vi, 5 to viii, I. (SB)

the entry of Mary into the Temple, just seventeen years before the Birth of Christ, Herod ordered that work should be done in the Temple.[9] It was not a rebuilding of the Temple, but alterations and embellishments were made here and there. The Flight into Egypt took place when Christ was nine months old, and the Massacre of the Innocents was in His second year.

[She mentioned, in addition, many other things—incidents, features, and journeys—from Herod's life, which showed how clearly she saw everything, but it was impossible to collect and arrange these very numerous communications, some of which she recounted only in fragments.]

The Birth of Christ occurred in a year which the Jews reckoned as having thirteen months. This must have been some such arrangement as our leap-years.[10] I think I have forgotten something about the Jews having months of twenty-one and twenty-two days twice a year. I heard something about feastdays connected with this, but have only a dim recollection of it all. I also saw how at different times something was altered in their calendar. It was after their coming out of a captivity, and the Temple was being added to at the same time. I saw the man who altered the calendar and I knew his name. [Here she tried to remember and said in her low German dialect with a smiling pretence of impatience, "I can't remember the fellow's name."] I

---

9. Josephus tells us *(Ant.,* XV, xi, I) that Herod began the rebuilding of the Temple in his eighteenth year, i.e. 20-19 B.C., and that work continued for one and a half years *(ib.,* 6). The Gospel *(John* 2:20), referring to the beginning of Our Lord's ministry, A.D. 29, mentions forty-six years of the Temple, which would give the date 17 B.C., perhaps, for its completion. Perhaps AC's "seventeen years before the birth of Christ" can be understood as 17 B.C., but there is a slight confusion here. (SB)

10. The twelve Hebrew lunar months (of alternatively twenty-nine and thirty days) gave a year of 354 days, so that every few years an error accumulated which was corrected by the insertion after the twelfth month, Adar, of a thirteenth or "intercalary" month, called Second Adar. The need for this intercalation was, at the time of Christ, still determined empirically, in such a way that the celebration of the Pasch at the full moon or fourteenth day of the first month, Nisan, should always occur after the spring equinox (Mar. 21st). The intercalary month was of the same length as the other months, running from new moon to new moon. (Cf. Schürer, *The Jewish People in the Time of Christ,* I, ii, 369 sqq.) AC herself admitted the likelihood of confusion on her part about this technical matter. (SB)

think Christ was born in the month Kislev.[11] The reason why the Church keeps the feast exactly a month
later than the actual event is because at one time, when
an alteration in the calendar was made, some days and
seasons were completely omitted.[12] I once saw it very
plainly, but can no longer recall it properly.

[Sunday, November 25th (morning):] In the early dawn
after Christ's birth the three chief shepherds came from
their hill to the Cave of the Nativity with their presents, which they had gathered together beforehand.
These presents were little animals not unlike roe-deer.
If they were kids, those in that country look very different from ours here at home. They had long necks,
very clear beautiful eyes, and were very swift and grace-
ful. The shepherds led them behind and beside them
on long, thin cords. The shepherds also had strings of
dead birds hanging over their shoulders, and carried
some bigger live birds under their arms. When they
knocked shyly at the door of the cave, St. Joseph came
towards them with a friendly greeting. They told him
what the angel had announced to them that night, and
how they were come to worship the Child of the Promise
and to present their poor gifts to Him. Joseph took
their gifts with humble gratitude, and made them take
the animals into the little chamber the entrance of
which is by the southern door of the cave. Then he
accompanied them into the cave itself, and led the three
shepherds up to the Blessed Virgin, who was sitting on
the coverlet on the ground by the Crib, holding the
Child Jesus before her on her lap. The shepherds, holding their staffs in their hands, threw themselves humbly
on their knees before Jesus, weeping for joy. They remained a long time speechless with bliss and then sang

---

11. Kislev was the ninth month, corresponding approximately to our Nov./Dec., and
    according to AC *(infra,* p. 247) Christ was born on the 12th Kislev, which that
    year was Nov. 25th. (SB)
12. The calendar was adjusted in 1582, when by order of Pope Gregory XIII ten days
    were omitted, so that the day following Oct. 4th in that year was Oct. 15th, and
    thus the spring equinox was restored to Mar. 21st. The ten days' error was the
    accumulation since the previous adjustment at Nicaea in A.D. 325 (cf. Breviary,
    De Anno et ejus partibus). (SB)

the angels' hymn of praise which they had heard in the night, and a psalm which I have forgotten. When they got up to go away, the Blessed Virgin put the little Jesus into their arms one after the other. They gave Him back to her with tears and left the cave.

[Sunday, November 25th (evening): During the whole day Catherine Emmerich was in great distress of body and mind. She had hardly fallen asleep in the evening when she at once felt herself transported to the Promised Land. During this year she had been also contemplating the first year of Our Lord's ministry, and particularly His forty-days' fast, and she exclaimed in childlike wonder: "What a moving sight! On one side I see Jesus as a man thirty years of age fasting and tempted in a cave in the wilderness, and on the other I see Him as a newborn child in the Cave of the Nativity, adored by the shepherds from the shepherds' tower." After these words the visionary rose from her couch with astonishing rapidity, ran to the open door of her room and called in an ecstasy of joy to some friends who were in the outer room: "Come quickly, quickly to adore the Child, He is in my room." She returned as rapidly to her couch, and began, quivering with rapture and devotion, to sing in a clear, inexpressibly moving voice the *Magnificat, Gloria in Excelsis,* and some other unknown hymns of praise. These were simple but profound and were partly in rhyme. In one hymn she sang second. She was in an unusually joyful and excited mood and said next morning:]

Yesterday evening several shepherds and shepherdesses and children from the Shepherds' Tower, which is four hours away, came to the Crib with presents. They brought eggs, birds, honey, woven stuffs of different colors, little bunches of what looked like raw silk, and bushes of a rush-like shrub with big leaves and ears full of thick grains. After handing their presents to St. Joseph, they came up humbly to the Crib, beside which the Blessed Virgin sat. They greeted her and the Child, and then, kneeling round her, they sang some lovely hymns, the *Gloria in Excelsis,* and a few short verses. I sang with them; they sang in parts. In one of the hymns I sang second. I remember the words more or less: "O little child, red as a rose, like a herald comest thou forth." When they made their farewell, they bent over the Crib as though they were kissing the Infant Jesus.

[November 26th:] Today I saw the three shepherds taking it in turns to help St. Joseph to arrange things more comfortably in the cave, round about it and in the side caves. I also saw several devout women with Our Lady, assisting her in various ways. These women were Essenes, and lived not far from the cave, as you went round to the east of the hill. They lived near each other in the deep part of the valley, in little chambers high up in the rock at a place where the hill had broken away. They had small gardens beside their dwellings and gave lessons to children belonging to their sect. St. Joseph had asked them to come; he knew this community since his childhood, for when as a boy he hid himself from his brothers in the Cave of the Nativity, he sometimes visited these pious women in their rock-dwellings. They took it in turns to come to the Blessed Virgin, bringing her bundles of wood and other small necessities, and cooking and washing for the Holy Family.

[November 27th:] Today I saw a very touching scene in the cave. Joseph and Mary were standing by the Crib, looking at the Infant Jesus with great devotion, when the donkey threw himself suddenly on his knees and bent his head down to the ground. Mary and Joseph wept. In the evening came messengers from Anna, Our Lady's holy mother. An elderly man and Anna's maid-servant, a widow who was related to her, arrived from Nazareth. They brought all kinds of little things which Mary needed. They were greatly moved at seeing the Infant, and the old manservant wept tears of joy. He soon started home again to bring Anna news. The maid-servant remained with the Blessed Virgin.

[November 28th:] Today I saw the Blessed Virgin with the Infant Jesus and the maidservant leaving the cave for several hours. I saw that after coming out of the door she turned to the right under the projecting thatched roof, then took a few steps and hid herself in the side cave. This was the cave where the fountain of water sprang up at Christ's birth and was captured by Joseph. She remained four hours in this cave, but later she spent a few days there. Joseph had been there at dawn to make a few arrangements for her comfort. They were given an inner warning to go there, for today there came to the cave from Bethlehem some men, emissaries of Herod, I think, because of the rumor, spread abroad by the shepherds' talk, that some wonderful thing had happened there connected with a child. I saw these men exchanging a few remarks with St. Joseph, whom they met in front of the Cave of the Nativity in the company of the shepherds. When they saw how poor and simple he was, they left him with supercilious smiles. The Blessed Virgin remained with the Infant Jesus about four hours in the side-cave, and then returned to the Crib. The Cave of the Nativity is pleasantly situated and very quiet. No one comes here from Bethlehem, except the shepherds whose duties bring them here. In general no one in Bethlehem pays any attention to what happens out here, for owing to the many strangers there is a great press of people coming and going in the town. There is much buying and slaughtering of beasts, as many of the people present pay their taxes with beasts. There are also many heathen there, who work as servants.

[This evening Catherine Emmerich said suddenly in her sleep: "Herod has had a pious man murdered who had an important post in the Temple. He invited him most warmly to visit him at Jericho and had him murdered on the way. He was opposed to Herod's pretensions regarding the Temple. In spite of Herod being accused of this murder, his power over the Temple increases." She again insisted that Herod had appointed two of his natural sons to high places in the Temple; that these were Sadducees and that they betrayed to him everything that went on there.]

[November 29th:] Early this morning the friendly innkeeper from the last inn, in which the Holy Family spent the night from November 22nd-23rd, sent a servant with presents to the cave, and in the course of the day he came himself to worship the Child. The appearance of the angels to the shepherds in the hour of Christ's birth has made the story of the wonderful Child of the Promise known to all good folk here in the valleys, and these people have come to worship the Child whom they had sheltered unknown to themselves.

[November 30th:] Today several shepherds and other good people came to the Cave of the Nativity and worshipped the Infant Jesus with great fervor. They were dressed in their best and were on their way to Bethlehem for the Sabbath. Among these people I saw the surly shepherd's good wife, who had given shelter to the Holy Family on November 20th. She might have taken a more direct road from her home to go to Jerusalem for the Sabbath, but she made a detour by Bethlehem in order to pay respect to the Holy Child and His dear parents. The good woman was full of happiness at having shown them loving-kindness. Today I also saw St. Joseph's relations, near whose dwelling the Holy Family had passed the night of November 22nd, come to the cave and greet the Child. Among them was the father of that Jonadab who at the Crucifixion brought Jesus a cloth to cover His nakedness. He had heard from the innkeeper of his village about Joseph's journey through the place and about the wonderful happenings at the birth of the Child, and had come here with presents for Him on his way to the Sabbath at Bethlehem. He greeted Mary and worshipped the Infant Jesus. Joseph was very friendly with him; he accepted nothing from him, but gave him the young she-ass (who had been running free with them) as a pledge, on condition that he could redeem her on repayment of the money. Joseph needed the money to pay for the presents and the meal at the circumcision ceremony. After Joseph had finished this business and everybody had gone to the synagogue in Bethlehem, he hung up in the cave the Sabbath lamp with seven wicks, lit it, and put beneath it a table covered with a red-and-white cloth on which lay prayer-scrolls. Here under the lamp he celebrated the eve of the Sabbath, reciting prayers with the Blessed Virgin and Anna's maidservant.[13] Two shepherds stood farther back in the entrance of the cave. The Essene women were also present, and afterwards they prepared the meal. Today, the eve of the Sabbath, the Essene women and the maidservant prepared several dishes for the next day. I saw the plucked and cleaned birds being roasted on a spit over the glowing embers. While roasting them they rolled them in a kind of flour made by pounding grains which grew in the ears of a rush-like plant. This plant grows wild only in damp, marshy places in that country and on the sunny side. In some places it is cultivated. It grows wild near Bethlehem and Hebron, but I never saw it near Nazareth. The shepherds of the tower had brought some of it to Joseph. I saw them making the grains into a thick shiny white paste, and they also baked cakes with the flour. I saw open holes under the fireplace, very hot, where they baked cakes as well as birds and other things. They kept for themselves very little of the many provisions given by the shepherds to St. Joseph. Most of it went as presents and as food for others, especially for the poor. Tomorrow evening, during the meal at the circumcision ceremony, there will be a great distribution.

---

13. The ritual of lighting the Sabbath lamp on Friday evening is described in the Mishnah, *Shabbath*, II, 5-7; III, 6. The Mosaic prohibition of making fire on the Sabbath is in *Exod.* 35:3. (SB)

THE CIRCUMCISION

[DECEMBER 1ST:] This afternoon I saw several more people who were keeping the Sabbath come to the Cave of the Nativity, and in the evening, after the Sabbath was over, I saw the Essene women and Mary's maidservant preparing a meal in an arbor in front of the entrance to the cave. Joseph had begun to put up this arbor with the shepherds several days before. He had also cleared out his room at the entrance to the cave, covering the floor with rugs and decorating everything as festively as his poverty allowed. He had made all these arrangements before the Sabbath began, for tomorrow at daybreak is the eighth day from the birth of Christ, when the child must be circumcised according to God's commandment. Towards evening Joseph had gone to Bethlehem, and returned with three priests, an elderly man, and a woman who seemed to act as a kind of nurse at this solemn ceremony. She brought with her a chair specially kept for these occasions, and a thick octagonal stone slab containing what was necessary. All these things were put down on mats spread out at the place where the ceremony was to take place. This was at the entrance to the cave, not far from the Crib, between the partition lately removed by Joseph and the hearth-place. The chair was really a box and could be drawn out to form a sort of low couch with an arm at one side. It was covered with red material. It was more for lying than sitting on. The octagonal stone slab must have been over two feet in diameter. In its center there was an octagonal cavity covered with a metal plate; in it were three boxes and a stone knife in separate compartments. This stone slab was placed beside the chair on a three-legged stool, which until now had always stood, covered with a cloth, on the place where Our Lord was born. When all had been arranged, the priests greeted the Blessed Virgin and the Infant Jesus. They spoke friendly words to her and took the Child in their arms with emotion. A meal was

then eaten in the arbor before the entrance, and a crowd
of poor people (who, as always happens on such occasions, had followed the priests) surrounded the table
and were given presents throughout the meal by Joseph
and the priests, so that soon everything was distributed. I saw the sun go down; it looked bigger than here
at home. I saw its low rays shining through the open
door into the Cave of the Nativity.

[Sunday, December 2nd. She does not mention
whether after yesterday's meal the priests again
returned to the town and did not come back till next
morning, or whether they passed the night at or near
the cave:] There were lamps lit in the cave and I saw
them often praying and singing during the night. The
circumcision took place at dawn, eight days after the
birth of Our Lord.[14] The Blessed Virgin was distressed
and anxious. She had herself prepared the little cloths
to catch the blood and to bandage the Child and had
kept them at her breast in a fold of her mantle. The
octagonal stone slab was covered by the priests first with
red and then with white. This was accompanied by
prayers and ceremonies. One of the priests then placed
himself in the chair, leaning back rather than sitting
in it, while the Blessed Virgin, who was veiled and
holding the Infant Jesus in her arms at the back of the
cave, handed the Child to the maidservant together
with the bandages. St. Joseph took Him from the maidservant and gave Him to the nurse who had come with
the priests. She laid the little Jesus, covered with a
veil, upon the cloth on the octagonal stone slab.

Prayers were again offered, then the woman
unwrapped the Child from His swaddling-clothes and
placed Him on the lap of the priest in the chair. St.
Joseph bent down over the priest's shoulders and held
the upper part of the Child's body. Two priests knelt
to right and left, each holding one of the Child's feet:

---

14. The conduct of the rite is accurately described (cf. *Jewish Encyc.,* art. "Circumcision," pp. 95 sqq.), though it seems that the *mohel* was usually a surgeon rather
than a priest. (SB)

the one who was to perform the holy ceremony knelt before the Child. The cover was removed from the stone to disclose the three boxes with healing ointments and lotions. The handle and the blade of the knife were both of stone. The smooth brown handle had a groove into which the blade could be shut down; the latter was of the yellow color of raw silk, and did not seem to me to be sharp. The cut was made with the hook-shaped point of the blade, which when opened must have been nine inches long. The priest also made use of his sharp fingernails for the operation. Afterwards he dabbed it with healing lotion and some soothing substance from the boxes. The part that was cut off he placed between two round discs of some precious material, shining and reddish-brown in color, and slightly hollowed out in the center, making a kind of flat box. This was handed to the Blessed Virgin. The nurse now took the Child, bandaged Him and wrapped Him again in His swaddling-clothes. Up till now these, which were red beneath and white above, had been wound round up to under the arms. Now the little arms were also wrapped round, and the veil was wrapped round His head instead of covering it. He was then again laid on the octagonal slab of stone, which was covered with its cloths, and more prayers were said over Him. Although I know that the angel had told Joseph that the child was to be called Jesus, yet I remember that the priest did not at once approve of this name, and therefore fell to praying. I then saw a shining angel appear before the priest, holding before his eyes a tablet (like that on the Cross) with the name of Jesus. I do not know whether he or any of the other priests saw this angel as I did, but he was awestruck, and I saw him writing this name by divine inspiration on a parchment.

The Infant Jesus wept loudly after the sacred ceremony, and I saw that He was given back to St. Joseph. He laid Him in the arms of the Blessed Virgin, who was standing with two women in the back of the cave.

She wept as she took Him, and withdrew into the corner where the Crib was. Here she sat down, wrapped in her veil and soothed the crying Infant by giving Him her breast. Joseph also gave her the little bloodstained cloths: the nurse kept the little bloody shreds of stuff that remained. Prayers were again said and hymns sung; the lamp was still burning, but day was breaking. After a while the Blessed Virgin came forward herself with the Child and laid Him down on the octagonal stone; the priests held out their hands to her, crossed over the Child. After this she retired, taking the Child with her. Before the priests left, taking with them all that they had brought, they ate a light meal in the arbor with Joseph and a few shepherds who had been standing at the entrance to the cave. I learnt that all those who took part in this holy ceremony were good people, and that the priests were later enlightened and obtained salvation. During the whole morning generous presents were given to poor people who came to the door. During the ceremony the donkey was tied up farther away. Today crowds of dirty, swarthy beggars went past the cave, carrying bundles, coming from the Valley of the Shepherds. They seemed to be going to Jerusalem for some feast. They were very violent in demanding alms, and cursed and raged horribly at the Crib because they were not satisfied with Joseph's presents. I do not know what was wrong with these people; I felt a great dislike for them. Today the nurse came again to the Blessed Virgin and bandaged the Infant Jesus. In the night that followed I saw the Child often restless with pain and crying a great deal. Mary and Joseph took Him in their arms in turns, carrying Him about and comforting Him.

[December 3rd:] This evening I saw Elisabeth coming from Jutta to the Cave of the Nativity. She was riding on a donkey led by an aged manservant. Joseph received her very warmly, and she and Mary embraced each other with intense joy. She pressed the Infant Jesus to her heart with tears. Her couch was prepared beside the place where Jesus was born. In front of this place there stood sometimes a high stand like a sawing-trestle, with a little box on it. They often laid the Infant Jesus in this box, standing round Him in prayer and caressing Him. This must be the custom there, for I saw in Anna's house the child Mary lying on a similar stand. Elisabeth and Mary talked to each other in the sweetest intimacy.

[December 4th:] Yesterday evening and again today I saw Mary and Elisabeth sitting together in sweet converse, and I felt myself to be with them and heard all their talk with heartfelt joy. The Blessed Virgin told her everything that had happened to her, and when she described their difficulty in finding a lodging in Bethlehem, Elisabeth wept in sympathy. She also told her much about the birth of the Infant Jesus, and I can remember something of this. She said that at the time of the Annunciation she had lost consciousness for ten minutes and had felt as if her heart had grown to double its size and as if she were filled with inexpressible grace. At the hour of the Birth of Christ she had been full of endless yearning, and had been rapt in ecstasy, feeling as though she were uplifted, kneeling, by angels; then she had felt as though her heart was split in twain, and that one half had gone from her. She had remained thus for ten minutes without consciousness, then she had had a feeling of inner emptiness and an intense yearning for an infinite salvation outside herself, whereas before she had always felt that it was within her. She had then seen a glow of light before her, in which the form of her Child seemed to grow before her eyes. Then she had seen His movements and heard His crying, and coming to herself, had taken Him up from the ground to her breast. At first she had been as in a dream, and had not dared to lift up the little Child surrounded with radiance. She also said that she had not been conscious of having given birth to the Child. Elisabeth said to her: "You have been more favored in giving birth than other women: the

birth of John was a joy indeed, but it was otherwise
than with you." That is all that I remember of their
talk.

Today I saw many people visiting the Blessed Virgin and the Infant Jesus. I also saw a lot of ill-behaved
folk like the day before going by and stopping at the
door to demand alms, cursing and raging. Joseph did
not give them any presents this time. Towards evening
Mary again hid herself with the Infant Jesus and Elisabeth in the cave at the side of the Cave of the Nativity, and I think Mary remained there the whole night.
This happened because all kinds of inquisitive and
important people from Bethlehem crowded to the Crib,
and the Blessed Virgin did not wish to be seen by them.

Today I saw the Blessed Virgin leave the Cave of the
Nativity with the Infant Jesus and go into another cave
to the right of it. The entrance was very narrow, and
fourteen steep steps led down first into a small cellar-
like chamber and then into a vaulted chamber which
was more spacious than the Cave of the Nativity. The
space near the entrance was semicircular, and Joseph
divided this off by a hanging curtain, leaving a rectangular room beyond. The light fell not from above but
through side-openings pierced in the thick rock. During the last few days I saw an old man clearing out of
this cave a lot of brushwood and bundles of straw or
rushes such as Joseph used for kindling. It must have
been a shepherd who helped in this way. This cave was
lighter and more spacious than the Cave of the Nativity. The donkey was not kept here. I saw the Infant
Jesus lying here in a hollowed trough on the ground.
In the last few days I often saw Mary showing her
Child to visitors who came singly. He was covered with
a veil, but otherwise had nothing on but a bandage
round His body. At other times I saw the little Child
all swaddled up again. I see the nurse often visiting
the Child. Mary gave her a generous share of the gifts
brought by the visitors, which she distributed amongst
the needy in Bethlehem.

XI

THE JOURNEY OF THE THREE HOLY KINGS TO BETHLEHEM[1]

[Catherine Emmerich had already, in the course of 1819 and 1820, communicated a series of visions of the three holy kings' journey to Bethlehem; but as at that time she was following the dates of the feasts of the Church in her contemplations, the period of thirteen days from Christmas to the Epiphany was too short for their long journey, and she communicated only some descriptions of single halting-places. As, however, in 1821 she dated the day of Christ's birth a month earlier, that is to say on November 25th, and saw the departure of the kings for Judaea on that day, there remained a space of about a month's time for the journey. She said, in defining its length, "I always saw the kings approaching Bethlehem when I was putting out the Crib in the convent"—that is to say, about December 25th.]

[NOVEMBER 25TH:] I have already related on Christmas Day how I saw the Birth of Christ being announced to the kings on Christmas night. I saw Mensor and the dark-skinned Sair gazing at the stars from a field in Mensor's country.[2] Everything was prepared for their departure. They were on a pyramid-shaped tower looking through long tubes at the Star of Jacob, which had

---

1. Communicated in 1821. *Matt.* 2:1-12.
2. The names of the three kings as given by AC, Mensor, Sair, and Theokeno, find no documentary parallel, nor is there anywhere any information about their homelands or their subsequent history *(infra,* p. 238). The apocryphal *Protev.* 21 adds nothing to St. Matthew's account. For latter names, see n. 7, p. 235. (SB)

a tail. The star split asunder before their eyes, and I saw a great shining virgin appear therein, before whom a radiant child hovered in the air. At his right hand a branch grew forth, bearing, like a flower, a little tower with several entrances. This tower was finally transformed into a city. I cannot remember the picture completely. Immediately after seeing this picture they both started off. Theokeno, the third king, lived a few days' journey farther to the east. He saw the same star-picture in the same hour, and set off at once in great haste in order to overtake his two friends quickly, which he succeeded in doing.

[November 26th: I went to sleep with a great longing to be with the Mother of God in the Cave of the Nativity, and to be given by her the Infant Jesus to hold in my arms for a little and to press Him to my heart. I did come there, at night. Joseph was asleep behind his partition to the right of the entrance, his head resting on his right arm. Mary sat at her usual place beside the Crib; she was awake, and held the Infant Jesus to her breast under her veil. When she sat watching in the daytime, a piece of her coverlet was rolled up to make a pillow behind her back as a support; now, at night, she lay back on her couch so that her head was lower. I fell on my knees and prayed with great longing that I might hold the Child for a little. Ah, she knew well what I wanted: she knows everything and accepts everything with such loving, touching sympathy if one prays with real faith; but she was so still, so quiet and so full of adoring mother-love, and she did not give me the Child—I think because she was suckling Him. I would not have either. But my longing increased continually, and joined in the stream of longing of all the souls who yearn for the Infant Jesus. This burning desire for Our Saviour was, however, nowhere so pure, innocent, childlike, and true as in the hearts of the beloved holy kings from the East, all of whose ancestors had for centuries waited for Him, in faith, hope, and love. So my longing drew me then to them,

and when I had finished my adoration, I crept softly
and reverently out of the cave, so as to make no disturbance, and was taken on a long journey, in the train
of the three holy kings. On this journey I saw many
things—many strange countries and dwellings and
many different peoples, their clothes and their manners and customs as well as many idolatrous ceremonies
that they performed; but I have forgotten most of it. I
will relate as well as I can what still remains clear in
my memory.

I was taken eastwards to a region where I had never
been before. It was mostly sand and desert. On some
of the hills lived people in groups of five to eight, like
families, inhabiting huts made of brushwood. The brushwood roof was built against the hill out of which the
living-rooms were hollowed. On going in, I saw that the
huts were divided into rooms by partitions. The front
and back rooms were larger than the central ones. Nothing at all grew in that region but low bushes, and here
and there a little tree bearing buds out of which the
people pulled white wool. Besides these I saw a few
larger trees under which they had placed their idols.
These men must have been still in a very wild state,
for they seemed to me to eat little but meat, and even
the raw flesh of birds. They seemed to live partly by
robbery. They were as dark as copper and had foxy yellow hair. They were small, thick-set, and rather fat, but
very skillful, agile, and active. They seemed to have no
domestic animals and no flocks or herds. They wore, I
saw, but little clothing. The men had short aprons hanging in folds under their girdle before and behind, and
wore on their breast a sort of narrow diagonally ribbed
scapulary, fastened across the shoulders and round the
neck. This narrow breast-covering seemed to be elas-
tic and could be pulled out longer. Their whole back
down to the girdle was uncovered except for the strap
across the shoulders. On their heads they wore hoods
tied round with a band, and having a sort of rosette
or knot on the forehead. The women wore short skirts

half-way down to the knee; the breast and the lower part of the body was covered with what looked like the front of a jacket, the edge of which came down to the girdle. This garment was closed at the neck with a strip of stuff of the shape and size of a stole; it was scalloped round the shoulders, but plain over the breast. Their head-covering was a cap crowned by a button shaped like a truncated goblet. This cap was drawn down to make a point over the forehead, and covered the ears and part of the cheek. Behind the ears and at the back of the head this cap had loose flaps of stuff between which cushions of hair could be seen. The breast-covering of the women was colored, and was quilted or embroidered with yellow and green designs. It was decorated in front down the middle with buttons and scalloped on the shoulders. The embroidery was rather coarse, as on old vestments. Their upper arms were covered with bracelets.

These people made blankets or something like them out of the white wool, which they took from the buds of the little trees. Two of them tied a wad of this wool round their bodies, and each walked backwards away from the other, spinning from the wool round the other one's body a very long cord as thick as a finger. These cords they then plaited together to make broad strips. When they had prepared a great number of them, they went in troops, bearing great rolls of these blankets on their heads, to sell them in a town.

Here and there in this region I saw their idols under great trees. They had heads of horned oxen with wide-open mouths, and lower down in their body was a wider opening where fire was lit, to burn the offerings placed in the smaller openings. Round these idol-trees stood little stone pillars on each of which were small figures of other animals, such as birds, dragons, and a figure with three dogs' heads and a coiled snake's tail.

At the beginning of my journey I had the feeling of there being a great piece of water to my right from which I was, however, always going farther away. After

I had left the region inhabited by these people, my path continually ascended, and I had to cross a mountain ridge of white sand, covered in many places with all kinds of little broken black stones, like broken pots and dishes. On the farther side of this ridge I came down a valley into a region covered with many trees growing in almost regular rows. There were trees there with scaly trunks and enormous leaves, also pyramid-shaped ones with very big, beautiful flowers; these last had yellowish-green leaves and branches with buds. I also saw trees with quite smooth heart-shaped leaves.

Thereafter I came into a region consisting of wide endless pasture-lands between hills, where there were countless flocks and herds of different kinds. Vines grew on the slopes of the hills, and were cultivated, for there were rows of them on terraces, protected by little wattle fences. The owners of the herds lived in tents with flat roofs; the entrance was closed by a door of light wickerwork. These tents were made of the white woollen stuff woven by the wild people I had seen, but they were covered over with pieces of brownish stuff overlapping each other like scales and hanging down in a shaggy edge. They looked as if they were made of moss or fur. One big tent stood in the middle, and many smaller ones in a wide circle round it. The flocks and herds, divided according to their kind, went out into the wide pastures, interspersed here and there in the distance with expanses of bushes, like low woods. I was able to distinguish herds of very different kinds of animals. I saw sheep with fleeces of long twisted wool and long woolly tails, and also very agile animals with horns like he-goats: these were as big as calves; others were the size of the horses which run wild on our moors at home. I also saw droves of camels and animals like them only with two humps. In one place I saw some elephants in an enclosure, white ones and spotted ones; they were quite tame and were used only for domestic work.

In this vision I was thrice interrupted by having my

attention turned in other directions, but I always came back—though at another time of day—to this picture of pastoral activity. These herds and pasturages seemed to me to belong to one of the kings now on their travels: I think it was Mensor and his family. They were tended by under-shepherds wearing coats reaching to the knee, rather like the coats worn by our peasants, only that they fitted tight round the body. I think that now that their chief was going away for some long time, all the herds were being examined and counted by overseers, and the under-shepherds had to render account, for from time to time I saw more important people arriving in long cloaks and inspecting everything. They went into the big central tent, and the herds were then driven past between it and the small tents to be counted and looked at. The persons who received the reckonings had in their hands tablets, I do not know of what material, on which they wrote something. I thought as I watched them: "How I wish our bishops would examine as diligently the flocks in the care of their under-shepherds."

When I again returned to the pasturages after the last interruption, it was night. A deep stillness rested on the place. Most of the shepherds were asleep under the small tents, only a few crept about, watching over the sleeping herds. These lay at rest in great enclosures, divided according to their kind, some crowded together and some less so. It was for me a deeply moving and edifying sight—this great pasture full of peacefully sleeping herds, the servants of mankind, and above them the immeasurable expanse of the deep-blue pastures of heaven, filled with countless stars—stars which had come forth at the bidding of their almighty Creator. They follow the voice of their shepherd like true sheep with greater obedience than the sheep of earth give to their mortal shepherds. And when I saw the waking shepherds wandering to and fro and turning their eyes more to the starry flocks above than to the earthly ones below who were entrusted to their care, I thought within myself: they are right to look up in astonishment and gratitude to where their ancestors have for centuries turned their expectant gaze in longing and prayer. The good shepherd seeks for the lost sheep and rests not till he has found it and brought it home; so does the Heavenly Father, the true Shepherd of all these countless flocks of stars in immeasurable space. When man, whom He had made lord of the earth, sinned, and as a punishment the earth became cursed to him, God sought out fallen man and his home the earth like the lost sheep. He even sent down His only-begotten Son to become man, to bring the lost sheep home, to take upon Himself, as the Lamb of God, the sins of mankind, and by dying Himself to make satisfaction for those sins to the divine justice. And now the coming of the promised Redeemer was at hand, and the kings of these shepherds, led by a star, had set forth the night before to pay homage to the newborn Redeemer. That was why the watchers of the flocks looked up in awe and adoration to the heavenly pastures, for the Shepherd of the shepherds came down from above, and His coming was announced first of all to the shepherds.

While I was meditating on all this in the wide pasture-land, I was aware of the stillness of the night being broken by the sound of hoofs hurriedly approaching: it was a troop of men riding on camels. They passed quickly by the sleeping herds to the main tent of the shepherds' encampment. Woken by the noise, some of the camels got up from their sleeping position and stretched their long necks towards the riders, and lambs woke up bleating. Some of the newcomers alighted from their beasts and woke the sleeping shepherds in the tents, while the nearest herdsmen came up to greet the riders. Soon all were awake and gathered round the new arrivals; there was much talking, and all looked and pointed at the stars. They were speaking of a star or of some apparition in the heavens, which must have already disappeared, for I did not see it. These newcomers were Theokeno and his train. He was the third king and the one who lived farthest away. He had seen in his home the same picture in the skies, and had at once set forth and journeyed to this place. He asked how far ahead of him Mensor and Sair might be, and whether the star whose guidance they had followed could still be seen. After receiving the news for which he asked, Theokeno and his followers went on their way quickly without any delay. This was the place where the three kings, coming from their separate homes, used generally to meet to observe the stars. The pyramidal tower, from which they looked at the stars through long tubes, was close by. Theokeno lived farther away than the others, beyond the region which was Abraham's first dwelling-place. They all lived near that region.

In the intervals between the visions of the three days during which I saw what was happening on that wide pasture-land, I was shown much about the places in which Abraham lived, but have forgotten most of it. Once, in the distance, I saw the mountain on which Abraham was preparing to sacrifice Isaac. Another time I was shown very clearly Agar and Ismael in the desert, although this happened a long way from here. I cannot remember in what connection this was. Abraham's first dwelling-place was high up, and the lands of the three kings were below and round it. I will here describe the picture of Ismael and Agar.[3]

At the side of Abraham's mountain, more towards the lower part of the valley, I saw Agar and her son wandering about in the bushes; she seemed quite beside herself. The boy was only a few years old and was wearing a long dress. His mother was wrapped in a long cloak which covered her head; under it she wore a short dress, the upper part of which was tight round her body, and her arms, too, were tightly wrapped round. She laid the child under a tree on a hill, and made

---

3. Agar and Ismael: *Gen.* 21:14-21. (SB)

signs on his forehead, on the middle of his right upper arm, on his breast, and on his left upper arm. When she went away I did not see the mark on his forehead, but the other marks, which had been made on his clothing, remained visible as if drawn in red-brown color. These marks were in the form of a cross, but not an ordinary one. They were like a Maltese cross, only the points of the four triangles were arranged in the shape of a cross round a ring. In the four triangles she wrote signs or letters, like hooks, whose significance I could not clearly retain in my mind; I saw her also write two or three letters in the ring, in the middle. She drew this very rapidly with some red color, which she seemed to have in her hand (or perhaps it was blood). As she did this she kept her thumb and forefinger pressed together. Thereupon she turned round, gazed up to heaven, and did not look round again at her son. She went about a gun-shot's distance away and sat down under a tree. She heard a voice from heaven; rose up and went farther away. Again she heard a voice, and saw a spring of water under the leaves. She filled her leather water-bottle at the spring, and going back to her son gave him to drink and led him to the spring, where she put another garment over the one she had marked with crosses. That is what I remember of this vision. I think that I saw Agar in the desert twice before, once before the birth of her son, and the second time with the young Ismael as now.

[The night of November 27th-28th. When Catherine Emmerich communicated in 1821 these visions of the journey of the three holy kings, she had already related the whole of Jesus' earthly ministry, and had amongst other things seen how, after the raising of Lazarus (which she saw happening on September 7th of the third year of His ministry), He withdrew beyond the Jordan. During His sixteen weeks' absence there, He visited the three holy kings who on their return from their journey to Bethlehem had settled all together, with their attendants, nearer to the Promised

Land.[4] Only Mensor and Theokeno were alive then. The dark-skinned Sair was in his grave when Jesus came there. It seems necessary to inform the reader about these events (which were thirty-two years later in date but described earlier by Catherine Emmerich) in order that certain references to them in what follows may be understandable.]

In the night of the 27th to the 28th of November I saw, as day began to dawn, Theokeno and his retinue overtake Mensor and Sair, after whom they had been hurrying, in a deserted city with great rows of isolated high columns. By the gates, which were square ruined towers, and in other places stood many large and beautiful statues not so stiff as in Egypt but in beautiful living attitudes. This region was very sandy and rocky. In the ruins of this deserted city people who looked like bands of robbers had settled themselves. They wore nothing but a skin round their bodies and carried spears in their hands. They were brown in color, short, and stocky, but remarkably agile. (I had a feeling that I had been in this place before, perhaps on those journeys which I made in my dreams to the mountain of the Prophet and the river Ganges.) After the three kings and their followers had met here, they left at dawn in haste to continue their journey. Many of the rabble who lived here joined them because of the kings' generosity. (After Christ's death two disciples, Saturninus and Jonadab, the half-brother of Peter, were sent by St. John the Evangelist to this deserted city to preach the Gospel.[5])

I now saw all the three holy kings together. The last arrival was the one who lived farthest away, Theokeno. His face was of a beautiful yellowish color. (I recognized him as the one who was lying ill in his tent,

---

4. No such visit of Our Lord to the abode of the three kings in Arabia is recorded in the Gospels. (SB)

5. She saw the procession of the kings passing through this town on the feast of St. Saturninus (Nov. 27th) of whom she possesses a relic; that is why she mentioned his connection with this place. The writer read later in the legend of this saint in *Fleurs des Vies Saintes* that Saturninus preached the Gospel in Asia as far as Media. (CB)

234   *The Life of the Blessed Virgin Mary*

when thirty-two years later Jesus visited the kings in their settlement nearer the Promised Land.) Each of the three kings had with him four near relations or friends of his family, so that, counting the kings, there were fifteen important people of the party, besides the crowd of servants and camel-drivers that followed them. Amongst the many youths in their retinue, who were quite naked from the waist upwards, and were astonishingly agile in leaping and running, I recognized the young Eleazar, who later became a martyr and of whom I possess a relic.[6]

[In the afternoon, when her confessor again asked her for the names of the three holy kings, she answered, "Mensor, the brown-faced one, after Christ's death received the name of Leander on his Baptism by St. Thomas. Theokeno, the old, yellow-faced one, who was ill when Jesus visited Mensor's camp in Arabia, was baptized Leo by St. Thomas. The brown-skinned one, who was already dead when Our Lord made His visit, was called Seir or Sair." Her confessor asked her: "How then was he baptized?" She answered smiling and without hesitation: "He was already dead and had received the baptism of desire." Her confessor then said: "I have never heard these names in my life: how then did they get the names of Kaspar, Melchoir, and Balthasar?" She replied: "They were called this because it goes with their character, for these names mean: 1) He goes with love; 2) He wanders about, he approaches gently and with ingratiating manners: 3) He makes rapid decisions, he quickly directs his will to the will of God." She said this with great friendliness, and expressed the meaning of the names by making pantomimic gestures with her hand on the bed-coverlet. It must remain for the language experts to decide how far these words can be made to bear these meanings.[7]]

---

6. There is no available evidence about the martyr Eleazar. (SB)
7. According to the Ramsgate *Book of Saints* (1947), the names Melchior, Kaspar, and Balthasar were attributed to the Magi in the eighth century. The names themselves are not known before this, although Balthasar appears as a by-form of Belshazzar (*Dan.* 5:1), which is a pagan Babylonian name *Bel-shar-usur* ("Bel protect the king"),

[November 28th:] It was not, I think, until a half-day's journey from the deserted city with its many columns and statues that I first really joined the three kings and their train. It was in a more fertile region. One could see shepherds' dwellings here and there, with walls of black and white stones. The travellers came to a spring of water in the plain near which there were several large sheds, open at the side. Three stood in the middle with others round them. This seemed to be a customary halting-place for caravans. I saw that the whole procession was divided into three separate parties; each had five leaders, one being the chief or king, who, like a master of the house, saw to everything, gave orders, and apportioned the work. The members of each of these three parties had faces of different colors. Mensor's tribe was of a pleasing brownish color, Sair's was brown, and Theokeno's a bright yellow. I saw none shining black in color except some slaves, who were in all three parties. The leaders sat on their high-loaded beasts between bundles covered with carpets. They had staffs in their hands. They were followed by other beasts, almost as big as horses and ridden by servants and slaves with luggage. When they arrived at the halting-place they dismounted, unloaded the beasts completely and watered them at the spring, which was surrounded by a little rampart on which was a wall with three openings in it. The cistern was at the bottom of this enclosure; it had a fountain with three water-pipes closed by pegs. The cistern was covered with a lid, which a man who had come with them from the deserted city opened in return for a fee. They had leather vessels, which could be folded up quite flat, with four partitions. These were filled with water, and four camels always drank from them at the same time. They were

---

and Melchior, if a Hebrew name *Malki-or*, could mean "My king is light." The meanings given by AC are most obscure. The *Legenda Aurea* (Jan. 6th) gives their names as Appellius, Amerius, and Damascus in Greek; Galgalat, Malgalat, and Sarathin in Hebrew; and Melchior, Kaspar, and Balthasar in Latin; and adds that their bodies were found by Helena and taken to Constantinople, whence later to Milan, and finally to Cologne. (SB)

very careful with the water, and not a drop was allowed
to be wasted. After drinking, the camels were led into
open enclosures near the spring, each in a separate
compartment. Fodder which had been brought with them
was shaken out into the stone troughs in front of them;
it consisted of grains of the size of acorns (perhaps
beans). Amongst the baggage there were also big square
bird-cages, narrow and high, hanging by the sides of
the camels under the larger packages. In these were
birds, single or in couples, according to their size; they
were as big as pigeons or hens, and were kept in separate compartments as food on the journey. They carried their loaves of bread, which were all of the same
size, in leather cases, packing the slabs tightly together
and taking out only so much as they needed each time.
They had with them very costly vessels of yellow metal,
some of them ornamented with precious stones. These
were almost exactly like our chalices and incense-boats
in shape; they drank from them and handed round food
on them. The rims of most of these vessels were set
with red jewels.

The three tribes differed somewhat in their clothing.
Theokeno, the yellow-skinned, and his family, as well
as Mensor, the light-brown one, wore high hoods embroidered in colors with a strip of thick white stuff wound
round them. Their coats, which were very simple, with
few buttons or ornaments on the breast, reached almost
to their ankles. They wrapped themselves in light cloaks,
very full and flowing, so that they trailed on the ground
behind them. Sair, the brown-skinned one, and his family wore caps with little white pads and round hoods
embroidered in colors on which was a disc of another
color. Their cloaks were shorter than the others,' but
longer at the back than in front; their coats were but-
toned to the knee and were decorated at the breast
with braid and tinsel and thickly set with shining buttons. On one side of the breast they wore a shining little shield like a star. All wore sandals, the soles of
which were fastened round their bare feet with cords.

The more important ones had short swords or long knives in their girdles, with many pouches and boxes hanging from their waists. Amongst the kings and their families were men of fifty, forty, thirty, and twenty years of age. Some had long and some short beards. The servants and camel-drivers were dressed much more simply, some wearing only one piece of stuff or an old blanket.

When the camels had been watered, fed, and stabled, the travellers, after drinking, made a fire in the middle of the shed under which they had camped. The firewood consisted of pieces some two-and-a-half feet long brought by poor people from nearby in very neat bundles; they seemed to have a store of it ready for travellers. The kings made a triangular fireplace and piled up the long pieces round it, leaving an opening on one side for the draught. It was very cleverly arranged. I am not sure how they made fire: I saw that one of them kept turning one piece of wood in another, as if in a box, and then pulled it out alight. They then lit the fire, and I saw them kill some of the birds and roast them. Each of the three kings acted towards his tribe like the head of a family: he distributed the food, laying the carved-up birds and little loaves of bread on small bowls or plates standing on short feet, and handed them round. In the same way he filled the goblets and gave drink to each. The lower servants, among whom there were Moors, lie on a blanket on the ground at one side of the fire, patiently awaiting their turn. They, too, receive their due share. I think that these are slaves.

Oh, how touching is the good temper and childlike simplicity of these beloved kings! They give to those who come to them a share of all they have; they even hold the golden vessels to their lips and let them drink out of them, like children.

Today I learnt much about the holy kings, including the names of their countries and cities, but in my helpless and agitated condition I have quite forgotten everything. I will tell what I know. Mensor, the brown-skinned

one, was a Chaldaean, his city had a name like Acajaja[8] and was surrounded by a river, like an island.
Mensor spent all his time in the fields with his herds.
Sair, the dark-skinned one, was on Christmas night all
ready to start on his journey from home. The name of
his country is connected in my memory with the sound
"Partherme."[9] Beyond his country, and higher up, was
a lake or sea. It was only he and his tribe who were
so brown, with red lips; the people round were white.
His country was quite small, no bigger than the province
of Münster. Theokeno, the pale one, came from a country still higher up, called Media, lying between two
seas.[10] I have forgotten the name of the city in which
he lived; it was an assemblage of tents erected on foundations of stones. Theokeno, the richest of the three,
was the one who left most behind him. I believe that
he could have taken a more direct way to Bethlehem,
and had to make a detour in order to travel in company with the others. I almost think that he had to go
by Babylon to join them.

Sair, the dark-skinned one, lived three days' journey
from the home of Mensor, the brown one, and Theokeno five days' journey. Each day's journey was reckoned as lasting twelve hours. Mensor and Sair were
together in the former's camp when they saw the vision
of the star of Our Lord's birth, and started off the next
day with their followers. Theokeno, the pale one, saw
the same vision in his home, and hurried after them
in great haste, catching up with the other two in the

---

8. In 1839, eighteen years after this word Acajaja was pronounced by Catherine
Emmerich, the writer found in Funke's dictionary: "Achajacula, a castle on an
island in the Euphrates in Mesopotamia (Ammian, 24, 2)" (CB)

   The reference is to the history by Ammianus Marcellinus covering the twenty-
six years from Constantius to Valens, entitled *Res Gestae,* in thirty-one books of
which eighteen are extant. The twenty-fourth book deals with the campaigns of
the Emperor Julian (A.D. 363), and in XXIV, ii, 2, the place Achaiachala, an island
fortress in the river Euphrates, is mentioned. (SB)

9. The name Partherme is otherwise unknown. It occurs again (of the same land),
infra, p. 390. (SB)

10. It would seem that Mensor, the Chaldaean, was from Mesopotamia, Theokeno from
Media (Persia), and Sair from the mountain country between Mesopotamia and
Persia. But the geographical information is not precise enough to determine any-
thing. (SB)

deserted city. I did know the length of their journey to Bethlehem, but have partly forgotten it. What I remember, more or less, is that their journey was about 700 hours and still another figure with six in it. They had about sixty days' journey, each reckoned at twelve hours, but they performed it in thirty-three days owing to the great speed of their beasts and to their often travelling day and night.

The star which led them was really like a round ball with light streaming out of it as from a mouth. It always seemed to me as if this ball, which was as it were swinging on a shaft of light, was guided by the hand of a supernatural being. In the daytime I saw a light brighter than daylight going before them. If one considers the distance they had to travel, the speed of their journey seems astonishing; but the pace of their beasts was so light and even that I see them moving onward with the order, rapidity, and rhythm of a flight of migrating birds. The homes of the three kings were at the three points of a triangle. Mensor, the brown one, and Sair, the dark, lived nearer to each other than Theokeno, the pale one, who was the farthest away of the three. They have, I think, already passed Chaldar where I once saw the enclosed garden in the temple. Theokeno's distant city has only its foundations of stone; above, it is all tents. There is water round it. It seems to me about the size of Münster.

After the kings had rested here until the evening, the people who had attached themselves to their company helped them to pack their baggage onto their beasts, and then carried home with them everything that was left behind. It was towards evening when they started off. The star was visible and was today reddish in color, like the moon in windy weather. Its long tail of light was pale. They went on foot for a while beside their beasts with uncovered heads, praying. On this part of the way it was impossible to go fast; later on, when they came to level ground, they mounted their beasts, which moved at a very quick pace. Sometimes they went more slowly, and then they all sang as they journeyed through the night; it was very moving to hear.

[November 29th to December 2nd:] I was again with the kings on their journey in the night of Thursday, November 29th, and during the following day. I cannot say enough how much I admired the order, nobility, and joyfulness which inspires all that they do. We are journeying through the night, always following the star, whose long tail reaches down to earth. These good men follow it with their eyes quietly and joyfully, talking to each other from their high saddles. Sometimes they sing short sentences by turns, in a very slow and beautiful melody, sometimes very high and sometimes deep in tone. It is very moving to hear it in the quiet night, and I feel all that they sing. They travel with perfect orderliness; first comes a big camel with boxes on each side of his hump covered with large carpets on which sits the leader with a goad in his hand and a sack at his side. Then follow smaller beasts, such as horses or big donkeys, carrying packages and ridden by the men belonging to this leader. Then comes another of the leaders on a camel and so on. The creatures walk so delicately with big steps, and put down their feet as if they were trying not to crush anything.

They carry their burdens with so little motion that it seems as though only their legs were alive, and the carriage of their heads on their long necks is wonderfully calm and quiet. The men, too, seem to do everything without having to take thought about it. Everything happens as in a quiet dream, peaceful and sweet. (I cannot help reflecting here how these good people, who as yet do not know the Lord, journey towards Him in such order, peace, and sweetness, whilst we, whom He has redeemed and loaded with graces, are so disorderly and disrespectful in our processions!) I think the region through which they passed tonight might well be the district between Atom, the home of Azarias, and the castle of the idolater, where I saw

Jesus at the end of the third year of His ministry when He was journeying through Arabia on His way to Egypt.

On Friday, November 30th, I saw the procession halting at night by a fountain in the fields. A man from a hut, of which there were several nearby, opened the fountain for them. They watered their beasts and rested for a short time without unloading. On Saturday, December 1st, I saw the kings, whose road had been going uphill the day before, on higher ground. On their right was a mountain range, and when their road descended again, they seemed to be in a place where houses, trees, and fountains often stood beside the road. It seemed to me to be the home of the people whom I had seen, last year and again lately, spinning and weaving cotton. They had stretched the threads between the trees and plaited broad coverings out of them. They worshipped images of oxen. They were generous in giving food to the rabble that followed the procession of the kings, but it surprised me to see that they never used the bowls again from which these had eaten.

On Sunday, December 2nd, I saw the three holy kings near a place whose name I remember as something like Causur, a city of tents on stone foundations.[11] They were given hospitality here by another king, to whom this city belonged. His tent-dwelling stood a little distance before it. Since their meeting in the deserted city, they had now travelled fifty-three or sixty-three hours. They told the king of Causur all that they had seen in the stars. He was very astonished, and looked through a tube at the star that was guiding them and saw in it a little child with a cross. He begged them to tell him everything on their return, when he would erect altars to the King and make sacrifices to Him. I am curious to see if he will keep his word when they return. I heard them recounting to him the origin of their star-watching, and remember

---

11. Perhaps "Geshur in Syria," Absalom's retreat in *2 Kgs.* (*Sam.*) 15:8. Fahsel notes Gessur, a Roman garrison town on the road from Damascus to Galilee, just south of Mount Hermon. (SB)

of their conversation what follows.

The ancestors of the kings descended from Job, who once lived in the Caucasus and possessed other far-off lands.[12] About 1,500 years before the birth of Christ only one tribe of them remained there. The prophet Balaam came from that region,[13] and one of his disciples spread abroad and expounded in that land his master's prophecy, "A star shall rise out of Jacob" [see *Num.* 24:17]. He had many followers, and they built a high tower upon a mountain, where many wise men and those learned in the stars lived by turns. I have seen that tower; it was like a mountain itself, broad at the base and pointed at the top. I saw, too, the openings in it where they lived. All that they discovered in the stars was noted and handed down by word of mouth. There were times when this observation of the stars fell into disuse owing to various happenings, and later it degenerated into the idolatrous horror of sacrificing children in order to hasten the coming of the promised Child.

About 500 years before the birth of Christ the observation of the stars had lapsed. At this time the race consisted of three tribes, founded by three brothers who lived with their families apart from each other. They had three daughters to whom God had given the spirit of prophecy and who wandered about the land in long cloaks prophesying, and teaching about the star and the Child that was to come out of Jacob. In this way the observation of the stars and the longing for the Child was again revived in these three tribes. The three holy kings were descended from these three brothers in a direct line of fifteen generations, covering some

---

12. The Bible tells us nothing whatever about the historical setting of the Book of Job, except that Job lived "in the land of Hus (or Uz)"—a place otherwise unknown. But see further in n. 24, p. 345. (SB)

13. That Balaam should come from a northern land is no surprise in view of *Num.* 22:5 in the Hebrew text, where we read that the king of Moab "sent messengers to Balaam, son of Beor, to Pethor, which is by the river of his people's land," and this Pethor is usually identified with Pitru of the Assyrian inscriptions, a city on the Euphrates (cf. *Cath. Comm.,* 206d). (The Vulgate reads "soothsayer" for Pethor, and "Ammon" for "his people.") Balaam's remote and pagan origin makes him a character of particular interest in the history of Israel. (SB)

500 years. Their complexions had, however, become different from each other as the result of intermarriage with other races.

For 500 years the ancestors of the kings had met at a building which they shared in common for the observation of the stars. According to what they saw, various alterations were made in their temple and its services. Unfortunately, for a long time they continued to sacrifice children and other human beings. As they watched the stars, they were shown in wonderful visions all the special events and times connected with the coming of the Messias. I saw many of these visions as they conversed, but can no longer describe them clearly. Since Mary's conception, fifteen years before, these visions had pointed ever more distinctly to the nearness of the Child. At last they had seen several indications of the Passion of Jesus.

They were able to calculate very exactly the coming of the star prophesied by Balaam, for they had seen Jacob's Ladder and were able to reckon precisely, as in a calendar, the approach of our salvation by the number of rungs in the ladder and by the pictures appearing on each. The end of the ladder led to the star, which was the uppermost picture on it. They saw Jacob's Ladder as a tree in the midst of which three rows of rungs were fastened, and on these appeared a series of pictures which they saw in the star as each was fulfilled, so they knew exactly which must be the next picture, and the intervals between the pictures told them how long they must wait for it. At the time of Mary's conception they had seen the Virgin holding a sceptre and evenly balanced scales with wheat and grapes. A little below her they saw the Virgin with the Child. They saw Bethlehem as a beautiful palace, a house where much blessing was stored and distributed. In it they saw the Virgin and Child surrounded by a great glory of light, and many kings bowing before Him and making offerings to Him. They also saw the heavenly Jerusalem, but between it and Bethlehem was a dark street, full of thorns, strife and blood.

All this was real to them. They thought that glory such as this surrounded the newborn King, and that all peoples were bowing before Him; that was why they came, bringing their gifts with them. They took the heavenly Jerusalem to be His earthly kingdom and thought they would come to it. The dark street they thought meant their own journey, or that some war was threatening the King; they did not know that it meant His *Via Dolorosa*. At the foot of the ladder they saw (as did I) an elaborate tower, like the one I saw on the mountain of the Prophet. They saw how the Virgin once took refuge in a storm under a projecting portion of this tower, which had many entrances. I cannot remember what this signified. (Perhaps the Flight into Egypt.) There was a whole series of pictures on this Jacob's Ladder, amongst others many prophetic symbols of the Blessed Virgin, such as the sealed fountain and the enclosed garden. There were also pictures of kings, some holding out sceptres and others branches to each other.

All these pictures they saw appearing in their turn in the stars as they were fulfilled. In the last three nights they saw these pictures continuously. The chief one of the three sent messengers to the others, and when they saw the picture of the kings making offerings to the newborn Child, they hurried on their way with their rich gifts, not wishing to be the last to arrive. All the tribes of the star-gazers had seen the star, but these were the only ones who followed it. The star which went before them was not the comet, but a shining brilliance borne by an angel. By day they followed the angel.

Because of all this they were full of expectation as they journeyed, and were afterwards astonished to find nothing like it. They were dismayed by Herod's reception of them and by the ignorance of all men about these things. When they came to Bethlehem and saw a desolate cellar instead of the glorious palace they had seen in the star, great doubt assailed them; but they remained true to their faith, and at the sight of Jesus they realized that all they had seen in the stars was fulfilled.

These observations of the stars were accompanied by fasting, prayer, religious ceremonies, and various forms of self-denial and purification. The visions did not come from looking at one single star, but from a grouping of certain separate stars. This star-worship exercised an evil influence on those who had a tendency towards evil. Such people were seized with violent convulsions in their star-gazing, and it was they who were responsible for the misguided sacrifices of children. Others, like the three holy kings, saw the pictures clearly and calmly, in a spirit of inner piety, and grew ever better and more devout.

[December 3rd to 5th:] When the kings left Causur, I saw that they were joined by a considerable number of distinguished travellers who were going the same way. On December 3rd and 4th I saw them crossing a wide plain. On the 5th they rested by a fountain but without unloading. They watered and fed their beasts and prepared food for themselves.

[In the last few days Catherine Emmerich while asleep in the evening often sang several short verses with very strange and moving melodies. When she was asked the reason for this, she said:] I am singing with my dear kings, they sing with great sweetness many short verses, such as:

> *Over the hills let us make our way*
> *Our homage to the new King to pay.*

They take it in turn to invent and sing these verses: one begins, and the others repeat the verse he has sung. Then another starts another verse, and so as they ride along they keep up their sweet and heartfelt singing.

In the heart of the star, or rather of the globe of light, which went before them to show them the way, I saw the appearance of a Child with a Cross. When they saw the appearance of the Virgin in the stars at the birth of Jesus, this globe of light appeared in front of the picture and suddenly began to move gently forward.

[December 5th:] Mary had had a vision of the approach of the three holy kings while they were resting in the tent of the king of Causur. She also saw that the latter intended to erect an altar in honor of her Child. She told this to St. Joseph and Elisabeth, and asked that they should clear out the Cave of the Nativity and make everything ready in time for the reception of the kings.

The people because of whom Mary had yesterday retreated into the other cave were visitors who had come out of curiosity. There were many such in the last few days. Today Elisabeth went home to Jutta with a servant who came to fetch her.

[December 6th to 8th:] These were quieter days in the Cave of the Nativity, and the Holy Family was generally alone. Only Mary's maidservant, a robust, serious, and unpretentious person of some thirty years, was there. She was a childless widow, related to Anna, who had given her a home. Her late husband had been very severe with her because she went so often to the Essenes, for she was very devout and was hoping for the salvation of Israel. So he was angry with her, just as today bad men are angry because their wives go to church too often. He left her and afterwards died.

In the last few days there came no more of those insistent beggars who had demanded alms at the cave with curses and abuse. They were on their way to Jerusalem for the Maccabees' Feast of the Consecration of the Temple.[14] This feast really begins on the 25th day of the month Kislev, but as this fell on the evening of Friday, December 7th, in the year of Jesus' birth, that is to say, on the eve of the Sabbath, it was postponed to the evening of Saturday, December 8th, or the 26th day of Kislev. It lasted eight days.

(Thus the sixth day after the Circumcision was the

14. Maccabean Dedication Feast; cf. *supra*, n. 51, p. 70. (SB)

25th day of Kislev, so that the Circumcision happened on the nineteenth day of Kislev, and Our Lord's birth on the twelfth day of Kislev.)

Joseph kept the Sabbath under the lamp in the Cave of the Nativity with Mary and the maidservant. On Saturday evening the Feast of the Consecration of the Temple began. Joseph had fastened lamp-brackets, in three places in the cave, on each of which he lit seven little lamps. All is quiet now; the many visitors came because they were on their way to the festival. The nurse came to Mary every day now. Anna often sends messengers with presents who take news back to her. Jewish women do not suckle their children for long without other nourishment, and even when He was only a few days old the Infant Jesus was given a pap made of the pith of some rush which is light, nourishing, and sweet to taste. In the daytime the donkey is generally outside at pasture and only spends the night in the cave.

[December 10th:] Yesterday, Sunday, December 9th, I did not see the nurse coming to the cave any more. Joseph lights his little lamps for the Consecration feast every morning and evening. It is very quiet here since the feast began in Jerusalem.

Today a manservant came from Anna. He brought Our Lady, amongst other things, materials for making a girdle, and a most beautiful little basket of fruit, covered over with fresh roses among the fruit. The basket was high and narrow, and the color of the roses different from ours: it was paler, almost flesh-colored. There were also big yellow and white roses, some open and some in bud. Mary seemed delighted with them and placed the basket beside her.

[Journey of the kings:] In the last few days I often saw the kings on their journey. The road was more hilly, and they came over the hills which I had seen covered with little pieces of stone like broken pottery. I should very much like to have some of them, they are so beautifully smooth. On other mountains in that region are many white transparent stones like birds' eggs, and a quantity of white sand. I saw the kings now in the place where they afterwards lived when Jesus visited them in the third year of His ministry. They were not in the city of tents, for at that time it did not exist.

[December 11th to 13th:] It seems to me as if Joseph would like to stay in Bethlehem and live there with Mary after the Purification. I think he was looking out for a house there. About three days ago some rather distinguished people came to the cave from Bethlehem; they wanted to take the Holy Family into their house. Mary hid herself from them in the other cave, and Joseph declined their offer. Anna is soon going to visit the Blessed Virgin. I saw her very busy lately, dividing up her herds again for the poor and for the Temple. The Holy Family, too, always gave away at once whatever they had. The Consecration festival was still celebrated every morning and evening, but on the 13th a new festival must have started. I saw various alterations being made in the festival in Jerusalem. I saw the windows in many houses being closed and curtained. I also saw a priest with a scroll in the cave with Joseph. They were praying together at a little table hung with white and red. It was as if he had wanted to see whether Joseph was keeping the feast, or as if he was announcing a new feast to him. [It seemed to her to be a feast-day, but she also thought that the feast of the new moon must now have begun. She was uncertain about this.] The Crib was quiet in these last few days, without visitors.

[December 14th to 18th:] With the Sabbath the Feast of the Consecration of the Temple came to an end, and Joseph ceased lighting the little lamps. On Sunday the 16th and Monday the 17th people from the neighborhood once more came to the Crib. The unruly beggars, too, were heard at the entrance. This was because people were now returning from the festival.

On the 17th two servants came from Anna with food and other things. Mary is much quicker than I am in distributing things, and everything was soon given away. I see Joseph beginning to tidy and clear up in the Cave of the Nativity, the side-caves and grave of Maraha, and he has brought in provisions. They are awaiting Anna's visit, and Mary is expecting the kings to arrive soon.

[December 17th:] Today, late in the evening, I saw the kings arrive in a little town of scattered houses, many of which were surrounded by high fences. It seemed to me that this was the first Jewish town they came to. Bethlehem was in a straight line from here, but they went off to the right, I suppose because the only road led in that direction.[15] As they approached this place they sang particularly loudly and beautifully, and were full of joy, for the star shone unusually brightly here. It was like moonlight and one could see quite clearly the shadows which it cast. The inhabitants seemed either not to see the star or to take no special interest in it, but they were good people and extremely helpful. Some of the travellers had dismounted, and the inhabitants helped them to water their beasts. (It made me think of Abraham's times, when all men were so good and helpful.) Several of the inhabitants, bearing branches, led the travellers through the town and went some of the way with them. I did not see the star always shining brightly before them; sometimes it was quite dim. It seemed to shine more brightly in places where good people lived, and when the travellers saw that it was very brilliant, they were greatly excited and thought that perhaps the Messias might be in that place.

[December 18th:] This morning they passed by a dark, misty city without stopping, and soon after crossed a river flowing into the Dead Sea. In the last two places many of the rabble which had followed them stayed behind. (I had a distinct impression that someone had

---

15. Medeba is about eighteen miles north of the brook Arnon, which flows into the Dead Sea, and Bethlehem lies due west from here across the Dead Sea, so that travellers would have to turn north to go round it. (SB)

taken refuge in one of these two places in a conflict before the reign of Solomon.[16] They crossed the river this morning and now came on to a good road.

[December 19th to 21st:] This evening I saw the kings on this side of this river.[17] Their generosity had attracted so many followers that their train must have numbered 200. They were nearing the town which was approached by Jesus on its western side on July 31st in the second year of His ministry, though He did not enter it. Its name sounded like Manathea, Metanea, Medana, or Madian.[18] It had a mixed population of heathens and Jews; they were evil people, and though a high road led through the town, they would not let the kings go through. They led them outside the town, on the eastern side, to a place enclosed by walls, where there were sheds and stables. The kings put up their tents here, fed and watered their beasts, and prepared a meal for themselves.

On Thursday the 20th and Friday the 21st I saw the kings resting here, but they were greatly distressed because here, as in the last town, nobody knew or cared about the newborn King. I heard them telling the inhabitants in a very friendly way a great deal about the cause of their long journey and all the circumstances attending it. Of what I heard I recollect this much.

They had received the announcement about the newborn King a very long time ago. I think it must have been not long after Job's time and before Abraham went to Egypt, when an army of some three thousand Medes from Job's country (they lived in other parts as well) came as far as the region of Heliopolis in a campaign

---

16. Medeba was the scene of David's battle with the Ammonites (*1 Par.* 19:7), and also (but after Solomon's time) one of the cities captured during the revolt of Mesha, King of Moab (*4 Kgs.* 3:4 sqq., *Is.* 15:2), as recorded on the Moabite Stone. (SB)

17. Since the Arnon flows east to west, we should understand "northern side" here. (SB)

18. St. Jerome mentions a Methane near Arnon, which gave its name to the Mathanites. See *1 Par.* 11:43. (CB)

    Nothing else is recorded in the Bible about the Mathanites. Fahsel marks a village Madian on the north bank of the Arnon. (SB)

against Egypt.[19] I cannot now clearly recollect why they had advanced so far, but I think their campaign was in aid of someone. It was not, however, for a good purpose, they were attacking something holy; whether holy men or a religious mystery connected with the fulfillment of the promise, I cannot remember. Near Heliopolis an angel appeared to several of their leaders at once, warning them to go no farther. He spoke to them of a Redeemer who was to be born of a Virgin and would be worshipped by their descendants. This was connected, I cannot remember how, with a command that they should advance no farther but should go home and observe the stars. After this I saw them arranging joyful feasts in Egypt, setting up triumphal arches and altars, and decorating them with flowers. Then they went home. They were Median star-worshippers, exceptionally tall, almost like giants, of very noble stature and of a beautiful yellowish-brown color. They journeyed with their herds from place to place and imposed their will everywhere by their great strength. I have forgotten the name of their chief prophet. They were much given to prophesying and the taking of omens from animals. Often on their journeys animals would suddenly place themselves across their road, standing with outstretched legs and letting themselves be killed rather than go away. That was an omen for them, and they turned away from these roads. The kings said that these Medes, returning from Egypt, were the first to bring the prophecy and to start the watching of the stars. When they passed away, it was continued by a disciple of Balaam and renewed 1,000 years after him by the three prophetess-daughters of the three kings who founded their dynasties. Now, 500 years after them, the star had come which they were following in order to adore the newborn King. All this they explained to the inquisitive listeners with the most child-like sincerity, and were dis-

---

19. According to AC *(infra,* p. 251) this took place about 1500 B.C., when "Medes(?) from Job's country" (the Caucasus according to AC) invaded Egypt. Is this to be identified with the Hittite invasions in the Amarna period (14th cent. B.C.)? (SB)

tressed that they did not seem at all to believe in what their ancestors had so patiently waited for during 2,000 years. In the evening the star was covered in mist, but when it appeared again at night large and clear between moving clouds, they rose from their camp and awoke the inhabitants living near to show them the star. These gazed in wonder at the sky, and some showed emotion; but many of them were vexed with the kings, and in general they merely sought to take advantage of their generosity.

I heard the kings saying what a long way they had travelled from their first meeting-place to here. They reckoned by day's journeys on foot, each of twelve hours. But their beasts, which were dromedaries and were faster than horses, enabled them to do thirty-six hours' journey each twenty-four hours, including the rest-hours. Thus the most distant of the three kings was able to accomplish his sixty hours' journey to the meeting-place in two days, and the two who were nearer did their thirty-six hours' journey in a day and a night. From the meeting-place to where they were now they had travelled 672 hours' journey, and had spent about twenty-five days and nights since starting off at the moment of the Birth of Christ.

[December 20th and 21st:] The kings and their train rested here both these days, and I heard what they told. On the evening of Friday the 21st the Jews who lived here began their Sabbath and crossed a bridge leading westwards across the water to a small Jewish village with a synagogue. At the same time the kings prepared for their departure and made their farewells. I noticed that the inhabitants looked at the star (when visible) which led the kings and expressed much astonishment, but it did not make them more respectful. They were shamelessly importunate, pestering the kings like swarms of wasps. In reply to their demands the kings with great forbearance gave them little triangular pieces of their gold and also grains of some darker metal. They must have been very rich.

They were escorted by the inhabitants when they left. Skirting the walls of the town (in which I saw temples surmounted by idols), they crossed the river by a bridge, and passed through the Jewish village, hurrying on towards the Jordan by a good road. From here they still had about twenty-four hours' journey to Jerusalem.

[December 19th to 22nd:] On the evening of December 19th I saw Anna, accompanied by her second husband, Maria Heli, a maid, and a manservant with two donkeys stopping for the night not far from Bethany on their way to Bethlehem. Joseph has finished the arrangements which he has been making in the Cave of the Nativity and in the side-caves in order to receive both the guests from Nazareth and the kings, whose arrival Mary had foreseen a short while ago when they were at Causur. Joseph and Mary had moved with the Infant Jesus into the other cave. The Cave of the Nativity had been entirely cleared out, and only the donkey, I saw, had been left in it. Even the fireplace and the things for preparing food had been moved out. Joseph had, if I remember rightly, already paid his second tax. There were again many inquisitive visitors coming to Mary from Bethlehem to see the Child. Some He allowed to take Him in their arms, from others He turned away crying. I saw the Blessed Virgin calm and peaceful in the new dwelling, which had now been arranged very comfortably. Her couch was against the wall. The Infant Jesus lay beside her in a long basket woven from broad strips of bark; it had a shelter for the head and stood on trestles. Our Lady's couch with Jesus' cradle was separated from the rest of the room by a wicker screen. In the daytime, except when she wished to be alone, she sat in front of this screen with the Child beside her. Joseph's resting-place was some way off at the side of the cave, and was divided off in the same way. A vessel holding a lamp stood on a piece of wood projecting from the wall high enough to light both these screened-off partitions. I saw Joseph bringing Our Lady a bowl of food and a jug of water.

[December 20th:] This evening was the beginning of a fast. All the food for the next day was prepared beforehand, the fire was covered over, the openings of the cave hung with curtains, and all the household utensils put away. (The 8th and 16th days of the month Shebet are Jewish fast days.) Anna has come to the cave with her second husband, Mary's elder sister, and a maidservant. I had seen Anna on her journey several days before. These visitors were to sleep in the Cave of the Nativity; this was why the Holy Family had moved into the side-cave, though the donkey had remained behind. Today I saw Mary lay the Infant in her mother's arms; Anna was greatly moved. She had brought with her coverlets, clothes, and provisions. Anna's maidservant was strangely dressed. Her hair was plaited and hung down to her girdle in a net; she had on a short dress reaching only to the knees. Her pointed bodice was fastened tightly round her hips and breast; it came high up above the latter as if to make a place for hiding something. She carried a basket hanging on her arm. The old man (Anna's husband) was very shy and humble. Anna slept where Elisabeth had slept, and Mary told her everything, as she had Elisabeth, in happy intimacy. Anna wept with the Blessed Virgin; they often interrupted their talk to caress the Infant Jesus.

[December 21st:] Today I saw the Blessed Virgin once more in the Cave of the Nativity and little Jesus once more in the Crib. When Joseph and Mary are alone with the little Child, I often see them adoring Him; and now I see Anna and the Blessed Virgin standing by the Crib with bowed heads, and gazing at the Infant Jesus with great devotion. I am not quite sure whether Anna's companions slept in the other cave or whether they had gone away. I almost think they had gone. Today I saw that Anna had brought the Mother and Child various things such as coverlets and swaddling-bands. Since she came here, Mary has been given a good many things; but she has very little of anything, because she at once gives away anything that is not absolutely necessary. I heard her telling Anna that the kings out of the East would soon be coming, bringing great gifts, and that this would cause a great sensation. I think that while the kings are on their way here, Anna will go to her sister, three hours' distance from here, and come back later.

[December 22nd:] This evening, after the Sabbath had ended, I saw Anna and her companions going away from the Blessed Virgin for a little time. She went three hours' journey away from here, to the Tribe of Benjamin, to a younger married sister who lived there. I do not remember the name of the village, which consisted only of a few houses and a field. It is half an hour away from the last resting-place of the Holy Family on their journey to Bethlehem, where Joseph's relations lived. They spent the night of November 22nd/23rd there.

The kings and their train left Mathanea and hurried through the night, following a high-road. They passed through no more towns, but skirted all the little places in which, at the end of July in the third year of His ministry, Jesus blessed the children and healed and taught; for example, Bethabara,[20] the place of the ferry across the Jordan, which they reached early in the morning. As it was the Sabbath, they met few people on their way.

Early in the morning, at seven o'clock, I saw them crossing the Jordan. Generally people were ferried across the river on a raft of beams, but for large companies a sort of bridge was put together. This was generally done by the ferrymen who lived on the bank and received payment for it, but as these could not work on the Sabbath the travellers did it themselves, with the help of some of the ferrymen's heathen servants, who were paid

---

20. Bethabara (thus named by AC) (="place of crossing") by the Jordan is mentioned in some codices of *John* 1:28 ("where John was baptizing"), while other codices have Bethania (="place of the ship")—probably two names for the same place. (SB)

for it. The Jordan was not broad here and was full of sand-banks. Planks were placed against the raft generally used for crossing, and the camels were led up them onto the raft. I saw that this sort of bridge was ferried backwards and forwards till all the train were landed on the western bank. It was quite a long time before all were safely across.

[In the evening at half-past five, she said:] They have left Jericho on their right and are now in a direct line with Bethlehem, but are turning more to the right in the direction of Jerusalem. There must be as many as a hundred men with them. In the distance I see a little town, which I know, beside a stream coming from Jerusalem in an eastward direction. I am sure they will have to pass through this town. They go on for some time with the stream on their left hand. I saw Jerusalem as they went; it sank out of sight and reappeared as the road rose or fell. [Later she said:] They did not pass through that town after all; they turned to the right towards Jerusalem.

Today [Saturday evening, December 22nd] I saw the three holy kings and their train arriving before Jerusalem. I saw the city towering up to heaven. The guiding star had here almost disappeared, it had become quite small and glowed only dimly behind the city. The travellers became more and more depressed the nearer they came to Jerusalem, for the star was not nearly so bright before them, and in Judaea they saw it but seldom. They had expected, too, to find everywhere great rejoicings and festivities at the newborn Saviour, for whose sake they had made so long a journey. When, however, they found nowhere the smallest trace of excitement about Him, they were distressed and full of doubts, thinking that they had perhaps gone completely astray.

Their train numbered, I am sure, more than 200 men, and took a quarter of an hour to pass by. A distinguished company had joined them as far back as Causur, and since then others had been added. The three kings rode on dromedaries (camels with two humps), with baggage all round them, and there were three other loaded dromedaries with their riders. Each king was accompanied by four men of his tribe; among them I noticed two young men (one of them was Azarias of Atom), whom I saw later as fathers of families when Jesus visited Arabia. The rest of the company rode mostly on very swift yellowish animals with delicate heads; I am not sure whether these were horses or donkeys. They looked quite different from our horses. The ones ridden by the more distinguished persons had richly ornamented saddles and bridles, and were hung with little gold chains and stars. Some of the company went up to the gate of the city and came back accompanied by guards and soldiers. Their arrival by this road with so large a train caused great surprise, as there was no festival and they were bringing no merchandise with them. When questioned, they explained why they had come, speaking of the star and the newborn Child, but not a soul there understood what they were talking about. This depressed them extremely; they thought that they must certainly have made a mistake, for they could find nobody here who seemed to know anything about the Saviour of the World. Everyone gazed at them in astonishment, and could not understand what they wanted. However, the gate-keepers went back into the city to report when they saw the generous alms given so kindly to the importunate beggars, and heard not only that the kings sought a lodging and would pay liberally, but also that they asked to speak with King Herod. Then followed an exchange of reports, messages, inquiries, and explanations between the kings and the authorities. While this was going on, the kings talked with the various people who had collected round them. Some of them had heard a rumor of a child said to have been born at Bethlehem, but it could not, they said, be He, for His parents were common people and poor. Others only laughed at them; and as they gathered, from what little the people said, that Herod knew nothing of a newborn child, and that, in general, they had no very high opinion of Herod, they became even more dejected, for they were troubled in their minds as to how to deal with the matter when speaking to Herod. However, calming themselves, they fell to praying and took courage again, saying to each other: "He who has led us here so quickly by the star will bring us happily home again."

When the gate-keepers at last came back, the kings and their train were taken round the outside of the city walls for some way and brought into it through a gate near Mount Calvary. They and their baggage-animals were taken to a circular enclosure not far from the fish-market. It was surrounded by houses and stables, and there were guards at the entrances. The animals were taken into the stables, while the kings established themselves in sheds near a fountain in the center of the court. The baggage-animals were watered at this fountain. One side of this circular court was on the slope of a hill; the two other sides were open, with trees in front. Officials now came two by two with torches and examined what the kings had in their baggage. I suppose they were customs officers.

Herod's palace was on higher ground, not far from here, and I saw the way thither illuminated with torches and braziers on poles. Herod sent a servant down and caused the oldest of the kings, Theokeno, to be brought to his palace in secret. It was after ten o'clock at night. He was received in a lower room by one of Herod's courtiers and questioned as to the object of his journey. He related everything in the most child-like manner, and begged him to ask Herod where to find the newborn King of the Jews whose star they had seen and followed in order to worship Him. When the courtier reported this to Herod, he was much startled, but he dissembled and sent in reply a message saying that he would cause inquiries to be made, but that in the meantime the kings were to rest: early next morning he would speak with them all himself and tell them what he had discovered. Theokeno was thus unable to give his companions any special encouragement when he returned to them, and they made no preparations for resting, but on the contrary ordered the repacking of much that had been unpacked. I did not see them sleeping that night at all; they were wandering about separately in the city with guides, looking at the sky as if they were seeking for their star. In Jerusalem itself all was quiet, but there was much talk and coming and going at the guard-house before the court. The kings were of the opinion that Herod probably knew everything but wished to keep it secret from them.

Herod was giving a feast when Theokeno was in the palace; the rooms were illuminated and full of guests, among them brazen-faced women in fine dresses. Theokeno's questions about a newborn King disturbed Herod greatly, and he at once summoned all the high priests and scribes. I saw them coming to him with their scrolls before midnight, wearing their priestly vestments and breast-plates and their girdles with letters. I saw as many as twenty of them about him. He asked them where Christ was to be born, and I saw them unrolling their scrolls before him and answering, pointing with their fingers: "In Bethlehem of Juda, for so it is written by the prophet Micheas: 'And thou Bethlehem in the land of Juda art not the least among the princes of Juda; for out of thee shall come forth the captain that shall rule my people Israel.'" Then I saw Herod walking about on the roof of the palace with some of them and looking in vain for the star of which Theokeno had spoken. He was in a strange state of unrest, but the learned priests made every effort to persuade him not to pay any attention to what the kings had said. These romantic people, they said, were always full of fantastic ideas about their stars; if such a thing had really happened, Herod and they themselves, in the Temple in the Holy City, would of course be the first to know of it.

[Sunday, December 23rd:] Very early this morning

Herod secretly summoned the three kings to his palace.[21] They were received under an archway and taken into a room, where I saw green branches and bushes arranged in vases to welcome them, with some refreshments. They remained standing for a while until Herod came in, and then, after bowing before him, they again asked him about the newborn King of the Jews. Herod concealed his uneasiness as well as he could and even pretended to be overjoyed. He still had some of the scribes with him. He inquired of the kings as to what they had seen, and Mensor described to him the last picture they had seen in the stars before setting off on their journey. This, he said, was a Virgin with a Child before her: on the right-hand side of the picture a branch of light grew forth, bearing on it a tower with several gates. This tower had grown into a great city, over which the Child had appeared as a king with crown, sword, and sceptre. They had then seen themselves and the kings of the whole world come and bow down before the Child in adoration, for His kingdom was to conquer all other kingdoms. Herod told them that a prophecy of this kind about Bethlehem Ephrata did indeed exist and asked them to go there at once very quietly, and when they had found and adored the Child, to come back and bring him word, that he, too, might go and adore Him. The kings, who had not touched any of the food set out for them by Herod, went back again. It was very early, for I saw the torches in front of the palace still alight. Herod spoke to them in secret because of all the talk in the city. The day then began to break, and they made all preparations for their departure. The stragglers who had followed them to Jerusalem had dispersed about the city the night before.

Herod was in a state of ill-humor and vexation in these days. At the time of Christ's birth he had been in his palace near Jericho and had committed a vile murder. He had insinuated adherents of his into the

---

21. That the second visit of the Magi to Herod was in private is recorded in *Matt.* 2:7. (SB)

higher posts of the Temple to find out what was going on there so as to warn him of anyone opposed to his designs. One of these in particular was a high official in the Temple, a good and upright man. He invited this man with friendly words to visit him at Jericho, but caused him to be waylaid and murdered in the desert on his way there, making it appear as the work of robbers. A few days later he came to Jerusalem in order to take part in the feast of the dedication of the Temple on the 25th day of the month Kislev, and there he became involved in a very disagreeable affair. He wanted to do something in his own way which would please the Jews and do them honor. He had a golden image made of a lamb, or rather of a kid, for it had horns. This was to be set up for the festival over the gate leading from the outer court of the women into the Court of Sacrifice. He proposed to force this arrangement on the Jews and yet expected to be thanked for it. The priests opposed it, so he threatened them with fines; whereupon they declared that they would pay the fine, but that their law forbade them ever to accept the image. Herod, bitterly angered, tried to put up the image in secret; but when it was brought into the Temple, it was seized by a zealous official and flung to the ground, so that it broke in two.[22] A tumult ensued, and Herod had the official imprisoned. This affair had so angered him that he regretted coming to the feast. His courtiers endeavored to distract him with all kinds of entertainments.

Now came the rumors of Christ's birth to add to Herod's uneasiness. Of late there had arisen among certain devout Jews a lively sense of the near approach of the Messias. The events attending the birth of Jesus had been spread abroad by the shepherds, but all this was looked on by important people as nonsensical gossip. It had come to Herod's ears, and he had secretly

---

22. This is probably the same story as that recorded by Josephus (*BJ.*, I, xxxiii, 2-4): Herod had put up a golden *eagle* over the main gate of the Temple. Some young Jews climbed up at noonday and smashed it with axes. About forty men were arrested. (SB)

made inquiries at Bethlehem. His messengers came to
the Crib three days after Christ's birth [see above, p.
215], and after talking with St. Joseph, a poor man,
they reported, as all arrogant people like them are wont
to do, that there was nothing to be seen but a poor
family in a miserable cave, and that the whole thing
was not worth talking about. To begin with they were
too arrogant to talk properly to St. Joseph, all the more
as they had been warned not to cause any sensation.
Now, however, Herod was suddenly confronted by the
three kings and their numerous company, and was filled
with fear and dismay, for they came from a long way
off and their story could not be dismissed as idle talk.
When however they inquired so particularly about the
newborn King, he feigned a desire to worship Him too,
much to their joy. He was in no way reassured by the
blind arrogance of the scribes, and was determined in
his own interests that the event should remain as unno-
ticed as possible. He did not at once oppose the statements made to him by the kings, nor did he at once
lay hands on Jesus, for by so doing he feared to give
the impression to the people (who were already in a
difficult frame of mind) that the kings' announcement
was true and of serious consequence to himself. He
therefore planned to gain more accurate information
from the kings before taking steps himself about it.
When the kings, warned by God, failed to return to
him, he announced that their flight was a proof that
they had either been disappointed in their search or
had been lying. He caused it to be spread abroad that
they had been ashamed and afraid to come back,
because they had so greatly deceived themselves and
others; what other reason could there be for their secret
flight, when they had been received by him in so friendly
a manner? In this way he stopped all further rumors
and merely let it be known in Bethlehem that no one
should have anything to do with that family and that
no attention should be paid to misleading rumors and
imaginations. When the Holy Family returned to

Nazareth a fortnight later, it put an end to the talk about an event which had never become clearly known to most people. The devout ones hoped in silence. When all was calm once more, Herod planned to do away with Jesus, but heard that the family with the Child had now left Nazareth. For a long time he caused search to be made for the Child, and when he was forced to give up hope of finding Him, his anxiety increased, and he had recourse to the desperate measure of the Massacre of the Innocents. He took stringent precautions and ordered a number of troop movements in order to prevent any insurrection. I think the children were murdered in seven different places.

I saw the kings and their train moving southwards out of the city gate. A crowd of people followed them as far as a brook outside the walls, and then turned back. After crossing the stream, the kings made a short halt to look for their star. When they saw it they broke into cries of joy, and went on their journey, singing their sweet songs. The star did not lead them by the direct road to Bethlehem, but by a westerly detour. They passed by a little town I know well, and towards midday I saw them stop in a pleasant place near a little village behind the town. A spring of water burst forth before their eyes, at which they were overjoyed. They dismounted and hollowed out a basin round the spring, surrounding it with clean sand, stones, and turf. They stayed several hours here, watering and feeding their beasts, and refreshing themselves with food; for in Jerusalem they had been too disturbed and anxious to rest. In later years I saw Our Lord stopping sometimes by this spring with His disciples and teaching there.

The star, which at night shone like a ball of fire, now looked like the moon in daylight. It was not a perfect round, but had as it were a jagged edge; I often saw it hidden by clouds. The direct road from Jerusalem to Bethlehem was full of travellers with donkeys and baggage, probably returning home from Bethlehem after the taxation, or going to the market or the Temple in

Jerusalem. The way taken by the kings was very quiet, and no doubt God led them by it so that they should not cause too much sensation and should not arrive in Bethlehem before the evening. When the sun was already low, I saw them starting off again. They travelled in the same order as when they first met. Mensor, the brownish one and the youngest, went first; then came Sair, the dark-brown one; and then Theokeno, the white-skinned one and the eldest.

Today, Sunday, December 23rd, at dusk, I saw the three holy kings and their train arrive at the same building outside Bethlehem where Joseph and Mary had been registered. It was the former ancestral house of David of which some masonry still remained; once it had belonged to Joseph's parents. It was a large house with several smaller ones round it; in front of it was a closed court, giving on to an open place with trees and a fountain. In this place I saw Roman soldiers; they were there because of the tax office which was in the building. When the kings and their train arrived, a crowd of inquisitive onlookers began pressing round them. The star had disappeared, and they were somewhat uneasy. Some men came up to them and questioned them. They dismounted, and were met by officials from the house bearing branches, who offered them a light refreshment of bread, fruit, and drink. This was a usual welcome for strangers like these. Meanwhile I saw their beasts being watered at the fountain under the trees. I thought to myself: these strangers are more courteously received than poor Joseph, because of the little gold pieces they distribute. They were told that the Shepherds' Valley was a good camping-place, but remained for some time undecided. I did not hear them ask for the newborn King of the Jews; they knew that according to the prophecy this was the place, but because of what Herod had said to them they were afraid of causing any comment. When, however, they saw a light shining in the sky beside Bethlehem, as though the moon were rising, they mounted again and rode beside a ditch and some ruined walls round the south side of Bethlehem towards the east, approaching the Cave of the Nativity from the field where the angels had appeared to the shepherds. On entering the valley behind the cave, near the grave of Maraha, they dismounted, and their people unpacked much of the luggage and set up a great tent which they had with them. They made all arrangements for an encampment with the help of some shepherds, who had pointed out the places to them.

The camp had been partly arranged when the kings saw the star appear bright and clear above the hill where the Cave of the Nativity was, the light that streamed from it descending in a vertical line on to the hill.[23] The star seemed to grow larger as it drew near until it became a body of light which looked to me as big as a sheet. I saw them at first gazing at it in great astonishment. It was already dark; they saw no house, only the outline of a hill, like a rampart. Suddenly they were filled with great joy, for they saw in the radiance the shining figure of a Child, like the one they had seen before in the star. All bared their heads in obeisance, and the three kings, going up to the hill, found the door of the cave. Mensor opened the door and saw the cave full of heavenly light, and in the back of it the Virgin sitting with the Child, just as they had seen them in their visions. He went back at once and told this to his companions; in the meantime Joseph, accompanied by an aged shepherd, came out of the cave to meet them. They told him, in childlike simplicity, how they had come to adore the newborn King of the Jews, whose star they had seen, and to bring Him gifts. Joseph welcomed them warmly, and the old shepherd accompanied them to their encampment and helped them with their arrangements; some of the shepherds who were there gave them the use of some sheds. They themselves prepared for the solemn ceremony that was before them.

---

23. Cf. *Matt.* 2:9: The star "came and stood over where the child was." (SB)

I saw them putting on big white cloaks with long trains. The material had a yellowish sheen, like raw silk, and was beautifully fine and light. They wore these fluttering robes for all their religious ceremonies. All three wore girdles on which many pouches and gold boxes (like sugar-basins with knobs) were suspended by little chains among the ample folds of their cloaks. Each of the kings was followed by four members of his family. Besides these there there several of Mensor's servants holding a small tablet like a tray, a rug with tassels, and some strips of thin stuff.

They followed St. Joseph in an ordered procession to the shelter at the entrance of the cave, where they covered the tray with the tasselled rug. Each king then placed on it some of the golden boxes and vessels which he took from his girdle; this was the offering which they made in common. Mensor and all the others took their sandals from off their feet, while Joseph opened the door of the cave. Two youths from Mensor's following went before him, spreading out a strip of stuff on the floor of the cave before his feet and then retiring. Two others came close behind him with the tray of presents, which he took from them when he was before the Blessed Virgin, and falling on his knee placed them at her feet on a low stand. Those who had carried the tray went back. Behind Mensor stood the four members of his family, humbly bowing down. Sair and Theokeno with their followers stood at the entrance and under the shelter outside. They were all as though drunk with ecstasy and seemed transfused by the light which filled the cave, though no light was there save the Light of the World. Mary was lying, rather than sitting, on a carpet to the left of the Infant Jesus; she was leaning on her arm. The Child lay in a trough covered with a rug and raised on a high stand, opposite the entrance to the cave and at the place where He was born. As the kings entered, the Blessed Virgin raised herself into a sitting position, covered herself with a veil and took the Infant Jesus on to her lap under her ample veil. When Mensor knelt down and spoke touching words of homage as he put down his presents, humbly bowing his bared head and crossing his hands on his breast, Mary undid the red-and-white wrappings from the upper part of the Child's body, which gleamed softly from behind her veil. She supported His head with one hand and held Him with the other. He was holding His little hands before His breast as if in prayer. He was shining with welcome, and now and then made friendly little gestures with His hands.

Oh what heavenly peace surrounds the prayers of these good men from the East! As I saw them, I said to myself: how clear and untroubled are their hearts, as full of goodness and innocence as the hearts of pious children. There is nothing violent in them, and yet they are all fire and love. I am dead, I am a spirit, otherwise I could not see it, for it is not happening now—and yet it *is* now, for it is not in time; in God is no time, in God everything is present. I am dead, I am a spirit. As these strange thoughts came to me, I heard myself being told: "What is that to thee? Be not troubled, look, and praise the Lord who is eternal and in whom are all things."

I now saw Mensor bringing out of a pouch hanging at his girdle a handful of little thick shining bars. They were as long as one's finger, pointed at the top, and speckled with little gold-colored grains in the middle. He offered these to Our Lady as his gift, laying them humbly on her knee beside the Child. She accepted the gold with loving gratitude, and covered it with a corner of her cloak. These little bars of natural gold were Mensor's gift, because he was full of fidelity and love and was seeking for the holy truth with unshaken fervor and devotion. He then withdrew with his four companions, and Sair, the dark-brown one, came forward with his following and, falling with great humility on both knees, offered his present with touching words of homage. This was a little golden incense-boat full of little greenish grains of gum, which he laid on the table before the Infant Jesus. Incense was his gift because he embraced the Will of God, and followed it willingly, reverently, and lovingly. He knelt there for a long time with deep devotion before withdrawing. After him came Theokeno, the white-skinned one and the oldest. He was very old and heavy and was not able to kneel down; but he stood bowing low and placed on the table a golden vessel containing a delicate green plant. It seemed to be rooted; it was a tiny green upright tree, very delicate, bearing curly foliage with little delicate white flowers. It was myrrh. His gift was myrrh, because it symbolizes mortification and the overcoming of passions; for this good man had conquered extreme temptations to commit idolatry, polygamy, and to give way to violence. He remained standing in deep emotion before the Infant Jesus with his attendants for a very long time, and I grew sorry for the other servants before the Crib having to wait so long to see the Child. The addresses made by the kings and their followers were extremely touching and childlike. As they knelt down and offered their presents, they said: "We have seen His star, we have seen that He is king over all kings, and we come to worship Him and to pay Him homage with our gifts"—or something like this. They seemed to be in an ecstasy, and with childlike and rapturous prayers committed to the Infant Jesus themselves and their families, their lands and their peoples, all their goods and possessions and everything of value that they owned. They besought the newborn King to accept their hearts and souls and all their thoughts and deeds, begging Him to enlighten them and to grant them every virtue and, while they were on earth, happiness, peace, and love. While thus praying, they were overflowing with loving humility; and tears of joy coursed down their cheeks and beards. They were blissfully happy, they thought that they had now reached the very star for which their ancestors had watched for centuries with faithful yearning. All the joy of promises fulfilled after many centuries was theirs.

The Mother of God accepted all these gifts with humble gratitude. At first she said nothing, but a gentle movement under her veil showed the joy and emotion that she felt. The Child's bare body, which she had wrapped in her veil, seemed to shine from under her cloak. Afterwards she spoke a few, friendly, humble words of gratitude to each king, throwing her veil back a little as she did so. Ah, I said to myself, I have been given another lesson. With what sweet and loving gratitude she accepts each gift—she, who needs naught, who possesses Jesus Himself, accepts with humility every loving gift. From this I can surely learn how loving gifts should be received; I, too, in future will accept every kindness with thankfulness and all humility. How kind Mary and Joseph are; they kept nothing at all for themselves, but gave it all away to the poor.

When the kings with their attendants had left the Cave and gone to their encampment, their servants came in. They had put up the tent, unloaded the baggage animals and, after arranging everything, were waiting in patient humility before the entrance. There must have been at least thirty of them, as well as a host of boys who had nothing on but loin-cloths and little cloaks. The servants always came in fives, led by one of the important personages to whom they belonged. They knelt round the Child and venerated Him in silence. Afterwards the boys came in all together, knelt round and worshipped the Infant Jesus with childlike innocence and joy. The servants did not stay long in the cave, for the kings came back again, making a solemn entry this time. They had put on other cloaks of thin stuff which floated round them in ample folds; they carried censers in their hands and censed with great reverence the Child and the Blessed Virgin and St. Joseph and the whole cave, withdrawing afterwards with low obeisances. This was a customary form of worship amongst these people.

During all this Mary and Joseph were as full of sweet joy as I ever saw them; tears of happiness often ran

down their cheeks. The recognition and solemn veneration of the Infant Jesus, whom they had been obliged
to lodge so poorly, and whose infinite glory was a secret
hidden in their humble hearts, brought them endless
consolation. By God's almighty Providence they saw the
Child of the Promise being given, in spite of the blindness of mankind, what they themselves could not give
him—the worship of the great ones of the earth with
all the sacred splendor due to Him, prepared since centuries and sent from a far country. They worshipped
Jesus with the holy kings, happy in the honor paid to
Him.

The kings' encampment was set up in the valley behind
the Cave, stretching as far as the tomb of Maraha. The
beasts of burden were fastened in rows to posts between
ropes. Beside the big tent, which was near the hill of
the Cave of the Nativity, was an enclosure roofed with
mats where part of the baggage was stored, though most
of it was taken into Maraha's tomb. The stars had come
out when all had left the Crib, and they all assembled
in a circle near the old terebinth tree which stood above
Maraha's tomb and there, with solemn hymns, held
their service to the stars. I cannot express how mov-
ingly their singing echoed through the quiet valley. For
so many centuries their forebears had gazed at the stars,
prayed, and sung; and today all their yearning was fulfilled. They sang in raptures of gratitude and joy.

Meanwhile Joseph, helped by two of the old shepherds, had set out a light meal in the kings' tent. They
brought plates with bread, fruit, honey-comb, bowls with
vegetables, and flasks of balsam, arranging it all on a
low table on a carpet. Joseph had got together all these
provisions for the kings in the morning, having been
forewarned of their arrival by the Blessed Virgin. When
the kings and the members of their families returned
to the tent after their evening hymn, I saw Joseph
receiving them with great friendliness and begging them
to be his guests and accept this modest meal. He reclined
among them round the low table as they ate. He was

not at all shy, and was so happy that he shed tears of joy. (When I saw this, I thought of how my dead father, who was a poor peasant, was obliged to sit at table with so many grand people when I was clothed at the convent. He was very humble and simple and had dreaded this sorely, but afterwards he was so happy that he wept for joy. Without wanting it he became the guest of honor.) After this slight meal Joseph left them. Some of the more important persons accompanying the kings betook themselves to an inn at Bethlehem, the others lay down to rest on their couches spread out in a circle in the big tent.

When Joseph returned to the Crib, he put all the presents in a corner of the wall to the right of the Crib, placing a screen before it so that what was kept there could not be seen. Anna's maidservant, who had remained behind to wait on the Blessed Virgin, had stayed all this time in the small side-cave, of which the door was in the entrance to the Cave of the Nativity. She did not come out until all had left the Crib. She was very serious and modest. I never saw either the Holy Family or this maidservant showing any worldly pleasure at the sight of the kings' gifts. Everything was accepted with humble gratitude, and given away again with gentle charity.

When the kings had arrived that evening at the tax-collecting office in Bethlehem, I had seen a certain amount of disturbance there and much movement in the town; some people followed the kings to the Valley of the Shepherds, but soon came back again. Afterwards, while the kings, radiant with holy joy, were worshipping and offering their gifts at the Crib, I saw some Jews lurking at a distance in the country round and murmuring angrily, and then going about in Bethlehem spreading all kinds of rumors. These miserable men made me shed bitter tears; I was grieved at heart for the evil people who, nowadays as in those distant times, stand about muttering and grumbling and spreading lies in their wrath; salvation is so close to them, and they thrust it from them. How unlike they are to the good kings who, in their trusting faith in the Promise, have come from so far and have found salvation. How I pity the hardhearted and blind!

In Jerusalem during this day I saw Herod again with several scribes. They were reading from scrolls and talking of the statement made by the kings. Afterwards it was no more spoken of, as though the whole matter were to be ignored.

[December 24th:] Very early today I saw the kings and some of their followers pay separate visits to the Infant Jesus and the Blessed Virgin. During the whole day I saw them busy in their camp beside their beasts of burden distributing all kinds of things. They were full of joy and happiness, and gave away many gifts, as I have always seen done on joyful occasions. The shepherds who had rendered services to the kings and their train were given many presents, and I saw many poor people receiving gifts. I saw them hanging coverlets over the shoulders of some poor old women who crept up to them all bent. Several of the kings' followers took a great liking to the Shepherds' Valley, wishing to stay there and join the shepherds. They submitted this wish to the kings, who allowed them to leave their service and gave them rich presents. They were given blankets, household utensils, grains of gold, and also the donkeys on which they had ridden. When I saw the kings distributing a quantity of bread, I at first wondered where so much bread came from. Then I remembered having seen that sometimes, when they halted, they used their provision of flour to bake little thin flat loaves like rusks in iron molds, which they carried with them. These loaves they packed tightly in light leather boxes, which they hung on their pack-animals. Today many people came from Bethlehem and pestered the kings for gifts of all kinds. Some of these searched their baggage, and on various pretexts made greedy demands of them. Here, and in Jerusalem too, the sensation caused by their numerous following had been a great annoy-

ance to the kings. They had arrived in a kind of triumphal procession, thinking to find general rejoicings
over the newborn King, but after what had happened
they now resolved to start their return journey quietly
and with a smaller following, which would enable them
to travel more rapidly. They therefore dismissed today
many of their followers; some of whom remained behind
in the Valley of the Shepherds, while others went on
ahead to meeting-places arranged beforehand. I was
surprised to see how much their train had diminished
by the evening. The kings no doubt intended to travel
the next day to Jerusalem and to tell Herod that they
had found the Child; but they wanted to do this more
quietly, and this was why they sent many on ahead,
thus making the journey easier. They and their dromedaries could overtake them without difficulty.

In the evening they went to the Crib to say farewell.
Mensor went in first, alone. Mary placed the Infant
Jesus in his arms; he shed tears and his face was shining with joy. After him the two others came and wept
as they said farewell. They brought yet more gifts,
many pieces of different stuffs, some looking like
undyed silk, some red and some with flowered patterns, and a number of beautiful thin coverlets; they
also left behind their ample, thin cloaks. These were
pale yellow and seemed to be woven of the finest wool;
they were so light that they moved with every breath
of air. They also brought many bowls standing one on
the other, and boxes filled with grains, and a basket
with pots of little delicate green bushes with small
white flowers. There were three of these in the center
of each pot, so arranged that another pot could be
placed on the edge; the pots were built up above each
other in the basket. This was myrrh. They also gave
Joseph long narrow baskets containing birds; they had
had a number of these hanging on their dromedaries
for killing and eating.

They all shed many tears when they left the Child
and Mary. I saw the Blessed Virgin standing up beside

them as they said farewell. She held the Infant Jesus in her arms wrapped in her veil, and went a few steps with the kings towards the door of the cave. There she stood still, and in order to give these holy men a remembrance, she took from her head the thin yellow veil covering the Infant Jesus and herself and handed it to Mensor. The kings received this gift with deep obeisances, and their hearts overflowed with awe and gratitude when they saw the Blessed Virgin standing before them unveiled with the Infant Jesus. They were weeping with ioy as they left the Cave. Henceforth the veil was the holiest treasure that they possessed.

The manner in which the Blessed Virgin accepted presents, although it did not show pleasure in the things themselves, was particularly touching in its humility and in its real gratitude towards the giver. During this wonderful visit I saw in her no trace of self-interest, except that to begin with, out of love for the Infant Jesus and out of pity for Joseph, she allowed herself in all simplicity the joy of hoping that now they might perhaps find a shelter in Bethlehem and not be so contemptuously treated as on their arrival. She had been truly sorry for Joseph's distress and confusion at this.

After the kings had said farewell it grew dark, and the lamp was lit in the cave. The kings went with their followers to the great old terebinth tree above Maraha's grave, there to hold their evening service as they had the day before. A lamp was burning beneath the tree. When they saw the stars coming out, they prayed and sang their sweet songs. The voices of the boys sounded particularly lovely among the others. After this they went into their tent, where Joseph had once more prepared a light meal for them; and then some returned to the inn in Bethlehem, while the rest lay down in the tent.

At midnight I suddenly saw a vision. I saw the kings lying asleep in their tent on rugs, and I saw the appearance of a shining youth among them. It was an angel. Their lamp was burning, and I saw them sitting up, half asleep. The angel woke them and told them to leave immediately, and not to go by Jerusalem but through the desert round the Dead Sea. They sprang in haste from their couches; some hurried to rouse their followers, one went to the Cave and woke St. Joseph, who hastened to Bethlehem to summon those who were in the inn. These, however, met him on his way there, for they had had the same vision. The tent was taken down, packed, and the rest of the encampment removed, all with wonderful speed. While the kings were taking once more a touching farewell of Joseph before the Crib, their followers were already hurrying southwards through the desert of Engaddi along the shores of the Dead Sea. They travelled in separate parties so as to progress more quickly.

The kings begged that the Holy Family should fly with them, for danger most certainly threatened them, or at least that Mary should hide herself with the Child so as not to be molested because of them. They cried like children, embracing Joseph and speaking in the most moving manner. Then they mounted their dromedaries, which carried but little baggage, and hastened away across the desert. I saw the angel with them out in the fields, showing them their way; they seemed to be gone in an instant. They took different ways, about a quarter of an hour's distance apart from each other. First they went for an hour towards the east, and then southwards into the desert. Their way home led through the region which Jesus traversed on His return from Egypt in the third year of His ministry.

[December 25th:] The angel had warned the kings just in time, for the authorities in Bethlehem—perhaps on a secret order from Herod, but I think from their own zeal of office—meant to arrest today the kings who were sleeping in the inn at Bethlehem and to imprison them in the cellars deep under the synagogue. They were then going to denounce them to Herod as disturbers of the peace. However, when their departure became known this morning, they were already near

Engaddi, and the valley where they had encamped was quiet and deserted as usual, with nothing but the trodden grass and a few tent-poles to show that they had been there. In the meantime the appearance in Bethlehem of the kings and their train had caused a considerable stir. Some regretted that they had refused Joseph a lodging; others said that the kings were strange fanatical adventurers; while others connected their arrival with the rumors of what the shepherds had seen. The authorities of the place (perhaps as the result of a warning from Herod, but of this I am not sure) decided that steps must be taken to deal with the situation. In the center of the town, in an open place with a fountain surrounded by trees, I saw near the synagogue a large house with steps leading up to it. All the inhabitants were summoned to the square in front of the house, and I saw a warning or command being given to them from the steps. They were told that all perverse talk and superstitious rumors must be stopped, and from now onwards there must be no more running backwards and forwards outside the town to the dwelling of the people who had been the cause of all this talk. After the assembled people had dispersed, I saw St. Joseph summoned by two men and being examined in that house by some aged Jews. I saw him go back to the Crib and then again go to the court-house. When he went there the second time, he took with him some of the gold from the kings' gifts and gave it to them, upon which they let him go in peace. It seemed to me that the whole examination was a sort of blackmail. I saw, too, that a path leading towards the Crib was blocked by the authorities by felling a tree across it. This was not the path through the town-gate, but the one which led over a hill or rampart to the Cave of the Nativity from the place where Mary had waited under a big tree on arriving at Bethlehem. They even put up a guard-house by the tree, and stretched ropes across the road which were attached to a bell in the guard-house, so that they could hold up anyone who tried to pass. In the afternoon I saw a band of sixteen of Herod's soldiers talking to Joseph; they were probably sent on account of the kings, who had been accused of being disturbers of the peace. Finding, however, everything quiet and lonely, with nobody but a poor family in the cave, and having been warned not to alarm these in any way, they went quietly back to report what they had found. The presents and other things left by the kings had been hidden away by Joseph partly in Maraha's grave and partly in some secret places in the hill of the Cave of the Nativity, which he knew of since his boyhood when he had often hidden there from his brothers. These separate hiding-places dated from the time of the patriarch Jacob, who had once set up his tents here on this hill. At that time there were only a few tents on the site of Bethlehem.

This evening I saw Zacharias of Hebron coming to see the Holy Family for the first time. Mary was still in the cave. He wept with joy, took the Infant Jesus in his arms, and repeated (in part or somewhat altered) the hymn of praise which he had uttered at the circumcision of John.

[December 26th:] Today Zacharias went away again, but Anna came back to visit the Holy Family with her eldest daughter, her second husband and the maidservant. Anna's eldest daughter is bigger than her mother and really looks older than Anna. Anna's second husband is taller and older than Joachim was. His name is Eliud, and he had a post at the Temple connected with the supervision of the sacrificial animals. Anna had a daughter by him, also called Mary. At Christ's birth she must have been six or eight years old. This Eliud died soon after this, and it was God's Will that Anna should marry for the third time. Of this marriage there was a son, who was called one of Christ's brethren.

The maidservant brought by Anna from Nazareth a week ago is still with the Blessed Virgin. While Our Lady was living in the Cave of the Nativity, this maid-

servant lived in the little cave at the side; but now, as
Mary is in the cave at the side, the maidservant sleeps
under a shelter put up for her by Joseph in front of
the cave. Anna and her companions sleep in the Cave
of the Nativity.

The Holy Family is now deeply joyful. Anna is blissfully happy. Mary often lays the Infant Jesus in her
arms for her to nurse. I did not see her do that with
anyone else. I saw, to my great wonderment, that the
Infant's hair, which is yellow and curly, ends in little
fine rays of light intersecting each other. I think they
make His hair curly, for I see them rubbing His head
after washing it. They put a little cloak round Him the
while. I always see in the Holy Family the most touching and devout honor being paid to the Infant Jesus,
but it is all quite simple and human, as it always is
with holy and elect ones. The Child turns to His Mother
with love such as I have never seen in one so young.

Mary told her mother all about the visit of the three
holy kings, and Anna was greatly moved on hearing
that the Lord God had summoned them from so far to
acknowledge the Child of the Promise. She was shown
the gifts of the kings, which were hidden in a wicker
basket in a covered niche in the wall. She recognized
them as tokens of homage and gazed at them with deep
humility. She helped to give away some of them and to
arrange and pack up the rest. All is now quiet in the
neighborhood; all the paths except the one through the
gate of the town have been closed by the authorities.
Joseph no longer goes to Bethlehem for what he wants;
the shepherds bring him everything needful. The
kinswoman with whom Anna stayed in Benjamin is
Mara, the daughter of Elisabeth's sister Rhode. She is
poor, and had several sons, who became disciples. One
of them was called Nathanael and was later the bridegroom at Cana. This Mara was present at the Blessed
Virgin's death at Ephesus.

This Nathanael is not the one whom Jesus saw under
the fig-tree. Nathanael, Mara's son, was present as a

boy at the children's festival given by Anna for the twelve-year-old Jesus, when He came home after His first teaching in the Temple. The boy Jesus told on this occasion a parable of a wedding where water was to be turned into wine, and of another wedding, where wine was to be turned into blood. He told the boy Nathanael, as if in jest, that one day He would be present at Nathanael's wedding. The bride of Cana came from Bethlehem, from Joseph's family. After the miracle at Cana the bridegroom and the bride made a mutual vow of continence. Nathanael at once became a disciple and received the name Amator in Baptism. Later he was made a Bishop and was in Edessa; he was also in the island of Crete with Carpus. He then went to Armenia, and because of the many conversions he made he was captured and sent into exile to the shores of the Black Sea. On being set free he came into Mensor's land, where he worked a miracle (which I have forgotten) on a woman and baptized so many people that he was done to death, in the city of Acajacuh on an island in the River Euphrates.[24]

Today Anna sent away her husband Eliud with a loaded donkey and the maidservant, her relation, with two big packs. She carried one on her back and one in front. These contain part of the kings' gifts, stuffs of various kinds and golden vessels, which in later years were used at the first Christian religious services. They are sending everything away in secret, for some sort of investigation is always going on about here. It seems as though they are only taking these things to some place on the way to Nazareth whence they will be fetched by servants, for in earlier visions I saw Eliud back in Bethlehem at Anna's departure thence, which will soon take place. Anna was now alone with Mary in the side-cave. I saw that they were working together, plaiting and

---

24. Nathanael under the fig-tree: *John* 1:45-51; the Marriage of Cana: *John* 2:1-11. Of the subsequent events there is no documentary record, unless Carpus in Crete is to be identified with St. Paul's friend at Troas (*2 Tim.* 4:13). For the city of Acajacuh, see n. 8. p, 238. (SB)

knitting a coarse blanket. The Cave of the Nativity is now completely cleared out. Joseph's donkey is hidden behind wicker screens. Today there were again officers of Herod in Bethlehem, searching in a number of houses for a newborn child. Soldiers came, too, looking for a newborn son of a king. They were particularly persistent in their questioning of a distinguished Jewish woman who had lately given birth to a son. They did not go near the Cave of the Nativity; they had been there before and found only a poor family, so took for granted that it was nothing to do with these. Two old men, shepherds I think, came to Joseph and warned him of these inquiries. That was why I saw the Holy Family and Anna escaping into Maraha's grave with the Infant Jesus. There was nothing left in the Cave of the Nativity to show that it had been lived in; it looked quite deserted. I saw them going through the valley in the night with a covered light. Anna held the Infant Jesus before her in her arms, Mary and Joseph walking beside her. The shepherds accompanied them, carrying the blankets and other things to make resting-places for the holy women and the Infant Jesus. (I had a vision meanwhile; I do not know whether the Holy Family saw it, too. Round the Infant Jesus at Anna's breast I saw a glory of seven figures of angels, intertwining and superimposed on each other. Many other figures appeared in this glory, and beside Anna, Joseph, and Mary I saw figures of light who seemed to be leading them by the arms.) On reaching the passage into the cave, they shut the door and then went into the cave itself and prepared their resting-places there.

[December 27th:] The Blessed Virgin told her mother all about the three kings, and they looked at all the things that the latter had yesterday left behind in Maraha's grave. I saw two shepherds come and warn the Blessed Virgin that people were coming from the authorities to look for her Child. Mary was in great distress at this, and soon after I saw St. Joseph come in and take the Infant Jesus from her arms. He wrapped

Him in a cloak and took Him away; I can no longer remember where to. I now saw the Blessed Virgin for at least half a day alone in the cave without the Infant Jesus and full of a mother's fear and anxiety. When the time came near for her to be called to give suck to the Child, she did as all good mothers are wont to do after being alarmed or upset: before suckling the Child she pressed out from her breast the disturbed milk, letting it fall into a little hollow in the white stone bench in the cave. This she told to a good devout shepherd who came to her (probably to lead her to the Child). He, deeply sensible of the holiness of the Mother of the Redeemer, afterwards scooped carefully out with a sort of spoon the virgin milk enclosed in the little white hollow of the stone. In his simple faith he brought it to his wife, who was suckling a child but had not enough milk to feed it. The good woman drank this holy nourishment with reverent trustfulness, and at once her faith was rewarded, so that she was able to feed her child abundantly. Since then the white stone in this cave was given a similar healing power, and I saw that right up to our own day even Mohammedans, though unbelievers, use it as a remedy in this as in other bodily ailments. The earth from this place was for ages cleansed and pressed into small molds by the guardians of the Holy Land and distributed throughout Christendom as a pious remembrance. These relics bear the inscription *"de lacte sanctissimae Virginis Mariae"* ("of the milk of the Most Holy Virgin Mary").

Joseph did not remain hidden in the grave of Maraha. I saw him making all sorts of arrangements in the Cave of the Nativity with the two old shepherds. I saw the shepherds carrying in wreaths of leaves and flowers, but did not at first know why they were doing this; afterwards I saw that they were the preparations for a very touching ceremony. I saw Eliud, Anna's second husband, there once more, and also the maidservant. They had brought two donkeys with them. They had probably met Anna's menservants when the latter had come only part of the way from Nazareth with the animals, and had then sent the men and the baggage back to Nazareth and brought the donkeys to Bethlehem themselves. When I saw them on their way back here, I thought for some time that they were people from an inn outside Jerusalem where I saw the Holy Family staying later. Joseph had made use of the absence of the Blessed Virgin in Maraha's grave to decorate the Cave of the Nativity, with the help of the shepherds, in honor of the anniversary of their wedding. When all was in order, he fetched the Blessed Virgin with the Infant Jesus and Anna, and led them into the decorated Cave of the Nativity. Eliud and the maidservant and the three old shepherds were already there. How moving it was to see their joy when the Blessed Virgin carried the Infant Jesus into the cave! The roof and walls of the cave were hung with wreaths of flowers, and a table was set for a meal in the center. Some of the three holy kings' beautiful carpets were spread on the floor and table and hung on the walls. On the table a pyramid of foliage and flowers rose to an opening in the roof: on the topmost twig there was a dove which had, I think, been made for the occasion. I saw the whole cave full of lights and brightness. They had put the Infant Jesus sitting up in His basket-cradle on a stool. Mary and Joseph, crowned with wreaths, stood beside Him and drank out of one goblet. Besides the relations the old shepherds were present. They sang hymns and partook happily of a light meal. I saw choirs of angels and heavenly powers appearing in the cave. All present were filled with emotion and fervor. After this ceremony the Blessed Virgin with the Infant Jesus and Anna again betook themselves to the grave of Maraha.

[December 28th to 30th:] In the last few days and again today I have seen St. Joseph making various preparations for the approaching departure of the Holy Family from Bethlehem. He got rid every day of some of his household belongings. He is giving the shepherds all the light wicker screens and other contrivances for making the cave comfortable, and they are taking them all away. This afternoon there were again many people at the cave on their way to Bethlehem for the Sabbath, but finding it forsaken they soon went on. Anna is going back to Nazareth after the Sabbath. Today they are arranging and packing up everything. Anna is taking with her on two donkeys many of the gifts of the three holy kings, especially carpets, coverings, and stuffs. They kept the Sabbath this evening in Maraha's grave, and continued keeping it next day (Saturday), when all was quiet in the neighborhood. When the Sabbath was ended, all preparations were made for the departure for Nazareth of Anna and Eliud and their servants. Once, and again tonight for the second time, I saw the Blessed Virgin carry the Infant Jesus in the dark from the grave of Maraha into the Cave of the Nativity. She laid Him on a carpet at the place of His birth and knelt down in prayer beside Him. I saw the whole cave full of heavenly light as at the moment when Our Lord was born. I think that the dear Mother of God must have seen that, too.

[Sunday, December 30th:] At early dawn I saw Anna, with her husband and servants, start for Nazareth after taking a tender farewell of the Holy Family and the three old shepherds. Anna's maidservant went with them, and I was again astonished by her strange cap, which was almost like a "cuckoo-basket," the name given by our peasant children at home to a pointed cap they plait from reeds in their games. (The reason why I thought for some time that Anna's husband and maidservant were people from the inn outside Jerusalem may have been that I had seen them spending the night in that inn and conversing with its owners.) They took all that still remained of the kings' gifts and packed them on their beasts. While they were doing this, I was very much astonished to see them taking with them a package belonging to me. I felt that it was there, and could not at all make out what had induced Anna to take my property away with her.

[Soon after this expression of surprise that Anna should take away from Bethlehem something belonging to her, Sister Emmerich, the following dialogue took place between the latter (who was in a visionary state of great intensity) and the writer.

[Sister Emmerich: "When Anna went away, she took with her many of the kings' gifts, especially stuffs. Some of these were used in the first Christian Church, and pieces have survived until our own time. A piece of the cloth that covered the little table on which the kings laid their presents and a piece of one of their cloaks are among my own relics."[25] Since some of these relics were in a little cupboard beside her bed, while others were in the writer's house, he asked: "Are these relics of stuff here?"

[Catherine Emmerich: "No, over there in the house."

[The writer: "In my house?"

[Catherine Emmerich: "No, in the pilgrim's house (her usual name for the writer). They are in a little bundle, the piece of the cloak is faded. People will not believe it, but it is true, all the same, and I see it before my eyes." When the writer brought the relics kept in his house in what might certainly be described as "little bundles," she opened one of these at once and identified a little piece of dark red silk as part of the kings' stuffs, without, however, giving any more precise explanation about it. She then said: "I am sure I have another little piece of the kings' stuffs. They had several cloaks, a thick strong one for bad weather, a yellow one and a red one of very thin light wool. These cloaks blew in the wind as they went. At their cere-

---

25. Catherine Emmerich was in the highest degree sensitive to the hidden qualities of all material objects consecrated by the Church, and in particular to relics of the saints. In the presence of their bones, or of stuff which they had worn, she was able to give their names and often the smallest details of their stories. She identified numbers of relics rescued from destroyed churches, private houses, and even old curiosity shops, sometimes first telling where they were to be found. She was given many of these, including two large reliquaries full of relics from early times, which were presented to her by one of her spiritual directors. (CB)

monies they wore cloaks of shining undyed silk, embroidered at the edge with gold. These had long trains which had to be carried. I think that a piece of a cloak like this must be near me, and that is why tonight and before that I was watching silk being produced and woven in the country of the kings. I remember that in an eastern land, between Theokeno's and Sair's countries, there were trees full of silkworms, with little ditches of water round each tree to prevent the silkworms from escaping. I sometimes saw them strewing leaves under the trees, and I saw little boxes hanging from their branches. Out of these boxes they took little round things more than a finger in length. I thought, at first, they were some strange kind of birds' eggs, but I soon saw that they were the cocoons which the worms had spun round themselves, for I saw people winding off threads as fine as gossamer. I saw them fastening a mass of this on their breasts and spinning from it a fine thread, rolling it up on something they held in their hands. I saw them also weaving among trees: the loom looked white, it was quite simple, and the woven stuff must have been about the breadth of my sheet."

[A few days later she said:] "My doctor has often questioned me about a piece of very curiously woven silk. A short time ago I saw a similar piece in my room, but do not know what has become of it. I have been thinking over it, and realized that I had a vision of the women weaving silk in a country to the east of the countries of the three kings. It was in the country that St. Thomas visited. I made a mistake, it does not belong to the holy kings' stuff, the pilgrim must cross that out. Somebody gave it to me as a senseless sort of test, without considering what I was contemplating internally at that moment: this causes sad confusion. Now, however, I have seen the relics again and know where they are. Several years ago I gave a little packet, sewn together like a knob, to my sister-in-law who lives at Flamske. It was before her last confinement, and she

had begged me for some kind of holy relic to support
her; so I gave her this little bundle, which I saw shining and as though it had once been in contact with the
Mother of God. I cannot remember whether I looked
through its whole contents at the time, but the good
woman got great comfort from it. It contains a little
piece of dark red carpet and two little pieces of thin
woven stuff, like crêpe, of the color of raw silk; also a
piece of some stuff like green calico, a tiny piece of
wood, and a few little splinters of white stone. I have
sent a message to my sister-in-law to bring them back
to me."

[A few days later her sister-in-law paid her a visit
and brought the little packet, which was about the size
of a walnut. The writer undid it very carefully at home,
and separated the remnants of stuff which were twisted
together in it, moistening them and pressing them flat
between the leaves of a book. These consisted of about
two square inches of thick coarse woollen stuff woven
in a very faded flowered pattern, in color dark reddish
brown and in places dark purple; there were also strips,
two fingers in length and breadth, of loose, thin woven
stuff like muslin, of the color of raw silk; and a little
piece of wood and a few splinters of stone. In the evening
he held the pieces of stuff, which he had put inside
note-paper, in front of her eyes. Not knowing what it
was, she said first: "What am I to do with these letters?" Then, as soon as she had taken the closed letters one by one in her hand, she said: "You must keep
that carefully and not allow one thread of it to be lost.
The thick stuff that looks brown now was once a deep
red; it was part of a carpet as big as my room; the servants of the kings spread it out in the Cave of the
Nativity, and Mary sat on it with the Infant Jesus while
the kings swung their censers. Afterwards she always
kept it in the cave, and she put it on the donkey when
she went to Jerusalem for the Presentation of the Infant
Jesus in the Temple. The thin crêpe-like stuff is a piece
of a short cloak of three separate strips of stuff which

the kings wore fastened to their collars. It was like a ceremonial stole and fluttered over back and shoulders. It had a fringe with tassels. The splinters of wood and stone are of a later time: they come from the Promised Land."

[During these days she saw, in her consecutive visions of the Ministry of Jesus, the events of January 27th in the year of His death. She saw Our Lord on His way to Bethany in an inn near Bethoron[26] with seventeen disciples. "He taught them about their calling and kept the Sabbath with them: the lamp was burning the whole day. Among these disciples is one who has lately followed Him from Sichar. I saw him so plainly, some of his bones must be among my relics, a little thin white splinter. His name sounds like Silan or Vilan, those are the letters I see." Finally she said: "Silvanus," adding after a while: "I have once more seen the little pieces of stuff which I possess belonging to the three kings. There must be another little bundle there; among its contents are a piece of King Mensor's cloak, a piece of a red silk covering which was beside the Holy Sepulchre in old days, and a piece of the red and white stole of a saint. I also see the little bone-splinter of the disciple Silvanus in it."[27] After an interval of absence of mind, she said: "I see now where that little bundle is. Eighteen months ago I gave it to a woman here to hang round her neck. She is still wearing it, and I will ask her to give it back to me. She was so sympathetic when I was arrested[28] that I gave it to her to wear to console her. I did not then know its exact contents, I only saw that it shone, that it was a holy relic and had been in contact with the Mother of God. Now that I have seen everything to do with the three holy kings so clearly, I recognize everything round me that has to do

---

26. Bethoron is about twenty miles northwest of Jerusalem. Cf. n. 1, p. 10. (SB)
27. Silvanus: is this St. Paul's friend, called Silas in *Acts* (55:22, etc.) and Silvanus by St. Paul (*1 Thess.* 1:1; *2 Cor.* 1:19) and by St. Peter (*1 Ptr.* 5:12)? (SB)
28. "Arrested"—AC was a nun at the Augustinian Convent at Dülmen, when in 1812 Jerome Bonaparte, King of Westphalia, closed the convent and dispersed the nuns, who were compelled to live as seculars and find refuge in private houses. (SB)

with them, including these relics of stuffs. I had forgotten where all these things were."

[A few days later, when the little package returned,
she gave it to the writer to open, as she herself was
ill. He undid the little old bundle (which had been
firmly sewn up years before) in the room opening into
Catherine Emmerich's, and found the following objects
in it, tightly wrapped round each other:

(1) A narrow little strip (like a rolled-up hem)
of natural-colored woven material of some very
soft wool too fragile and thin to unfold.

(2) Two pieces of yellowish cotton material,
loosely woven but quite strong, a finger in length
and half that in breadth.

(3) A square inch of patterned crimson silk
material.

(4) A square quarter-inch of silk brocade, yellow and white.

(5) A little piece of green and brown silk
material.

(6) In the middle of all this was a folded
paper containing a white stone the size of a
pea.

[The writer put all these objects in separate pieces
of paper, except No. (6), which he left in its old paper.
When he brought them to Catherine Emmerich, who
did not seem to be in a visionary state, she coughed
and complained of violent pains, but then said: "What
are those letters you have? They are shining: what treasures we possess, more valuable than a kingdom." She
then took the closed letters (the contents of which it
was impossible for her to know) one by one, weighing
each in her hand. She was silent for a few moments,
as though looking within herself, and, as she handed
each back, gave the following information about their
contents without making a single mistake (for the writer
tested what she said by at once opening the letters,

which were all exactly alike, as she handed them back).

(1) This comes from a coat of Mensor's, it is of very fine wool. It had arm-holes and no sleeves. A piece of stuff hung from the shoulder to the elbow like the half of a slit-up sleeve. She then exactly described the shape, material, and color of the relic.

(2) This is from a cloak left behind by the kings. She again described the nature of the relic.

(3) This is a piece of a covering of thick red silk which was spread out on the floor of the Holy Sepulchre when the Christians were still in possession of Jerusalem. When the Turks conquered the city, this silk was still as good as new. It was cut into pieces when the knights divided everything, and each one received a piece as a remembrance.

(4) This is from the stole of a very holy priest named Alexius. I think he was a Capuchin, and he was always praying at the Holy Sepulchre. The Turks mishandled him grievously. They stabled their horses in the church, and made an old Turkish woman go and stand before the Holy Sepulchre where he was praying. He paid no attention and went on with his prayers. Finally they walled him up there, and made the old woman give him bread and water through an opening. I remember this much from a great deal that I saw lately when I saw the little bundle and its contents without knowing for certain where they were.

(5) This is not a holy relic, but is worthy of respect. It is taken from the seats and benches on which the princes and knights sat in a circle in the Church of the Holy Sepulchre. This, like the red silk, was divided up amongst them.

(6) In this is a little stone from the chapel

above the Holy Sepulchre, and also the little splinter of the bone of Sylvanus, the disciple of Sichar.

[When the writer said that there was no bone-splinter in it, she said "Go and look." He went at once into the next room to the light, opened the folded-up paper carefully, and found in a fold of it a fine white splinter of bone, of the thickness of a finger-nail, irregular in shape and the size of a sixpenny piece, exactly as she had described it. She recognized it at once. All this happened in the evening in the darkness of her room. The light was burning in the ante-room.]

XII

THE PURIFICATION[1]

THE days being nearly fulfilled when the Blessed Virgin must, according to the Law, present and redeem her firstborn in the Temple,[2] all was prepared for the Holy Family's journey first to the Temple and then to their home in Nazareth. On the evening of Sunday, December 30th, the shepherds had been given everything left behind by Anna's servants. The Cave of the Nativity, the side-cave, and Maraha's grave were all completely swept out and emptied. Joseph left them all quite clean. In the night of Sunday, December 30th, to Monday, December 31st, I saw Joseph and Mary with the Child visiting the Cave of the Nativity once more and taking leave of that holy place. They spread out the kings' carpet on Jesus' birthplace, laid the Child on it and prayed, and finally laid it on the place where He had been circumcised, kneeling down in prayer there, too. At dawn on Monday, December 31st, I saw the Blessed Virgin mount the donkey, which the old shepherds had brought to the cave all equipped for the journey. Joseph held the Child while she settled herself comfortably; then he laid Him in her lap. She sat sideways on the saddle with her feet on a rather high support, facing backwards. She held the Child on her lap wrapped in her big veil and looked down on Him with an expression of great happiness. There were only a

1. *Luke* 2:22-39. (SB)
2. The laws about "Purification" and offerings after childbirth are in *Lev.* 12:4-8, and the "sanctification" of the firstborn is directed in *Exod.* 13:2 and *Num.* 3:13. (SB)

few rugs and small bundles on the donkey. Mary sat between them. The shepherds accompanied them part of their way before taking a moving farewell of them. They did not take the way by which they had come, but went between the Cave of the Nativity and the grave of Maraha, round the east side of Bethlehem. Nobody noticed them.

[January 30th:] This morning I saw them going very slowly on the short journey from Bethlehem to Jerusalem: they must have made many halts. At midday I saw them resting on benches round a fountain with a roof over it. I saw some women coming to the Blessed Virgin and bringing her jugs with balsam and small loaves of bread. The Blessed Virgin's sacrifice for the Temple hung in a basket at the side of the donkey. This basket had three compartments, two of which were lined with something. These contained fruit. The third was of open wicker-work and a couple of doves could be seen in it. Towards evening I saw them enter a small house beside a large inn about a quarter of an hour from Jerusalem. This was kept by an old childless couple who welcomed them with particular affection. I now know why I mistook Anna's companions yesterday for the people from an inn in Jerusalem: I had seen them stopping here with these good old people on their way to Bethlehem, when they had no doubt arranged about a lodging for the Blessed Virgin. The old couple were Essenes and related to Joanna Chusa. The husband was a gardener by trade, trimmed hedges, and was employed in work on the road.

[February 1st:] I saw the Holy Family with these old innkeepers near Jerusalem during the whole of today. The Blessed Virgin was generally alone in her room with the Child, who lay on a rug on a low ledge projecting from the wall. She was praying all the time, and seemed to be preparing herself for the coming ceremony. It was revealed to me at the same time how one should prepare oneself for receiving Holy Communion.

I saw the appearance of a number of holy angels in

her room, worshipping the Infant Jesus. I do not know whether the Blessed Virgin also saw these angels, but I think so, because I saw her rapt in contemplation. The good people of the inn did everything possible to please the Blessed Virgin: they must have been aware of the holiness of the Infant Jesus.

About seven o'clock in the evening I had a vision of the aged Simeon. He was a thin, very old man with a short beard. He was an ordinary priest, was married, and had three grownup sons, the youngest of whom might have been about twenty. I saw Simeon, who lived close to the Temple, going through a narrow dark passage in the Temple walls into a small vaulted cell, built in the thickness of the wall. I saw nothing in this room but an opening through which one could look down into the Temple. I saw the aged Simeon kneeling here rapt in prayer. Then the appearance of an angel stood before him and warned him to take heed of the little child who should be first presented early next morning, for this was the Messias for whom he had so long yearned. After he had seen Him, he would soon die. I saw this so plainly; the room was illuminated, and the holy old man was radiant with joy. Then I saw him going to his house and telling his wife with great joy what had been announced to him. After his wife had gone to bed, I saw Simeon betake himself to prayer again.

I never saw devout Israelites and their priests praying with such exaggerated gestures as the Jews today. I did, however, see them scourging themselves. I saw the prophetess Anna praying in her cell and having a vision about the Presentation of the Infant Jesus in the Temple.

[February 2nd:] This morning, while it was still dark, I saw the Holy Family, accompanied by the people of the inn, leaving the inn and going to Jerusalem to the Temple with the baskets of offerings and with the donkey laden for the journey. They went into a walled courtyard in the Temple. While Joseph and the innkeeper stabled the donkey in a shed, the Blessed Virgin and her Child were kindly received by an aged woman and led into the Temple by a covered passage. A light was carried, for it was still dark. No sooner had they entered this passage than the aged priest Simeon came, full of expectation, towards the Blessed Virgin. After addressing a few friendly words to her, he took the Child Jesus in his arms, pressed Him to his heart, and then hurried back to the Temple by another way. Yesterday's message from the angel had so filled him with longing to see the Child of the Promise, for whom he had sighed so long, that he had come out here to the place where the women arrived. He was dressed in long garments such as the priests wear when not officiating. I often saw him in the Temple, and always as an aged priest of no elevated rank. His great devoutness, simplicity, and enlightenment alone distinguished him.

The Blessed Virgin was led by her guide to the outer courts of the Temple where the ceremony took place, and she was here received by Noemi, her former teacher, and Anna, who both lived on this side of the Temple. Simeon, who now once more came out of the Temple to meet the Blessed Virgin, led her, with her Child in her arms, to the customary place for the redemption of the firstborn. Anna, to whom Joseph gave the basket with the offerings, followed her with Noemi. The doves were in the lower part of the basket; above them was a compartment with fruit. Joseph went by another door into the place set apart for men.

It must have been known in the Temple that several women were coming for the presentation ceremony, for everything was arranged. The room where the ceremony took place was as big as the parish church here in Dülmen. Many lamps were burning on its walls, forming pyramids of light. The little flames are at the end of a bent tube projecting from a golden disc which shines almost as brightly as the flame. Hanging from this disc by a woven cord is a little extinguisher which is used to put out the light without making any smell and removed again when the lamps are lit.

An oblong chest had been brought out by several priests and set before a kind of altar with what looked like horns at each corner. The doors of this chest were opened to form a stand on which a large tray was laid. This was covered first with a red cloth, and then with a transparent white one, which hung down to the ground on each side. Burning lamps with several branches were placed at the four corners of this table, in the middle of which was an oblong cradle flanked by two oval bowls containing two baskets. All these things had been brought out of drawers in the chest, with priests' vestments, which were laid on the other permanent altar. The table which had been set up for the offering was surrounded by a railing. On each side of this room were seats, raised one above the other, in which were priests saying prayers.

Simeon now approached the Blessed Virgin, in whose arms the Infant Jesus lay wrapped in a sky-blue covering, and led her through the railing to the table, where she laid the Child in the cradle. From this moment I saw an indescribable light filling the Temple. I saw that God Himself was in it, and above the Child I saw the Heavens opening to disclose the Throne of the Holy Trinity. Simeon then led the Blessed Virgin back to the women's place. Mary wore a pale sky-blue dress, with a white veil, and was completely enveloped in a long yellow cloak. Simeon then went to the permanent altar on which the vestments had been laid out, and he and three other priests vested each other for the ceremony. They had a kind of little shield on their arms, and on their heads were caps divided like mitres. One went behind and the other in front of the table of offering, while two others stood at the narrow ends of it praying over the Child. Anna now came up to Mary and handed her the basket of offerings, which contained fruit and doves in two separate compartments, one above the other. She led her to the railing in front of the table, and there both remained standing. Simeon, who was standing before the table, opened the railing, led Mary up to the table, and placed her offering on it. Fruit was placed in one of the oval dishes and coins in the other: the doves remained in the basket.[3] Simeon remained standing with Mary before the table of offering, and the priest who stood behind it lifted the Infant Jesus from the cradle and held Him up towards the different sides of the Temple, making a long prayer the while. He then gave the Child to Simeon, who laid Him once more in Mary's arms and prayed over her and the Child from a scroll hanging on a stand beside him. Simeon then led the Blessed Virgin back to where Anna was waiting for her in front of the railing, after which Anna took her back to the railed-off women's enclosure. Here some twenty women were waiting to present their firstborn. Joseph and the other men were standing farther back in the place for men.

The priests at the permanent altar now began a service with incense and prayers. The priests in the seats took part in this service, making gestures, but not such violent ones as the Jews of today. At the close of this ceremony, Simeon came up to where Mary was standing, took the Infant Jesus from her into his arms, speaking long and loudly over Him in raptures of joy and thanking God that He had fulfilled His Promise. He ended with his *Nunc Dimittis* [*Luke* 2:29-32]. After the Presentation Joseph came up, and he and Mary listened with great reverence to Simeon's inspired words

---

3. In 1823, when recounting Jesus' stay in Hebron during the third year of His ministry, some ten days after the death of the Baptist, Catherine Emmerich said that she saw Our Lord teaching, on Friday the 29th day of the month of Thebet (i.e. Jan. 17th), from the Sabbath reading taken from Exodus, Chapter 10 to Chapter 13:17. He taught about the Egyptian plague of darkness and about the redemption of the firstborn. In connection with the latter she recounted once more the whole ceremony of the Presentation of Christ in the Temple, including the following, omitted from the description given in the text:

"The Blessed Virgin did not present Our Lord in the Temple until the forty-third day after His birth. Because of the feast, she waited for three days with the good people of the inn outside the Bethlehem gate of Jerusalem. Besides the customary offering of doves, she presented to the Temple five triangular pieces of gold from the kings' gifts, as well as several pieces of beautiful stuff for embroidery. Before leaving Bethlehem, Joseph sold to his cousin the young she-ass which he had given him in pledge on Nov. 30th. I have always thought that the she-ass, on which Jesus rode into Jerusalem on Palm Sunday, was a descendant of hers." (CB)

to Our Lady [*Luke* 2:34]. When Simeon had finished speaking, the prophetess Anna was also filled with inspiration, and spoke long and loudly about the Infant Jesus, hailing His Mother as blessed. I saw that those who were present were greatly moved by all this, and the priests, too, seemed to hear something of what was happening; but no sort of disturbance was caused thereby. It seemed as if this loud inspired praying was nothing unusual, as if it often happened, and as if it must all be so. At the same time I saw that the hearts of all the bystanders were much moved, and all showed great reverence to the Child and His Mother. Mary was like a heavenly rose in radiance.

The Holy Family had, in appearance, made the most humble offering; but Joseph gave Anna and the aged Simeon many of the triangular yellow pieces in secret, to be used specially for poor girls who were being brought up in the Temple and could not afford the expense.

I saw the Blessed Virgin and her Child being accompanied by Anna and Noemi back to the outer court, whence they had fetched her, and there they took leave of each other. Joseph was there already with the two people from the inn; he had brought the donkey which carried Mary and the Child, and they started at once on their journey from the Temple through Jerusalem to Nazareth. I did not see the presentation of the other firstborn children that day, but I feel that they were all given a special grace, and that many of them were among the massacred Innocents.

The Presentation must have ended about nine o'clock this morning, for it was at this time that I saw the departure of the Holy Family. That day they travelled as far as Bethoron, where they spent the night at the house which had been the last stopping-place of the Blessed Virgin when she was brought to the Temple thirteen years before. The owner of this house seemed to me to be a school-teacher. Servants sent by Anna were waiting here for them. They went to Nazareth by a much more direct road than on their way to Bethlehem, when they had avoided all towns and had only stopped at lonely houses. Joseph had left in pledge with his relations the young she-ass which had shown him the way on their journey to Bethlehem, for he still intended to return to Bethlehem and build a house in the Shepherds' Valley. He had spoken to the shepherds about it, and told them that he was taking Mary to her mother only for a time until she should have recovered from the discomfort of her lodging. With this plan in his mind, he had left a good many things with the shepherds. Joseph had a strange kind of money with him; I think he must have been given it by the three kings. Inside his robe he had a kind of pouch, in which he carried a quantity of little, thin, shining, yellow leaves rolled up in each other. Their corners were rounded and something was scratched on them. Judas' pieces of silver were thicker and tongue-shaped; the whole pieces were rounded at both ends and the half pieces at one end only.

At this time I saw all three kings together again beyond a river. They had a day of rest and kept a feast. At this place there was one big house with several smaller ones. The direction taken by the kings on their way home lies between the road they followed on their journey to Bethlehem and that by which Jesus came out of Egypt in the third year of His ministry. At first they travelled very quickly, but after this resting-place their pace was much slower than when they came. I always saw a shining youth going before them and sometimes talking with them. They left Ur on the right.

[February 3rd:] Simeon had a wife and three sons, of whom the eldest was about forty and the youngest twenty years old. All three served in the Temple, and were later secret friends of Jesus and His followers. All became disciples of Our Lord, but at different times: before His death or after His ascension. At the Last Supper one of them prepared the Paschal Lamb for Jesus and the Apostles; but these were perhaps grand-

sons, not sons, of Simeon; I am not sure. Simeon's sons
did much to help the friends of Our Lord at the time
of the first persecutions after the Ascension. Simeon
was related to Seraphia, who was later given the name
Veronica, and also, through her father, to Zacharias. I
saw that Simeon fell ill yesterday immediately on
returning home after his prophecy at the Presentation
of Jesus, but he spoke very joyfully with his wife and
sons. Tonight I saw that today was to be the day of
his death. Of the many things I saw I can only remember this much. Simeon, from the couch where he lay,
spoke earnestly to his wife and children, telling them
of the salvation that was come to Israel and of everything that the angel had announced to him. His joy
was touching to behold. Then I saw him die peacefully
and heard the quiet lamentation of his family. Many
other old priests and Jews were praying round his bed.
Then I saw them carry his body into another room.
They placed it on a board pierced with holes, and washed
it with sponges, holding a cloth over it so that its
nakedness could not be seen. The water ran through
the board into a copper basin placed beneath it. Then
they covered the body with big green leaves, surrounded
it with bunches of sweet herbs, and wrapped it in a
great cloth in which it was tied up with long bandages
like a child in swaddling bands. The body lay so straight
and rigid that I thought the bands must have been
tied right round the board.

In the evening Simeon was buried. His body was carried to the grave by six men bearing torches. It lay on
a board more or less the shape of a body, but surrounded by an edge higher in the middle of its four
sides and lower at the corners. The wrapped-up corpse
lay on this board without any other covering. The bearers and those who followed them walked quicker than
is usual at our burials. The grave was on a hill not
very far from the Temple. The door of the sepulchre
was set slanting against a little hill; it was walled inside
with a strange kind of masonry, like that which I saw

St. Benedict working at in his first monastery.[4] The walls, like those in the Blessed Virgin's cell in the Temple, were decorated with stars and other patterns in colored stones. The little cave in the middle of which they laid the corpse was just large enough to allow them to pass round the body. There were some other funeral customs such as laying various things beside the dead man—coins, little stones, and I think also food, but I am not sure.

In the evening I saw the Holy Family arrive at Anna's house, which is about half an hour's distance from Nazareth in the direction of the valley of Zabulon. There was a little family festival like the one when Mary left home for the Temple. A lamp was burning above the table. Joachim was dead, and I saw Anna's second husband as master of the house. Anna's eldest daughter, Maria Heli, was there on a visit. The donkey was unloaded, for Mary meant to stay here for some time. All were full of joy over the Infant Jesus, but it was a tranquil inner joy; I never saw any of these people giving way to very violent emotions. Some aged priests were there, and all present partook of a light meal. The women ate separately from the men, as is always the custom at meals.

I saw the Holy Family still in Anna's house a few days later. There are several women there, Maria Heli, Anna's eldest daughter, with her child Mary Cleophas, a woman from Elisabeth's home, and the maidservant who was with Mary in Bethlehem. This maidservant

---

4. In a vision of the life of St. Benedict which Catherine Emmerich had on Feb. 10th, 1820, she saw amongst other things that as a boy he was shown by his teacher how to use colored stones to make all kinds of ornaments and arabesques in the sand of the garden in the manner of the old pavements. Later she saw him, a hermit, decorating the roof of his cell or cave with a reproduction in rough mosaic of a vision of the Last Judgment. Still later she saw St. Benedict's followers imitating and extending this form of decoration. After contemplating in its smallest details the whole history and development of his Order from its foundation, she said: "Because in the Benedictines the inner spirit became less active and alive than its outer shell, I saw their churches and monasteries becoming too much ornamented and decorated. I thought to myself, that comes from the picture Benedict made in his cell; it has shot up like a weed, and when once this superstructure collapses, it will bring descendant of hers [sic]." (CB)

did not wish to marry again after the death of her husband, who had not been a good man, and came to Elisabeth at Jutta, where the Blessed Virgin made her acquaintance when she visited Elisabeth before John's birth. From here this widow came to Anna. Today I saw Joseph in Anna's house packing many things on donkeys and going in front of the donkeys (of which there were two or three) towards Nazareth, accompanied by the maid.

I cannot remember the details of all that I saw today in Anna's house, but I must have had a very vivid impression of it all, for while I was there I was in an intense activity of prayer, which is now hardly comprehensible to me. Before I came to Anna's house I had been in spirit with a young married couple who supported their old mother; they are both mortally ill, and if they do not recover, the mother will perish. I know this poor family, but have had no news of them for a long time. In desperate cases like this I always invoke St. Anne, and when I was in her house today in my vision, I saw, in spite of the season of the year, and though the leaves had all fallen, many pears, plums, and other fruit hanging on the trees in her garden. When I went away I was allowed to pick these, and I took the pears to the young couple who were ill and so cured them. After that I was made to give some to many other poor people, known and unknown to me, who were restored to health by them. No doubt these fruits signified graces obtained through the intercession of St. Anne. I fear that these fruits mean much pain and suffering for me, which always comes after visions in which I pick fruit in the gardens of the Saints; this has always to be paid for. Perhaps these souls are under the protection of St. Anne, and are thus entitled to fruit from the garden; or perhaps it happened because, as I have always recognized, she is a patroness in desperate cases.

[When asked what sort of weather she saw in Palestine at this time of the year, she answered:] I always forget to mention that, because it seems to me all so natural that I always think everyone knows about it. I often see rain and mist, and sometimes a little snow, but this melts at once. I often see leafless trees with fruit still hanging on them. I see several crops in the year, and I see them beginning to harvest in our spring. Now that it is winter I see people going along the roads wrapped up, with their cloaks over their heads.

[February 6th:] This afternoon I saw the Blessed Virgin going from Anna's house to Joseph's house in Nazareth. She was accompanied by her mother, who carried the Infant Jesus. It is a very pleasant walk of half an hour among hills and gardens. Anna sends provisions from her own house to Joseph and Mary in Nazareth. How beautiful is the life of the Holy Family! Mary is at once the mother and the humblest handmaid of the Holy Child and at the same time she is Joseph's servant. Joseph is her faithful friend and humblest servant. When the Blessed Virgin rocks the Infant Jesus to and fro in her arms, how marvellous to see the all-merciful God, who made the world, allowing Himself out of His great love to be treated like a helpless little child! How dreadful in comparison the coldness and self-will of deceitful and hard-hearted men!

CANDLEMAS

THE Feast of Candlemas was represented to me in a great picture, but one very difficult to describe, although I recollect much of what I saw.

I saw a feast being celebrated in the Church, transparent and floating above the earth, as I always am shown the Catholic Church when I am to contemplate it, not as some particular local church, but as the Universal Church itself. I saw this Church filled with choirs of angels surrounding the Most Holy Trinity. Since, however, I saw the Second Person of that Most Holy Trinity being presented and redeemed in the Temple, incarnate in the form of the Infant Jesus and yet present in the Most Holy Trinity, it seemed to me, as it did a short time ago, that the Child Jesus was sitting near me and comforting me at the same time that I saw a vision of the Holy Trinity. I saw the appearance of the Word become Flesh, the Infant Jesus, at my side, connected with the vision of the Trinity as it were by a path of light. I could not say, "He is not there, since He is with me," nor could I say, "He is not with me, since He is there"; and yet in the instant when I had a vivid sensation of the Child Jesus being near me, the representation of the Most Holy Trinity was shown to me, but in a different form from that in which I see it when it is a picture of the Godhead alone.

I saw an altar appear in the center of the Church— not an altar like those in our churches today, but just an altar. On this altar stood a little tree of the same kind as the Tree of Knowledge in the Garden of Eden, with broad hanging leaves. Then I saw the Blessed Virgin rise before the altar with the Infant Jesus in her arms as if she had come up out of the earth; and I saw the tree on the altar bow before her and then wither away. And I saw a great angel in priest's vestments, with only a ring round his head, approach Mary. She gave him the Child, whom he placed on the altar, and in the same moment I saw the Child thus offered up pass into the picture of the Holy Trinity, which I now saw once more in its usual form. I saw, too, that the angel gave the Mother of God a little bright globe surmounted by the figure of a child in swaddling-bands, and that Mary floated with this gift towards the altar. I saw crowds of poor people coming to her from all sides bearing lights: she handed all these lights to the Child on the globe, into whom they passed. And I saw a light and a radiance being thrown by these lights on Mary and the Child, illuminating everything. Mary had a flowing mantle which spread over the whole earth. The picture was then transformed into a festal ceremony.

I think that the withering of the Tree of Knowledge at Mary's appearance, and the passing of the Child on the altar into the Holy Trinity signified the reunion of mankind with God. That is why I saw all the scattered individual lights handed to the Mother of God and given by her to the Child Jesus: for He was the light enlightening all mankind, in whom alone all the scattered lights became one light to enlighten the whole world, symbolized by the globe, the orb of a king. The lights presented to Our Lady signified the Blessing of the Candles at today's feast.

XIII

THE FLIGHT INTO EGYPT AND
ST. JOHN THE BAPTIST IN THE DESERT[1]

[ON Saturday, February 10th, 1821, Catherine Emmerich, who was ill at the time, was worried by material cares about where she was to live. She fell asleep full of these cares, but soon woke up quite happy. She said that a good friend of hers who had lately died (a pious old priest) had just been with her and had comforted her. "How wise that wise man now is, and how well he can now speak! He said to me: 'Do not be anxious about a dwelling for yourself; take care only that you are swept and garnished within to receive Our Lord when He comes to you. When Joseph came to Bethlehem, he sought a lodging for Jesus, not for himself, and swept the Cave of the Nativity till it was beautifully clean.'" She told of several other profound utterances of this friend, all characteristic of one who knew her temperament so well. She added that he said to her: "When St. Joseph was told by the angel to flee into Egypt with Jesus and Mary, he did not worry about a dwelling-place, but set off at once as he was told." As she had seen something of the flight into Egypt the year before at this time, the writer thought that this was happening again, so asked her: "Was it today that Joseph started for Egypt?" to which she answered very clearly and decisively: "No, the day he started on the flight was what is now February 29th." Unfortunately there was

---

1. *Matt.* 2:13-18. (SB)

no opportunity of obtaining precise information from her about this, as she was very ill during these communications. Once she said: "The Child may well be more than a year old, I saw Him playing about by a balsam-bush at one of the halting-places on the journey, and sometimes His parents led Him by the hand for a little way." Another time it seemed to her that Jesus was nine months old. It must be left to the reader to conjecture the age of Jesus from the various circumstances of Catherine Emmerich's account, and in particular from a comparison with the age of the little John the Baptist, which seems to confirm the theory of Our Lord being nine months old.]

[Sunday, February 25th:] I saw the Blessed Virgin doing knitting or crochet work. She had a roll of wool fastened at her right hip and she held in her hands two needles (of bone, I think) with little hooks. One must be half a yard long, the other is shorter. The needle is prolonged beyond the hook, and it is round this prolongation that the thread is looped to make the stitch in working. The part already knitted hangs down between the two needles. She did this work standing or sitting beside the Infant Jesus lying in a basket. I saw St. Joseph plaiting long strips of yellow, brown, and green bark to make panels for screens or for walls and ceilings. He had a store of these panels lying on top of each other in a shed near the house. He wove various patterns into them—stars, hearts, and other things. I felt sorry for him; he had no idea that he would soon have to flee into Egypt. Our Lady's mother comes regularly every day to visit her; it is nearly an hour's walk from her house.

I had a view of Jerusalem, and saw Herod having numbers of men summoned, as when soldiers are called up with us. These were led into a large courtyard and given clothes and weapons. They wore something like a half-moon on one arm. They carried spears and short broad swords like chopping knives. They wore helmets, and many of them had wrappings tied round their legs.

All this must have been connected with the Massacre of the Innocents. Herod was in a very uneasy frame of mind.

[February 26th:] I still see Herod exceedingly uneasy, just as he was when the three kings asked him about the newborn King of the Jews. I saw him taking counsel with several old scribes, who read from very long parchment scrolls, fastened on rods, which they had brought with them. I saw, too, that the soldiers who had been given new clothes two days ago were sent to Bethlehem and to various places round Jerusalem. I think they were sent to occupy the places whence the children were to be brought by their unsuspecting mothers to Jerusalem. The soldiers were intended to prevent any insurrection when the reports of the massacre reached the children's homes.

[February 27th:] Today I saw Herod's soldiers who had started yesterday from Jerusalem arriving at three places. They came to Hebron, Bethlehem, and another place, lying between those two in the direction of the Dead Sea. I have forgotten its name. The inhabitants had no idea why these soldiers had been sent to them and were somewhat disturbed. Herod was crafty, he kept his own counsel and sought in secret for Jesus. The soldiers stayed in these towns for some time; then, when Herod completely failed to find the child born in Bethlehem, he massacred all the children under two years of age.

[This evening at dusk Catherine Emmerich fell asleep and after a few minutes said, without any apparent reason: "God be thanked a thousand times that I came at the right moment! What a blessing that I was there! The poor child is saved; I prayed that she should bless and kiss it, and after that she could no longer have thrown it into the pond." The writer, on hearing this sudden exclamation, asked, "Whom do you mean ?" She continued: "It is an unfortunate girl who has been seduced. She was going to drown her newborn child not far from here. During the last few days I have besought

God so earnestly that no poor innocent child should die without being baptized and blessed. I prayed thus because the time of the martyrdom of the Holy Innocents is drawing near. I adjured God by the blood of His first blood-witnesses. One must profit by the times and seasons, and every year, when the rose-buds open in the garden of the Church Triumphant, one must pluck them on earth. God has heard my prayer and enabled me to help the mother and her child. Perhaps one day I shall see that child." This is what she said immediately after her vision, or rather after the action she took in spirit. Next morning she said: "My guide took me quickly to M. Near there I saw a girl who had been seduced who had just given birth to her child behind a bush. She carried it in her apron towards a deep pond on which green scum was floating, meaning to throw the child into the water. I saw a tall dark figure beside her from which a dreadful kind of light was thrown; I think it was the evil one. I went close up to her, praying with my whole heart, and saw the dark figure withdraw. Then she took the child and kissed and blessed it, after which she could no longer bring herself to drown it. She sat down again, weeping most terribly and not knowing where to turn. I comforted her and gave her the idea of going to her confessor and begging him to help her. She did not see me, but her guardian angel gave her this advice. Her parents were, I think, far away. She seemed to belong to a middle-class family.]

[February 28th:] This evening I saw Anna and her eldest her house to Nazareth [sic] with the maidservant who was related to her—the one she had left with the Blessed Virgin in Bethlehem after Christ's birth. The maid had a bundle hanging at her side, and carried a basket on her head and another in her hand. They were round baskets, and you could see through one of them. There were birds in them. They were taking provisions to Mary, who did no house-keeping and was provided for by Anna.

[February 28:] This evening I saw Anna and her eldest daughter with the Blessed Virgin. Maria Heli had with her a sturdy little boy four or five years old, her grandson, the eldest son of her daughter Mary Cleophas. Joseph had gone to Anna's house. I watched the women sitting there, talking confidentially to each other, playing with the Infant Jesus and pressing Him to their breasts or giving Him to the little boy to hold in his arms. Women are always the same, I thought; it was all just as it is with us today.

Maria Heli lived in a little village some three hours to the east of Nazareth. Her house was almost as good as her mother's: it had a walled courtyard with a fountain and pump. You trod on something beneath it, and water poured out at the top into a stone basin. Her husband was called Cleophas, and her daughter Mary Cleophas, who was married to Alphaeus, lived at the other end of the village.

In the evening I saw the women praying. They stood before a little table covered with a red-and-white cloth and standing against the wall. A scroll lay on this table, which the Blessed Virgin unrolled and hung up on the wall. A figure was embroidered on it in pale colors; it looked like a dead man in a long white cloak, wrapped up like a child in swaddling-bands. The head was wrapped in the cloak, which was wider round the arms. The figure held something in its arms. I had already seen this figure at the ceremony in Anna's house, when Mary was taken to the Temple. It reminded me then of Melchisedech, for he seemed to have a chalice in his arms; but another time I thought it represented Moses. A lamp was burning during the prayer. Mary, with her sister beside her, stood in front of Anna. They crossed their hands on their breasts, folded them, and then extended them. Mary read from a scroll lying before her, unrolling it as she read. They prayed in a particular tone and rhythm which reminded me of the chanting in the convent choir.

[The night of Thursday, March 1st, to the morning

of Friday, March 2nd:] They are gone, I saw them start forth. Joseph came back early in the morning of yesterday, Thursday, from Anna's house. Anna and her eldest daughter were still here in Nazareth. They had all only just gone to bed when the angel came to warn Joseph.[2] Mary and the Infant Jesus had their bedroom to the right of the hearth; Anna's was to the left, and her eldest daughter's room was between hers and Joseph's. These rooms were compartments divided off and sometimes roofed by wicker screens. Mary's room had yet another curtain or screen dividing it off. The Infant Jesus lay on a rug at her feet, and she could pick Him up without getting out of bed.

I saw Joseph in his room lying on his side asleep with his head on his arm. I saw a shining youth come up to his bed and speak with him. Joseph sat up, but was heavy with sleep and lay down again. The youth took his hand and pulled him up, when Joseph came to his senses and got up, on which the youth disappeared. Joseph then went to the lamp burning in front of the fireplace in the center of the house and lit his own lamp at it. He knocked at the Blessed Virgin's room and asked whether he might come in. I saw him go in and speak with Mary, who did not open the screen before her bed; then I saw him go to his donkey in the stable, and afterwards into a room where all kinds of things were kept. He prepared everything for their departure. As soon as Joseph had left the Blessed Virgin's room, she got up and dressed for the journey, before going to her mother and telling her of God's commands. Anna got up, as did Maria Heli and her little boy, but they let the Infant Jesus go on sleeping. For these good people God's Will came first of all; sad at

2. Since Matthew alone gives the account of the Magi and of the Flight into Egypt, and Luke alone that of the Presentation, it is not easy to decide the exact order of events. According to AC the Magi came to Bethlehem *before* the Presentation, and the angel's warning came to Joseph at Nazareth some time *after* it, if Jesus was by then nine months old. In this case the words of *Matt.* 2:13, "And after they [the Magi] were departed, behold an angel . . .," refer to the passage of over seven months and a removal to Nazareth. This interval between the visit of the Magi and the Flight into Egypt certainly offers an explanation of a chronological problem. (SB)

heart though they were, they hastened to make all preparations for the journey before allowing themselves to give way to the sorrow of parting. Anna and Maria Heli helped to get everything ready for the journey. Mary did not take nearly so much with her as she had brought from Bethlehem. They packed up nothing but a moderate-sized bundle and a few blankets, which were taken out to Joseph to be loaded on the donkey. Everything was done quietly and very quickly, as was proper for a journey undertaken secretly after a warning at dead of night. When Mary fetched her Child, she was in such haste that I did not even see her wrap Him in fresh swaddling-clothes. Then came the farewells, and I cannot describe how moving it was to see the distress of Anna and her eldest daughter. They embraced the Infant Jesus with tears, and the little boy, too, was allowed to take Him in his arms. Anna embraced the Blessed Virgin again and again, weeping as bitterly as if she were never to see her more. Maria Heli flung herself onto the ground in tears.

It was not yet midnight when they left the house. Anna and Maria Heli accompanied the Blessed Virgin on foot for a short part of the way from Nazareth, Joseph following with the donkey. The way led towards Anna's house, but rather more to the left. Mary carried the Infant Jesus, wrapped in swaddling-clothes, before her in a sort of sling, which went round her shoulders and was fastened behind her neck. She wore a long cloak which wrapped both herself and the Child, and a big square veil, fastened round the back of her head and hanging in long folds beside her face. They had not gone far when Joseph came up with the donkey, which was carrying a skin of water and a basket with several compartments containing little loaves of bread, small jugs, and live birds. The baggage and blankets were packed round the side-saddle, which had a footrest hanging from it. They embraced again with tears, and Anna blessed the Blessed Virgin, who then seated herself on the donkey, led by Joseph, and they started off. [Whilst Catherine Emmerich was describing the grief of Anna and Maria Heli, she wept copiously herself, saying that in the night, too, when she saw this vision, she could not help shedding many tears.]

[March 2nd:] Early in the morning I saw Maria Heli with her little boy going to Anna's house and sending the master of the house and a manservant to Nazareth, after which she went to her own house. I saw Anna putting everything in order in Joseph's house and packing away many things. In the morning there came two men from Anna's house; one of them was dressed in nothing but a sheepskin, and had on his feet thick sandals strapped round his legs. The other had a long robe on; he seemed to me to be Anna's present husband. They helped to arrange everything in Joseph's house, and to pack up what was movable and take it to Anna's house.[3]

During the night of the Holy Family's flight from Nazareth, I saw them passing through various places and resting in a shed before dawn. Towards the evening, when they could go no farther, I saw them stopping at a village called Nazara in the house of people who lived apart and were rather despised. They were not proper Jews, and their religion had something heathen about it. They worshipped in the Temple on Mount Garizim, near Samaria, approached by a difficult mountain path several miles long.[4] They were oppressed by many hard duties, and were obliged to work like slaves at forced labor in the Temple at Jerusalem and other public buildings. These people gave a warm welcome to the Holy Family, who remained there the whole of the following day. On their return from Egypt the Holy Family once more visited these good people, and again when Jesus

---

3. According to this account Joseph evidently intended to give up the house at Nazareth, and presumably to carry out his plan of moving to Bethlehem (cf. AC, p. 170, and p. 248). All this helps to explain why we get the impression from *Matt.* 2:22-23 that Joseph really wanted to settle in Judaea but came to Nazareth almost *faute de mieux*. (SB)

4. Clearly the despised Samaritans, cf., e.g., *John* 4:9, 20 (where their worship on Mount Garizim is mentioned). (SB)

went to the Temple in His twelfth year and returned thence to Nazareth.[5]

This whole family later received baptism from John and became followers of Our Lord. This place is not far from a strange town, high up, the name of which I can no longer remember. I have seen and heard the names of so many towns in this district, among them Legio and Massaloth, between which, I think, Nazara lies. I believe that the town whose situation I thought so strange is called Legio, but it has another name as well.[6]

[Sunday, March 4th:] Yesterday, Saturday evening, at the close of the Sabbath, the Holy Family travelled on from Nazara through the night, and during the whole of Sunday and the following night I saw them in hiding by that big old terebinth tree where they had stopped in Advent on their journey to Bethlehem, when the Blessed Virgin was so cold. It was Abraham's terebinth tree, near the grove of Moreh, not far from Sichem, Thenat, Silo and Arumah. The news of Herod's pursuit had spread here, and the region was unsafe for them. It was near this tree that Jacob buried Laban's idols. Josue assembled the people near this tree and erected the tabernacle containing the Ark of the Covenant, and it was here that he made them renounce their idols. Abimelech, the son of Gedeon, was hailed here as king by the people of Sichem.[7]

[March 5th:] This morning I saw the Holy Family resting in a fertile part of the country and refreshing themselves beside a little stream where there was a balsam bush. The Infant Jesus lay on the Blessed Virgin's knees with His little feet bare. Incisions had been made here and there in the branches of the balsam

---

5. Fifteen years after Catherine Emmerich's death, when the writer was putting together her account of the Flight into Egypt, he wondered why the Holy Family should have remained in Nazara a whole day. It was only then that he discovered that the Sabbath began on the evening of March 2nd, 1821, so that the Holy Family must have kept it in secret here, though Catherine Emmerich made no mention of this. (CB)

6. The identification of Nazara, Legio, and Massaloth is uncertain, but they are probably in the hill country south of the Vale of Esdraelon, and are so placed by Fahsel. (SB)

7. The Biblical references to all these places are given *supra*, p. 174. (SB)

shrub, which had red berries, and from these incisions a liquid dripped into little pots hanging on the branches. I was surprised that these were not stolen. Joseph filled the little jugs, which he had brought with him with the balsam juice. They ate little loaves of bread and berries which they picked from the bushes growing near. The donkey drank from the stream and grazed nearby. On their left I saw Jerusalem high up in the distance. It was a very lovely scene.

[March 6th:] Zacharias and Elisabeth had also received a message warning them of imminent danger. I think the Holy Family had sent them a trusty messenger. I saw Elisabeth taking the little John to a very hidden place in the wilderness, a few hours' distance from Hebron.[8] Zacharias accompanied them for only a part of the way, to a place where they crossed a small stream on a wooden beam. He then left them and went towards Nazareth by the way which Mary followed when she visited Elisabeth. I saw him on his journey to Nazareth, where he is probably going to obtain further details from Anna. Many of the friends of the Holy Family there are much distressed at their departure. Little John had nothing on but a lamb's skin; although scarcely eighteen months old, he was sure on his feet and could run and jump about. Even at that age he had a little white stick in his hand, which he treated as a plaything. One must not think of his wilderness as a great desert of waste sand, but rather as a desolate place with rocks, caves, and ravines, where bushes and wild fruits and berries grew. Elisabeth took the little John into a cave in which Mary Magdalene lived for some time after Jesus' death. I cannot remember how long Elisabeth remained here hidden with her young child, but it was probably only until the alarm about Herod's persecution had subsided. She then returned to Jutta, about two hours' distance away, for I saw her escaping

---

8. The story of Elisabeth's concealing the boy John the Baptist is found in *Protev.* 22, but with a typical addition in the fanciful detail of the mountain splitting to receive them into hiding. (SB)

again into the wilderness with John when Herod summoned the mothers with their little sons up to two years
of age, which happened quite a year later.

[Catherine Emmerich, who had up to this point communicated pictures of the Flight day by day, was here
interrupted by illness and other disturbances. On resum-
ing her story a few days later she said:] I cannot distinguish the days so clearly now, but will describe the
separate pictures of the Flight into Egypt as nearly as
possible in the order in which I remember seeing them.

I saw the Holy Family, after they had crossed some
of the ridges of the Mount of Olives, going in the direction of Hebron beyond Bethlehem. They went into a
large cave, about a mile from the wood of Mambre, in
a wild mountain gorge. On this mountain was a town
with a name which sounded like Ephraim. I think that
this was the sixth halting-place on their journey. I saw
the Holy Family arriving here very exhausted and distressed. Mary was very sad and was weeping. Everything they needed was lacking, and in their flight they
kept to by-ways and avoided towns and public inns.
They spent the whole day here resting. Several special
favors were granted to them here. An angel appeared
to them and comforted them, and a spring of water
gushed forth in the cave at the prayer of the Blessed
Virgin, while a wild she-goat came to them and allowed
herself to be milked. A prophet used often to pray in
this cave, and I think Samuel came here several times.
David kept his father's sheep near here;[9] he used to
pray here, and it was here that he received from an
angel the order to undertake the fight against Goliath.[10]

9. David kept his father's sheep near Bethlehem: *1 Kgs.* (*Sam.*) 17:15. Bethlehem is
about twelve miles from Mambre. (SB)
10. In her general description of the Flight into Egypt she forgot to mention this refuge
of the Holy Family. The description given above is taken from her daily account
of Our Lord's ministry, at the time when, after His baptism, He visited with some
of His disciples all the places near Bethlehem where His Mother had been with
Him. She saw Jesus, after His Baptism by John, which she described on Friday,
Sept. 28th, 1821, staying in this cave with His disciples from Oct. 8th to Oct. 9th,
and she heard Him speak of the graces given in this place and of the hardships
and difficulties of the Flight into Egypt. He blessed this cave and told them that
one day a church would be built over it. On Oct. 18th she said: "This refuge of the
Holy Family was later called Mary's place of sojourn, and was visited by pilgrims

From this cave they journeyed southwards for seven hours, with the Dead Sea always on their left hand. Two hours after leaving Hebron they entered the wilderness where little John the Baptist was in hiding.[11] Their way led them only a bow-shot's distance from his cave. I saw the Holy Family wandering through a sandy desert, weary and careworn. The water-skin and the jugs of balsam were empty; the Blessed Virgin was greatly distressed, and both she and the Infant Jesus were thirsty. They went a little way aside from the path, where the ground sank and there were bushes and some withered turf. The Blessed Virgin dismounted, and sat for a little with the Child on her knees, praying in her distress. While the Blessed Virgin was thus praying for water like Agar in the wilderness, I was shown a wonderfully moving incident. The cave in which Elisabeth had hidden her little son was quite near here, on a wild rocky height, and I saw the little boy not far from the cave wandering about among the stones and bushes as if he were anxiously and eagerly waiting for something. I did not see Elisabeth in this vision. To see this little boy roaming and running about in the wilderness with such confidence made a great impression on me. Just as beneath his mother's heart he had leaped up at the approach of his Lord, so now he was moved by the nearness of his Redeemer, thirsty and weary. I saw the child wearing his lamb's-skin over his shoulders and girt round his waist, and carrying in his hand a little stick with a bit of bark waving on it. He felt

---

who were, however, ignorant of its real history. Later only poor people lived there." She gave a precise description of the place, and some time afterwards the writer found to his great astonishment an account by the Minorite friar Antonio Gonzalez of his journey to Jerusalem (Antwerp, 1679, Part I, p. 556), in which he stated that he had been in a "village of Mary's," a short mile on the left of the road from Hebron to Bethlehem, where she had taken refuge on the Flight. It was, he said, on a hill, and a church with three vaults and three doors was still standing there, with a picture on its wall of Mary and her Child on the donkey, led by Joseph. Below the hill on which stood the village and church was a beautiful spring of water, known as Mary's fountain. All of this agrees with the place described by Catherine Emmerich. Arvieux says in the second volume of his Memoirs (Leipzig, 1783): "Between Hebron and Bethlehem we came through the village of the Blessed Virgin, who is said to have rested here during her Flight." (CB)

11. None of the many details of the life of the young John the Baptist in the desert are found in any available document. (SB)

that Jesus was passing near and that He was thirsty; he threw himself on his knees and cried to God with outstretched arms, then jumped up, ran, driven by the Spirit, to the high edge of the rocks and thrust with his staff into the ground, from which an abundant spring burst forth. John ran before the stream to the edge, where it rushed down over the rocks. He stood there and watched the Holy Family pass by in the distance.[12]

The Blessed Virgin lifted up the Infant Jesus high in her arms, saying to Him, "Look! John in the wilderness!"; and I saw John joyfully leaping about beside the rushing water, and waving to them with the little flag of bark on his stick. Then he hurried back into the wilderness. After a little time the stream reached the travellers' path, and I saw them crossing it and stopping to refresh themselves at a pleasant place where there were some bushes and thin turf. The Blessed Virgin dismounted with the Child; they were all joyful. Mary sat down on the grass, and Joseph dug a hollow a little way off for the water to fill. When the water became quite clear, they all drank, and Mary washed the Child. They sprinkled their hands, feet, and faces with water. Joseph led the donkey to the water, of which it drank deeply, and he filled his water-skin. They were all happy and thankful; the withered grass, now saturated with water, grew straight again, and the sun came out and shone on them. They sat there refreshed and full of quiet happiness. They rested for two or three hours in this place.

The last place where the Holy Family sheltered in Herod's territory was not far from a town on the edge

---

12. Catherine Emmerich heard Our Lord Himself relate this touching incident in her visions of Our Lord's ministry. It was in January (Tuesday, the 26th day of the month Thebet) of the third year of His ministry, in the house of John's parents at Jutta, in the presence of the Blessed Virgin, Peter, John and three trusty disciples of the Baptist. A carpet had been spread out before them, which had been worked by Mary and Elisabeth after the Visitation: it had been embroidered with many significant texts. Our Lord was speaking with comforting words of the Baptist's murder, which had taken place on the 20th of the month Thebet (Jan. 8th) at Herod's birthday feast at Machaerus. He spoke much about John on this occasion and said that He had only seen him twice in the flesh; that time on the Flight to Egypt and the second time at His baptism. (CB)

of the desert, a few hours' journey from the Dead Sea. Its name sounded like Anem or Anim. They stopped at a solitary house which was an inn for those travelling through the desert. There were several huts and sheds on a hill, and some wild fruit grew round them. The inhabitants seemed to me to be camel-drivers, for they kept a number of camels in enclosed meadows. They were rather wild people and had been given to robbery, but they received the Holy Family well and showed them hospitality. In the neighboring town there were also many disorderly people who had settled there after fighting in the wars. Among the people in the inn was a man of twenty called Reuben.[13]

[March 8th:] I saw the Holy Family journeying in a bright starlit night through a sandy desert covered with low bushes. I felt as if I were travelling through it with them. It was dangerous because of the numbers of snakes which lay coiled up among the bushes in little hollows under the leaves. They crawled towards the path, hissing loudly and stretching out their necks towards the Holy Family, who, however, passed by in safety surrounded by light. I saw other evil beasts there with long black bodies, short legs, and wings like big fins. They shot over the ground as if they were flying, and their heads were fish-like in shape. I saw the Holy Family come to a fall in the ground like the edge of a sunken road; they meant to rest there behind some bushes.

I was alarmed for the Holy Family. The place was sinister, and I wanted to make a screen to protect them on the side left open, but a dreadful creature like a

---

13. The first mention by Catherine Emmerich of this inn was in her account of Christ's ministry. On Oct. 8th after His baptism Our Lord came here alone from the Valley of the Shepherds. He converted Reuben and healed several sick people while His disciples waited for Him in the cave of refuge near Ephraim. He taught at the places where the Holy Family had rested and taken food, and explained to the inhabitants that the grace given to them now was the fruit of the hospitality shown by them to the Holy Family. On His journey between here and the cave near Ephraim He passed by Hebron. A place called Anim or Anem, nine miles south of Hebron in the district of Daroma, is mentioned by Jerome and also by Eusebius. (CB)

Anim is mentioned among the hill cities of Juda in *Jos.* 15:50, together with Jutta (Douay Jota) in 55 and Hebron in 54. (SB)

bear made his way in, and I was in terrible fear. Then there suddenly appeared to me a friend of mine, an old priest who had died lately. He was young and beautiful in form, and he seized the creature by the scruff of its neck and threw it out. I asked him how he came to be here, for surely he must be better off in his own place, to which he replied: "I only wanted to help you, and shall not stay here long." He told me more, adding that I should see him again.

The Holy Family always travelled a mile eastwards of the high road. The name of the last place they passed between Judaea and the desert sounded very like Mara. It reminded me of Anna's home, but it was not the same place. The inhabitants here were rough and wild, and the Holy Family could obtain no assistance from them. After this they came into a great desert of sand. There was no path and nothing to show their direction, and they did not know what to do. After some time they saw a dark, gloomy mountain-ridge in front of them. The Holy Family were sorely distressed, and fell on their knees praying to God for help. A number of wild beasts then gathered round them, and at first it looked very dangerous; but these beasts were not at all evil, but looked at them in just the same friendly way as my confessor's old dog used to look at me when he came up to me.[14] I realized then that these beasts were sent to show them the way. They looked towards the mountain and ran in that direction and then back again, just like a dog does when he wants you to follow him somewhere. At last I saw the Holy Family follow these animals and pass over a mountain-ridge into a wild and lonely region. It was dark, and the way led past a wood. In front of this wood, at some distance from the path, I saw a poor hut, and not far from it a light hanging in a tree, which could be seen from a long way off, to attract travellers. This part of the road

14. The apocryphal *Ps-Matt.* 18-19 includes details of wild beasts in the desert on the way to Egypt, but the account is very fanciful and tells how they wagged their tails in reverence, and so forth, and how the Child Jesus spoke to the creatures and comforted His mother. (SB)

was sinister: trenches had been dug in it here and there, and there were also trenches all round the hut. Hidden cords were stretched across the good parts of the road, and when touched by travellers rang bells in the hut and brought out its thieving inhabitants to plunder them. This robbers' hut was not always in the same place, it could be moved about and put up wherever its inhabitants wanted it.[15]

When the Holy Family approached the light hanging in the tree, I saw the leader of the robbers with five of his companions closing round them. At first they were evilly disposed, but I saw that at the sight of the Infant Jesus a ray, like an arrow, struck the heart of the leader, who ordered his comrades to do no harm to these people. The Blessed Virgin also saw this ray strike the robber's heart, as she later recounted to Anna the prophetess when she returned.[16]

The robber now led the Holy Family through the dangerous places in the road into his hut. It was night. In the hut was the robber's wife with some children. The man told his wife of the strange sensation that had come over him at the sight of the Child. She received the Holy Family shyly, but was not unfriendly. The travellers sat on the ground in a corner, and began to eat some of the provisions which they had with them. The people in the hut were at first awkward and shy (quite unlike, it seemed, their usual behavior), but gradually drew nearer and nearer to the Holy Family. Some of the other men, who had in the meantime stabled Joseph's donkey, came in and out, and eventually they

---

15. The encounter with robbers occurs in the *Arabic Gospel of the Infancy*, 23, where the robbers Titus and Dymachus are the future thieves at the Crucifixion. According to AC it was at the robbers' hut that a boy was cured of leprosy by being washed in Our Lord's bath-water, and this boy (nameless) became the Good Thief at the Crucifixion *(infra*, p. 322). The same Arabic source has the episode of the bath-water on three occasions (17, 31, 32). In the apocryphal *Gospel of Nicodemus*, 10, the Good Thief is called Dismas (his traditional name), and the Bad Thief Gestas (or Gistas). (SB)

16. We quote the whole of this incident, as well as many others of the Flight into Egypt, from the accounts given by Catherine Emmerich of the conversations with Jesus of Eliud, an aged Essene, who accompanied Our Lord on His journey from Nazareth to be baptized by John. Eliud said that Anna the prophetess had told him that she had heard of this incident from the Blessed Virgin. (CB)

all became more familiar and began to talk to the travellers. The woman brought Mary little loaves of bread with honey and fruit, as well as goblets with drink. A fire was burning in a hollow in a corner of the hut. The woman arranged a separate place for the Blessed Virgin, and brought at her request a trough with water for washing the Infant Jesus. She washed the linen for her and dried it at the fire. Mary bathed the Infant Jesus under a cloth. The man was very much agitated and said to his wife: "This Hebrew child is no ordinary child, He is a holy Child. Ask His mother to allow us to wash our leprous little boy in His bath-water, perhaps it will do him good." As the woman came up to Mary to ask her this, Our Lady told her, before she had said a word, to wash her leprous boy in the bath-water. The woman brought her three-year-old son lying in her arms. He was stiff with leprosy and his features could not be seen for scabs. The water in which Jesus had been bathed seemed clearer than it had been before, and as soon as the leprous child had been dipped into it, the scales of his leprosy fell off him to the ground and the child was cleansed. The woman was beside herself with joy and tried to embrace Mary and the Infant Jesus, but Mary put out her hand and would not let her touch either herself or Jesus. Mary told the woman that she was to dig a well deep down to the rock and pour this water into it; this would give the well the same healing power. She spoke long with her, and I think the woman promised to leave this place at the first opportunity. The people were extremely happy at the restoration of their child to health, and showed him to their comrades who came in and out during the night, telling them of the blessing that had befallen them. The new arrivals, some of them boys, stood round the Holy Family and gazed at them in wonderment. It was all the more remarkable that these robbers were so respectful to the Holy Family, because in the very same night, while they were housing these holy guests, I saw them seizing some other travellers who had been enticed into their lair by the light and driving them into a great cave deep in the wood. This cave, whose entrance was hidden and grown over by wild plants so that it could not be seen, seemed to be their real dwelling-place. I saw several boys in this cave, from seven to nine years of age, who had been stolen from their parents; and there was an old woman who kept house there. I saw all kinds of booty being brought in— clothes, carpets, meat, young kids, sheep, and bigger animals too. The cave was big and contained an abundance of things.

I saw that Mary slept little that night; she sat still on her couch most of the time. They left early in the morning, well supplied with provisions. The people of the place accompanied them a short way, and led them past many trenches on to the right road. When the robbers took leave of the Holy Family, the man said with deep emotion: "Remember us wherever you go." At these words I suddenly saw a picture of the Crucifixion, and saw the Good Thief saying to Jesus, "Remember me when Thou shalt come into Thy kingdom," and recognized in him the boy who had been healed. The robber's wife gave up this way of life after some time, and settled with other honest families at a later resting-place of the Holy Family, where a spring of water and a garden of balsam shrubs came into being.

After this I again saw the Holy Family journeying through a desert, and when they lost their way, I again saw various kinds of creeping beasts approach them, lizards with bats' wings and snakes, but they were not hostile and seemed only to want to show them the way. Later on, when they had lost every trace of their path and direction, I saw them guided by a very lovely miracle; on each side of the path the plant called the rose of Jericho appeared with its curling leaves surrounding the central flower and the upright stalk. They went up to it joyfully, and on reaching it they saw in the distance another plant of it spring up, and so throughout the whole desert. I saw, too, that it was revealed to the

Blessed Virgin that in later times the people of the country would gather these flowers and sell them to passing strangers to gain their bread. (I saw this happening afterwards.) The name of the place sounded like Gase or Gose [? Gosen]. Then I saw them come to a place called by a name like Lepe or Lape [? Pelusium]. There was a lake there with ditches, canals, and high embankments. They crossed the water on a raft with a sort of big tub on it in which the donkey was put. Mary sat with her Child on a piece of timber. Two ugly, brown, half-naked men with flattened noses and protruding lips ferried them over. They passed only the outlying houses of this place, and the people here were so rough and unsympathetic that the travellers went on without speaking to anyone. I think that this was the first heathen town. They had been ten days in the Jewish country and ten days in the desert.

I now saw the Holy Family on Egyptian territory. They were in flat country, with green pastures here and there on which cattle were feeding. I saw trees to which idols had been fastened in the shape of infants wrapped in broad swaddling-bands inscribed with figures or letters. Here and there I saw people thick-set and fat, dressed like the cotton-spinners whom I once saw near the frontiers of the three kings. I saw these people hurrying to worship their idols. The Holy Family went into a shed; there were beasts in it, but these went out to make room for them. Their provisions had given out, and they had neither bread nor water. Nobody gave them anything, and Mary was hardly able to feed her Child. They did, indeed, endure every human misery. At last some shepherds came to water the beasts at a closed spring, and at Joseph's urgent request gave them a little water. Then I saw the Holy Family going through a wood, exhausted and helpless. On coming out of it they saw a tall, slender date-palm with its fruit growing all together like a bunch of grapes at the very top of the tree. Mary went up to the tree with the Infant Jesus in her arms, and prayed, lifting the Child up to it; the tree bowed down its head to them, as if it were kneeling, so that they were able to pick all its fruit.[17] The tree remained in that position. I saw a rabble of people from the last town following the Holy Family, and I saw Mary distributing the fruit from the tree among the many naked children who were running after her. About a quarter of an hour from the first tree they came to an unusually big sycamore tree with a hollow trunk. They had got out of sight of the people who were following them, and hid in the tree so as to let them pass by. They spent the night here.

Next day they continued through waste and sandy deserts, and I saw them sitting on a sand-hill quite exhausted, for they had no water with them. The Blessed Virgin prayed to God, and I saw an abundant spring of water gush forth at her side and run in streams on the ground. Joseph levelled a little sand-hill and made a basin for the water, digging a little channel to carry off the overflow. They refreshed themselves with the water and Mary washed the Infant Jesus. Joseph watered the donkey and filled the water-skin. I saw tortoises, and ugly creatures like big lizards coming to drink at the water. They did the Holy Family no harm, but looked at them in a friendly way. The stream of water flowed in a wide circle, disappearing again in the ground near its source. The space which it enclosed was wonderfully blessed: it soon became green and produced the most delicious balsam shrubs, which grew big enough to give refreshment to the Holy Family on their return from Egypt. Later it became famous as a balsam garden. A number of people came to settle there; amongst them, I think, the mother of the leprous child who had been healed in the robbers' den. Later I had visions of this place. A beautiful hedge of balsam shrubs surrounded the garden, in the middle of which were big fruit-trees. Later a deep well was dug there, from

---

17. The palm-tree that bowed appears (on the Flight) in *Ps-Matt.* 20, but there the little Jesus is figured as addressing the tree and also commanding it to straighten itself afterwards. (SB)

which an abundant supply of water was drawn by a wheel turned by an ox. This water was mixed with the water from Mary's well so as to supply the whole garden. The water from the new well would have been harmful if used unmixed. It was shown me that the oxen who turned the wheel did no work from midday on Saturday till Monday morning.

After refreshing themselves here they journeyed to a great city called Heliopolis or On. It had wonderful buildings, but much of it had been laid waste. When the children of Israel were in Egypt, the Egyptian priest Putiphar lived here, and had in his house Aseneth (the daughter of Dina of the Sichemites) whom Joseph married.[18] Here also Dionysius the Areopagite lived at the time of Christ's death. The city had been devastated by war, but numbers of people had made themselves homes in the ruined buildings.

The Holy Family crossed a very high bridge over a broad river which seemed to me to have several arms. They came to an open place in front of the city-gate, which was surrounded by a kind of promenade. Here there was a pedestal, thicker below than above, surmounted by a great idol with an ox's head bearing in its arms something like a child in swaddling-bands. The idol was surrounded by a circle of stones like benches or tables, and people came in crowds from the city to lay their offerings on them. Not far from this idol was a great tree under which the Holy Family sat down to rest. They had rested there for only a short time when there came an earthquake, and the idol swayed and fell to the ground.[19] There was an uproar among the people, and a crowd of canal-workers ran up from near at hand. A good man who had accompanied the Holy Family on their way here (I think he was a drain-digger) led them hurriedly into the town, and they were leaving the place where the idol had stood when the

---

18. Joseph married Aseneth: *Gen.* 41:50. (SB)
19. The idol falling when the Holy Family reached Egypt is mentioned in *Ps-Matt.* 23 (all the idols) and in the *Arabic Gospel of the Infancy*, 10, Cf. *supra*, p. 52 and n. 37. (SB)

frightened crowd observed them and began assailing them with threats and abuse for having been the cause of the idol's collapse. They had not, however, time to carry out their threats, for another shock came which uprooted and engulfed the great tree till nothing but its roots showed above ground. The gaping space where the idol had stood became full of dark and dirty water, in which the whole idol disappeared except for its horns. Some of the most evil among the raging mob were swallowed up in this dark pool. Meanwhile the Holy Family went quietly into the city, and took up their abode near a great heathen temple in the thickness of a wall, where there were a great number of empty rooms.

[Catherine Emmerich also communicated the following fragments of visions of the subsequent life of the Holy Family in Heliopolis or On:]

Once at a later time I came over the sea to Egypt, and found the Holy Family still living in the great devastated city. It is very extensive, and is built beside a great river with many arms. The city can be seen from afar, standing high up. In many places the river flows underneath the buildings. The people cross the arms of the river on rafts which lie there in the water ready for use. I saw quite astonishingly huge buildings in ruins, great masses of solid masonry, halves of towers and whole, or nearly whole, temples. I saw pillars as big as towers, with winding staircases outside. I saw high tapering pillars completely covered with strange figures, and also a number of big figures like reclining dogs with human heads.

The Holy Family lived in the galleries of a great stone building supported at one side by short thick pillars, some square and some round. People had built themselves dwellings against and under these pillars; above the building ran a road with much traffic on it; it passed a great heathen temple with two courts. In this building was a space with a wall on one side of it and on the other a row of short thick pillars. In front of this Joseph had constructed a light wooden building, divided off by wooden partitions, for them to live in. I saw them there all together. The donkeys were there, too, but separated by screens such as Joseph always used to make. I noticed for the first time that they had a little altar against the wall, hidden behind one of these screens—a little table covered with a red cloth and a transparent white one over it. There was a lamp above it, and they used to pray there. Later I saw that Joseph had arranged a workshop in his home, and also that he often went out to work. He made long staffs with knobs at the end, and little, low, round, three-legged stools with a handle at the back to carry them by. He also made baskets and light wicker screens. These were afterwards smeared with some substance which made them solid, and were then used to make huts and compartments against and in the massive masonry of the walls. He also made little light hexagonal or octagonal towers out of long thin planks, ending in a point crowned by a knob. These had an opening and could be used to sit in like sentry-boxes. They had steps leading up to them. I saw little towers like these here and there in front of the heathen temples, and also on the flat roofs. People sat inside them. They were perhaps sentry-boxes, or little summer-houses used to give shade.

I saw the Blessed Virgin weaving carpets. I also saw her with other work; she had a stick beside her with a lump fastened to the top of it, but I do not know what she was doing, whether spinning or something else. I often saw people visiting her and the Infant Jesus, who lay in a sort of cradle on the floor beside her. Sometimes I saw this cradle raised on a stand like a sawing-trestle. I saw the Child lying very contentedly in His cradle, sometimes with His arms hanging out on each side. Once I saw Him sitting up in it. Mary sat close by knitting, with a basket at her side. There were three women with her.

The people in this half-destroyed city were dressed just like those cotton-spinning people whom I saw when

I went to meet the three kings, except that they wore aprons, like short skirts. There were not many Jews here, and they seemed to live here on sufferance. North of Heliopolis, between it and the Nile, which there divides into many arms, was the land of Gessen. Amongst its canals was a place where a large number of Jews lived. Their religion had become very degraded. Some of these Jews became acquainted with the Holy Family, and Mary made various things for them, in return for which they gave her bread and provisions. The Jews in the land of Gessen had a temple which they likened to Solomon's temple, but it was very different.[20]

I again saw the Holy Family in Heliopolis. They were still living near the heathen temple under the vaulting of the massive walls. Not far off Joseph built a place of prayer in which the Jews living in the city assembled together with the Holy Family. Before this they had had no meeting-place for prayer. The room had a lightly built dome above it, which they could open so as to be under the open sky. In the middle of the room stood a sacrificial table or altar, covered with white and red, and having scrolls upon it. The priest or teacher was a very old man. The men and women were not so strictly separated at their prayers as in the Promised Land: the men stood on one side and the women on the other. I had a sight of the Blessed Virgin visiting this place of prayer with the Infant Jesus for the first time. She sat on the ground leaning on one arm; the Child was sitting before her in a little sky-blue dress, and she put His hands together on His breast. Joseph stood behind her, as he always does here, though the other men and women stand and sit in separate groups on each side of the room. I was often shown how the little Jesus was already growing bigger, and how He was often visited by other children. He could already speak and run quite well; He was

---

20. The presence of a Jewish temple built on the ruins of Leontopolis, on the outskirts of Heliopolis, is well known from Josephus (*Ant.*, XIII, iii, 1-4), who explains that it was built by Onias (IV) after his flight from Palestine, *c.* 170 B.C., "like indeed to that at Jerusalem, but smaller and poorer." Cf. also *BJ*, VII, x, 3. (SB)

much with Joseph, and I think went with him when
he worked away from home. He wore a little dress like
a shirt, knitted or woven in one piece. Some of the idols
fell down in the temple near which they lived, just as
the statue near the gate had collapsed on their entry
into the city; many people said that this was a sign of
the wrath of the gods against the Holy Family, and in
consequence they suffered various persecutions.

THE MASSACRE OF THE INNOCENTS

TOWARDS the middle of Jesus' second year the Blessed
Virgin was told of Herod's Massacre of the Innocents
by an angel appearing to her in Heliopolis. She and
Joseph were greatly distressed, and the Child Jesus
wept that whole day. I saw what follows.

When the three kings did not return to Jerusalem,
Herod's anxiety decreased to some extent; he was at
that time much occupied with family affairs. His anxiety revived again, however, when various reports
reached him about Simeon's and Anna's prophecies in
the Temple at the Presentation of the Infant Jesus. At
this moment the Holy Family had been some time in
Nazareth.

Under various pretexts he dispatched soldiers to different places round Jerusalem, such as Gilgal, Bethlehem, and Hebron, and ordered a census of the children
to be made. The soldiers remained, I think, about nine
months in these places. Herod was in the meantime in
Rome,[21] and it was not until soon after his return that
the children were massacred. John the Baptist was two
years old when it happened, and had again been for
some time at home with his parents in secret. Before
Herod issued the order that all mothers were to bring

---

21. This was recounted while Catherine Emmerich was seriously ill; she mentioned
several journeys and other matters connected with Herod's family, but very obscurely.
The statement that Herod had been in Rome in the meantime was the only clear
one. Some fifteen years after this communication, the writer reread the history
of Herod the Great given by the Jewish historian Josephus, but found no mention of any journey of Herod's to Rome at this time. (CB)

before the authorities their male children up to two
years old, Elisabeth had been warned by the appearance of an angel and had once more fled into the wilderness with her little son. Jesus was nearly eighteen
months old and could already run about.[22] The children
were massacred in seven different places. The mothers
had been promised rewards for their fruitfulness. They
came from their homes in the surrounding country to
the government offices in the various towns, bringing
with them their little boys in holiday dress. The husbands were turned back, and the mothers were separated from their children. These were stabbed by the
soldiers behind the walls of lonely courtyards; their
bodies were heaped together and then buried in trenches.

[Catherine Emmerich communicated her vision of
the Massacre of the Innocents on March 8th, 1821, i.e.
a year after her account of the Flight into Egypt, so
that it may be presumed that the massacre took place
a year later than the Flight.]

This afternoon I saw the mothers with their little
sons up to two years of age come to Jerusalem from
Hebron, Bethlehem, and a third place. Herod had sent
soldiers there, and had later communicated his orders
through the authorities of these towns. The women
came to the city in separate groups. Some had two
children with them and rode on donkeys. They came
to the city in joyful expectation, for they thought they
were to receive a reward for their fruitfulness. They
were all taken into a large building, and the men accompanying them were sent home. This building was somewhat isolated; it was not far from the house where
later Pilate lived. It was so enclosed that it was difficult to see from outside what was happening within
it. It must once have been a place of execution, for I

---

22. It has already been observed (n. 2, p. 310) that *Matt.* 2:13, according to AC, involves
the passing of over seven months. Here we are told that Jesus was nearly eighteen months old, so that *Matt.* 2:16, *"Then* Herod perceiving that he was deluded
. . . sending killed . . . ,"* shows the passage of a further nine months to the murder of the Innocents. The Gospel has no details beyond the fact of the massacre.
(SB)

saw in its courtyard stone pillars and blocks with chains fastened to them, as well as trees which were tied together and then allowed to spring apart so as to tear in pieces the men fastened to them. It was a dark, strong building, and its courtyard was quite as big as the graveyard on one side of Dülmen parish church. A gate led through two walls into this courtyard, which was enclosed by buildings on three sides. To the right and left these were one story high; the center one had two stories and looked like an ancient, deserted synagogue. There were gates opening into the courtyard from all three buildings.

The mothers were led through the courtyard into the two side-buildings and there imprisoned. At first I had the impression of their being in a kind of hospice or inn. They became alarmed when they saw themselves deprived of liberty and began to weep and moan, continuing their laments throughout the whole night.

[On the next day, March 9th, she said:] This afternoon I saw a terrible picture. I saw the Massacre of the Innocents taking place in that house of execution. The big building at the back of the court was two stories high: the lower storey consisted of a great deserted hall like a prison or a guard-room; above it was a large room with windows looking down into the courtyard. I saw a number of officials assembled there as if in a court of justice; before them was a table on which lay scrolls. I think Herod was there, too, for I saw a man in a red cloak lined with white fur with little black tails on it. He was wearing a crown. I saw him, surrounded by others, looking out of the window of the room.

The mothers were summoned one by one with their children from the side-buildings into the great hall below the building at the back of the courtyard. As they came in, their children were removed from them by soldiers and taken through the gate into the courtyard, where some twenty soldiers were at the murderous work of thrusting swords and spears into their throats and hearts. Some were children still at the breast, wrapped in swaddling-bands; others were tiny boys wearing long embroidered dresses. They did not trouble to take off their clothes, they ran their swords through their throats and hearts, and then seized their bodies by an arm or leg and flung them onto a heap. It was a ghastly sight. The mothers were thrust back one by one by the soldiers into the great hall. When they saw what was done to their children, they raised a terrible outcry, clinging to each other and tearing their hair. They were so closely packed at the end that they could hardly move. I think the massacre went on until towards evening.

The children's bodies were afterwards buried in a pit in the same courtyard. Their number was shown to me, but I have no clear recollection of it. I think it was 700, and another number with 7 or 17 in it. The number was explained to me by an expression in which I remember a sound like "Ducen": I think I had to reckon two c's together several times.[23]

I was absolutely horrified by what I had seen, and did not know where it had happened: I thought it was here. It was only when I woke up that I was able gradually to recollect myself. The next night I saw the mothers being taken back by the soldiers to their homes, bound, and in separate groups. The place of the Massacre of the Innocents in Jerusalem was used later as a court of justice; it was not far from Pilate's judgment seat, but by his time it had been a good deal altered. At Christ's death I saw the grave of the massacred children fall in and saw their souls appear and depart from thence.

I was shown how Elisabeth, warned by the angel, once more fled into the desert with the little John to escape the Massacre of the Innocents.

---

23. Perhaps this refers to the Roman numeral DCC=700 (AC always saw Roman numerals). She mentions *(supra,* p. 330) that the massacres took place in seven different places, and the Gospel *(Matt.* 2:16) indicates a whole district: "Bethlehem and all the borders thereof." (SB)

Elisabeth searched for a long time till she found a cave which seemed to her sufficiently hidden, and then stayed there with the boy for about forty days. When she went home, an Essene from the community on Mount Horeb came to the boy in the wilderness, brought him food, and gave him all the help he needed. This Essene (whose name I keep forgetting) was a relation of Anna of the Temple. He came at first every eight days, then every fourteen; but in a short time John no longer needed help, for he was soon more at home in the wilderness than among men. It was ordained by God that he should grow up in the wilderness without contact with mankind and innocent of their sins. Like Jesus, he never went to school; the Holy Ghost taught him in the wilderness. I often saw at his side a light, or shining figures like angels. The desert here was not waste and barren; many plants and bushes grew in it, bearing many kinds of berries, and among the rocks were strawberries, which John picked and ate as he passed. He was uncommonly familiar with the beasts, and especially with the birds: they flew to him and perched on his shoulders, he spoke to them and they seemed to understand him and to act as his messengers. He wandered along the banks of the streams, and was just as familiar with the fishes. They swam near to him when he called them, and followed him in the water as he went along the bank.

I saw now that he moved far away from his home, perhaps because of the danger which threatened him. He was so friendly with the beasts that they helped him and warned him. They led him to their nests and lairs, and he fled with them into their hiding-holes if men came near. He lived upon fruit, berries, roots, and herbs. He had no need to search long for them; he either knew himself where they grew, or the beasts showed him. He always had his sheepskin and his little staff, and from time to time went still deeper into the wilderness. Sometimes he would go nearer his home. Several times he rejoined his parents, who were always longing for him. I think they must have known about each other by revelation, for whenever Elisabeth and Zacharias wanted to see him, he always came from a long way off to meet them.

After staying in Heliopolis for a year and a half, until Jesus was about two years old, the Holy Family left the city because of lack of work and various persecutions. They moved southwards in the direction of Memphis. When they passed through a small town not far from Heliopolis and sat down to rest in the open porch of a heathen temple, the idol fell down and broke in pieces. (It had the head of an ox with three horns, and there were holes in its body in which sacrifices were placed to be burnt.) This caused an uproar amongst the heathen priests, who seized and threatened the Holy Family. As the priests were consulting together, one of them said that for his part he thought it wise to commend themselves to the God of these people, reminding them of the plagues that had befallen their ancestors when they persecuted the Israelites, and how in the night before their exodus the firstborn had died in every Egyptian house. They followed his advice and dismissed the Holy Family unmolested.

They made their way to Troja, a place on the east bank of the Nile, opposite Memphis. It was a big town, but filthy. They thought of staying here, but were not taken in; indeed, they could not even obtain the drink of water or the few dates for which they asked. Memphis was on the west bank of the Nile, which was here very broad, with islands. Part of the city was on the east bank, and here in the time of Pharao was a great palace with gardens and a high tower, to the top of which Pharao's daughter used often to ascend to survey the country round. I saw the place where the child Moses was found among the tall rushes. Memphis was composed as it were of three different towns, one on each side of the Nile, and another called Babylon which seemed to belong to it. This was farther downstream

on the east bank. Indeed, in Pharao's time the whole
region round the Nile between Heliopolis, Babylon, and
Memphis was so covered with canals, buildings, and
stone embankments that it all seemed to form one uninterrupted city. Now, at the time of the Holy Family's
visit, it had all become separated with great waste
spaces between. From Troja they went northwards downstream towards Babylon, which was ill-built, dirty, and
desolate. They skirted this city between it and the Nile,
and retraced their steps for some distance. They went
downstream, following an embankment along which
Jesus travelled later, when He journeyed through Arabia to Egypt after the raising of Lazarus and before
meeting His disciples again at Jacob's Well at Sichar.
They travelled downstream for some two hours; there
were ruined buildings at intervals all along their path.
They had to cross a small arm of the river or canal,
and came to a place whose name as it was at that time
I cannot remember; afterwards it was called Matarea,
and was near Heliopolis.[24] This place, which lay on a
promontory surrounded by water on two sides, was very
desolate. Its scattered buildings were mostly very badly
made of palm wood and thick mud, roofed with reeds.
Joseph found much work here in strengthening the
houses with wattles and building galleries onto them.

In this town the Holy Family lived in a dark vaulted
room in a lonely quarter at the landward side of the
town, not far from the gate by which they had entered.
As before, Joseph built a room in front of the vaulted
one. Here, too, when they arrived, an idol fell down in
a small temple, and afterwards all the idols fell. Here,
too, a priest pacified the people by reminding them of
the plagues of Egypt. Later, when a little congregation
of Jews and converted heathens had gathered round
the Holy Family, the priests handed over to them the

---

24. Troja and Babylon near Memphis, and Matarea near Heliopolis or On, are all
   readily identifiable in the region of the modern Cairo. At Matarea it is said that
   the "Tree of Our Lady" is still shown. The tree is also mentioned in the *Arabic
   Gospel of the Infancy,* 24. (SB)

little temple where the idol had fallen, and Joseph arranged it as a synagogue. He became, as it were, the father of the congregation, and introduced the proper singing of the Psalms, for their previous services had been very disorderly. There were only a few very poor Jews living here in wretched holes and ditches, though in the Jewish town between On and the Nile there were many Jews and they had a regular temple there. They had, however, fallen into dreadful idolatry; they had a golden calf, a figure with an ox's head surrounded by little figures of animals like polecats or ferrets with little canopies over them. These were animals which protected people against crocodiles. They also had an imitation Ark of the Covenant, with horrible things in it. They carried on a revolting idolatrous worship, which consisted of immoral practices performed in a subterranean passage and supposed to bring about the coming of the Messias. They were very obstinate and refused to amend their lives. Afterwards many of them left this place and came to where the Holy Family lived, not more than two hours' journey away. Owing to the many dikes and canals, they could not travel direct but had to make a detour round On.

The Jews in the land of Gessen had already become acquainted with the Holy Family in the city of On, and Mary had done much work for them—knitting, weaving, and sewing. She would never work at things which were superfluous or mere luxuries, only at what was necessary and at praying garments. I saw women bringing her work to do which they wanted, from vanity, to be made in a fashionable style; and I saw Mary giving back the work, however much she needed the money. I saw, too, that the women insulted her vilely.

To begin with, they had a very hard time in Matarea. There was great shortage of good water and wood. The inhabitants cooked with dry grass or reeds. The Holy Family generally had cold food to eat. Joseph was given a great deal of work in improving the huts, but the people there treated him just like a slave, giving him only what they liked; sometimes he brought home some money for his work, sometimes none. The inhabitants were very clumsy at building their huts. Wood was lacking, and though I saw trunks of trees lying about here and there, I noticed that there were no tools for dealing with them. Most of the people had nothing but stone and bone knives like turf-cutters. Joseph had brought his necessary tools with him. The Holy Family soon arranged their dwelling a little. Joseph divided the room very conveniently by light wicker screens; he prepared a proper fireplace and made stools and little low tables. The people here all ate off the ground.

They lived here for several years, and I have seen many scenes from Our Lord's childhood. I saw where Jesus slept. In the thickness of the wall of Mary's sleeping-room I saw a niche hollowed out by Joseph in which was Jesus' couch. Mary slept beside it, and I have often seen her during the night kneeling before Jesus' couch and praying to God. Joseph slept in another room.

I also saw a praying-place which Joseph had arranged in their dwelling. It was in a separate passage. Joseph and the Blessed Virgin had their own special places, and the Child Jesus also had His own little corner, where He prayed sitting, standing, or kneeling. The Blessed Virgin had a kind of little altar before which she prayed. A little table, covered with red and white, was let down like a flap before a cupboard in the wall, of which it generally formed the door. In the thickness of the wall were preserved sacred relics. I saw little bushy plants in pots shaped like chalices. I saw the end of St. Joseph's staff with its blossom, whereby the lot had fallen upon him in the Temple to become Mary's spouse. It was fixed in a box an inch and a half in thickness. Besides this, I saw another precious relic, but can no longer explain what it really was. In a transparent box I saw five little white sticks of the thickness of big straws. They stood crossed and as if tied in the middle; at the top they were curly and broader, like a little sheaf. [She crossed her fingers to explain and spoke also of bread.]

During the sojourn of the Holy Family in Egypt the child John must have again stayed in secret with his parents at Jutta, for I saw him at the age of four or five being once more taken into the wilderness by Elisabeth. When they left the house, Zacharias was not there; I think he had gone away beforehand so as not to see the departure, for he loved John beyond measure. He had, however, given him his blessing, for each time he went away he used to bless Elisabeth and John.

Little John had a sheepskin hanging over his left shoulder round his breast and back, fastened together under his right arm. Afterwards in the desert I saw him wearing this sheepskin sometimes over both shoulders, sometimes across his breast, sometimes round his waist—just as it suited him. This sheepskin was all that the boy wore. He had brownish hair darker than Jesus', and he still carried in his hand the little white staff which he had brought from home before. I always saw him with it in the wilderness.

I now saw him hurrying along hand in hand with his mother Elisabeth, a tall woman with a small face and delicate features. She was much wrapped up and walked quickly. The child often ran on ahead; he was quite natural and childlike, but not thoughtless. At first their way led them northwards for some time, and they had water on their right hand; then I saw them crossing a little stream. There was no bridge, and they crossed on logs lying in the water, which Elisabeth, who was a very resolute woman, ferried across with a branch. After crossing the stream they turned more eastwards and entered a rocky ravine, the upper part of which was waste and stony, though the lower slopes were thick with bushes and fruits, among them many strawberries, of which the boy ate one here and there.

After they had gone some way into this ravine, Elisabeth said good-bye to the boy. She blessed him, pressed him to her heart, kissed him on his forehead and on both cheeks, and started on her journey home. She turned round several times on her way, and wept as she looked back towards John. The boy himself was quite untroubled and wandered on farther into the ravine with sure steps.

As during these visions I was very ill, God granted me the favor of feeling as if I were myself a child in presence of all that happened. It seemed to me that I was a child of John's own age, accompanying him on his way; and I was afraid that he would go too far from his mother and would never find his way home again. Soon, however, I was reassured by a voice which said: "Do not be troubled, the boy well knows what he is about." Then I thought that I went quite alone with him into the wilderness as if he had been a familiar childhood's playmate of mine, and I saw many of the things that happened to him. Yes, while we were together, John himself told me much about his life in the wilderness; for example, how he practiced self-denial in every way and mortified his senses, how his vision grew ever brighter and clearer, and how he had been taught, in an indescribable way, by everything round him.

All this did not astonish me, for long ago as a child, when I was all by myself watching our cows, I used to live in familiar fellowship with John in the wilderness. I often longed to see him, and used then to call into the bushes in my country dialect: "Little John with his little stick and his sheepskin on his shoulder is to come to me": and often little John with his little stick and his sheepskin on his shoulder did come to me, and we two children played together, and he told me and taught me all kinds of good things. And it never seemed to me strange that in the wilderness he learnt so much from plants and beasts, for when I was a child, whether in the woods, on the moors, in the fields, with the cows, or plucking ears of corn, pulling grass, gathering herbs, I used to look at every little leaf and every flower as

at a book; every bird, every beast that ran past me,
everything round me, taught me something. Every
shape and color that I saw, every little veined leaf,
filled my mind with many deep thoughts. But if I spoke
of these, people either listened with surprise or else,
more often, laughed at me, so that at last I accustomed
myself to keeping silence about such things. I used to
think (and sometimes think still) that it must be so
with everyone, and that nowhere could one learn better, because here God Himself had written our alpha-
bet for us.

So now, when again in my visions I followed the boy
John into the wilderness, I saw as before all that he
was about. I saw him playing with flowers and beasts.
The birds especially were at home with him. They flew
on to his head as he walked or as he knelt in prayer.
I often saw him lay his staff across the branches; then
at his call flocks of bright-colored birds came flying to
perch on it in a row. He gazed at them and spoke famil-
iarly with them as if they were his schoolchildren. I
saw him, too, following wild animals into their lairs,
feeding them and watching them attentively.

When John was about six years old, Elisabeth took
the opportunity of Zacharias' absence on a journey to
the Temple with herds for sacrifice to pay a visit to her
son in the wilderness. Zacharias, I think, never went
to see him there, so that he might truthfully say, if
asked by Herod where his son was, that he did not
know. In order, however, to satisfy his intense longing
to see John, the latter came several times from the
wilderness to his parents' house in great secrecy and
by night, and stayed there a short time. Probably his
guardian angel led him there at the right moment when
there was no danger. I saw him always guided and protected by higher Powers, and sometimes accompanied
by shining figures like angels.

John was destined to live in the wilderness, separated from the world and from ordinary human food,
and to be taught and trained by the Spirit of God.

Providence so ordained matters that outer circumstances made him take refuge in the desert to which his natural instincts drew him with irresistible force; from his earliest childhood I always saw him thoughtful and solitary. Just as the Child Jesus fled to Egypt as the result of a divine warning, so did John, His precursor, fly to a hiding-place in the wilderness. Suspicion was directed to him, too, for there had been much talk in the land about John ever since his early days. It was well known that wonders had attended his birth, and that he was often seen surrounded by light, for which reasons Herod was particularly suspicious of him. He had caused Zacharias to be questioned several times as to the whereabouts of John, but had never yet laid hands on the old man. This time, however, as he was on his way to the Temple, he was attacked by Herod's soldiers in a sunken road outside the Bethlehem Gate of Jerusalem, from which the city was not yet visible. These soldiers, who had been lying in wait for him, dragged him brutally to a prison on the slope of the Hill of Sion, where later I used often to see Jesus' disciples making their way up to the Temple. The old man was here subjected to ill-treatment and even torture, in order to force from him a confession of his son's whereabouts. When this had no effect, he was, by Herod's soldiers, stabbed to death.[25] His friends buried his body not far from the Temple. This was not the Zacharias who was murdered between the Temple and the altar. When the dead came out of their graves at the death of Christ, I saw the grave of that Zacharias falling out of the Temple walls near the praying-room of the aged Simeon, and himself coming forth from it. At that moment several other secret graves in the Temple burst open. On the occasion when that Zacharias was murdered between the Temple and the altar, there were many disputes going on about the descent of the Messias, and about certain rights and privileges in the

---

25. The murder of Zacharias, the father of John the Baptist, is recounted in *Protev.* 23, with subsequent portents added. (SB)

Temple of various families. For instance, not all families were allowed to have their children brought up in the Temple. (This reminds me that I once saw in the care of Anna in the Temple a boy whose name I have forgotten; I think he was a king's son.) Zacharias was the only one among the disputants who was murdered. His father was called Barachias.[26] I saw that later the bones of that Zacharias were found again, but have forgotten the details.

Elisabeth came home from the desert expecting to find Zacharias returned from Jerusalem. John accompanied her for some of the way; when they parted, she blessed him and kissed him on the forehead, and he hastened back, untroubled, to the wilderness. On reaching home Elisabeth heard the terrible news of the murder of Zacharias. She grieved and lamented so sorely that she could find no peace or rest at home, and so left Jutta forever and hastened to join John in the wilderness. She died there not long after, before the return of the Holy Family from Egypt. She was buried in the wilderness by the Essene from Mount Horeb who had always helped little John.

After this John moved farther into the wilderness. He left the rocky ravine for more open country, and I saw him arrive at a small lake in the desert. The shore was flat and covered with white sand, and I saw him go far out into the water and all the fishes swimming fearlessly up to him. He was quite at home with them. He lived here for some time, and I saw that he had made himself in the bushes a sleeping-hut of branches. It was quite low, and only just big enough for him to lie down in. Here and later I saw him accompanied

---

26. The earlier Zacharias killed near the altar is in *2 Par.* 24:20-21. There is a well-known difficulty in *Matt.* 23:35, where this Zacharias is called "son of Barachias," when 2 Par. gives his father's name as Joiada. It is generally agreed that the verse in Matthew includes a scribal error, arising from the fact that the much better-known Prophet Zacharias' father was called Barachias (*Zach.* 1:1), and that the two names were thus linked in the scribe's memory. This supposition is borne out by the omission of a father's name in Matt. in Codex Sinaiticus. The parallel in *Luke* 11:51 has no father's name. Yet all texts of Matthew before the discovery of Sinaiticus in 1859 include the name, and it is hardly surprising that AC should do so too. (SB)

very often by shining figures or angels, with whom he associated humbly and devoutly, but unafraid and in childlike confidence. They seemed to teach him and to make him notice all kinds of things. I saw that his staff had a little crosspiece, so that it formed a cross; fastened to it was a broad band of bark which he waved about in play like a little flag.

A daughter of Elisabeth's sister now lived in John's family house at Jutta near Hebron. It was well supplied with everything. When John was grown up he came there once in secret, and then went still farther into the wilderness, remaining there until he appeared among mankind. Of this I shall tell later.

In Matarea, where the inhabitants had to quench their thirst with the muddy water of the Nile, a fountain sprang up as before in answer to Mary's prayers. At first they suffered great want, and were obliged to live on fruit and bad water. It was long since they had had any good water, and Joseph was making ready to take his water-skins on the donkey to fetch water from the balsam spring in the desert, when in answer to her prayer an angel appeared to the Blessed Virgin and told her to look for a spring behind their house. I saw her go beyond the enclosure round their dwelling to an open space on a lower level surrounded by broken-down embankments. A very big old tree stood here. Our Lady had a stick in her hand with a little shovel at the end of it, such as people in that country often carried on their journeys. She thrust this into the ground near the tree, and thereupon a beautiful clear stream of water gushed forth. She ran joyfully to call Joseph, who on digging out the spring discovered that it had been lined with masonry below, but had dried up and was choked with rubbish. Joseph repaired and cleaned it, and surrounded it with beautiful new stonework. Near this spring, on the side from which Mary had approached it, was a big stone, just like an altar, and, indeed, I think it had once been an altar, but I forget in what connection. Here the Blessed Virgin used to dry Jesus' clothes and wrappings in the sun after washing them. This spring remained unknown and was used only by the Holy Family until Jesus was big enough to do various little commissions, such as fetching water for His Mother. I once saw that He brought other children to the spring, and made a cup with a leaf for them to drink from. The children told this to their parents, so others came to the spring, but, as a rule, it was used only by the Jews. I saw Jesus fetching water for His Mother for the first time. Mary was in her room kneeling in prayer, and Jesus crept out to the spring with a skin and fetched water; that was the first time. Mary was inexpressibly touched when she saw Him coming back, and begged Him not to do it again, in case He were to fall into the water. Jesus said that He would be very careful and that He wanted to fetch water for her whenever she needed it.

The Child Jesus performed all kinds of services for His parents with great attention and thoughtfulness. Thus I saw Him, when Joseph was working near his home, running to fetch some tool which had been left behind. He paid attention to everything. I am sure that the joy He gave His parents must have outweighed all their sufferings. I also saw Jesus going sometimes to the Jewish settlement, about a mile from Matarea, to fetch bread in return for His Mother's work. The many loathsome beasts to be found in this country did Him no harm; on the contrary, they were very friendly with Him. I have seen Him playing with snakes.

The first time that He went alone to the Jewish settlement (I am not sure whether it was in His fifth or seventh year) He was wearing a new brown dress with yellow flowers round its edge which the Blessed Virgin had made and embroidered for Him. He knelt down to pray on the way, and I saw two angels appearing to Him and announcing the death of Herod the Great. Jesus said nothing of this to His parents, why I do not know, whether from humility or because the angel had forbidden Him to, or because He knew that the time had not yet come for them to leave Egypt. Once I saw Him going to the settlement with other Jewish children, and when He returned home, I saw Him weeping bitterly over the degraded state of the Jews living there.

The spring which appeared at Matarea in answer to the Blessed Virgin's prayers was not a new one, but an old one which gushed forth afresh. It had been choked but was still lined with masonry. I saw that Job had been in Egypt long before Abraham and had dwelt on this spot in this place.[27] It was he who found the spring, and he made sacrifices on the great stone lying here. Job was the youngest of thirteen brothers. His father was a great chieftain at the time of the building of the Tower of Babel. His father had one brother who was Abraham's ancestor. The tribes of these two brothers generally intermarried. Job's first wife was of the tribe of Phaleg: after many adventures, when he was living in his third home, he married three more wives of the same tribe. One of them bore him a son whose daughter married into the tribe of Phaleg and gave birth to Abraham's mother. Job was thus the great-grandfather of Abraham's mother. Job's father was called Joktan, a son of Heber. He lived to the north of the Caspian Sea, near a mountain range one side of which is quite warm, while the other is cold and ice-covered. There were elephants in that country. I do not think elephants could have gone to the place where Job first went to set up his own tribe, for it was very swampy there. That place was to the north of a mountain range lying between two seas, the westernmost of which was before the Flood a high mountain

---

27. The Book of Job gives no clue to the ancestry, offspring, or homeland of Job, and (as AC remarks, *infra.*, p. 349) it is difficult to recognize the true history of Job from it. Job is only mentioned elsewhere in the Old Testament as a just man, together with Noe and Daniel (*Ezech.* 14:14, 16, 20).

   Rabbinic lore has, however, many accounts of the circumstances of Job's family; some texts place Job as a contemporary of Abraham, while others place him earlier or later. There are several accounts of his visit to Egypt. The list of such Rabbinic texts is too great to insert here, but a general account of them will be found in the *Jewish Encyclopedia*, art. Job, p. 193b. (SB)

inhabited by evil angels by whom men were possessed.[28] The country there was poor and marshy; I think it is now inhabited by a race with small eyes, flat noses, and high cheek-bones. It was here that Job's first misfortune befell him, and he then moved southwards to the Caucasus and began his life again. From here he made a great expedition to Egypt, a land which at that time was ruled by foreign kings belonging to a shepherd people from Job's fatherland. One of these came from Job's own country; another came from the farthest country of the three holy kings. They ruled over only a part of Egypt, and were later driven out by an Egyptian king.[29] At one time there was a great number of these shepherd people all collected together in one city; they had migrated to Egypt from their own country.

The king of these shepherds from Job's country desired a wife for his son from his family's tribe in the Caucasus, and Job brought this royal bride (who was related to him) to Egypt with a great following. He had thirty camels with him, and many menservants and rich presents. He was still young—a tall man of a pleasing yellow-brown color, with reddish hair. The people in Egypt were dirty brown in color. At that time Egypt was not thickly populated; only here and there were large masses of people. There were no great buildings either; these did not appear until the time of the children of Israel.

The king showed Job great honor, and was unwilling to let him go away again. He was very anxious for him to emigrate to Egypt with his whole tribe, and appointed as his dwelling-place the city where afterwards the Holy Family lived, which was then quite different. Job remained five years in Egypt, and I saw

---

28. It is remarkable that she said on another occasion that the Black Sea had been before the Flood a high mountain on which evil angels held sway. This seems to show that the mountain range behind which Job's first dwelling-place was situated must have been the Caucasus. (CB)

29. The Hyksos or "Shepherd Kings" were foreign rulers in Egypt, *c.* 1730-1580 B.C., who were finally driven out by a native dynasty. (SB)

that he lived in the same place where the Holy Family lived, and that God showed him that spring. When performing his religious ceremonies, he made sacrifice on the great stone.

Job was to be sure a heathen, but he was an upright man who acknowledged the true God and worshipped Him as the Creator of all that he saw in nature, the stars, and the ever-changing light. He was never tired of speaking with God of His wonderful creations. He worshipped none of the horrible figures of beasts adored by the other races of mankind in his time, but had thought out for himself a representation of the true God. This was a small figure of a man with rays round its head, and I think it had wings. Its hands were clasped under its breast, and bore a globe on which was a ship on waves. Perhaps it was meant to represent the Flood. When performing his religious ceremonies he burnt grains before this little figure. Figures of this kind were afterwards introduced into Egypt, sitting in a kind of pulpit with a canopy above.

Job found a terrible form of idolatry here in this city, descending from the heathen magical rites practiced at the building of the Tower of Babel. They had an idol with a broad ox's head, rising to a point at the top. Its mouth was open, and behind its head were twisted horns. Its body was hollow, fire was made in it, and live children were thrust into its glowing arms. I saw something being taken out of holes in its body. The people here were horrible, and the land was full of dreadful beasts. Great black creatures with fiery manes flew about in swarms, scattering what seemed like fire as they flew. They poisoned everything in their path, and the trees withered away under them. I saw other animals with long hind-legs and short fore-legs, like moles; they could leap from roof to roof. Then there were frightful creatures lurking in hollows and between stones, which wound themselves round men and strangled them. In the Nile I saw a heavy, awkward beast with hideous teeth and thick black feet. It was the size of a horse

and had something pig-like about it. Besides these I saw
many other ugly creatures; but the people here were
much more horrible than any of them. Job, whom I saw
clearing the evil beasts from around his dwelling by his
prayers, had such a horror of these godless folk that he
often broke out in loud reproaches of them, saying that
he would rather live with all these dreadful beasts than
with the infamous inhabitants of this land. I often saw
him at sunrise gazing longingly towards his own country, which lay a little to the south of the farthest country of the three holy kings. Job saw prophetic pictures
foreshadowing the arrival in Egypt of the children of
Israel; he also had visions of the salvation of mankind
and of the trials that awaited himself. He would not be
persuaded to stay in Egypt, and at the end of five years
he and his companions left the country.

There were intervals of calm between the great misfortunes that befell Job: the first interval lasted nine
years, the second seven, and the third twelve. The words
in the Book of Job: "And while he (the messenger of
evil) was yet speaking" mean "This misfortune of his
was still the talk of the people when the following befell
him." [30] His misfortunes came upon him in three different places. The last calamity—and also the restoration of all his prosperity—happened when he was living
in a flat country directly to the east of Jericho. Incense
and myrrh were found here, and there was also a gold-
mine with smithies. At another time I saw much more
about Job, which I will tell later. For the present I will
only say that Job's story of himself and of his talking
with God were written down at his dictation by two
trusty servants of his, like treasurers. Their names were
Hai and Uis or Ois.[31] This story was preserved by his

---

30. The phrase "while he was yet speaking" occurs in *Job* 1:16, 17, 18. The text certainly suggests a quick succession of calamities, but if AC's statement of intervals of nine, seven, and twelve years between the calamities is correct, it is easier
to suppose the story to have been telescoped for the purpose of the drama as we
know it, than to interpret the text (as AC suggests) as meaning "while it was still
the talk of the people." (SB)
31. In 1835 the writer heard that the founder of the Armenian race was so named.
(CB)

descendants as a sacred treasure, and was handed down from generation to generation until it reached Abraham and his sons. It was used for purposes of instruction, and came into Egypt with the children of Israel. Moses used it to comfort and console the Israelites during the Egyptian oppression and their journey through the desert, but in a summarised version, for it was originally of much greater length, and a great deal of it would have been incomprehensible to them. Solomon again remodelled it, so that it is a religious work full of the wisdom of Job, Moses, and Solomon. It was difficult to recognize the true history of Job from it, for the names of persons and places had been changed to ones nearer Chanaan, and it was thought that Job was an Edomite because the last place where he lived was inhabited long after his death by Edomites, the descendants of Esau. Job might still have been alive when Abraham was born.

When Abraham was in Egypt, he also had his tents beside this spring, and I saw him teaching the people here.[32] He lived in the country several years with Sara and a number of his sons and daughters whose mothers had remained behind in Chaldaea. His brother Lot was also here with his family, but I do not remember what place of residence was assigned to him. Abraham went to Egypt by God's command, firstly because of a famine in the Land of Chanaan, and secondly to fetch a family treasure which had found its way to Egypt through a niece of Sara's mother. This niece was of the race of the shepherd-people belonging to Job's tribe who had been rulers of part of Egypt. She had gone there to be serving maid to the reigning family and had then married an Egyptian. She was also the

---

32. Flavius Josephus (lib. I, *Antiquitat. Jud.,* c. 8) and others state that Abraham instructed the Egyptians in arithmetic and astrology. (CB)

   Abraham in Egypt: *Gen.* 12:13. That Lot was with him is shown by 13:1. He pretended that his wife was his sister a second time (20:2) after which the explanation referred to is given (20:12). That Abraham taught the Egyptians is an old Jewish tradition, preserved in Josephus, *Ant.,* I, viii, 2, and there are many Rabbinic stories about his sojourn in Egypt, especially in the Midrash (e.g. *Genesis Rabba,* XLI and XLIV). (SB)

foundress of a tribe, but I have forgotten its name. Agar, the mother of Ismael, was a descendant of hers and was thus of Sara's family.[33]

The woman had carried off this family treasure just as Rachel had carried off Laban's household gods, and had sold it in Egypt for a great sum. In this way it had come into the possession of the king and the priests. This treasure was a genealogy of the children of Noe (especially of the children of Sem) down to Abraham's time. It looked like a scales hanging on several chains from inside a lid. This lid was made to shut down on to a sort of box which enclosed the chains in it. The chains were made of triangular pieces of gold linked together; the names of each generation were engraved on these pieces, which were thick yellow coins, while the links connecting them were pale like silver and thin. Some of the gold pieces had a number of others hanging from them. The whole treasure was bright and shining. I heard, but have forgotten, what was its value in shekels. The Egyptian priests had made endless calculations in connection with this genealogy, but never arrived at the right conclusion.

Before Abraham came into their country, the Egyptians must have known, from their astrologers and from the prophecies of their sorceresses, that he and his wife came from the noblest of races and that he was to be the father of a chosen people. They were always searching in their prophetic books for noble races, and tried to intermarry with them. This gave Satan the opportunity of attempting to debase the pure races by leading the Egyptians astray into immorality and deeds of violence.

Abraham, fearing that he might be murdered by the Egyptians because of the beauty of Sara, his wife, had

---

33. Catherine Emmerich says elsewhere of Agar: "She was of Sara's family, and when Sara herself was barren, she gave Abraham Agar for his wife and said she would build from her and have descendants through her. She looked upon herself as one with all the women of her tribe, as if it were a female tree with many blossoms. Agar was a vessel, or flower of her tribe, and she hoped for a fruit of her tribe from her. At that time the whole tribe was as one tree and each of its blossoms formed part of it." (CB)
Gen. 16:1 simply states that Agar was an Egyptian. (SB)

given out that she was his sister. This was not a lie, since she was his step-sister, the daughter of his father Tharah by another wife (see *Gen.* 20:12). The King of Egypt caused Sara to be brought into his palace and wished to take her to wife. Abraham and Sara were then in great distress and besought God for help, whereupon God punished the king with sickness, and all his wives and most of the women in the city fell ill. The king, in alarm, caused inquiry to be made, and when he heard that Sara was Abraham's wife, he gave her back to him, begging him to leave Egypt as soon as possible. It was clear, he said that Abraham and his wife were under the protection of the gods.

The Egyptians were a strange people. On the one hand they were extremely arrogant and considered themselves to be the greatest and wisest among the nations. On the other hand they were excessively cowardly and servile, and gave way when they were faced by a power which they feared was greater than theirs. This was because they were not sure of all their knowledge, most of which came to them in dark ambiguous soothsayings, which easily produced conflicts and contradictions. Since they were very credulous of wonders, any such contradiction at once caused them great alarm.

Abraham approached the king very humbly with a request for corn. He won his favor by treating him as a ruler over the nations, and received many rich presents. When the King gave Sara back to her husband and begged him to leave Egypt, Abraham replied that he could not do this unless he took with him the genealogy that belonged to him, describing in detail the manner in which it had come to Egypt. The king then summoned the priests, and they willingly gave Abraham back what belonged to him, only asking that the whole transaction might first be formally recorded, which was done.[34] Abraham then returned with his following to the land of Chanaan.

---

34. *Gen.* 12:20 (literally from the Hebrew): "And Pharao gave men orders concerning him, and sent him away, and his wife, and all that belonged to him." (SB)

I have seen many things about the spring at Matarea right down to our own times, and remember this much: already at the time of the Holy Family it was used by lepers as a healing well. Much later a small Christian church was built on the site of Mary's dwelling. Near the high altar of this church one descended into the cave where the Holy Family lived until Joseph had arranged their dwelling. I saw the spring with human habitations round it, and I saw it being used for various forms of skin eruptions. I also saw people bathing in it to cure themselves of evil-smelling perspirations. That was when the Mohammedans were there. I saw, too, that the Turks always kept a light burning in the church over Mary's dwelling. They feared some misfortune if they forgot to light it. In later times I saw the spring isolated and at some distance from any houses. There was no longer a city there, and wild fruit-trees grew about it.

XIV

THE RETURN OF THE HOLY FAMILY FROM EGYPT[1]

AT last I saw the Holy Family leaving Egypt. Though Herod had been dead for some time, they were not yet able to return, for there was still danger. Their sojourn in Egypt became increasingly difficult for St. Joseph. The people there practiced an abominable idolatry, sacrificing deformed children, and even thinking it an act of special piety to offer healthy ones to be sacrificed. Besides this, they practiced obscene rites in secret. Even the Jews in their settlement had become infected by these horrors. They had a temple which they said was like Solomon's temple, but this was idle boasting, for it was utterly different. They had an Ark of the Covenant in imitation of the real one, but it contained obscene figures, and their ceremonies were abominable. They no longer sang the Psalms. Joseph, on the other hand, had arranged everything admirably in the school at Matarea. He had been joined there by the heathen priest who had taken the Holy Family's part when the idols collapsed in the little town near Heliopolis. Others had accompanied him and had attached themselves to the Jewish community.

I saw St. Joseph busy at his carpentry on the eve of the Sabbath. He was in great distress because he was not given the payment due to him, and he had nothing to take home, where money was much needed. In

---

1. *Matt.* 2:19-23.

his trouble he knelt down under the open sky in a corner and prayed to God to help him in his need. The
next night I saw that an angel came to him in a dream,
saying that those who had sought the life of the child
were dead, and that he was to rise up and make ready
to journey home from Egypt by the high road; he was
to have no fear, for the angel would accompany him. I
saw St. Joseph communicating to the Blessed Virgin
and to the Child Jesus this command that he had
received from God, and I saw them preparing as
promptly and obediently for their journey home as they
had done when warned to flee into Egypt.

When their decision became known next morning,
many people came to them in great distress to say
farewell, bringing with them all kinds of presents in
little vessels of bark. They were mostly Jews, but some
were converted heathens and all were truly grieved.
(The Jews in this country were so sunk in idolatry as
hardly to be recognized. There were some people here
who were glad at the departure of the Holy Family,
looking on them as sorcerers who owed their power to
the mightiest among the evil spirits.) Amongst the good
people who brought presents I saw mothers with their
little boys who had been Jesus' playfellows. Among these
I particularly noticed a prominent woman of that town
with her small son whom she used to call "the son of
Mary"; for this woman, who was named Mira, had long
hoped for children, and had, by the prayers of the Blessed
Virgin, been granted this son by God. She had called
him Deodatus. [When Catherine Emmerich saw Jesus
passing through Egypt on His way to Jacob's Well after
the raising of Lazarus, she said that He took this Deodatus with Him as a disciple.] I saw this woman giving money to Jesus—yellow, white, and brown pieces,
triangular in shape. Jesus looked at His Mother as He
accepted this gift.

As soon as Joseph had packed on the donkey all that
they needed, they started on their journey, accompanied by all their friends. The donkey was the same one

on which Mary had journeyed to Bethlehem. (On their flight into Egypt they had also had a she-ass with them, but Joseph had been obliged to sell her when they were in want.) They went between On and the Jewish settlement, and then turned southwards to the spring which had gushed forth in answer to Mary's prayer before they came to On or Heliopolis. All was now green here, and the stream from the spring encircled a garden, surrounded on all four sides (except for the entrance) by a hedge of balsam shrubs. This garden was as big as Duke Croy's riding-school at Dülmen, and in it were young fruit-trees, date-palms and sycamores. The balsam shrubs were already as big as good-sized vines. Joseph had made little vessels of bark, very smooth and delicate except for the places where they were smeared with pitch. While they were resting he often made vessels like these for various uses. He broke off the trefoil-shaped leaves from the reddish tendrils of the balsam, and hung his little bark bottles on the shrub to catch the falling drops of balsam for them to take with them on their journey. Their companions now took a tender farewell of them, after which the Holy Family remained some hours here. The Blessed Virgin washed and dried some things, and after refreshing themselves with water and filling their water-skin, they started on their journey along the highway. I saw many pictures of them on this journey home, always free from danger. The Child Jesus, Mary, and Joseph had on their heads, to protect them from the sun, a round piece of thin bark tied under their chins with a cloth. Jesus had His brown dress on, and wore shoes of bark which Joseph had made for Him. They were arranged so as to cover half His feet. Mary wore only soles. I saw that she was often worried because the Child Jesus found it so difficult to walk in the hot sand. I often saw her stopping to shake the sand out of His shoes. He often had to ride on the donkey so as to rest. I saw them go through several towns and pass by others. Their names have escaped me, though I still remember the name

Ramesses. They crossed some water which they had also crossed on their journey into Egypt. It runs from the Red Sea to the Nile.

Joseph did not really want to go back to Nazareth, but wished to settle in his ancestral home of Bethlehem. He was, however, still irresolute, since on arriving in the Promised Land he heard that Judaea was governed by Archelaus, who like Herod was very cruel. I saw that the Holy Family stayed about three months in Gaza, where there were many heathens. Here an angel again appeared to Joseph in a dream and commanded him to go to Nazareth, which he did at once.[2] Anna was still alive. She and a few relations knew where the Holy Family had been living. The return from Egypt happened in September. Jesus was nearly eight years old.

---

2. Joseph's obedience to the angel in the choice of Nazareth: *Matt.* 2:22. (SB)

XV

THE DEATH OF THE BLESSED VIRGIN AT EPHESUS

The following communications, made in different years, generally in the middle of August before the Feast of the Assumption, are here arranged in chronological order.

[On the morning of August 13th, 1822, Catherine Emmerich said: "Last night I had a great vision of the death of the Blessed Virgin, but have completely forgotten it all." On being asked, in the middle of a conversation on everyday matters, how old the Blessed Virgin was when she died, Catherine Emmerich suddenly looked away and said: "She reached the age of sixty-four years all but three and twenty days: I have just seen the figure X six times, then I, then V; is not that sixty-four?" (It is remarkable that Catherine Emmerich was not shown numbers with our ordinary Arabic figures, with which she was familiar, but never saw anything but Roman figures in her visions).]

AFTER Our Lord's Ascension Mary lived for three years on Mount Sion, for three years in Bethany, and for nine years in Ephesus, whither St. John took her soon after the Jews had set Lazarus and his sisters adrift upon the sea.[1]

---

1. The chronology here is not quite plain. The years given here probably include parts of years, since on p. 372 AC states clearly that Mary lived fourteen years and two months after the Ascension, or, as on p. 379, thirteen years and two months. If the Ascension took place in A.D. 30, the date of the Assumption would be A.D. 43 or

Mary did not live in Ephesus itself, but in the country near it where several women who were her close friends had settled.[2] Mary's dwelling was on a hill to the left of the road from Jerusalem some three and a half hours from Ephesus.[3] This hill slopes steeply towards Ephesus; the city as one approaches it from the southeast seems to lie on rising ground immediately before one, but seems to change its place as one draws nearer. Great avenues lead up to the city, and the ground under the trees is covered with yellow fruit. Narrow paths lead southwards to a hill near the top of which is an uneven plateau, some half-hour's journey in circumference, overgrown, like the hill itself, with wild trees and bushes. It was on this plateau that the Jewish settlers had made their home. It is a very lonely place, but has many fertile and pleasant slopes as well as rock-caves, clean and dry and surrounded by patches of sand. It is wild but not desolate, and scattered about it are a number of trees, pyramid-shaped, with big shady branches below and smooth trunks.

John had had a house built for the Blessed Virgin before he brought her here. Several Christian families and holy women had already settled here, some in caves in the earth or in the rocks, fitted out with light woodwork to make dwellings, and some in fragile huts or tents. They had come here to escape violent persecution. Their dwellings were like hermits' cells, for they

44, which will fit with the subsequent martyrdom of James the Great under Herod (42-44). See n. 11, p. 376. If she was then sixty-four years old (as AC says here), she was born in 20 B.C. But here there are difficulties about other statements: from AC's remarks on p. 211 we can deduce that she was eighteen at the birth of Christ, though from p. 130 we gather she was fourteen when she left the Temple and was married. The matter is also confused by the historical problems of the date of the birth of Christ and the date of the Crucifixion and Ascension, and cannot be decided with any certainty. (SB)

2. None of the apocryphal legends of the Assumption suggest that Our Lady lived at Ephesus: most suggest Jerusalem, and the Greek legend *(John,* 4) gives Bethlehem. (SB)

3. The "road from Jerusalem," one would suppose, would be the main road eastwards through Colossae, etc., but the suggestion that Mary's house was, "nearer the sea" than Ephesus (p. 359) indicates a road southward along the coast. The issue is obscured by AC's supposition that Ephesus "must be several hours distant from the coast" (*ib.*). There seems to be some geographical confusion here, although the precise geographical history of Ephesus is rendered difficult through the silting-up of its harbor. (SB)

used as their refuges what nature offered them. As a rule, they lived at a quarter of an hour's distance from each other. The whole settlement was like a scattered village. Mary's house was the only one built of stone. A little way behind it was the summit of the rocky hill from which one could see over the trees and hills to Ephesus and the sea with its many islands. The place is nearer the sea than Ephesus, which must be several hours' journey distant from the coast. The district is lonely and unfrequented. Near here is a castle inhabited by a king who seems to have been deposed. John visited him often and ended by converting him. This place later became a bishop's see. Between the Blessed Virgin's dwelling and Ephesus runs a little stream which winds about in a very singular way.

Mary's house was built of rectangular stones, rounded or pointed at the back; the windows were high up near the flat roof. The house was divided into two compartments by the hearth in the center of it. The fireplace was on the floor opposite the door; it was sunk into the ground beside a wall which rose in steps on each side of it up to the ceiling. In the center of this wall a deep channel, like the half of a chimney, carried the smoke up to escape by an opening in the roof. I saw a sloping copper funnel projecting above the roof over this opening. The front part of the house was divided from the room behind the fireplace by light, movable, wicker screens on each side of the hearth. In this front part, the walls of which were rather rough and also blackened by smoke, I saw little cells on both sides, shut in by wicker screens fastened together. If this part of the house was needed as one large room, these screens, which did not nearly reach to the ceiling, were taken apart and put aside. These cells were used as bedrooms for Mary's maidservant and for other women who came to visit her. To the right and left of the hearth, doors led into the back part of the house, which was darker than the front part and ended in a semicircle or angle. It was neatly and pleasantly arranged; the walls were covered with wickerwork, and the ceiling was vaulted. Its beams were decorated with a mixture of panelling and wickerwork, and ornamented with a pattern of leaves. It was all simple and dignified.

The farthest corner or apse of this room was divided off by a curtain and formed Mary's oratory. In the center of the wall was a niche in which had been placed a receptacle like a tabernacle, which could be opened and shut by pulling at a string to turn its door. In it stood a cross about the length of a man's arm in which were inserted two arms rising outwards and upwards, in the form of the letter Y, the shape in which I have always seen Christ's Cross. It had no particular ornamentation, and was more roughly carved than the crosses which come from the Holy Land nowadays. I think that John and Mary must have made it themselves. It was made of different kinds of wood. It was told me that the pale stem of the cross was cypress, the brown arm cedar, and the other arm of yellow palmwood, while the piece added at the top, with the title, was of smooth yellow olive-wood. This cross was set in a little mound of earth or stone, like Christ's Cross on Mount Calvary. At its foot there lay a piece of parchment with something written on it; Christ's words, I think. On the cross itself the figure of Our Lord was roughly outlined, the lines of the carving being rubbed with darker color so as to show the figure plainly. Mary's meditation on the different kinds of wood forming the cross were communicated to me, but alas I have forgotten this beautiful lesson. Nor can I for the moment be sure whether Christ's Cross itself was made of these different kinds of wood, or whether Mary had made this cross in this way only for devotional reasons. It stood between two small vases filled with fresh flowers. I also saw a cloth lying beside the cross, and had the impression that it was the one with which the Blessed Virgin had wiped the blood from all the wounds in Our Lord's holy body after it was taken down from the Cross. The reason why I had this impression was that, at the sight of the cloth, I was shown that manifestation of Our Lady's motherly love. At the same time I had the feeling that it was the cloth which priests use at Mass, after drinking the Precious Blood, to cleanse the chalice; Mary, in wiping the Lord's wounds, seemed to me to be acting in the same way, and as she did it she held the cloth just as the priest does. Such was the impression I had at the sight of the cloth beside the cross.

To the right of this oratory, against a niche in the wall, was the sleeping-place or cell of the Blessed Virgin. Opposite it, to the left of the oratory, was a cell where her clothes and other belongings were kept. Between these two cells a curtain was hung dividing off the oratory. It was Mary's custom to sit in front of this curtain when she was working or reading. The sleeping-place of the Blessed Virgin was backed by a wall hung with a woven carpet; the side-walls were light screens of bark woven in different-colored woods to make a pattern. The front wall was hung with a carpet, and had a door with two panels, opening inwards. The ceiling of this cell was also of wicker-work rising into a vault from the center of which was suspended a lamp with several arms. Mary's couch, which was placed against the wall, was a box one and a half feet high and of the breadth and length of a narrow plank. A covering was stretched on it and fastened to a knob at each of the four corners. The sides of this box were covered with carpets reaching down to the floor and were decorated with tassels and fringes. A round cushion served as pillow, and there was a covering of brownish material with a check pattern. The little house stood near a wood among pyramid-shaped trees with smooth trunks. It was very quiet and solitary. The dwellings of the other families were all scattered about at some distance. The whole settlement was like a village of peasants.

The Blessed Virgin lived here alone, with a younger woman, her maidservant, who fetched what little food they needed. They lived very quietly and in profound peace. There was no man in the house, but sometimes they were visited by an Apostle or disciple on his travels. There was one man whom I saw more often than others going in and out of the house; I always took him to be John, but neither here nor in Jerusalem did he remain permanently near the Blessed Virgin. He came and went in the course of his travels. He did not wear the same dress as in Our Lord's time. His garment was very long and hung in folds, and was of a thin greyish-white material. He was very slim and active, his face was long, narrow, and delicate, and on his bare head his long fair hair was parted and brushed back behind his ears. In contrast with the other Apostles, this gave him a womanish, almost girlish appearance. Last time he was here I saw Mary becoming ever quieter and more meditative: she took hardly any nourishment. It was as if she were only here in appearance, as if her spirit had already passed beyond and her whole being was far away. In the last weeks before she died I sometimes saw her, weak and aged, being led about the house by her maidservant. Once I saw John come into the house, looking much older too, and very thin and haggard. As he came in he girt up his long, white, ample garment in his girdle, then took off this girdle and put on another one, inscribed with letters, which he drew out from under his robe. He put a sort of maniple on his arm and a stole round his neck. The Blessed Virgin came in from her bedchamber completely enveloped in a white robe, and leaning on her maidservant's arm. Her face was white as snow and as though transparent. She seemed to be swaying with intense longing. Since Our Lord's Ascension her whole being seemed to be filled with an ever-increasing yearning which gradually consumed her. John and she went together to the oratory. Our Lady pulled at the ribbon or strap which turned the tabernacle in the wall to show the cross in it. After they had knelt for a long time in prayer before it, John rose and drew from his breast a metal box. Opening it at one side, he drew from it a wrapping of material of fine wool, and out of this took a little folded cloth of white material. From this he took out the Blessed Sacrament in the form of a small square white particle. After speaking a few solemn words, he gave the Sacrament to the Blessed Virgin. He did not give her a chalice.

Behind the house, at a little distance up the hill, the Blessed Virgin had made a kind of Way of the Cross. When she was living in Jerusalem, she had never failed, ever since Our Lord's death, to follow His path to Calvary with tears of compassion. She had paced out and measured all the distances between the Stations of that *Via Crucis,* and her love for her Son made her unable to live without this constant contemplation of His sufferings. Soon after her arrival at her new home I saw her every day climbing part of the way up the hill behind her house to carry out this devotion. At first she went by herself, measuring the number of steps, so often counted by her, which separated the places of Our Lord's different sufferings. At each of these places she put up a stone, or, if there was already a tree there, she made a mark upon it. The way led into a wood, and upon a hill in this wood she had marked the place of Calvary, and the grave of Christ in a little cave in another hill. After she had marked this Way of the Cross with twelve Stations, she went there with her maidservant in quiet meditation: at each Station they sat down and renewed the mystery of its significance in their hearts, praising the Lord for His love with tears of compassion. Afterwards she arranged the Stations better, and I saw her inscribing on the stones the meaning of each Station, the number of paces and so forth. I saw, too, that she cleaned out the cave of the Holy Sepulchre and made it a place for prayer. At that time I saw no picture and no fixed cross to designate the Stations, nothing but plain memorial stones with inscriptions, but afterwards, as the result of constant visits and attention, I saw the place becoming increasingly beautiful and easy of approach. After the Blessed Virgin's death I saw this Way of the Cross being visited by Christians, who threw themselves down and kissed the ground.

After three years' sojourn here Mary had a great longing to see Jerusalem again, and was taken there by John and Peter. Several of the Apostles were, I believe, assembled there: I saw Thomas among them and I think a Council was held at which Mary assisted them with her advice. On their arrival at Jerusalem in the dusk of the evening, before they went into the city, I saw them visiting the Mount of Olives, Calvary, the Holy Sepulchre, and all the holy places outside Jerusalem. The Mother of God was so sorrowful and so moved by compassion that she could hardly hold herself upright, and Peter and John had to support her as they led her away.

She came to Jerusalem from Ephesus once again,[4] eighteen months before her death, and I saw her again visiting the Holy Places with the Apostles at night, wrapped in a veil. She was inexpressibly sorrowful, constantly sighing, "Oh my Son, my Son." When she came to that door behind the palace where she had met Jesus sinking under the weight of the Cross, she too sank to the ground in a swoon, overcome by agonizing memories, and her companions thought she was dying. They brought her to Sion, to the Cenacle, where she was living in one of the outer buildings. Here for several days she was so weak and ill and so often suffered from fainting attacks that her companions again and again thought her end was near and made preparations for her burial. She herself chose a cave in the Mount of Olives, and the Apostles caused a beautiful sepulchre to be prepared here by the hands of a Chris-

---

4. These visits to Jerusalem may be the source of the legends that suppose her death to have taken place there. Several, the Latin (3), the Greek (3), and Pseudo-Joseph of Arimathea (4), refer to her visit to the sepulchre. The Council cannot be that of *Acts* 15, which took place some years later. (SB)

tian stonemason. [At another time Catherine Emmerich said that St. Andrew had also helped in this work.] During this time it was announced more than once that she was dead, and the rumor of her death and burial was spread abroad in Jerusalem and in other places as well. By the time, however, that the sepulchre was ready,[5] she had recovered and was strong enough to journey back to her home in Ephesus, where she did in fact die eighteen months later. The sepulchre prepared for her on the Mount of Olives was always held in honor, and later a church was built over it, and John Damascene (so I heard in the spirit, but who and what was he?)[6] wrote from hearsay that she had died and been buried in Jerusalem. I expect that the news of her death, burial-place, and assumption into Heaven were permitted by God to be indefinite and only a matter of tradition in order that Christianity in its early days should not be in danger of heathen influences then so powerful. The Blessed Virgin might easily have been adored as a goddess.

Amongst the holy women living in the Christian settlement near Ephesus and visiting the Blessed Virgin in her house was the daughter of a sister of Anna, the prophetess of the Temple. I saw her once travelling to Nazareth with Seraphia (Veronica) before Our Lord's baptism. This woman was related to the Holy Family through Anna, for Anna was related to St. Anne and still more closely to Elisabeth, St. Anne's niece. Another of the women living in Mary's neighborhood, whom I had also seen on her way to Nazareth before Our Lord's baptism, was a niece of Elisabeth's called Mara. She was related to the Holy Family in the following way: St. Anne's mother Ismeria had a sister called Emerentia, both living in the pasture-lands of

---

5. Her tomb at Gethsemani is mentioned in the Greek legend (48). The others indicate the Vale of Josaphat, usually identified with the Kedron Valley between Jerusalem and the Mount of Olives. Gethsemani is on one side of the valley. (SB)
6. St. John Damascene, a monk at Jerusalem, died *c.* A.D. 754, and is a Doctor of the Church. His sermon (2 *de Dormitione Deiparae*) relates her burial at Jerusalem. It is recited in the Breviary on the Octave-Day or during the Octave, and is in fact the simplest collection of popular legends about the Assumption. (SB)

Mara between Mount Horeb and the Red Sea. She was told by the head of the Essenes on Mount Horeb that among her descendants would be friends of the Messias. She married Aphras, of the family of the priests who had carried the Ark of the Covenant. Emerentia had three daughters: Elisabeth, the mother of the Baptist, Enue (who was present as a widow at the birth of the Blessed Virgin in St. Anne's house), and Rhode, whose daughter Mara was, as I have said, now at Ephesus. Rhode had married far away from the home of her family: she lived first in the region of Sichem, then in Nazareth and at Casaloth on Mount Thabor. Besides Mara she had two other daughters, and the sons of one of these became Our Lord's disciples. One of Rhode's two sons was the first husband of Maroni, who, when he died, married as a childless widow Eliud, a nephew of St. Anne, and went to live at Naim. Maroni had by this Eliud a son whom Our Lord raised from the dead in Naim after his mother had become a widow for the second time. He was the young man of Naim who became a disciple and received the name of Martial in Baptism. Rhode's daughter Mara, who was present at Mary's death at Ephesus, was married and lived near Bethlehem. At the time of Christ's birth, when St. Anne absented herself from Bethlehem on one occasion, it was to Mara that she went. Mara was not well off, for Rhode had (like the rest of her family) left her children only a third of her property, the other two-thirds going to the Temple and the poor. I think that Nathanael, the bridegroom of Cana, was a son of this Mara, and received the name of Amator in Baptism. She had other sons who all became disciples.

Last night and the night before I had much to do with the Mother of God at Ephesus. I followed her Way of the Cross with her and some five other holy women. The niece of Anna the prophetess was there, and also Elisabeth's niece, the widow Mara. The Blessed Virgin went in front of them all. I saw that she was weak, her face was quite white and as though transparent.

Her appearance was indescribably moving. It seemed to me as if I were following her here for the last time. While she was making the Stations, John, Peter, and Thaddaeus were I think, already in her house. I saw the Blessed Virgin as very full of years, but no sign of old age appeared in her except a consuming yearning by which she was as it were transfigured. There was an indescribable solemnity about her. I never saw her laugh, though she had a beautiful smile. As she grew older, her face became ever paler and more transparent. She was very thin, but I saw no wrinkles; there was no sign whatever in her of any withering or decay. She was living in the spirit, as it were.

The reason why I saw the Blessed Virgin with such particular clearness in this vision may be my possession of a little relic of a garment which she wore on this occasion. I will endeavor to describe the garment as clearly as I can. It was an over-garment. It completely covered only the back, where it fell to the feet in a few long folds. At the neck it was crossed over the breast and shoulders, and was held on one shoulder by a button, making a kind of scarf. It was fastened round the waist by a girdle and fell from under her arms to the feet on each side of the brown undergarment. Below the girdle it was folded back to show the lining, which had red and yellow stripes running down and across it. The little piece in my possession comes from the right-hand side of this fold, but not from the lining. It was a festival garment, worn in this way according to old Jewish custom. Our Lady's mother wore one, too. This garment covered only the back of the brown undergarment, leaving the bodice and whole front of the latter visible. The sleeves, which were full, showed only from the elbows downwards. Our Lady's hair was hidden in the yellowish cap which she wore; this was stretched rather tightly across her forehead and drawn together in folds on the back of her head. Over it she wore a soft black veil which hung down to her waist. I saw her wearing this dress at the wedding of Cana.

In the third year of Jesus' ministry, when Our Lord was healing the sick and teaching beyond the Jordan at Bethabara (also called Bethania), I saw the Blessed Virgin wearing this dress in Jerusalem, where she was living in a beautiful house near the house of Nicodemus, who, I think, owned that house also. Again at Our Lord's crucifixion I saw her wearing this garment, completely hidden under her praying and mourning cloak. No doubt she wore this ceremonial dress here at the Way of the Cross in Ephesus in memory of having worn it during Our Lord's sufferings on His way to Calvary.

[The morning of August 9th, 1821:] I came into Mary's house, some three hours' journey from Ephesus. I saw her lying on a low, very narrow couch in her little sleeping-alcove all hung with white, in the room behind and to the right of the hearth-place. Her head rested on a round cushion. She was very weak and pale, and seemed as though completely consumed with yearning. Her head and whole figure were wrapped in a long cloth; she was covered by a brown woollen blanket. I saw several women (five, I think) going into her room one after the other, and coming out again as though they were saying farewell to her. As they came out they made affecting gestures of prayer or grief. I again noticed amongst them Anna the niece of the prophetess, and Mara, Elisabeth's niece, whom I had seen at the Stations of the Cross. I now saw six of the Apostles already gathered here—Peter, Andrew, John, Thaddaeus, Bartholomew, and Matthias—and also one of the seven deacons, Nicanor, who was always so helpful and anxious to be of service. I saw the Apostles standing in prayer together on the right-hand side of the front part of the house, where they had arranged an oratory.

[August 10th, 1821:] The time of the year when the Church celebrates the death of the Blessed Virgin is no doubt the correct one, only it does not fall every year on the same day.

Today I saw two more Apostles coming in with girt-up garments like travellers.[7] These were James the Less and Matthew, who is his step-brother, since Alphaeus married when a widower Mary the daughter of Cleophas, having had Matthew by a former wife. Yesterday evening and this morning I saw the assembled Apostles holding a service in the front part of the house. For this purpose they had taken away or arranged differently the movable wickerwork screens which divided it into sleeping compartments. The altar was a table covered with a red cloth with a white one over it. It was brought from its place to the right of the hearth (which was in daily use) to be set up against the wall and used at the service, after which it was put back again. In front of the altar was a stand covered with a cloth over which hung a scroll. Lamps were burning above the altar. On the altar had been placed a vessel in the shape of a cross made of a substance lustrous with mother-of-pearl. It was barely nine inches in length and breadth and contained five boxes closed by silver lids. In the center one was the Blessed Sacrament, and in the others chrism, oil, salt, other holy things, and some shreds of what was perhaps cotton. Everything was tightly closed and packed together to prevent any leakage. It was the Apostles' custom to carry this cross on their travels hanging on their breasts under their garments. They were then greater than the high priest when he carried on his breast the holy treasure of the Old Covenant. I cannot clearly recollect whether there were holy bones in one of the boxes or elsewhere. But I do know that in the Sacrifice of the New Covenant they always had near the altar the bones of prophets and later of martyrs, just as the Patriarchs at their sacrifices always placed on the altar the bones of Adam or of other progenitors on whom the Promise rested. At the Last Supper Christ had taught the Apostles to do the same.

---

7. AC's matter-of-fact account of the arrival of the Apostles (and cf. p. 374 on their tiredness) contrasts strikingly with that of the legends. In most of these the Apostles are transported by clouds to Mary's deathbed, and in the Syriac legend some are already dead and come to life for the occasion. (SB)

Peter stood in priestly vestments before the altar, with the others behind him as if in choir. The women stood in the background.

[August 11th, 1821:] Today I saw a ninth Apostle, Simon, arrive. James the Greater, Philip and Thomas were the only ones missing. I also saw that several disciples had arrived, among whom I remember John Mark and the aged Simeon's son or grandson, who had killed Jesus' last Easter lamb and had the duty of supervising the sacrificial animals in the Temple. There were now some ten men assembled there. There was again a service at the altar, and I saw some of the new arrivals with their garments girt up high, so that I thought they must be intending to leave immediately afterwards. In front of the Blessed Virgin's bed stood a small, low, three-cornered stool, like the one on which the kings had laid their presents before her in the Cave of the Nativity. On it was a little bowl with a small brown transparent spoon. Today I saw nobody in the Blessed Virgin's room except one woman.

I saw Peter again bringing her the Blessed Sacrament after the service; he brought It to her in the cross-shaped vessel. The Apostles stood in two rows reaching from the altar to her couch, and bowed low as Peter passed between them bearing the Blessed Sacrament. The screens round the Blessed Virgin's couch were pushed back on all sides.

After witnessing all this in Ephesus, I had a longing to see what was going on in Jerusalem at this time, but shrank from the long journey thither from Ephesus. Whereupon the holy virgin and martyr Susanna[8] came to me and encouraged me, saying that she would be my companion on the journey. (Today is her feast-day, and I have a relic of her, and she was with me the whole night.) So I went with her over sea and land, and we soon reached Jerusalem. She was, however, quite different from me, as light as air, and when I tried to

---

8. St. Susanna was a Roman maiden, martyred in A.D. 295. (SB)

take hold of her I could not do it. As soon as I came to a definite place, as for instance Jerusalem yesterday, she disappeared; but in all my passages from one vision to another, she was there to accompany and encourage me.

I came to the Mount of Olives, and found it all changed and laid waste since I had seen it before, though I was able to recognize each place I had known. The house near the garden of Gethsemani where the disciples had stayed had been pulled down, and a number of trenches and walls had been made there to prevent access to it. After this I betook myself to Our Lord's Sepulchre. It had been walled up and buried under rubbish, and above, on the top of the rock, a building like a little temple was being put up. So far only the bare walls had been built. As I looked about me, distressed at all the devastation, my heavenly Bridegroom appeared to me in the form in which He had once appeared to Mary Magdalene in this place, and comforted me.

I found Mount Calvary built up and desolate. The little hill on which the Cross had stood had been levelled and surrounded by banks and ditches to prevent access to it. I did, however, make my way there to pray, and again Our Lord came to strengthen and comfort me. When Our Lord appeared to me I no longer saw St. Susanna beside me.

Afterwards I entered into a vision of Christ's miracles and acts of healing near Jerusalem, and saw many of these healings again. This made me think of the power of healing in the name of Jesus which is specially bestowed upon priests, and how in our days this grace has been particularly manifested in the person of Prince Hohenlohe.[9] I saw him healing many kinds

---

9. Prince Alexander Leopold Hohenlohe-Waldenburg-Schillingsfürst was born in 1794. Ordained priest in 1815, he became a canon of Bamberg in 1821. About this time he began to perform some outstanding miraculous cures. The most outstanding was that performed on June 21st, 1821, when Princess Mathilda von Schwarzenberg was released from her paralysis of the previous eight years. The date at the heading of this section of AC's statement shows that she was speaking less than two months after this event, which therefore had a great topical interest. The holy man became a titular bishop in 1844 and died in 1849. (SB)

of illnesses by his prayers; sometimes he cured people who had long suffered from ulcers hidden under their dirty rags. I am not sure whether these were really ulcers or only symbols of old burdens on their consciences. At the same time I found myself in the presence of other priests who possessed this power of healing in the same degree, but failed to exercise it owing to distractions, preoccupations with other things, fear of other people, or lack of perseverance. One of these I saw particularly clearly; to be sure, he helped many people whose hearts were, I saw, being gnawed by ugly creatures (these, no doubt, signified sins), but others, who lay stricken with bodily illness and whom he could certainly have helped, he neglected to assist owing to distractions, which caused disturbances and obstacles within him.

[August 12th, 1821:] There are now not more than twelve men gathered together in Mary's house. Today I saw a service being held in her sleeping-alcove; Mass was said there. Her little room was open on all sides. A woman was kneeling beside Mary's couch and every now and then held her upright. I see this being done throughout the day, and I see the women giving the Blessed Virgin a spoonful of liquid from the bowl. Mary had a cross on her couch, half an arm's length long and shaped like the letter Y, as I always see the Holy Cross. The upright piece is somewhat broader than the arms. It seems to be made of different woods, and the figure of Christ is white. The Blessed Virgin received the Blessed Sacrament. After Christ's Ascension she lived fourteen years and two months.

[As Catherine Emmerich fell asleep that evening, she sang hymns to the Mother of God very softly and peacefully in a most moving manner. When she woke up again, the writer asked her what she was singing, and she answered, still heavy with sleep: "I was following in the procession with that woman there: now she has gone!" Next day she again spoke of this singing. "In the evening I was following two of Mary's friends on the

Way of the Cross behind her house. Every day they take it in turns to go there, morning and evening, and I creep up quietly to join in behind them. Yesterday I could not help starting to sing and then everything was gone."]

Mary's Way of the Cross has twelve Stations. She paced out all the measurements, and John had the memorial stones set up for her. At first they were just rough stones to mark the places, afterwards everything was made more elaborate. There were now low smooth white stones with many sides—I think eight—with a little depression in the center of the surface. Each of these stones rested on a base of the same stone whose thickness was hidden by the close turf and the beautiful flowers surrounding them. The stones and their bases were all inscribed with Hebrew letters. These Stations were all in hollows like little round basins. They were enclosed, and a path encircled the stones broad enough for one or two people to approach in order to read the inscriptions. The spaces round the stones, covered with grass and beautiful flowers, varied in size. These stones were not always uncovered; there was a mat or cover fastened at one side which, when nobody was praying there, was pulled over the stone and held down on the other side with two pegs. These twelve stones were all alike, all engraved with Hebrew inscriptions, but their positions were different. The Station of the Mount of Olives was in a little valley near a cave, in which several people could kneel at prayer. The Station of Mount Calvary was the only one not in a hollow, but on a hill. To reach the Station of the Holy Sepulchre one went over this hill and came to the stone in a hollow. Still lower down at the foot of the hill, in a cave, was the Sepulchre in which the Blessed Virgin was buried. I believe that this grave must still exist under the earth and will one day come to light.

I saw that the Apostles, holy women, and other Christians, when they approached these Stations to pray before them, kneeling or lying on their faces, brought out from under their robes a Y-shaped cross about a foot long, which they set up in the hollow on the various stones by means of a prop at its back. [August 13th, 1821:] I saw the service being celebrated today as before. I saw the Blessed Virgin being lifted up several times in the day to be given nourishment from the spoon. In the evening about seven o'clock she said in her sleep: "Now James the Greater has come from Spain by Rome with three companions, Timon, Eremensear, and still another." Later Philip came with a companion from Egypt. I saw the Apostles and disciples arrive mostly in a very tired condition.[10] They had long staffs with crooks and knobs of different shapes in their hands which showed their rank. They wore long, white, woollen cloaks which they could draw over their heads as hoods. Underneath they wore long white priests' robes of wool; these were open from top to bottom, closed by little knob-like buttons and slit straps of leather. I always saw them like this, but forgot to say so. When they were on their travels they wore their garments girt up high round their waists. Some of them had a pouch hanging from their girdles.

The newcomers tenderly embraced those who were already there, and I saw many of them weeping for joy and for sorrow, too—happy to see each other again and grieved that the occasion for their meeting was so sad. They laid aside their staffs, cloaks, girdles, and pouches, letting their long white undergarments fall to their feet. They put on broad girdles which they carried with them, engraved with letters. After their feet had been washed, they approached Mary's couch and greeted her with reverence. She could only say a few words to them. I saw that they took no nourishment except little loaves; they drank from the little flasks hanging from their girdles.

---

10. The mission-fields of the various Apostles as mentioned by AC on these pages generally correspond to the traditional legends as preserved in the Lives of the Saints, the Breviary, the *Acta Bollandiana,* and local cult.

Timon was one of the seven deacons (*Acts* 6:15), and is so called by AC (*infra,* p. 381). The identity of Eremensear is unknown, but AC 381 states (p. 378) that he joined James and Timon later and had been a disciple of Our Lord. (SB)

A short time before the Blessed Virgin's death, as she felt the approach of her reunion with her God, her Son, and her Redeemer, she prayed that there might be fulfilled what Jesus had promised to her in the house of Lazarus at Bethany on the day before His Ascension. It was shown to me in the spirit how at that time, when she begged Him that she might not live for long in this vale of tears after He had ascended, Jesus told her in general what spiritual works she was to accomplish before her end on earth. He told her, too, that in answer to her prayers the Apostles and several disciples would be present at her death, and what she was to say to them and how she was to bless them. I saw, too, how He told the inconsolable Mary Magdalene to hide herself in the desert, and her sister Martha to found a community of women; He Himself would always be with them.

After the Blessed Virgin had prayed that the Apostles should come to her, I saw the call going forth to them in many different parts of the world. At this moment I can remember what follows.

In many of the places where they had taught, the Apostles had already built little churches. Some of them had not yet been built in stone, but were made of plaited reeds plastered with clay; yet all those I saw had at the back the semicircular or three-sided apse, like Mary's house at Ephesus. They had altars in them and offered the Holy Sacrifice of the Mass there.

I saw all, the farthest as well as the nearest, being summoned by visions to come to the Blessed Virgin. The indescribably long journeys made by the Apostles were not accomplished without miraculous assistance from the Lord. I think that they often travelled in a supernatural manner without knowing it, for I often saw them passing through crowds of men apparently without anyone seeing them.

I saw that the miracles which the Apostles worked amongst various heathen and savage peoples were quite different from their miracles described in Holy Writ.

Everywhere they worked miracles according to the needs of the people. I saw that they all took with them on their travels the bones of the Prophets or of martyrs done to death in the first persecutions, and kept them at hand when praying and offering the Holy Sacrifice.

When the Lord's summons to Ephesus came to the Apostles, Peter, and I think also Matthias, were in the region of Antioch. Andrew, who was on his way from Jerusalem, where he had suffered persecution, was not far from him. In the night I saw Peter and Andrew asleep on their journey in different places but not very far apart from each other. Neither of them were in a town, but were taking their rest in public shelters such as are found by the roadside in these hot countries. Peter was lying against a wall. I saw a shining youth approach and wake him by taking him by the hand and telling him to rise and hurry to Mary, and that he would meet Andrew on the way. I saw that Peter, who was already stiff from age and his exertions, sat up and rested his hands on his knees as he listened to the angel. Hardly had the vision vanished when he got up, wrapped himself in his cloak, fastened his girdle, grasped his staff and set forth. He was soon met by Andrew, who had been summoned by the same vision; later they met with Thaddaeus, to whom the same message had been given. Thus all three came to Mary's house, where they met John.

James the Greater, who had a narrow, pale face and black hair, came from Spain to Jerusalem with several disciples, and stayed some time in Sarona near Joppa. It was here that the summons to Ephesus reached him. After Mary's death he went with some six others back to Jerusalem and suffered a martyr's death.[11] The man who denounced him was converted, was baptized by him, and beheaded with him.

---

11. The martyrdom of James the Great is the only death of an Apostle narrated in the New Testament (*Acts* 12:1), and the persecutor is named: Herod, i.e. Herod Agrippa I. This Herod reigned A.D. 42-44. AC suggests that James went directly to his martyrdom after the Assumption, in which case the Assumption must have taken place in A.D. 44 at the latest. (SB)

Judas Thaddaeus and Simon were in Persia when the summons reached them.

Thomas was of low stature and had red-brown hair. He was the farthest off, and did not arrive until after Mary's death.[12] I saw the summoning angel come to him. He was a very long way off. He was not in any town, but in a reed-hut, where he was praying, when the angel told him to go to Ephesus. I saw him alone in a little boat with a very simpleminded servant crossing a wide expanse of water—then journeying across country without, I think, touching at any town. He was accompanied by a disciple. He was in India when he received the warning, but before that he had decided to go farther north to Tartary, and could not make up his mind to abandon this plan. (He always tried to do too much and so often arrived too late.) So he went still farther north, right across China, to where Russia is now, where he received a second summons which sent him hurrying to Ephesus. The servant whom he had with him was a Tartar whom he had baptized. This man played a part in later events, but I forget what it was. Thomas did not return to Tartary after Mary's death. He was killed in India by being pierced with a lance. I saw that he set up a stone in that country on which he knelt and prayed, and that the marks of his knees were imprinted upon the stone. He foretold that when the sea should reach this stone, another would come to that country preaching Jesus Christ.

John had been in Jericho a short time before; he often travelled to the Promised Land. He usually stayed in Ephesus and its neighborhood, and it was here that the summons reached him.

Bartholomew was in Asia, east of the Red Sea. He was handsome and very gifted. His complexion was pale, and he had a high forehead, large eyes, and black curly hair. He had a short, black, curly beard, divided

---

12. The late arrival of Thomas is included in the tradition preserved by St. John Damascene, but among the early legends only in that entitled "of Joseph of Arimathea" (17). It might easily be supposed to be invented in view of *John* 20:24, but it might equally easily be supposed to be truly in character. (SB)

in the middle. He had just converted a king and his family. I saw it all and will recount it in due course. When he returned there he was murdered by the king's brother.

I forget where James the Less was when the summons reached him. He was very handsome and had a great resemblance to Our Lord, whence he was called by all his brethren the brother of the Lord.

About Matthew I again saw today that he was the son of Alphaeus by a former marriage, and was thus the stepson of Alphaeus' second wife Mary, the daughter of Cleophas.

I forget about Andrew.

Paul was not summoned. Only those were summoned who were relations or acquaintances of the Holy Family.

During these visions I had by my side, amongst the many relics I possess, those of Andrew, Bartholomew, James the Greater, James the Less, Thaddaeus, Simon Zelotes, Thomas, and several disciples and holy women. All these came up to me in that order more clearly and distinctly than the others, and then entered into the vision that I saw. I saw Thomas come up to me like the others, but he did not come into the vision of Mary's death; he was far away and came too late. I saw that he was the only one of the twelve who was missing. I saw him on his way at a great distance.

I also saw five disciples, and can remember with particular clearness Simeon Justus and Barnabas (or Barsabas), whose bones were beside me.[13] Among the three others was one of the shepherd's sons (Eremensear), who accompanied Jesus on His long journeys after the raising of Lazarus. The other two came from Jerusalem. I also saw coming into Mary's house Maria Heli, the elder sister of the Blessed Virgin, and her younger stepsister, a daughter of Anna by her second

---

13. Simeon Justus and Barnabas or Barsabas. There may be a confusion here (unless other persons are intended): Joseph Barsabas Justus was the candidate proposed with Matthias in *Acts* 1:23; Joseph Barnabas, later the companion of St. Paul, first appears in *Acts* 4:36. (SB)

husband. Maria Heli (who was the wife of Cheophas, the mother of Mary Cleophas, and the grandmother of the Apostle James the Less, Thaddaeus, and Simon) was by then a very old woman. (She was twenty years older than the Blessed Virgin.) All these holy women lived nearby; they had come here some time before to escape the persecution in Jerusalem. Some of them lived in caves in the rocks which had been arranged as dwellings by means of wickerwork screens.

[On the afternoon of August 14th Catherine Emmerich said to the writer: "Now I will tell of the death of the Blessed Virgin if only I am not disturbed by visits. Tell my little niece not to interrupt me but to wait patiently in the other room for a time." The writer, having done this and returned, said to her, "Now tell", whereupon she answered, gazing before her with a fixed stare: "Where am I, then? Is it morning or evening?" The writer: "You are going to tell of the death of the Blessed Virgin." "Well, there they are, the Apostles, ask them yourself, you are much more learned than I am, you can ask them better than I can. They are following the Way of the Cross and are preparing the grave of the Mother of God." When she said this, she was already seeing what happened after Mary's death. After a pause she continued, marking on her fingers the figures she mentioned: "See this number, a stroke I and then a V, does not this make four? Then again V and three strokes, does not that make eight? This is not properly written out; but I see them as separate figures because I do not understand big sums in Roman letters. It means that the year 48 after Christ's Birth is the year of the Blessed Virgin's death. Then I see X and III and then two full moons as they are shown in the calendar, that means that the Blessed Virgin died thirteen years and two months after Christ's Ascension into Heaven. This is not the month in which she died—I think I already saw this vision several months ago. Ah, her death was full of sorrow and full of joy." In this continued state of fervor she then recounted the following:]

Yesterday at midday I saw that there was already great grief and mourning in the Blessed Virgin's house. Her maidservant was in the utmost distress, throwing herself on her knees and praying with outstretched arms, sometimes in corners of the house and sometimes outside in front of it. The Blessed Virgin lay still and as though near death in her little cell. She was completely enveloped in a white sleeping coverlet, even her arms being wrapped in it. It was like the one I described when she went to bed in Elisabeth's house at the Visitation. The veil over her head was arranged in folds across her forehead; when speaking with men she lowered it over her face. Even her hands were covered except when she was alone. In the last days of her life I never saw her take any nourishment except now and then a spoonful of juice which her maidservant pressed from a bunch of yellow berries like grapes into a bowl near her couch. Towards evening the Blessed Virgin realized that her end was approaching and therefore signified her desire, in accordance with Jesus' Will, to bless and say farewell to the Apostles, disciples and women who were present. Her sleeping cell was opened on all sides, and she sat upright on her couch, shining white as if suffused with light. The Blessed Virgin, after praying, blessed each one by laying her crossed hands on their foreheads. She then once more spoke to them all, doing everything that Jesus had commanded her at Bethany. When Peter went up to her, I saw that he had a scroll of writing in his hand. She told John what was to be done with her body, and bade him divide her clothes between her maidservant and another poor girl from the neighborhood who sometimes came to help. The Blessed Virgin in saying this pointed to the cupboard standing opposite her sleeping cell, and I saw her maidservant go and open the cupboard and then shut it again. So I saw all the Blessed Virgin's garments and will describe them later. After the Apostles, the disciples who were present approached the Blessed Virgin's couch and received the same blessing. The men then went back into the front part of the house and prepared for the service, whilst the women who were present came up to the Blessed Virgin's couch, knelt down and received her blessing. I saw that one of them bent right down over Mary and was embraced by her.

In the meantime the altar was set up and the Apostles vested themselves for the service in their long white robes and broad girdles with letters on them. Five of them who assisted in offering the Holy Sacrifice (just as I had seen done when Peter first officiated in the new church at the pool of Bethsaida after Our Lord's Ascension) put on the big, rich, priestly vestments. Peter, who was the celebrant, wore a robe which was very long at the back but did not trail on the ground. There must have been some sort of stiffening round its hem, for I see it standing out all round. They were still engaged in putting on their vestments when James the Greater arrived with three companions. He came with Timon the deacon from Spain, and after passing through Rome had met with Eremensear and still another. The Apostles already present, who were just going up to the altar, greeted him with grave solemnity, telling him in few words to go to the Blessed Virgin. He and his companions, after having had their feet washed and after arranging their garments, went in their travelling dress to the Blessed Virgin's room. She gave her blessing first to James alone, and then to his three companions together, after which James went to join in the service. The latter had been going on for some time when Philip arrived from Egypt with a companion. He at once went to the Mother of Our Lord, and wept bitterly as he received her blessing. In the meantime Peter had completed the Holy Sacrifice. He had performed the act of Consecration, had received the Body of the Lord, and had given Communion to the Apostles and disciples. The Blessed Virgin could not see the altar from her bed, but during the Holy Sacrifice she sat upright on her couch in deep devotion. Peter, after he and the other Apostles had received

Communion, brought Our Lady the Blessed Sacrament and administered Extreme Unction to her. The Apostles accompanied him in a solemn procession. Thaddaeus went first with a smoking censer, Peter bore the Blessed Sacrament in the cruciform vessel of which I have spoken, and John followed him, carrying a dish on which rested the Chalice with the Precious Blood and some small boxes. The Chalice was small, white and thick as though of cast metal; its stem was so short that it could only be held with two or three fingers. It had a lid, and was of the same shape as the Chalice at the Last Supper. A little altar had been set up by the Apostles in the alcove beside the Blessed Virgin's couch. The maidservant had brought a table which she covered with red and white cloths. Lights (I think both tapers and lamps) were burning on it. The Blessed Virgin lay back on her pillows pale and still. Her gaze was directed intently upwards; she said no word to anyone and seemed in a state of perpetual ecstasy. She was radiant with longing; I could feel this longing, which was bearing her upwards—ah, my heart was longing to ascend with hers to God!

Peter approached her and gave her Extreme Unction, much in the way in which it is administered now. From the boxes which John held he anointed her with holy oil on her face, hands, and feet, and on her side, where there was an opening in her dress so that she was in no way uncovered. While this was being done the Apostles were reciting prayers as if in choir. Peter then gave her Holy Communion. She raised herself to receive It, without supporting herself, and then sank back again. The Apostles prayed for a while, and then, raising herself rather less, she received the Chalice from John. As she received the Blessed Sacrament I saw a radiance pass into Mary, who sank back as though in ecstasy, and spoke no more. The Apostles then returned to the altar in the front part of the house in a solemn procession with the sacred vessels and continued the service. St. Philip now also received Holy

Communion. Only a few women remained with the Blessed Virgin.

Afterwards I saw the Apostles and disciples once more standing round the Blessed Virgin's bed and praying. Mary's face was radiant with smiles as in her youth. Her eyes were raised towards Heaven in holy joy. Then I saw a wonderfully moving vision. The ceiling of Our Lady's room disappeared, the lamp hung in the open air, and I saw through the sky into the heavenly Jerusalem. Two radiant clouds of light sank down, out of which appeared the faces of many angels. Between these clouds a path of light poured down upon Mary, and I saw a shining mountain leading up from her into the heavenly Jerusalem. She stretched out her arms towards it in infinite longing, and I saw her body, all wrapped up, rise so high above her couch that one could see right under it. I saw her soul leave her body like a little figure of infinitely pure light, soaring with out-stretched arms up the shining mountain to Heaven. The two angel-choirs in the clouds met beneath her soul and separated it from her holy body, which in the moment of separation sank back on the couch with arms crossed on the breast.[14] My gaze followed her soul and saw it enter the heavenly Jerusalem by that shining path and go up to the throne of the most Holy Trinity. I saw many souls coming forward to meet her in joy and reverence; amongst them I recognized many patriarchs, as well as Joachim, Anna, Joseph, Elisabeth, Zacharias, and John the Baptist. The Blessed Virgin soared through them all to the Throne of God and of her Son, whose wounds shone with a light transcending even the light irradiating His whole Presence. He received her with His Divine Love, and placed in her hands a sceptre with a gesture towards the earth as

---

14. All the ancient legends describe the pure soul of Mary leaving her body. The dogmatic decree of Nov. 1st, 1950, however, makes no pronouncement about the death of Our Lady. It is worth here quoting the actual definition: "*Immaculatam Deiparam semper Virginem Mariam, expleto terrestris vitae cursu, fuisse corpore et anima ad caelestem gloriam assumptam.*"—"That Mary, the Immaculate and ever Virgin Mother of God, at the end of the course of her life on earth, was taken up, body and soul, into the glory of Heaven." (SB)

though indicating the power which He gave her. Seeing her thus entered into the glory of Heaven, I forgot the whole scene round her body on the earth. Some of the Apostles, Peter and John for example, must have seen this too, for their faces were raised to heaven, whilst the others knelt, most of them bowed down low to the earth. Everywhere was light and radiance, as at Our Lord's Ascension. To my great joy I saw that Mary's soul, as it entered Heaven, was followed by a great number of souls released from Purgatory; and again today, on the anniversary, I saw many poor souls entering Heaven, amongst them some whom I knew. I was given the comforting assurance that every year, on the day of Our Lady's death, many souls of those who have venerated her receive this reward.

When I once more looked down to earth, I saw the Blessed Virgin's body lying on the couch. It was shining, her face was radiant, her eyes were closed and her arms crossed on her breast. The Apostles, disciples, and women knelt round it praying. As I saw all this there was a beautiful ringing in the air and a movement throughout the whole of nature like the one I had perceived on Christmas night. The Blessed Virgin died after the ninth hour, at the same time as Our Lord.

The women now laid a covering over the holy body, and the Apostles and disciples betook themselves to the front part of the house. The fire on the hearth was covered, and all the household utensils put aside and covered up. The women wrapped and veiled themselves and, sitting on the ground in the room in front of the house, they began to lament for the dead, kneeling and sitting in turns. The men muffled their heads in the piece of stuff which they wore round their necks and held a mourning service. There were always two praying at the head and foot of the holy body. Matthew and Andrew followed Our Lady's Way of the Cross till the last Station, the cave which represented Christ's sepulchre. They had tools with them with which to enlarge the tomb, for it was here that the Blessed Virgin's body was to rest. The cave was not as spacious as Our Lord's and hardly high enough for a man to enter it upright. The floor sank at the entrance, and then one saw the burial-place before one like a narrow altar with the rock-wall projecting over it. The two Apostles did a good deal of work in it, and also arranged a door to close the entrance to the tomb. In the burial-place a hollow had been made in the shape of a wrapped-up body, slightly raised at the head. In front of the cave there was a little garden with a wooden fence round it, as there had been in front of Christ's sepulchre. Not far away was the Station of Calvary on a hill. There was no standing cross there, but only one cut into a stone. It must have been half an hour's journey from Mary's house to the tomb.

Four times did I see the Apostles relieve each other in watching and praying by the holy body. Today I saw a number of women, among whom I remember a daughter of Veronica and the mother of John Mark, coming to prepare the body for burial. They brought with them cloths, as well as spices to embalm the body after the Jewish fashion. They all carried little pots of fresh herbs. The house was closed and they worked by lamplight. The Apostles were praying in the front part of the house as though they were in choir. The women took the Blessed Virgin's body from her deathbed in its wrappings, and laid it in a long basket which was so piled up with thick, roughly woven coverings or mats that the body lay high above it. Two women then held a broad cloth stretched above the body, while two others removed the head-covering and wrappings under this cloth, leaving the body clothed only in the long woollen robe. They cut off the Blessed Virgin's beautiful locks of hair to be kept in remembrance of her. Then I saw that these two women washed the holy body; they had something crinkled in their hands, probably sponges. The long robe covering the body was severed. They carried out their task with great respect and reverence, washing the body with their hands without looking at it, for the

cloth which was held over it hid it from their eyes.
Every place touched by the sponge was covered up again
at once; the middle of the body remained wrapped up
and nothing whatever was exposed. A fifth woman wrung
out the sponges in a bowl and then dipped them into
fresh water; three times I saw the basin emptied into
a hollow outside the house and fresh water being
brought. The holy body was dressed in a new robe, open
in front, and reverently lifted, by means of cloths passed
under it, on to a table where the grave-clothes and
swaddling-bands had been arranged for convenient use.
They wound them tightly round the body from the ankles
to below the breast, leaving the head, breast, hands,
and feet free.

In the meantime the Apostles had assisted at the
Holy Sacrifice offered by Peter and received Communion with him, after which I saw Peter and John, still
in great bishops' cloaks, going from the front part of
the house to the death-chamber. John carried a vessel
with ointment, and Peter, dipping the finger of his right
hand into it, anointed the breast, hands, and feet of
the Blessed Virgin, praying as he did so. (This was not
Extreme Unction; she had received that while still alive.)
He touched her hands and feet with ointment, marking forehead and breast with the Sign of the Cross. I
think that this was done as a mark of respect for the
holy body, as at the burial of Our Lord. After the Apostles had gone away, the women continued their preparation of the body for burial. They laid bunches of myrrh
in the armpits and bosom, and filled with it the spaces
between the shoulders and round the neck, chin, and
cheeks; the feet, too, were completely embedded in
bunches of herbs. Then they crossed the arms on the
breast, wrapped the holy body in a great grave-cloth,
and wound it round with a band fastened under one
arm so that it looked like a child in swaddling-clothes.
A transparent handkerchief was folded back from the
face, which shone white between the bunches of herbs.
They then placed the holy body in the coffin which

stood near; it was like a bed or a long basket. It was a kind of board with a low edge and a slightly arched lid. On the breast was laid a wreath of white, red, and sky-blue flowers as a token of virginity. The Apostles, disciples, and all others present then came in to see the beloved face once more before it was covered up. They knelt quietly, shedding many tears, round the Blessed Virgin's body, touching Mary's hands wrapped up on her breast in farewell, and then went away. The holy women, after making their farewells, covered the holy face and placed the lid on the coffin, which they fastened round with grey bands at each end and in the middle. Then I saw the coffin lifted onto a bier and carried out of the house on the shoulders of Peter and John. They must have changed places, for later on I saw six of the Apostles acting as bearers—at the head James the Greater and James the Less, in the center Bartholomew and Andrew, and behind Thaddaeus and Matthew. There must have been a mat or piece of leather attached to the carrying-poles, for I saw the coffin hanging between them as if in a cradle. Some of the Apostles and disciples went on ahead, others followed with the women. It was already dusk, and four lights were carried on poles round the coffin.

XVI

THE BURIAL AND ASSUMPTION OF
OUR LADY

THE funeral procession followed the Way of the Cross set up by Our Lady right up to the last Station, and then went over the hill in front of that Station and stopped at the right of the entrance to the tomb. Here they laid down the holy body, and then four of them carried it into the burial-chamber in the rock and laid it in the place hollowed out for it. All those present went in one by one and laid spices and flowers beside the body, kneeling down and offering up their prayers and their tears. Many lingered there in love and sorrow, and night had fallen when the Apostles closed the entrance to the tomb. They dug a trench before the narrow entrance of the rock-tomb, and planted in it a hedge of various shrubs brought with their roots from elsewhere. Some had leaves, some blossoms, and some berries. They made the water from a nearby spring flow in front of the hedge, so that no trace of the entrance to the tomb could be seen and none could enter the cave without forcing a way round behind the hedge. They went away in scattered groups, some remaining to pray and watch by the tomb, others stopping to pray here and there at the Stations of the Cross. Those who were on their way home saw from the distance a strange radiance over Mary's tomb, which moved them to wonder, though they did not know what it really was. I saw it, too, but of all that I saw I remember only the following. It was as if a shaft of light descended from Heaven towards the tomb, and in this shaft was a lovely form like the soul of the Blessed Virgin, accompanied by the form of Our Lord; then the body of Our Lady, united to the shining soul, rose shining out of the grave and soared up to Heaven with the figure of Our Lord. All this lies in my memory as something half realized and yet distinct.

In the night I saw several of the Apostles and holy women praying and singing in the little garden in front of the rock-tomb. A broad shaft of light came down from Heaven to the rock, and I saw descending in it a triple-ringed glory of angels and spirits surrounding the appearance of Our Lord and of the shining soul of Mary. The appearance of Our Lord, whose wound-marks were streaming with light, moved down in front of her soul. Round the soul of Mary, in the innermost circle of the glory, I saw only little figures of children; in the mid-most circle they appeared as six-year-old children; and in the outermost circle as grown-up youths. I could see only the faces clearly, all the rest I saw as shimmering figures of light. As this vision, becoming ever clearer, streamed down upon the rock, I saw a shining path opened and leading up to the heavenly Jerusalem. Then I saw the soul of the Blessed Virgin, which had been following the appearance of Our Lord, pass in front of Him and float down into the tomb. Soon afterwards I saw her soul, united to her transfigured body, rising out of the tomb far brighter and clearer, and ascending into the heavenly Jerusalem with Our Lord and with the whole glory. Thereupon all the radiance faded again, and the quiet starry sky covered the land.

I do not know whether the Apostles and holy women praying before the tomb saw all this in the same manner, but I saw them looking upwards in adoration and amazement, or throwing themselves down full of awe with their faces to the ground. I saw, too, how several of those who were praying and singing by the Way of the Cross as they carried home the empty bier turned back with great reverence and devotion towards the light above the rock-tomb.

Thus I did not see the Blessed Virgin die in the usual manner, nor did I see her go up to Heaven; but I saw that first her soul and then her body were taken from the earth.

On returning to the house the Apostles and disciples partook of a little food and then went to rest. They slept outside the house in sheds built on to it. Mary's maidservant, who had remained in the house to set things in order, and the other women who had stayed there to help her, slept in the room behind the hearth. During the burial the maidservant had cleared everything out of this, so that it now looked like a little chapel; and thenceforward the Apostles used it for prayer and for offering the Holy Sacrifice. This evening I saw them still in their own room, praying and mourning. The women had already gone to rest. Then I saw the Apostle Thomas and two companions, all girt up, arrive at the gate of the courtyard and knock to be let in. There was a disciple with him called Jonathan, who was related to the Holy Family.[1] His other companion was a very simple-minded man from the land of the farthest of the three holy kings, which I always call Partherme,[2] not being able to recall names exactly. Thomas had brought him from there; he carried his cloak and was an obedient, child-like servant. A disciple opened the gate, and Thomas went with Jonathan into the Apostles' room, telling his servant to sit at the

---

1. She recognized this disciple by a relic of him which was in her possession but had no name on it. She said of him on July 25th and 26th, 1821: "Jonathan or Jonadab received the name of Elieser in baptism. He was of the tribe of Benjamin and came from the region of Samaria. He was with Peter and then with Paul, but was too slow for him: he was also with John, and came with Thomas from far away at Our Lady's death. He was, like Thomas' simple Tartar servant, very childish in character, but became a priest. I saw him still here in Ephesus three years after Mary's death. Later I saw him left lying here, stoned and half dead, and then taken into the city, where he died. Afterwards his bones were brought to Rome, but his identity remained unknown." (CB)

This Jonathan or Jonadab is not identifiable in any available document.

2. Partherme was indicated before (p. 238) as the land of Sair, though the land of Theokeno, Media, was stated *(ibid.)* to be the remotest. (SB)

gate and wait. The good brown man, who did everything that he was told, at once sat quietly down. Oh, how distressed they were to learn that they had come too late! Thomas cried like a child when he heard of Mary's death. The disciples washed his and Jonathan's feet, and gave them some refreshment. In the meantime the women had woken and got up, and when they had retired from Our Lady's room, Thomas and Jonathan were taken to the place where Our Lady had died. They threw themselves to the ground and watered it with their tears. Thomas knelt long in prayer at Mary's little altar. His grief was inexpressibly moving; it makes me cry even now when I think of it. When the Apostles had finished their prayers (which they had not interrupted), they all went to welcome the new arrivals. They took Thomas and Jonathan by the arms, lifted them from their knees, embraced them, and led them into the front part of the house, where they gave them honey and little loaves of bread to eat. They drank from little jugs and goblets. They prayed together once more, and all embraced each other.

But now Thomas and Jonathan begged to be shown the tomb[3] of the Blessed Virgin, so the Apostles kindled lights fastened to staves, and they all went out along Mary's Way of the Cross to her tomb. They spoke little, stopping for a short time at the stones of the Stations, and meditating on the *Via Dolorosa* of Our Lord and the compassionate love of His Mother, who had placed these stones of remembrance here and had so often wetted them with her tears. When they came to the rock-tomb, they all threw themselves on their knees. Thomas and Jonathan hurried towards the tomb, followed by John. Two disciples held back the bushes from the entrance, and they went in and knelt in reverent awe before the resting-place of the Blessed Virgin. John then drew near to the light wicker cof-

---

3. Thomas' late arrival was the immediate occasion of Our Lady's tomb being opened and found empty. This is also a feature of the general legend preserved by St. John Damascene and recited in the Breviary. (SB)

fin, which projected a little beyond the ledge of rock, undid the three grey bands which were round it and laid them aside. When the light of the torches shone into the coffin, they saw with awe and amazement the grave-clothes lying before them still wrapped round as before, but empty. About the face and breast they were undone; the wrappings of the arms lay slightly loosened, but not unwound. The transfigured body of Mary was no longer on earth. They gazed up in astonishment, raising their arms, as though the holy body had only then vanished from among them; and John called to those outside the cave: "Come, see, and wonder, she is no longer here." All came two by two into the narrow cave, and saw with amazement the empty grave-clothes lying before them. They looked up to Heaven with uplifted arms, weeping and praying, praising the Lord and His beloved transfigured Mother (their true dear Mother, too) like devoted children, uttering every kind of loving endearment as the spirit moved them. They must have remembered in their thoughts that cloud of light which they had seen from afar on their way home immediately after the burial, how it had sunk down upon the tomb and then soared upwards again. John took the Blessed Virgin's grave-clothes with great reverence out of the wicker coffin, folded and wrapped them carefully together, and took them away, after closing the lid of the coffin and fastening it again with the bands. Then they left the tomb, closing the entrance again with the bushes. They returned to the house by the Way of the Cross, praying and singing hymns. On their return they all went into Our Lady's room. John laid the grave-clothes reverently on the little table before the place where Our Lady used to pray. Thomas and the others prayed again at the place where she died. Peter went apart as if in spiritual meditation; perhaps he was making his preparation, for afterwards I saw the altar being set up before Our Lady's place of prayer where her cross stood, and I saw Peter holding a solemn service there, the others standing behind him in rows and praying and singing alternately. The holy women stood farther back by the doors, behind the hearth.

Thomas' simple-minded servant had followed him from the distant land which he had last visited. His appearance was very strange. He had small eyes, a flat forehead and nose, and high cheekbones. His skin was of a browner color than one sees here. He had been baptized; apart from that he was just like an ignorant, obedient child. He did everything that he was told—stood still where he was put, looked in the direction he was told to, and smiled at everybody. He remained seated in the place where Thomas had said he was to wait, and when he saw Thomas in tears, he wept bitterly, too. This man always stayed with Thomas; he was able to carry great weights, and I have seen him dragging up enormous stones when Thomas was building a chapel.

After the Blessed Virgin's death I saw the assembled Apostles and disciples often standing together in a group and telling each other where they had been and what had befallen them. I heard it all, and if it be God's Will I shall recollect it.

[August 20th, 1820 and 1821:] After performing various devotions most of the disciples have taken leave and returned to their duties. The Apostles are still at the house, with Jonathan, who came with Thomas, and also Thomas' servant; but they will all be leaving as soon as they have finished their work. They are working at freeing Mary's Way of the Cross from weeds and stones and are planting it with beautiful shrubs, herbs, and flowers. While working they pray and sing, and I cannot express how moving it is to see them: it is as if, in their love and sorrow, they were performing a solemn religious service, sad but beautiful. Like devoted children they adorn the footsteps of God's Mother and their Mother—those footsteps which followed, in compassionate devotion, her Divine Son's path of suffering to His redeeming death upon the Cross.

They entirely closed up the entrance into Mary's tomb

by earthing up more firmly the bushes planted in front of it and strengthening the trench. They arranged and beautified the little garden before the tomb, and dug out a passage at the back of the hill leading to the back wall of the tomb, chiselling out an opening in the rock through which one could see the place where the Holy Mother's body had rested—that Mother whom the Redeemer when dying on the Cross had entrusted to John and thus to them all and to His Church. Oh, they were true and faithful sons, obedient to the Fourth Commandment, and long will they and their love live upon the land! Above the tomb they made a kind of tent-chapel with carpets; it had wattle walls and roof. They built a little altar in it, with a stone step and a big flat stone supported on another stone. Against the wall behind this altar they hung a little carpet on which the picture of the Blessed Virgin had been woven or embroidered, very plainly and simply. It was in bright colors, showing her in festal attire, brown with blue and red stripes. When all was finished they held a service there, all praying on their knees with uplifted hands. They made Mary's room in the house into a church. Mary's maidservant and a few women continued to live in the house; and two of the disciples, one of whom came from the shepherds beyond the Jordan, were left here to provide for the spiritual comfort of the faithful living in the neighborhood.

Soon afterwards the Apostles separated to go their different ways. Bartholomew, Simon, Jude, Philip, and Matthew were the first to leave for the countries of their missions, after taking a moving farewell of the others. The others, except John, who stayed on for a while, went all together to Palestine before separating. There were many disciples there, and several women went with them from Ephesus to Jerusalem. Mary Mark did much for the Christians there; she had established a community of some twenty women who to a certain extent led a conventual life. Five of them lived in her own house, which was a regular meeting-place for the disciples.[4] The Christians still owned the church at the Pool of Bethsaida.

[On August 22nd she said:] John is the only one left in the house. All the others have already gone. I saw John carrying out the Blessed Virgin's wishes and dividing her clothes between her maidservant and another girl who sometimes came to help her. Some of the stuffs given by the three holy kings were among them. I saw two long white robes and several long cloaks and veils, as well as coverings and carpets. I also saw quite clearly that striped over-dress which she wore at Cana and on the Way of the Cross—the one of which I possess a little strip. Some of these things became the property of the Church; for instance, the beautiful sky-blue wedding-dress, ornamented with gold thread and strewn with embroidered roses, was made into a vestment for the Holy Sacrifice for the Bethsaida church in Jerusalem. There are relics of it in Rome still. I see them, but do not know if they are recognized there. Mary wore it only for her wedding and never again.

All that I have described happened in stillness and quiet. There was secrecy but (unlike today) no fear. Persecution had not yet reached the stage of spies and informers, and there was nothing to disturb the serenity and peace.

---

4. Mary Mark's house at Jerusalem, a meeting-place for disciples, was the natural place for Peter to go to after his escape from prison (*Acts* 12:12). It is evident that this event was after the Assumption, because Peter's arrest was part of the same persecution which caused the martyrdom of James the Great (*Acts* 12:1) which, according to AC, happened after his return to Jerusalem from Ephesus (*supra*, p. 376). (SB)

GENEALOGICAL TABLE

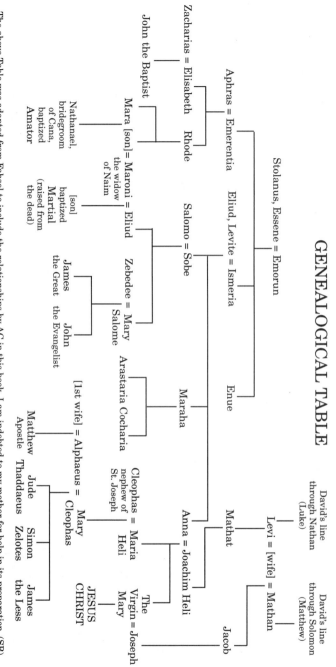

The above Table was adapted from Fahsel to include the relationships by AC in this book. I am indebted to my mother for help in its preparation. (SB)